T0330548

POLICY SIMULATIONS IN THE EUROPEAN UNION

The papers in this much-needed collection employ Applied General Equilibrium methodology to address a wide variety of policy concerns within the European Union. In examining such a variety of issues with varying modelling features the contributors illustrate the flexibility of the approach, and demonstrate how Applied General Equilibrium methodology is an increasingly important tool for economic development.

Policy issues investigated include:

- Problems related to the integration of international markets, and recent or proposed commercial policy reforms
- Modelling labour and capital markets
- The problem of abating the effects of carbon dioxide on the environment
- International policy issues, technological innovation and unilateral government deficit abatement
- The analysis of the efficiency and distributional effects of a number of proposed reforms of income tax in Germany.

Amedeo Fossati is Professor of Public Economics at the University of Genova, Italy. He serves on several editorial boards, and his most recent publications examine local finance and tax reform. **John Hutton** is Professor of Economics and Econometrics at the University of York, UK. He was, for several years, Managing Editor of the *Economic Journal* and serves on several editorial boards. His recent publications are concerned with international issues, including pollution and tax reform.

ROUTLEDGE NEW INTERNATIONAL STUDIES IN ECONOMIC MODELLING
Series Editor: H.M. Scobie

1. MODELS FOR ENERGY POLICY
Edited by Jean Baptiste Lesourd, Jacques Percebois and François Valette

2. BUDGETARY POLICY MODELLING
Public expenditures
Edited by Pantélis Capros and Danièle Meulders

3. ECONOMIC MODELLING AT THE BANK OF FRANCE
Financial deregulation and economic development in France
Edited by Michel Boutillier and Jean Cordier

4. POLICY SIMULATIONS IN THE EUROPEAN UNION
Edited by Amedeo Fossati and John Hutton

POLICY SIMULATIONS IN THE EUROPEAN UNION

*Edited by Amedeo Fossati
and John Hutton*

London and New York

First published 1998
by Routledge
2 Park Square, Milton Park, Abingdon, Oxon, OX14 4RN

Simultaneously published in the USA and Canada
by Routledge
270 Madison Ave, New York NY 10016

Transferred to Digital Printing 2009

Typeset in Garamond by
J&L Composition Ltd, Filey, North Yorkshire

British Library Cataloguing in Publication Data
A catalogue record for this book is available
from the British Library

Library of Congress Cataloging in Publication Data
Policy simulations in the European Union/edited
by Amedeo Fossati and John Hutton
p. cm.
Includes bibliographical references and index.
1. European Union countries – Economic policy – Econometric models.
2. Europe – Economic integration – Econometric models.
3. International economic integration – Econometric models.
4. Applied general equilibrium – Econometric models.
I. Fossati, Amedeo, 1937– . II. Hutton, John J., 1940–
HC240.P59377   1998
337.4–dc21   97–28275
                                                        CIP

ISBN 0–415–15335–2

Publisher's Note
The publisher has gone to great lengths to ensure the quality of this reprint
but points out that some imperfections in the original may be apparent.

CONTENTS

CONTENTS

CONTENTS

FIGURES

TABLES

CONTRIBUTORS

Stella Balfoussias, Researcher, Centre of Planning and Economic Research, Athens, Greece
e-mail: stbalf@kepe.ath.forthnet.gr

Christoph Böhringer, Assistant Professor, Institut für Energiewirtschaft und Rationelle Energieanwendung, University of Stuttgart, Germany
e-mail: cb@ier.uni-stuttgart.de

Maurizio Bussolo, Researcher, Fedesarrollo, Bogotá, Colombia

Barbara Cavalletti, Assistant Professor, Istituto di Finanza, University of Genova, Italy
e-mail: cavallet@economia.unige.it

Roberto A. De Santis, Researcher, University of Warwick, Coventry, UK
e-mail: ecrek@frost.csv.warwick.ac.uk

Alan Duncan, Professor of Public Finance, University of York and Institute for Fiscal Studies, UK
e-mail: asd1@york.ac.uk

T. Huw Edwards, Honorary research fellow, University of Birmingham, UK
e-mail: 101322.1225@compuserve.com

Hans Fehr, Assistant Professor, University of Tübingen, Germany
e-mail: hans.fehr@uni-tuebingen.de

John Hutton, Professor of Economics and Econometrics, University of York, UK
e-mail: jph1@york.ac.uk

Hans Kremers, Researcher, Istituto di Finanza, University of Genova, Italy
e-mail: kremers@economia.unige.it

Fouad Laroui, Researcher, University of York, UK
e-mail: fl6@mailer.york.ac.uk

Rosella Levaggi, Assistant Professor, Istituto di Finanza, University of Genova, Italy
e-mail: levaggi@economia.unige.it

Eckhard Lübke, Assistant Professor, Institute of Public Finance, University of Münster, Germany
e-mail: 13eclu@wiwi.uni-muenster.de

Georg Müller-Fürstenberger, Researcher, Department of Applied Micro-Economics, University of Berne, Switzerland

Alberto Pench, Assistant Professor, Scuola Superiore S. Anna, Pisa, Italy
e-mail: Pench@sssupl.sssup.it

Giancarlo Pireddu, Master Director, Scuola Superiore Enrico Mattei, Milan, Italy
e-mail: pireddu@feem.it

Clemente Polo, Professor of Economics, Barcelona Autónoma University, Spain
e-mail: cpolo@volcano.uab.es

Pascal Previdoli, Researcher, Department of Applied Micro-Economics, University of Berne, Switzerland

Kenneth A. Reinert, Assistant Professor of Economics, Kalamazoo College, USA
e-mail: kreinert@kzoo.edu

David Roland-Holst, Professor of Economics, Mills College, USA and CEPR
e-mail: dwzh@mills.edu

Roberto Roson, Assistant Professor, Dipartimento di Scienze Economiche, Cà Foscari University, Venice, Italy
e-mail: roson@unive.it

Anna Ruocco, Researcher, University of Tübingen, Germany
e-mail: wwvru01@fiwi02.wiwi.uni-tuebingen.de

Gunter Stephan, Professor of Economics, Department of Applied Micro-Economics, University of Berne, Switzerland
e-mail: gunter.stephan@vwi.unibe.ch

Wolfgang Wiegard, Professor of Public Finance, University of Tübingen, Germany
e-mail: wolfgang.wiegard@uni-tuebingen.de

PREFACE

This book brings together a set of fifteen papers on integration issues within the European Union. The majority concern tax and tariff reform, ranging from its impact on labour and capital markets, agriculture, and the distribution of income, extending to include the effects of enlargement of the Union, and the environmental issues of greenhouse gas abatement policy. Most of the papers were presented and discussed at a meeting in Genova on 20–21 November 1996 of members of a network, funded by the Commissions of the European Union under the Human Capital and Mobility programme. The network links together six universities (in Tübingen, Genova, Pisa, York, Barcelona and Athens). This book also brings together papers by experts from outside the network which contribute to the chosen theme of policy simulation in predominantly open economies modelled as general equilibrium systems.

The common methodology of these papers is Applied (or Computable) General Equilibrium modelling, static or dynamic, single or multicountry, according to the specific topic of each paper. The papers are variously methodological and policy oriented, though mainly the latter. The theoretical frameworks adopted all derive from the Walrasian tradition, but in addressing a wide variety of current concerns in Europe, demonstrate the flexibility of that approach, encompassing a wide variety of market impediments and institutional features. A further unifying feature of this collection is that five of the fifteen papers presented here[1] use models that, although quite different in many respects, have their common source in a multicountry static model developed earlier by two members of the network,[2] the FRW model. The book is divided into five parts, according to the policy issues investigated and to specific modelling features.

Part I is devoted to problems related to the integration of international

1 Duncan, Hutton, Laroui and Ruocco (Chapter 4); Kremers (Chapter 11); Levaggi; Fehr and Polo (Chapter 14); and Cavalletti and Ruocco (Chapter 15).
2 Fehr and Wiegard: see Fehr, Rosenberg and Wiegard (1995), *Welfare Effects of Value Added Tax Harmonisation in Europe: A Computable General Equilibrium Analysis*, Berlin: Springer.

markets, and in particular to recent or proposed commercial policy reforms. The two opening chapters confront aspects or consequences of the formation of regional trading blocs; the third investigates the consequences of a common trade reform, the European Union common agricultural policy.

In the first chapter Maurizio Bussolo and Giancarlo Pireddu address the topical problems of economic integration between North Africa and the Economic Union. The 'eastward' enlargement of the European Union causes concern among the Mediterranean developing countries that enjoy trade preferences, and poses important questions concerning regional trade agreements. Is the final agreement advantageous to both parties? What are the final effects on the structure of production of the economies involved? Bussolo and Pireddu use both static and recursive dynamic CGE models for Italy and Algeria to simulate possible integration scenarios and to assess their static welfare effects and growth interactions. The results confirm the findings of previous studies: comparative static simulations show gains whose magnitude is directly linked to the initial level of protection, trade dependency and relative size of the economies participating in the regional agreement. To study the sequencing issue of trade reforms, a dynamic model shows that the adjustments costs generated by the non-instantaneous sectoral reallocation of resources represent a major problem in implementing more liberal commercial policies. Bussolo and Pireddu present a comparison of different trade reforms, together with estimates of the effects of relative adjustment costs and growth rates.

Kenneth A. Reinert and David Roland-Holst (Chapter 2) address similar issues of international integration, even if in the different context of the economic effects of Chile's accession to the North American Free Trade Agreement. They use a static and multicountry model, a framework which appears suitable for the kind of problems investigated. Their results indicate that such an accession has significant implications for Chile, but very limited effects upon NAFTA incumbents, i.e. the US, Canada and Mexico. This follows, perhaps intuitively, from the size and proximity of the participating economies, but the sectoral and employment adjustments in Chile are complex and would be difficult to anticipate from heuristic, partial equilibrium or aggregate analysis. Generally speaking, Chile would be a significant beneficiary of the agreement, but the ensuing adjustments intensify traditional patterns of comparative advantage for this economy and, in the absence of other coordinated policies, might undermine modernisation and sustainable growth. These results have implications for many NAFTA and EU aspirants, but should not be generalised too freely: each prospective entry should be evaluated by the same detailed empirical analysis as is proposed for the Chilean case by Reinert and Roland-Horst.

In Chapter 3 Stella Balfoussias and Roberto De Santis attempt to evaluate the resource allocation effects on the Greek economy of the 1992 reform of the European Union common agricultural policy (CAP). For this purpose a static, single-country model of the Greek economy is developed, representing the agricultural and food sectors in a fairly detailed manner and bench-marked to data for 1990. The model incorporates a number of important CAP parameters, such as the levels of production and export subsidies, thus allowing simulation of both the actual package of recent CAP changes and a broad set of possible future ones. The simulations trace the intersectoral consequences of liberalisation not only between agricultural and non-agricultural sectors but also between those agricultural sectors that are subject to reform and those sectors that are not directly involved. The empirical results show that the 1992 CAP reform caused a significant reduc-tion in the production and exports of grains, milk and other animal products. Resources are reallocated to a minor extent to mining and the industrial sectors but mostly towards agricultural sectors not affected by the reform. Thus value added in agriculture and agribusiness industries decreases by only 1 per cent whereas the value added in non-agricultural sectors increases by 0.9 per cent, in real terms. It therefore appears that the aggregate welfare implications of such reforms are rather modest.

Part II is devoted to the study of modelling labour and capital markets, in order to ascertain the dependence of policy recommendations on this aspect of model specification. Alan Duncan, John Hutton, Fouad Laroui and Anna Ruocco develop the original FRW static, multicountry model of the EU to allow involuntary unemployment and the dependence of transfers on the levels of unemployment. The outcomes of VAT harmonisation are shown to depend on alternative closure rules: whether real wages are modelled as fixed; whether some form of equilibrium level of unemployment (e.g. the non-accelerating inflation rate of unemployment – NAIRU) exists; or whether equilibrium conforms to a wage curve. They also open up the single representative consumer-household by allowing for part-time and full-time labour supply, with only the part-time labour market clearing. Their results flow from the assumption that income taxes will be used to offset revenue changes from harmonisation, thus directly affecting labour supply decisions. In general, the more flexibility households are permitted, the greater the simulated benefits from tax reform, and the fixed real wage closure rule produces the worst outcomes.

The static approach is also used by Roberto Roson (Chapter 4), who proposes a general equilibrium model of the Italian economy to assess the implications of alternative assumptions about the functioning of labour and capital markets. For labour markets, specifications based on imperfect com-petition and wage curves are compared with others based on flexible and fixed real wages. For capital markets, hypotheses of fixed endowments are compared with hypotheses of international capital mobility and fixed interest rates. Combining the alternative assumptions, eight model versions are created and used to simulate the imposition of a trade balance constraint on the Italian economy. Results of the simulation exercises are compared with real data describing some structural adjustment processes which occurred in Italy in the early 1990s. The comparison of real data with model results provides some useful insights about the realism of the alternative model specifications.

In Eckhard Lübke's Chapter 5, on inheritance and pension policy, a dynamic single country model of the Auerbach–Kotlikoff type is adopted and expanded to allow analysis of demographic changes characteristic of Germany in particular, but relevant throughout Europe. First, a population model based on the cohort-component projection method is integrated into an AGE model in order to reproduce real-life demographic processes in detail. Second, an inheritance model is incorporated into the AGE framework. Since inheritance transfers are made on the basis of first-degree family relationships, the population model is expanded to determine these relationships. Third, the life-cycle model included in this AGE model takes account of the likelihood that a certain age will be reached. One consequence of this extension is the occurrence of unintentional inheritances. It is only within a model of this kind that the detailed effects of private pension insurance can be investigated. There is no contradiction between the results of Lübke's simulations and results obtained from other AGE models: his findings, however, are much more detailed than those reported by other researchers. For example, it can be shown how the population waves observed by demographers result in fluctuations in economic development and in changes in the volume of inheritances.

In Part III the problem of abatement of the effects of carbon dioxide on the environment is analysed from the perspective of the equity-efficiency trade-off. Gunter Stephan, Georg Müller-Fürstenberger and Pascal Previdoli (Chapter 6) present a dynamic model of an international market economy with five geopolitical regions where the effects of global carbon limits are experienced: the US, the OECD, the former Soviet Union, China and the Rest of the World. Each generation has the option to invest either in physical capital or in future environmental quality. Reducing the growth of the concentration of atmospheric greenhouse gases must be viewed as investment in the environmental quality that will be enjoyed by our offspring. The following questions suggest themselves: What is the optimal level of (costly) abatement of greenhouse gas? How might the burden be equitably shared between generations and regions? Is it feasible to separate the issue of efficiency in greenhouse gas abatement from that of inter- and intra-generational equity? Discussing these aspects within the framework of a computable overlapping generations model is the aim of their chapter, starting from the assumption that policy-makers have agreed on a 'weak' policy for CO_2 stabilisation. The simulations suggest that global welfare will not be improved, while regional gains or losses of welfare depend on the initial distribution of carbon rights.

In Chapter 7 Christoph Böhringer studies the unilateral taxation of environmental externalities in a static, multicountry model. He investigates the implications of sector-specific exemptions from unilateral carbon taxes on leakage for the international competitiveness of emission- and export-intensive industries and for global efficiency. The numerical analysis is based on a large-scale and detailed general equilibrium model for the EU, with twenty-three production sectors across six major EU member countries. The key finding is that for the standard (Armington) trade specification, where domestic, imported and exported varieties of traded goods are differentiated by origin, leakage rates are not high enough to justify exemptions on global-efficiency grounds. For a given domestic reduction target, exemptions reduce leakage but induce significant excess costs as compared to uniform taxes. Not surprisingly, exemptions decrease adjustment costs for export- and carbon-intensive industries but this is achieved at the expense of society as a whole. The numerical results support previous single-country analyses which identify substantial excess costs of tax exemptions.

T. Huw Edwards uses a single-country, static CGE model in Chapter 8 to analyse energy market distortions and their effect on the cost of introduction of a possible carbon tax in Japan and Germany. He combines CGE modelling with the more traditional partial equilibrium approach, though using demand changes from the CGE model, in order to explain how each assumed market distortion affects the cost of a hypothetical carbon tax. On his assumptions, a 15 per cent reduction in CO_2 emissions in 1990 would reduce welfare in Japan by a mere 0.073 per cent of national income, before taking account of pollution, whereas in Germany there is actually a net benefit from abatement. Edwards shows that these results occur because in Japan a carbon tax tends to increase the cost of existing distortions, while in Germany the tax tends to reduce this cost.

Alberto Pench (Chapter 9) employs a static CGE model of the Italian economy to examine the efficiency and distributional effects of two kind of ecotaxes and to point out the effects on the emissions of some of the most relevant pollutants. The first tax simulation concerns an exogenous tax on total output of oil products compensated by an equiproportional reduction in the personal income tax to keep public expenditure constant in real terms. In the second simulation an exogenous tax has been imposed on the same good but only on the purchases by households, with the same compensation as before. Even if the effects of these taxes on emissions are computed in a very crude manner and, at this stage, can only give a rough idea of their real impact, some interesting lessons can be drawn from the simulations proposed. It emerges that large reductions in emissions are not easy to achieve, at least within the current version of the model. Another result is that both simulations generate a welfare gain, even without including the effect of the reduction in emissions in households' utility functions; the aggregate welfare gain derives mainly from terms of trade effects. Finally, the distributive impact of the simulations is quite different: the main conclusion is that, unless we aim at a consistent reduction in emissions, a tax on consumers' purchases is preferable, on distributive grounds, to a tax on total output. In any case, both simulations tend to have a regressive impact.

Part IV comprises two chapters dealing with important but rather neglected international policy issues, technological innovation and unilateral government deficit abatement, using similar static, multicountry models. In Chapter 10 Hans Kremers seeks to analyse the consequences of technological innovation for employment in the European Union. To this end he extends the FRW model to include minimum wages in each EU country, so creating the possibility of unemployment. Three simulations are reported into the effect of forms of technological innovation: in the use of value-added in the production process; in the use of other commodities as inputs in the production process; and a combination of these two types. Under all counterfactuals, technological innovation occurring outside the EU leads to an improvement of welfare in the various EU countries. The main source of the welfare gain is the cheaper commodities produced outside the EU. On the contrary, the change in real gross national product is not unanimously positive, since The Netherlands, Belgium and Luxemburg, Germany and the United Kingdom show a decrease in real gross national product, because the fall in the activity levels of some sectors in these countries is not compensated by an increase in the activity levels of the remaining sectors.

Rosella Levaggi (Chapter 11) studies the effects of government deficit reduction, a policy issue of great significance in the EU of the 1990s in which the size of the deficit is one of the convergence criteria agreed as conditions for participation in monetary union. She employs an FRW-type model, in which perfect international mobility of capital is assumed, but in which the government deficit affects the degree of international competitiveness through a mark-up on the rental cost of capital. The fiscal policies analysed are the reduction of gross transfers, a cut in public expenditure and an increase in direct income taxation, in two alternative situations in which the mark-up on the cost of capital is fixed at its benchmark level or in which it decreases as the deficit is reduced. A reduction in gross transfers is, due to the structure of the model, neutral from the consumer's side and so one can identify the effects of international competitiveness alone. In this case, nations with relatively high deficits are better off when their deficits are reduced. A decrease in public expenditure also has important effects, but their welfare impact is difficult to evaluate in the absence of a model of the value attached to public expenditure. Finally, an increase in direct income taxation may have positive welfare effects in all the countries considered when the mark-up on the cost of capital is reduced with the public deficit. The model also shows the importance of taking account of the effects of government activity on the productive side of the economy in evaluating fiscal policies.

Part V concerns the analysis of efficiency, redistribution and welfare aspects of income and value added taxes. Hans Fehr and Wolfgang Wiegard (Chapter 12) contribute to the literature on income tax reform by examining the efficiency and distributional effects of a number of proposed reforms of the German income tax. Their analysis is based on an overlapping generations model of the German economy of the Auerbach–Kotlikoff (AK) type. The traditional AK framework is extended by distinguishing between two different households, rich and poor, within each age cohort. Model variants include a small open economy and a closed economy. Three alternatives are considered for replacing the current linear-progressive income tax schedule: a linear-progressive structure with reduced marginal tax rates at the beginning and the end of the tax rate schedule; a flat tax with very few tax brackets; and the abolition of interest income taxation. For each reform scenario the distributional and allocative consequences across and within generations are calculated, and the total generational specific welfare effect is decomposed into efficiency and redistributional components. This allows quantitative comparison of the implied intra- and inter-generational income effects and the efficiency effects. In contrast to the conventional economic debate which focuses almost exclusively on efficiency effects, this chapter suggests that redistributional effects dominate efficiency effects. For the tax reform proposals considered in the chapter, the differences in aggregate efficiency are relatively small, and the main differences concern the implied inter- and intra-generational redistribution. Hence, when choosing between different tax reform proposals, redistributive effects may matter more than pure efficiency considerations.

The last two chapters are concerned with the destination and origin principles for value added tax revenue allocation in similar applied general equilibrium models, in a static and multicountry framework. Hans Fehr and Clemente Polo examine in Chapter 13 the quantitative effects of various value added tax options for the EU. They compare the adoption of uniform tax rates within the current transitional system, and within various reformed systems representing the most recent policy proposals to replace the transitional system. For each reform scenario the country-specific welfare effects are decomposed into tax export and efficiency components. The results indicate quite substantial welfare gains for the EU from tax rate harmonisation, and strongly suggest that the equivalence of the destination regime and two origin regimes, a theoretical possibility depending on rather strong assumptions, does not hold in practice.

Finally, in Chapter 14 Barbara Cavalletti and Anna Ruocco examine the welfare effects of VAT rate harmonisation in the EU, also focusing on the implementation of the origin principle, and in particular on the viable alternatives for financing this policy. The issue is investigated within an FRW-type model, in which each government provides certain levels of public goods and in which national fiscal systems are modelled in detail. Their results suggest that the origin principle may be an important feature of a harmonised VAT regime: in particular, rate harmonisation within the origin regime is supported as potentially welfare improving compared to the actual VAT regime. Furthermore, income taxation proves to be a viable method for financing this harmonisation policy.

AMEDEO FOSSATI   JOHN HUTTON

ACKNOWLEDGEMENT

This book is the result of the scientific collaboration of the partners of the European Union Human Capital and Mobility Programme, Grant No. ERBCHRX-CT94-0493. Financial support is gratefully acknowledged.

Part I

INTERNATIONAL MARKET
INTEGRATION

1

A GENERAL EQUILIBRIUM ANALYSIS OF MEDITERRANEAN ECONOMIC INTEGRATION

The case of Italy and Algeria

Maurizio Bussolo and Giancarlo Pireddu[*]

1.1 INTRODUCTION

This chapter offers an examination of the Italian and Algerian economic relationship and studies the possible effects of the trade policy reforms currently discussed for the Mediterranean area. The economic benefits of further integration in terms of increased welfare, trade and growth rates are assessed using a multicountry computable general equilibrium (CGE) model.

The main results confirm the findings of previous studies concerned with similar set-ups of trade integration among partners at different levels of development.[1] Comparative static simulations of removing trade barriers show considerable gains, whose magnitude is directly linked to the initial level of protection, trade dependency and relative size of the economies participating in the regional agreement.

An additional objective of this chapter is to examine the sequencing issue of trade reforms. Adjustment costs generated by the non-instantaneous realignment of goods and factor prices represent a major concern of policy-makers implementing more liberal commercial policies. By using a recursive dynamic version of the multicountry CGE model, a comparison of different trade reforms is presented with an estimation of their effects in terms of adjustment costs and growth rates.

The simulations are based on the most recent policy package considered during the 1995 Barcelona conference between European Union (EU) ministers and representatives of non-EU Mediterranean countries. Although the European Mediterranean policy covers a broad range of measures and countries

[*] This project was partially financed by SNAM SpA, Milan.

– from full EU membership discussed with Malta, Cyprus and Turkey, to minor political links with other countries – the analysis here is further restricted to the proposal of trade integration between Algeria and the EU. In particular, the Euro-Med Conference in Barcelona set 2010 as a target date for a free trade area (FTA) between the EU and its twelve Mediterranean partners, as far as industrial goods are concerned.

Various factors contributed to the realisation by the European governments of the high negative externalities they would face with an inadequate development of the southern Mediterranean region. Earlier EU policy towards the Maghreb region led these countries to a narrow export specialisation, highly dependent of preferential trade agreements, and contested by emerging developing countries with lower labour costs. Differences in income per capita between the two sides of the Mediterranean are very high, resulting in high migratory pressure. At the current unemployment rates and growth forecasts, European labour markets are not able to accommodate a steady flow of migrant workers. Other global concerns include common environmental problems, political instability and crime. The idea of an FTA in the region has emerged as a solution compatible with this changing environment. It is to be implemented first on a bilateral basis (each Mediterranean country *vis-à-vis* the EU), before being extended to a regional FTA, as Mediterranean countries will sign bilateral free trade agreements among themselves.

The approach used to measure the economic effects of the formation of such an FTA or other possible options of trade policy reform has been to construct a prototype two-country CGE model which includes all the main characteristics of a larger multicountry model of the Mediterranean area. The countries chosen for the prototype are Algeria and Italy. In order to provide a fuller picture of the integration process, a comparative static and a recursive dynamic version of the same CGE model are used. In this way, it is possible to assess the static welfare effects and also the growth interactions of alternative trade policy scenarios. The plan for the chapter is as follows. The next section introduces the basic features of the CGE model. Section 1.3 describes the policy experiments and reports, in two subsections, the results of the comparative static and dynamic versions of the model. Some brief conclusions are presented in the final section.

1.2 THE EMMA MODEL: AN OVERVIEW

This section presents a brief overview of the Economic Model of the Mediterranean Area (EMMA) used to simulate our policies. It consists of a two-country Computable General Equilibrium model that can be used in two modes: comparative statics and recursive dynamics.[2]

Dimensions

The EMMA model consists of two detailed regional sub-models for Italy and Algeria. The main link between them is given by their bilateral trade which is fully endogenous (price and quantities are determined by the equilibrium conditions). The other key dimension of the model is given by its sectoral disaggregation: the version used here details fourteen sectors/commodities as shown in Table 1.1 in the appendix to this chapter. Also the model examines supply and demand for one type of capital and one type of labour. Finally, the benchmark year is 1989 and the time horizon for the model runs to 2003 with equilibrium values reported for five solution periods (1991, 1994, 1997, 2000 and 2003).[3]

Production

Standard assumptions are made for the production structure of the EMMA model: producers minimise costs under constant returns to scale technology and in a perfect competitive environment. Their input choices are modelled using a standard nested structure, reproduced in Figure 1.1. At the top level, output is a composite of fixed shares of value added and non-energy inter-mediate inputs. It is assumed that these are consumed in fixed proportion according to a Leontief input–output technology. At the next level, value added is separated into two components: a labour aggregate and a capital–energy bundle. Constant elasticity of substitution (CES) functions are used to set the degree of substitutability and substitution between imported and domestic goods à la Armington is assumed for intermediates. Further down, the capital–energy bundle is decomposed into two parts. A vague degree of substitutability is assumed at this level. The components of final demand include government expenditure, investment and variation of stocks. It is assumed that aggregate real government expenditures and variation of stocks are fixed, and, according to the closure rule, aggregate real investment depends on savings. These aggregated variables are mapped into commodity specific demands according to fixed shares derived from the social accounting matrix (SAM).

Trade

The main assumption about trade consists of modelling traded goods origi-nating (destined) from (to) different regions as imperfect substitutes. This allows for cross-hauling and rules out the extreme cases of complete specia-lisation. In the case of imports this is captured using an Armington nested CES system. At a first level, for each commodity, demand is in terms of a composite good which is an aggregate of domestic and imported compo-nents. The imported component is further decomposed into region-specific

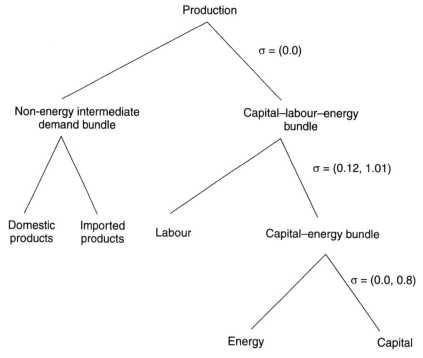

Figure 1.1 Production structure
Note: CES substitution elasticities are differentiated by capital vintage, with higher elasticities for new capital. The values used here are shown in parentheses with first the elasticity value for old capital, followed by that for new capital (note though that no substitution is possible at the top level of the nest).

elements. Exports are treated in a symmetric fashion. Domestic producers optimally allocate supply to domestic and international markets according to relative prices. Constant elasticity of transformation (CET) production possibility frontiers are used to determine the degree of substitutability.

Import demands and export supplies are price sensitive, so an increase in prices in one region with respect to the other region or domestic prices induces substitution. In the EMMA model a distinction is made between endogenous and exogenous regions. For the former, namely Algeria and Italy, border import prices of one country correspond to the export prices of the other and are calculated as equilibrium prices in the model. Whereas for the exogenous region, the Rest of the World, the standard small-country assumption holds, so border imports or export prices are equal to (fixed) world prices.

Equilibrium

The market-clearing condition for commodities sets domestic supply plus imports equal to domestic demand plus exports. The equilibrium conditions for factor markets are more complicated and vary according to whether the dynamic or the static version of the model is used. In the static version, it is assumed that capital stock is fixed and can be either fully mobile across sectors or sectorally specific. Labour supply is modelled in one of two extreme ways: perfectly elastic supply, implying a fixed real wage, or fully rigid supply.[4] Labour can move freely across sectors so that, for each skill, one economy-wide wage rate is computed. The variations in the dynamic version are examined below.

Closure

In addition to material balance and factor markets equilibrium, three additional macroeconomic 'budget constraints' for the government account, the investment-savings account and the balance of payments account are satisfied in the equilibrium. The first assumes that real government savings are fixed and, given that real expenditures are also fixed, the household tax schedule is shifted to balance any loss or gain in other tax (tariff and indirect taxes) revenues. This is equivalent to a lump-sum tax or transfer to the household sector.

The second closure rule concerns the savings–investment balance. In each sub-model investments are set equal to aggregate savings resulting from the sum of household savings, the net government budget position (which is fixed in real terms) and foreign savings (fixed, see below). Increased demand for investment can, therefore, be satisfied only by a corresponding increased supply in savings.

Third, it is assumed that the trade balance is equal to the exogenous level of foreign savings. This implies that, following trade liberalisation, to finance the increased import demand the country has to expand its exports. This is possible at rigid terms of trade, only if export sectors attract resources whose relative prices have declined due to structural adjustment in other sectors.

Dynamics

The recursive-dynamic structure of the EMMA model is rather simple and depends on three main features: factor accumulation, capital vintages and productivity growth. Each solution year in the period 1989–2003 is solved as a static equilibrium. There is no forward-looking behaviour in the model and the link among static equilibria is fully given by transition equations that govern capital accumulation.

For each period of the dynamic version of the model, capital is differentiated into two vintages: old and new. Old capital is equal to the capital of the previous period minus depreciation, and new capital is equal to the previous period's level of investment. Old capital is only partially mobile across sectors whereas the new one is perfectly mobile. The two vintages also have different elasticities of substitution between capital and the other inputs, with old capital having a lower degree of substitutability. This implies that larger investments result in a more flexible economy over time, given that the aggregate substitutability is an average of old and new vintages elasticities. Labour supply increases at an exogenous rate corresponding to the population growth rate.

Productivity gains are determined by increases in energy, labour and capital efficiency 'shifters' in the production function. Labour and energy productivity growth is exogenously specified, whereas capital efficiency is first endogenously calculated in the model base run and then fixed to that value in all subsequent simulations. In the base run, regional GDP growth rates are exogenous, and the instruments used to attain them are determined by the endogenously calculated regional capital productivity changes. During the simulations, GDP growth rates become endogenous and can increase or decrease with respect to the benchmark due to alterations in policy parameters.

1.3 MEDITERRANEAN INTEGRATION

As already noted, trade policy reforms are an essential part of the new agreement reached among the European Union and the other Mediterranean countries. These reforms aim at the constitution of a free trade area in the Mediterranean basin. Technically, a free trade area consists of the elimination of all trade barriers among participating countries, but it does not require that each country adopt a common trade policy (for example the same tariff rates) towards third countries. This, in fact, would be a requirement for the formation of a customs union. The three experiments performed here are based on the following distinct scenarios:

1   Formation of a free trade area between Italy and Algeria;[5]
2   Creation of a customs union between these two countries;
3   Complete elimination of all trade barriers.

Clearly, the only difference between these policies is the geographical extent of the liberalisation. Moreover, between scenarios 1 and 2, Italian trade policy is not changed, as the customs union scenario consists of setting Algerian tariffs on imports from the rest of the world equal to the Italian ones. The following sub-sections examine these policies with the EMMA model in comparative statics and recursive dynamics mode.

Comparative statics experiments and results

Each of the three experiments is performed under two closure rules for the labour markets. In both cases labour is fully mobile across sectors, but with the first closure it is assumed that aggregate labour is in excess supply. The domestic economy-wide wage is fixed, and aggregate employment adjusts to meet demand (in Table 1.3 results for this closure are below the label 'Flat labour supply'). Full employment is assumed for the second closure, and so demand increases will only affect wage rates. Clearly, these two closures represent extreme cases and the resulting estimates of the policies effect should be treated as bounds within which the exact values will lie. A discussion of the experimental results follows.

Aggregate results

Trade liberalisation aggregate results are easy to predict. The removal of import distortions, through enhanced comparative advantage and expanded trade, promotes greater efficiency and increases welfare. The structural adjustment which the economies undergo is more uncertain but, given that trade policy reform usually creates winners and losers, it might be important for its sustainability in the long term to have some *ex ante* detailed sectoral information on the possible outcomes. This is discussed below under 'Sectoral results'.

Table 1.3 presents aggregate results for the three scenarios under each of the two closure rules for the labour market. Results are shown as percentage differences with respect to the benchmark equilibrium.

Equivalent variation aggregate welfare gains, measured as a percentage of base gross domestic product, are positive for both labour market closures except in the FTA case for Algeria where it is −0.07 and −0.04 per cent. As expected, welfare gains increase with the degree of liberalisation. They are only slightly sensitive to the labour market closure rule used. It should be noticed that, for Italy, negligible welfare variations are registered for the two first experiments, whereas some gains are observed, around 0.3 per cent, in the case of full liberalisation. This is entirely due to the size of Italy relative to Algeria and its relatively low trade dependency on its southern partner. Algerian gains are also maximised in the case of full liberalisation, reaching the value of 1.7 per cent, but it is interesting to note that more than 70 per cent of these welfare improvements could be obtained simply by signing a customs union treaty with Italy.

Clearly, real GDP can change only in the case of expandable employment, as is shown in rows 2 and 3. In the case of fixed resources, i.e. a fixed capital stock and a vertical labour supply, GDP variations are negligible. Factor price variations depend on the structural adjustment in the economies and on the assumption made for the labour markets. With flat labour supply, nominal wages vary by the same amount as the consumer price index, as can be observed in row 6, whereas the rental rate responds to variations in demand and productivity. With more liberal trade, Algeria expands its capital-intensive sector, energy, and substitutes domestic production of labour-intensive goods with cheaper imports; this explains the decrease in employment and the increase in rental rate. Italian employment increases due to higher labour demand, and this drives up the rental rate of capital that becomes more productive. In the case of vertical labour supply, changes in labour demand and factor prices depend only on the pattern of structural adjustment in the economy and factor intensities in the various sectors.

Trade increases for both countries in all the simulations, except for Algeria in the FTA case[6] for both labour market closures. It is possible to consider separately changes in total trade (rows 'Total M' and 'Total Ex') and in bilateral trade ('Medit. M' and 'Medit. Ex'), but a clearer picture of the trade diversion effects following the various policies is provided by the indices[7] of import and export diversion in rows 12 and 13. These indices measure the percentage of imports or exports diverted from one market to another; positive values indicate diversion into the region and away from the rest of the world.

In order to appreciate the policy-induced trade diversion effects, it is necessary to consider these indices with the import and export price indices in the last two rows of Table 1.3. This is necessary because bilateral trade prices are endogenously determined. Algeria (Italy) faces a downward-sloping demand for its exports to Italy (Algeria) and an upward-sloping supply for its partner's import supply. This means that terms of trade effects are not ruled out in the bilateral trade relationship[8] and that their size depends on the elasticities of the trade functions.

Consider, for example, import diversion for Italy in the case of flat labour supply. It can be noticed first that although bilateral import increases by almost 7 per cent, 8 per cent and 5 per cent in the three scenarios (row 10), total import is only slightly affected (see row 8), and only a quite low impact is registered for the Italian diversion indices (row 12). Moving from the FTA to the customs union experiment, the Italian import diversion and the import price indices remain constant. When liberalisation is extended to the whole world, import diversion now decreases (from 0.07 to 0.03) as expected. The export diversion index for Italy moves in the same direction as the export price index, decreasing with the degree of liberalisation.

A similar reasoning holds in the case of Algeria. Import diversion clearly diminishes in the case of a customs union and reaches levels close to those of a fuller liberalisation. In this latter case diversion effects are caused by bilateral price changes.

The final set of aggregate results worth noting are presented in rows 14 and 15 in a compact format of adjustment indices[9] of capital and labour. These indices give the extent of the domestic resources reallocation conse-quent on the adoption of trade liberalisation, and are measured in a similar manner to the trade diversion indices. Clearly, the larger the value of these adjustment indices, the more resource reallocation and structural adjustment the economy undergoes.

Two main features are highlighted. First, the results confirm that the smaller the size of the economy, the higher the trade dependency and the size of the initial tariffs; hence, the larger the adjustment required after the policy shock. Second, given the relatively low substitution elasticity among labour and capital, although some variations in the adjustment indices are observable between the two closures, they are not very significant and their ratio (not shown) is almost constant.

Sectoral results

In a disaggregated CGE model such as EMMA, sectoral results are essential in the analysis of the real structural adjustment and reallocations occurring in response to policy change. Since it is individual sectors that seek import protection, aggregate real income or equivalent variation measures do not usually play a decisive role in the formulation of trade policy. In order to implement sustainable reforms it is crucial to have detailed information on sectoral adjustments and other trade-offs not discernible at the aggregate level.

Table 1.4 presents sectoral information on real GDP, real consumption, labour and capital demands, imports and exports inside and outside the Mediterranean region for the Custom Union and the full liberalisation (free trade) experiments. Results are shown as percentage differences from the initial equilibrium.

For Italy, results suggest that a customs union with Algeria has little impact. Although trade with its partner increases significantly with respect to the benchmark, this still represents a low proportion of Italian total trade, and the registered trade diversion effects are of minor importance. These conclusions change when full liberalisation, free trade, is considered. In this case, most manufacturing industries increase their production, whereas agriculture and food processing show a reduction. This is mainly a response to increases in domestic and foreign demand for the expanding sectors and substitution of cheaper imports for the decreasing ones.

Accompanying the output expansion is a growth in employment. Capital, due to its low substitutability with labour, is reallocated according to labour expansion.[10]

Algeria undergoes a remarkably larger structural adjustment, especially for both the policy scenarios considered. Almost two-thirds of its sectors contract and the others expand, including energy. In this case the extent of capital and labour reallocation is particularly interesting. As illustrated in Table 1.3, with both labour supply closures, capital returns go up. Factors' rewards depend on the sectoral adjustments brought about by changes in relative prices. As implied by the Stolper–Samuelson theorem: if relative prices of capital-intensive goods increase with respect to those of labour-intensive goods, the rental rate is expected to rise with respect to wages.

Examining the pattern of output changes and of capital intensities, in Table 1.2[11] and Table 1.4, it can be seen that the most capital-intensive sector of the Algerian economy, energy, is expanding with 'other manufacturing and construction'.

Both aggregate and sectoral results confirm expectations about the ranking of Italy and Algeria in terms of welfare effects and adjustment. Algeria benefits more than Italy, given its size and trade dependency. Clearly, the advantages increase with the degree of liberalisation, although larger resource reallocations are incurred. As far as comparative statics results are concerned, the best option for Algeria, in terms of the combination of positive effects, balanced adjustment costs and political feasibility, seems to be represented by a custom union treaty. The main risk for Algeria is represented by an excessive dependency on energy, with Dutch disease consequences.

Dynamic simulations and results

The benchmark scenario

The 1989–2003 benchmark scenario for the Mediterranean economies should not be considered a realistic prediction, but simply as a scenario in which the current economic policy parameters remain unaltered. This Business as Usual (BaU) scenario is obtained by making assumptions on the future behaviour of those variables that govern the dynamics of the model, namely: factor growth rates and productivity change. During the dynamic calibration of the model, labour growth rate in efficiency units is set exogenously together with a *target* real GDP growth rate, while the *instrument* is the capital productivity growth rate. Once this is calculated, it is fixed throughout all the simulations, and the GDP growth rate becomes an endogenously determined result.[12]

The BaU assumed growth rates are summarised in Table 1.5. The labour force rate is assumed to be equal to the national population growth rates; labour productivity rates are differentiated by country; and real GDP growth rates are simple trend extrapolations of past growth rates. The table also shows the region-specific capital stock depreciation rates. In addition to the data shown here, the assumptions on government and foreign savings also influence the dynamic behaviour of the model. For simplicity, and consistent with long-run equilibrium, it is assumed that Italian and Algerian governments have balanced budgets by the year 2003, and that foreign savings are fixed to the initial values shown in the SAM for 1989.

Trade liberalisation policies can have multiple effects on growth performance. First, they can improve *allocative efficiency* by affecting relative prices and they can make investment goods cheaper. Second, more liberal trade can have positive effects in terms of increased *technical efficiency* and productivity. The best-known attempts to link outward orientation and productivity are based on 'X-efficiency', economies of scale, capacity utilisation, increased competition and technological catch-up.[13] Finally, these policies can trigger virtuous circles by attracting more foreign capital.[14] In the EMMA model, given the closure rules chosen in the recursive dynamics mode, in particular setting aggregate investment equal to aggregate savings, and given the exogeneity of productivity changes, only the first effect is properly taken into account. In practice, as already demonstrated in the comparative statics section, by changing relative prices Mediterranean economic integration induces a more efficient allocation of resources and expands incomes. More savings become available and they can be devoted to larger investments. This is magnified if the relative price of investment goods is reduced.[15] In fact, the growth effects of the usual three policy scenarios will be examined next by focusing mainly on the changes in real investment and its price.

Description and results of experiments

Table 1.6 details the changes in the policy parameters performed in the six simulations: the overall shock (from 1989 to 2003) of policies 1 to 3 is equivalent to the comparative statics experiments. A final observation is necessary before proceeding to the description of the simulation results. Long-term growth implications of alternative trade strategies are of clear interest to policy-makers but, as already stated in the previous section, the model only partially captures policy effects on growth. It remains heavily dependent on the assumptions made on the exogenous variables (factor growth, productivity, depreciation, and expectations).

Table 1.7 reproduces the main results of the dynamic simulations. For each policy, i.e. proportional tariff reduction for a free trade area (FTA), a customs union, and free trade, real GDP growth rates, real investment, investment and GDP prices are presented as percentage differences with respect to the base year.

Not surprisingly, even in these dynamic simulations Algeria registers larger effects than Italy in terms of the variables considered. More open trade regimes boost growth in the southern Mediterranean country by up to 2 per cent of the base run growth rate in the proportional free trade option in the final year. In terms of GDP growth, the relatively small difference between the custom union and full free trade policy options is partially confirmed. For Italy the experiments show a small increase of up to 0.04 per cent in the free trade scenario of GDP growth rate to be correlated with more liberal trade. In order to explain these changes in GDP growth rates it is necessary to consider the other variables in Table 1.7. Growth of capital stock is the main endogenous mechanism influencing real GDP growth performance. The crucial equation is the investment-saving closure equation:

$$P^I \, I^{TOT} = S_h + S_g + P^{SAVF} \, S_f + Y^{DEPR} - \sum_i PA_i \, X_i^{ASTOCK}$$

the right-hand side measures the current value for aggregate investment as the product of real investment (I^{TOT}) and its price index; this value equals the current value of aggregate savings: the sum of household, government and foreign savings. In the dynamic simulation, real government savings starting at positive values for both Italy and Algeria go to zero by the year 2003, and foreign savings are fixed in real terms to the base year value.[16] Households' real savings, its price,[17] government's savings price[18] and the investment price are the endogenous variables determining capital accumulation and growth. From the above equation, at the same level of current savings, a reduction in investment prices produces increased real investment. Indeed, for both countries, investment grows and also becomes cheaper.[19]

In the case of Italy, reduced investment prices occur alongside increased real investment, at a lower rate. This is explained by noting the reduction in the price of GDP (the government savings price) which partly offsets the investment price contraction. The GDP price decreases due to the liberalisation process and lowers government savings (in current values). This reduction is only partially compensated by the increase in households' savings (in current value). Furthermore, given the balanced budget closure for the government account, during the trade liberalisation, tariff revenue losses are compensated by increased household direct taxes. This further depresses both household disposable income and increases in private savings.

In order to assess the reallocation costs of these liberalisation policies, labour adjustment indices were constructed and are shown in Table 1.8. The first-best policy is to set policy parameters to their long-run optimal levels as soon as possible. In fact, if factor and commodity prices adjust instantaneously among activities, the appropriate speed of liberalisation is a trivial issue.[20] In practice any change in policy is likely to generate adjustment costs both in terms of output forgone while resources are 'idle' in the process of moving between sectors and in the resources actually absorbed in this movement. Adjustment costs depend on the extent of inter- and intra-industry adjustment. An indirect measure of adjustment costs can be seen in the factor adjustment indices defined above (see note 9).

Table 1.8 displays two different types of normalised ratios. The labour adjustment index as a ratio of real GDP growth rates is shown in the base run rows. The same ratios are calculated for the experiments and divided by the base run. The resulting values are shown in the rows for each simulation. A value equal to 1 means that both the GDP growth rate and the adjustment index are increased (or decreased) in the same proportion with respect to the base run.

Clearly, in this type of CGE model, higher GDP values and higher growth rates are a direct consequence of increased allocative efficiency. Many of the values in Table 1.8 are close to 1, as expected. A closer inspection of this table reveals, though, that Algeria shows higher values for these normalised indices. It seems that in Algeria higher growth is attained with non-linearly augmenting adjustment costs. This is partially reversed in the last round of the period. Although further investigation is necessary to confirm the validity and robustness of these measurements, they give a preliminary indication of the likely balance between increased growth and adjustment associated with different types of policy. Credibility being a crucial success factor for trade policy reforms, policy-makers should be cautious not to be forced to reverse a blunt pro-growth policy due to the too large resource reallocation involved.

1.4 CONCLUDING COMMENTS

As stated in the introduction, this chapter has two primary objectives: to estimate the effects of trade policy reforms currently planned for the Mediterranean area and to extend the discussion of the sequencing issue of trade reform.

The first objective has been met by constructing a detailed two-country CGE model and using it to appraise the effects of trade liberalisation in three main scenarios: a customs union, a free trade area and a benchmark case of full liberalisation. The evidence obtained from the model results indicates that removing trade barriers may produce considerable gains, mainly in the full free-trade option. Their magnitude is in line with that shown in previous comparable studies, and is proportional to the initial level of protection, trade dependency and size of the economy.

To study the effect of differential levels of liberalisation of the current account, a dynamic version of the two-country CGE model was constructed. This was used to compare the effects on growth and adjustment costs of different scenarios. The results confirm that increased growth shown by policies implementing more extensive liberalisation derives from the stronger allocative efficiency they induce, but that it is also accompanied by higher adjustment costs.

NOTES

1 See for instance Roland-Holst *et al.* (1994) or Sobarzo, H. (1995) for CGE analysis of the NAFTA.
2 The model was developed in a doctorate thesis by M. Bussolo (1997). It was derived from a global model constructed at the OECD Development Centre for the 1994 *International Forum on Latin American Perspectives: Social Tensions, Employment Generation and Economic Policy in Latin America* (see Turnham *et al.* (eds), 1995).
3 The model is calibrated on a two-country social accounting matrix (SAM) for Italy and Algeria developed by the authors. Tables 1.1 and 1.2 display structural data derived from the SAM. It should be noted that a major contribution of this study has been the construction of this two-country SAM, not previously available. It was derived by merging the two single-country SAMs. This entailed various steps. First, 1989 was chosen as the base year, given that the most recent Algerian input–output

table was constructed for that year. The Italian table was adjusted from 1988 to 1989 using a RAS procedure. Second, sectors were aggregated to get a uniform classification and allow a clear measurement of bilateral trade. Third, the Italian IO table was reorganised into a system of national accounting (SNA) format. Finally, the two single-country matrices values expressed in local currency were converted into US dollars.

4 The factor markets closure rules as well as the investment–savings equilibrium condition reflect the macro aspects of CGE models. In particular, for the labour market, see Harrigan *et al.* (1992), Maechler and Roland-Holst (1996), McGregor, Swales, Yin (1996).

5 This and the following policy options consider tariff reductions for all sectors and not the manufacturing subset, as initially proposed in the Barcelona conference.

6 Algerian exports do not increase in this case for the following reason. Given the fixed current account balance closure, increased imports must be financed through increased exports, yet, due to the price rise of exports (0.17 in row 17) Algeria is able to finance its imports with less exports (in quantities).

7 These indices are defined as the normalised measure of the shifts in the composition of trade between the bilateral partner and the rest of the world. For example, the import diversion index is given by:

$$\delta(M_0,\ M_1) = 100\ \frac{\left\| M_1\ \frac{|M_0|}{|M_1|} - M_0 \right\|}{\|M_0\|}$$

where $M_0 = (M_0^b,\ M_0^r)$ and $M_1 = (M_1^b,\ M_1^r)$ are the two-tuple of bilateral and ROW imports in the base and after the experiment, respectively, and $\|\cdot\|$ and $|\cdot|$ denote Euclidean and simplex norms. The export diversion index is defined analogously.

8 Although, as already mentioned, both countries are assumed to be 'small' with respect to the rest of the world.

9 Labour adjustment index is given by:

$$\lambda(L_0,\ L_1) = 100\ \frac{\|L_1 - L_0\|}{\|L_0\|}$$

where $L_0 = (L_{0,i},\ L_{0,j},\ \ldots)$ and $L_1 = (L_{1,i},\ L_{1,j},\ \ldots)$ are the sectoral employment in the base and after the experiment, respectively. The index for capital is defined analogously.

10 Some sensitivity analysis has been carried out with changes in the elasticity of substitution of labour and capital, and the results confirm this observation.

11 Capital intensity is indirectly measured in column 6, the lower the value the higher the capital contribution.

12 With no shocks and by fixing the capital productivity growth rate calculated as described in the text, the model exactly recalculates the GDP growth rate chosen during the dynamic calibration.

13 Among the various papers on trade and growth explicitly referring to Maghreb are those by Haddad (1991) and Clerides *et al.* (1996).

14 See, for a study on Morocco, Haddad and Harrison (1992).

15 It is also possible to change exogenously productivity growth rates. For example, to mimic endogenous growth effects, labour productivity can be exogenously increased during a trade liberalisation experiment. This has been done for a

few simulations, but not reported here. As expected, the main effect is to enhance growth and incomes. In practice, this shows that the results reported in the main text, i.e. no productivity effects, should be considered a lower bound.

16 Given that the price of foreign savings is the numéraire of the model and it is fixed at 1, it is equivalent to defining foreign savings either in real or current terms.

17 Equal to the consumer price index.

18 This is equal to the price of GDP (i.e. equivalent to the GDP deflator).

19 A full analysis of the investment price reduction is based on the following decomposition:

$$\partial P^I = \alpha_d \, \partial P_d + \alpha_m \, \partial P_m \, (1 + \tau) + \alpha_m \, P_m \, \partial \tau$$

the variation in the price of investment depends on changes of the domestic price of investment (P_d), the import price (P_m) and the tariff rate (τ). Clearly the policy change directly affects the tariff, but domestic and imports prices for Algeria and Italy also change as a result of the policy shock affecting the price of investment. Note that import prices from the ROW region are fixed (small-country assumption).

20 See Falvey and Kim (1992), p. 919.

REFERENCES

Bussolo, M. (1977), 'A Mediterranean Region FTA: Some Economic and Environmental Effects Studied within a CGE Framework', unpublished PhD thesis, University of Warwick.

Carraro, C. and Galeotti, M. (1995), *Ambiente, Occupazione e Progresso Tecnico: Un modello per l'Europa*, Bologna: Il Mulino.

Clerides, S., Lach S. and Tybout, J. (1996), *Is Learning-by-exporting important? Micro-dynamic Evidence from Colombia, Mexico and Morocco*, NBER Working Paper No. 5715, New York: National Bureau of Economic Research.

Falvey, R. and Kim, C.D. (1992), 'Timing and Sequencing Issues in Trade Liberalisation', *Economic Journal*, 102: 906–24.

Haddad, M. (1991), 'The effect of trade liberalisation on multi-factor productivity: the case of Morocco', New York: World Bank, mimeo.

Haddad, M. and Harrison, A. (1992), 'Are there positive spillovers from direct foreign investment? Evidence from panel data for Morocco', New York: World Bank, mimeo.

Harrigan, F., McGregor, P.G., Swales, J.K. and Dourmashkin, N. (1992), 'Imperfect competition in regional labour markets: a Computable General Equilibrium Analysis', *Strathclyde Papers in Economics*, 92: 1.

Maechler, A.M. and Roland-Holst, D.W. (1996), 'Empirical Specification of Labour Market Structure and Conduct in a General Equilibrium Framework', in J.F. François and K.A. Reinert (eds), *Applied Trade Policy Modelling: A Handbook*, Cambridge: Cambridge University Press.

McGregor, P.G., Swales, J.K. and Yin, Y.P. (1996), 'Migration Equilibria in Regional Economics: a Multi-period CGE Analysis of an Improvement in Local Amenities', in J.C.J.M. Van den Bergh, P. Nijkamp and P. Rietveld (eds), *Recent Developments in Spatial Equilibrium Modelling*, Berlin: Springer-Verlag.

Pireddu, G. and Dufournaud, C.M. (1996), 'Eco-taxes in an Italian CGE model:

Double dividend effects and the distribution of tax burdens', in A. Fossati (ed.), *Economic Modelling under the Applied General Equilibrium Approach*, Aldershot, Hants: Avebury.

Roland-Holst, D.W., Reinert, K.A. and Shiells, C.R. (1994), 'A General Equilibrium Analysis of North American Economic Integration', in J.K. François and K.A. Reinert (eds), *Modelling Trade Policy: Applied General Equilibrium Assessments of North American Free Trade*, Cambridge: Cambridge University Press.

Royaume du Maroc (1994), *Nouvel accord Maroc Union Européenne. Mémorandum marocain*, Rabat.

Royaume du Maroc, Ministère de l'Agriculture (1994), *Accès au marches. Offre marocaine. Produits agricoles et leur dérives*, Rabat.

Sobarzo, H. (1992), 'A General Equilibrium Analysis of the Gains from Trade for the Mexican Economy of a North American Free Trade Agreement', *World Economy*, 15(1): 83–100.

Turnham, D., Foy, C. and Larraín, G. (eds) (1995), *Social Tensions, Job Creation and Economic Policy in Latin America*, New York: OECD Development Centre, Inter-American Development Bank.

APPENDIX: TABLES

Table 1.1 Basic structure of the Italian economy, 1989 (%)

		1 X	2 VA	3 D	4 E	5 M	6 L/K	7 E/X	8 M/D	9 MAlg/M	10 EAlg/E	11 Tariff
1	Agriculture	3	3	4	2	6	44	6	19	0.0	3.2	1.3
2	Energy	4	5	5	2	10	76	4	21	5.6	0.6	2.8
3	Heavy manfg	8	5	8	12	13	132	15	18	0.2	1.0	0.3
4	Chem., pharm., plast.	5	3	6	9	13	133	17	23	0.2	0.2	0.2
5	Capital goods	10	7	9	32	28	188	34	31	0.0	0.8	0.3
	Interm. invest. goods	23	15	23	53	54	154	24	25	0.1	0.7	0.3
6	Food, bever., tobac.	5	3	5	3	7	103	7	16	0.0	2.9	2.7
7	Textile, clothing	4	3	4	10	5	121	23	13	0.0	0.0	0.7
8	Leather	1	1	1	5	1	134	41	16	0.1	0.1	2.0
9	Wood products	2	1	2	3	1	92	14	9	0.1	0.1	0.1
10	Paper, publishing	2	1	2	2	3	129	8	13	0.0	0.6	0.8
	Final goods	14	9	13	22	17	114	16	14	0.0	0.5	1.6
11	Other manuf. & constn	7	6	7	2	1	91	3	2	0.0	0.1	4.8
	All industries	47	34	48	78	83	122	17	18	0.7	0.6	0.9
12	Commerce, hotel	14	17	14	7	3	35	5	2	0.0	0.0	0.0
13	Transp., commun.	5	6	5	9	2	111	17	4	0.0	0.0	0.0
14	Other services	30	40	30	3	6	99	1	2	0.1	0.0	0.1
	All services	50	62	49	20	11	79	4	2	0.0	0.0	0.1
	Economy-wide	100	100	100	100	100	88	10	10	0.6	0.6	0.8

Table 1.2 Basic structure of the Algerian economy, 1989 (%)

		1 X	2 VA	3 D	4 E	5 M	6 L/K	7 E/X	8 M/D	9 MAlg/M	10 EAlg/E	11 Tariff
1	Agriculture	13	19	14	0	10	11	0	16	6	1	0.7
2	Energy	21	20	8	84	1	7	57	2	14	11	3.5
3	Heavy manfg	5	4	8	1	15	454	3	41	9	36	7.8
4	Chem., pharm., plast.	2	1	4	1	11	2522	4	54	2	51	10.8
5	Capital goods	3	1	8	1	28	691	5	72	10	2	3.2
	Interm. invest. goods	10	6	20	3	54	567	4	56	7	27	5.9
6	Food, bever., tobac.	10	4	12	0	12	56	0	22	8	1	2.5
7	Textile, clothing	3	2	4	0	6	117	1	33	1	0	2.0
8	Leather	1	0	1	0	2	9315	2	39	3	26	1.3
9	Wood products	1	1	1	0	2	185	1	27	1	34	5.0
10	Paper, publishing	1	0	1	0	2	820	1	39	7	0	18.4
	Final goods	15	7	19	1	23	93	1	26	4	6	3.5
11	Other manuf. & constn	15	15	14	0	2	351	0	2	1	0	10.3
	All industries	61	47	62	87	80	81	20	27	6	12	5.3
12	Commerce, hotel	16	20	15	7	7	29	6	10	0	0	0.0
13	Transp., commun.	7	8	6	5	1	84	11	4	0	0	0.0
14	Other services	4	6	4	1	2	64	4	10	0	7	0.0
	All services	27	33	25	13	10	45	7	8	0	0	0.0
	Economy-wide	100	100	100	100	100	50	14	21	6	10	4.2

Table 1.3 Comparative statics: aggregate results (% difference from base run)

	Flat labour supply						Vertical labour supply					
	FTA		Customs union		Free trade		FTA		Customs union		Free trade	
	Italy	Algeria	Italy	Algeria	Italy	Algeria	Italy	Algeria	Italy	Algeria	Italy	Algeria
1 EV	0.00	-0.07	0.00	0.95	0.26	1.41	0.00	-0.04	0.00	1.23	0.30	1.71
2 Real GDP	0.00	-0.04	0.00	-0.40	0.06	-0.44	0.00	0.00	0.00	0.01	0.01	0.01
3 Employment	0.00	-0.13	0.00	-1.21	0.11	-1.33	0.00	0.00	0.00	0.00	0.00	0.00
4 Wage	0.00	0.07	0.00	-0.94	-0.36	-1.40	0.01	-0.20	0.00	-3.38	0.03	-4.05
5 Rent	0.01	0.20	0.00	0.30	0.05	0.16	0.00	0.25	0.00	0.74	-0.36	0.63
6 CPI	0.00	0.07	0.00	-0.95	-0.36	-1.40	0.00	0.04	0.00	-1.22	-0.41	-1.69
7 GDP deflator	0.01	0.15	0.00	-0.10	-0.13	-0.35	0.01	0.10	0.00	-0.63	-0.17	-0.93
8 Total M	0.03	0.42	0.02	2.04	1.29	2.95	0.03	0.36	0.02	1.48	1.17	2.34
9 Total Ex	0.03	-0.10	0.02	1.97	1.33	2.99	0.03	-0.17	0.02	1.39	1.21	2.36
10 Medit M	6.55	9.63	7.95	3.39	4.87	2.60	6.48	9.59	7.37	3.04	4.20	2.18
11 Medit Ex	9.63	6.55	3.39	7.95	2.60	4.87	9.59	6.48	3.04	7.37	2.18	4.20
12 Import diversion	0.06	0.81	0.07	0.12	0.03	0.03	0.06	0.81	0.07	0.13	0.03	0.01
13 Export diversion	0.08	0.71	0.03	0.63	0.01	0.20	0.08	0.71	0.02	0.63	0.01	0.19
14 Employ adjustment	0.01	0.16	0.00	1.77	0.22	1.78	0.00	0.14	0.00	1.72	0.17	1.66
15 Capital adjustment	0.00	0.34	0.00	1.67	0.18	2.48	0.00	0.26	0.00	0.91	0.16	1.69
16 Terms of trade	0.00	0.07	0.00	0.10	0.00	-0.01	0.00	0.07	-0.01	0.12	0.00	0.00
17 Ex price index	0.01	0.17	0.00	0.13	0.00	0.00	0.01	0.17	0.00	0.15	0.00	0.01
18 M price index	0.01	0.10	0.01	0.03	0.00	0.01	0.01	0.10	0.01	0.03	0.00	0.01

Table 1.4 Sectoral results: perfectly elastic labour supply (%)

	Customs union								Free trade							
	Real XP	Real Cons	LD	KD	Row M	Medit M	Row E	Medit E	Real XP	Real Cons	LD	KD	Row M	Medit M	Row E	Medit E
Italy																
Agriculture	0.0	0.0	0.0	0.0	0.0	3.0	0.0	1.2	−1.0	0.0	−1.0	−1.1	1.9	0.6	−0.4	−0.2
Energy	−0.1	0.0	−0.1	−0.1	−0.3	8.6	0.0	7.2	−1.5	0.3	−1.5	−1.5	5.3	5.3	−0.1	6.4
Heavy manfg	0.0	0.0	0.0	0.0	0.0	−0.3	0.0	7.3	0.6	0.0	0.6	0.5	0.3	−0.3	1.4	6.9
Chem., pharm., plast.	0.0	0.0	0.0	0.0	0.0	0.2	0.0	5.9	0.6	0.0	0.6	0.5	0.0	0.2	1.5	5.5
Capital goods	0.0	0.0	0.0	0.0	0.0	3.1	0.0	1.0	0.9	0.0	0.9	0.8	−0.1	3.0	1.8	0.7
Food, bever., tobac.	0.0	0.0	0.0	0.0	0.0	7.2	0.0	4.3	−1.0	0.1	−1.0	−1.0	5.7	3.0	0.2	2.3
Textile, clothing	0.0	0.0	0.0	0.0	0.0	2.3	0.0	1.4	0.4	0.0	0.4	0.3	0.8	1.4	1.3	0.6
Leather	0.0	0.0	0.0	0.0	0.0	10.2	0.0	0.1	0.9	0.2	0.9	0.9	3.4	6.8	2.4	−1.9
Wood products	0.0	0.0	0.0	0.0	0.0	0.4	0.0	5.6	0.3	0.0	0.3	0.3	−0.3	0.4	1.1	5.1
Paper, publishing	0.0	0.0	0.0	0.0	0.0	−1.8	0.0	16.4	0.0	0.0	0.0	−0.1	1.2	−2.8	0.8	14.9
Other manuf. & constn	0.0	0.0	0.0	0.0	0.0	15.3	0.0	20.4	0.0	0.0	0.0	−0.1	14.0	10.1	0.7	19.5
Commerce, hotel	0.0	0.0	0.0	0.0	0.0	0.0	0.0	−1.7	0.0	−0.1	0.0	0.0	−0.6	0.0	0.6	−2.3
Transp., commun.	0.0	0.0	0.0	0.0	0.0	0.0	0.0	0.0	0.3	0.0	0.3	0.3	−0.8	0.0	1.1	0.0
Other services	0.0	0.0	0.0	0.0	0.0	0.9	0.0	−1.6	0.0	−0.1	0.1	0.0	−0.1	1.0	0.6	−2.0
Algeria																
Agriculture	−0.4	−0.9	−0.3	−0.5	−2.1	1.2	−0.3	3.0	−1.4	−1.0	−1.3	−1.5	−0.1	−0.2	−0.6	0.6
Energy	2.4	−1.1	2.5	2.4	1.1	7.2	3.1	8.6	3.7	−1.1	3.8	3.6	8.7	6.4	5.2	5.3
Heavy manfg	−7.2	−0.1	−7.2	−7.3	8.9	7.3	−2.1	−0.3	−7.2	−0.3	−7.1	−7.2	8.7	6.9	−1.0	−0.3
Chem., pharm., plast.	−10.8	0.7	−10.8	−10.8	7.2	5.9	−0.8	0.2	−10.7	0.6	−10.7	−10.7	6.8	5.5	0.4	0.2
Capital goods	−1.4	−0.7	−1.4	−1.5	0.4	1.0	4.7	3.1	−1.1	−0.8	−1.1	−1.3	0.3	0.7	6.2	3.0
Food, bever., tobac.	−0.5	−0.8	−0.4	−0.5	−2.2	4.3	0.8	7.2	−2.0	−0.8	−1.9	−2.1	3.0	2.3	0.5	3.0
Textile, clothing	−1.3	−0.8	−1.2	−1.4	−0.1	1.4	1.4	2.3	−1.7	−0.9	−1.6	−1.8	0.3	0.6	2.1	1.4
Leather	3.2	−0.8	3.2	3.1	−5.6	0.1	10.0	10.2	1.5	−0.7	1.5	1.4	−3.2	−1.9	10.2	6.8
Wood products	−3.5	−0.8	−3.5	−3.6	7.1	5.6	0.1	0.4	−3.5	−1.0	−3.5	−3.7	6.5	5.1	1.1	0.4
Paper, publishing	−17.2	1.6	−17.1	−17.2	19.8	16.4	−7.3	−1.8	−17.8	1.5	−17.8	−17.9	20.0	14.9	−6.8	−2.8
Other manuf. & constn	0.3	−1.0	0.4	0.2	11.4	20.4	5.4	15.3	0.1	−1.1	0.2	0.0	26.5	19.5	6.3	10.1
Commerce, hotel	−1.4	−1.9	−1.3	−1.4	−2.3	−1.7	−0.6	0.0	−1.5	−2.1	−1.3	−1.5	−3.2	−2.3	0.1	0.0
Transp., commun.	−0.9	−1.7	−0.8	−0.9	−3.0	0.0	0.9	0.0	−0.5	−1.9	−0.5	−0.7	−3.9	0.0	2.0	0.0
Other services	−0.5	−1.8	−0.5	−0.6	−2.6	−1.6	1.0	0.9	−0.3	−2.0	−0.2	−0.4	−2.9	−2.0	2.1	1.0

Table 1.5 Growth rates in the recursive dynamics

	Italy					Algeria				
	1991	1994	1997	2004	2003	1991	1994	1997	2004	2003
Labour force	0.001	0.001	0.001	0.001	0.001	0.020	0.020	0.015	0.010	0.010
Labour productivity	0.010	0.010	0.010	0.010	0.010	0.020	0.020	0.020	0.020	0.020
RGDP	0.020	0.025	0.027	0.025	0.025	0.045	0.045	0.045	0.045	0.045
Depreciation	0.035	0.045	0.045	0.045	0.045	0.035	0.045	0.045	0.045	0.045

Table 1.6 Dynamic trade policy simulations: reduction coefficients and uniform rates values

Tariff of	On imports from	1990	1992	1995	1998	2001	2004
FTA							
Algeria	Italy	1.00	0.90	0.75	0.50	0.25	0.00
Algeria	Row	1.00	1.00	1.00	1.00	1.00	1.00
Italy	Algeria	1.00	0.90	0.75	0.50	0.25	0.00
Italy	Row	1.00	1.00	1.00	1.00	1.00	1.00
Customs union							
Algeria	Italy	1.00	0.90	0.75	0.50	0.25	0.00
Algeria	Row	1.00	0.75	0.50	0.25	= Italian tariff	= Italian tariff
Italy	Algeria	1.00	0.90	0.75	0.50	0.25	0.00
Italy	Row	1.00	1.00	1.00	1.00	1.00	1.00
Free trade							
Algeria	All	1.00	0.90	0.75	0.50	0.25	0.00
Italy	All	1.00	0.90	0.75	0.50	0.25	0.00

Table 1.7 Dynamic simulations: main results (% differences from base run)

			Italy					Algeria		
	1992	1995	1998	2001	2004	1992	1995	1998	2001	2004
Real GDP										
FTA	0.00	0.00	0.00	0.00	0.00	0.00	0.03	0.06	0.08	0.09
Customs union	0.00	0.00	0.00	0.00	0.00	0.18	0.81	1.29	1.55	1.41
Free trade	0.02	0.02	0.03	0.04	0.04	0.07	0.44	1.02	1.58	1.77
Real investment										
FTA	0.00	0.00	0.00	0.00	0.00	0.01	0.04	0.07	0.09	0.10
Customs union	0.00	0.00	0.00	0.00	0.00	0.48	0.98	1.49	1.70	1.74
Free trade	0.00	0.00	0.01	0.02	0.03	0.19	0.64	1.29	1.80	2.00
Investment price										
FTA	0.00	0.00	0.00	0.00	0.00	0.00	−0.01	−0.02	−0.03	−0.02
Customs union	0.00	0.00	0.00	0.00	0.00	−0.69	−1.25	−1.77	−1.85	−1.67
Free trade	−0.03	−0.10	−0.21	−0.29	−0.32	−0.28	−0.84	−1.66	−2.19	−2.21
GDP price										
FTA	0.00	0.00	0.01	0.01	0.01	0.01	0.03	0.07	0.09	0.09
Customs union	0.00	0.00	0.00	0.00	0.00	−0.17	−0.24	−0.29	−0.18	−0.10
Free trade	−0.02	−0.05	−0.11	−0.16	−0.18	−0.07	−0.18	−0.32	−0.39	−0.34

Table 1.8 Labour adjustment index as a ratio of real GDP growth

	1991	1994	1997	2000	2003
Italy					
Base run	1.034	0.422	0.444	0.546	0.347
FTA	1.000	1.000	0.999	1.001	1.000
Customs union	1.000	1.000	0.999	1.000	1.000
Free trade	1.000	0.994	0.986	1.004	1.001
Algeria					
Base run	1.276	2.033	1.356	1.198	1.200
FTA	1.002	1.002	1.005	1.004	1.000
Customs union	1.051	1.028	1.040	1.053	0.987
Free trade	1.021	1.027	1.059	1.044	0.997

2

CHILEAN ACCESSION TO THE NAFTA

General equilibrium estimates

*Kenneth A. Reinert and David Roland-Holst**

2.1 INTRODUCTION

The advent of the North American Free Trade Agreement (NAFTA) regional trading agreement has inspired a mixture of apprehension and anticipation elsewhere in the Americas. Unlike the Uruguay Round, this regional agreement implies pre-emptory exclusion of third parties, which raises questions about trade diversion and shrinking market access. On the other hand, the regional accord represents a model for other sub-regions in the hemisphere and even, in some countries' eyes, holds the implicit invitation of membership. By now, most economies in the Americas have envisioned the costs and benefits which would result from joining the initiative begun in North America, but like the ultimate effects of NAFTA itself there remain conjectures or tentative forecasts. Undoubtedly, many countries, particularly the smaller Central American economies, could experience substantial gains from better-articulated trade links to large northern markets, but the composition of such benefits and the structural adjustments they would occasion are not yet well understood.

Since Mexico, no Latin American country has aspired to NAFTA membership more vigorously than Chile. This is perhaps logical, given Chile's trade orientation *vis-à-vis* the United States and its aggressively reformist approach to external markets. Chile's adjustment experience is different from many other economies in the region, and helps to explain how it has arrived at this ambitious starting point for long-distance regionalism. Despite its unique history, however, the adaptation of its economy to a NAFTA+ commercial

* We would like to thank Dominique van der Mensbrugghe for helpful comments and Elena Alonso for expert technical assistance. The views expressed here are those of the authors and should not be attributed to their affiliated institutions.

union will be very instructive for other economies who might aspire to membership.

The course of Chile's trade orientation over the past three decades has been dictated by the alternating salience of policy preferences and economic necessity. Like many of its Latin American neighbours, Chile viewed the early growth opportunities of the 1960s as an opportunity for comprehensive domestic modernisation through increased domestic self-sufficiency in manufacturing.[1] This import-substitution strategy was fostered by an elaborate system of price distortions, including tariffs, quantity restraints and managed exchange rate regimes which biased domestic demand against imports and constricted the trading opportunities of the economy. By the early 1970s, average tariffs were over 100 per cent and foreign exchange rationing was extensive.

Political upheaval in the early 1970s brought with it a reversal of the country's trade and industrial policy orientations. Trade was rapidly liberalised, with average tariffs falling from 105 per cent to 12 per cent between 1974 and 1979. Domestic industry was extensively privatised and a wide array of government fiscal and regulatory instruments were relaxed. As Tybout (1989) has observed, this phase had three essential features: rapid growth in labour productivity (i.e. output rose much faster than employment after the recessionary retrenchments), a sharp deterioration in manufacturing terms of trade and import dependence, and high levels of industry consolidation. Despite an initial recessionary downturn, the economy recovered under this new regime and appeared to be on a sustained growth path into the 1980s.

By 1982, however, the economy had lost its momentum and headed into a steep recession. While this slump was concurrent with a global downturn and serious contractions elsewhere in Latin America, some unique features intensified the problems facing Chile at this time. A long period of exchange rate overvaluation and current account deficits had weakened foreign exchange earning potential, while at the same time increasing reliance on international capital inflows. When devaluation was undertaken, it was too late to stimulate tradable sectors and the economy contracted sharply, with the 1983 unemployment rate at 30 per cent.

This led to a new phase of public intervention, this time in capital markets. The government took control of the largest banks and rescheduled their private sector loan portfolios towards longer-term refinancing. This was combined with preferential access to foreign exchange for international debt payments and steep cuts in corporate tax rates. The trade regime was also liberalised a second time, and average tariff rates, which had crept up to 36 per cent by 1984, had fallen back to 15 per cent by 1988.

At the present time, Chile has emerged from its second major adjustment in as many decades with relatively competitive tradable sectors by international standards. Its trade and industrial policies have been described by some as *laissez-faire*, although the government is still actively engaged in credit management and trade promotion. This outward-oriented, reformist approach has most recently manifested itself in negotiations for the accession of Chile to the North American Free Trade Area.

This paper uses a four-country, calibrated general equilibrium (CGE) model to assess the economic effects of such an enterprise upon the members.[2] Our results indicate that substantial adjustments will indeed take place as a result of Chilean accession to the existing regional pact, but these are generally confined to Chile itself. Those effects which are ascribed to the incumbent economies are negligible and in most cases positive. The latter conclusion indicates that Chilean accession is more expansionary than diversionary from a trade perspective, and this result is likely to be due to its geographic isolation and differing economic structure. For this reason, this conclusion should be extended to more proximate Latin American NAFTA aspirants with care or not at all. The preferred approach would be a detailed, case-by-case empirical analysis of this kind for each candidate. This has two important advantages for policy-makers. First, it permits more accurate and timely anticipation of potential gains and losses and their implications for negotiation and adjustment assistance. Second, this kind of analytical support can greatly facilitate the design of coordinated domestic policies to limit the losses and more fully realize the gains of more liberal trade.

2.2 A CGE MODEL AND DATABASE FOR NAFTA+

This section presents a brief description of the computable general equilibrium (CGE) model and database we use to simulate the welfare and resource allocation effects of Chile joining Canada, the United States and Mexico in a free trade area (FTA). For readers interested in more details, a technical appendix is available upon request.

The CGE model

The four-country CGE model is based on a three-country kernel which has been used by the authors for several types of NAFTA appraisal[3] in the past. Typical of most comparative static, multisectoral, economy-wide models in use today, it simulates price-directed resource allocation in commodity and factor markets. These models maintain detailed information on sectoral prices, output, trade, consumption and factor use in a consistent framework which also accounts for aggregates such as income, employment and revenue. The present model differs from conventional CGE specifications in two important ways. First, it is a *detailed and complete four-country model*, so domestic supply, demand and bilateral trade for the United States, Canada, Mexico and Chile are fully endogenous at a 25-sector level of aggregation.

The extent of price adjustments as well as the volume and pattern of trade creation and trade diversion are important factors in determining the ultimate welfare and resource allocation effects of a multilateral trade policy. A second important feature of the model addresses these responses to FTA trade liberalization. The model employs differentiated product specifications of the demand and supply in tradable commodities. In each sector of each country, domestic demand consists of goods which are differentiated by origin (domestic goods, imports from each FTA partner, and imports from the rest of the world). These goods are aggregated using a non-nested, constant elasticity of substitution (CES) functional form into a single consumption good for both intermediate and final use. This specification allows for substitution among origins in response to commercial policy and exchange rate changes. Demand for the twenty-five aggregate goods in each country is modelled using a linear expenditure system (LES). Also in each sector of each country, domestic production is allocated using a non-nested, constant elasticity of transformation (CET) functional form among differentiated destinations (domestic market, exports to each FTA partner and exports to the rest of the world). This specification allows for substitution among destinations in response to commercial policy and exchange rate changes. Together, the above two trade specifications constitute product differentiation by country of origin and destination, allowing for intra-industry trade.[4] As such, the four countries maintain twelve pairs of 25-sector trade flows between them, governed by twelve endogenous price systems (US–Canada, US–Mexico, Canada–Mexico, US–Chile, Canada–Chile, and Mexico–Chile imports and exports). With respect to the rest of the world (ROW), each country faces import supply and export demand schedules, totalling four more price systems (US–ROW, Canada–ROW, Mexico–ROW, Chile–ROW imports and exports).[5]

Production takes place under constant returns to scale using constant elasticity of substitution functional forms, and there are perfectly competitive markets. In each domestic product market, we assume prices are normalised to a fixed numéraire price index weighted by the base composition of sectoral final demand. On the external accounts, we assume that for the ROW exchange rates are flexible while trade balances are fixed.

The CGE model was calibrated to a 1991 social accounting matrix (SAM) of North America and Chile, discussed in greater detail in the next subsection.[6] The calibration of the model to the SAM relied on a set of behavioural parameters equivalent to those described in Roland-Holst, Reinert and Shiells (1994b) and making use of the non-nested elasticities of substitution among import sources estimated by Shiells and Reinert (1993).[7]

The SAM database

The central data source for this chapter was a 1991 social accounting matrix for Canada, the United States, Mexico and Chile. Construction of the 1991 SAM began with the transformation of 1991 national accounts for each country into four separate macroeconomic SAMs. The Canadian macroeconomic SAM was constructed by mapping the macroeconomic data presented in two sources (Statistics Canada 1993a and 1993b) into a matrix format. The US macroeconomic SAM was constructed by transforming the US National Income and Product Account (NIPA) into a matrix format. For the Mexican macroeconomic SAM, we constructed a macroeconomic SAM using data from the OECD (1992), the Banco de México (1993), the Instituto Nacional de Estadística, Geographía e Informática (1992), and the International Monetary Fund (1993). Finally, the Chilean macroeconomic SAM was constructed using data from official sources.[8]

Next, the individual macroeconomic SAMs were joined together into an integrated macroeconomic SAM for the four countries. This process was completed in three steps. First, the Canadian, Mexican and Chilean macroeconomic SAMs were converted to 1991 US dollars using yearly averages of market exchange rates from the International Monetary Fund (1993). Second, trade flows among the four countries were added to the multicountry SAM and subtracted from the rest of the world account. Data on trade flows were taken from the International Monetary Fund (1992). Total Mexican trade was adjusted for maquiladora trade using data from the Banco de México (1993), since these activities were not reflected in the Mexican national accounts prior to 1992. Third, factor service flows and capital flows among the four countries were added, with the appropriate subtractions from the rest of the world account. These flows were taken from the US Department of Commerce (1992a) and Statistics Canada (1993b).

The detailed sectoral accounts were constructed by disaggregating the commodity account rows and columns of the four-country macroeconomic SAM into twenty-five sectors. The disaggregated accounts include labour value added, property value added, indirect business taxes, value added taxes (for Mexico), domestic final demand, imports, exports, and inter-industry transactions. This was done using 1990 Statistics Canada input–output accounts, 1987 US Department of Labor input–output accounts, 1989 SECOFI input–output accounts[9] for Mexico, and 1988 input–output accounts for Chile.

Sectoral trade flows were estimated using ten-digit HTS data for the United States and three-digit SITC data for all four countries. The former was obtained from the US Department of Commerce (USDOC) Bureau of the Census data tapes, and the latter was obtained from United Nations data tapes. Sectoral trade within North America was estimated using the import data from these tapes. Canadian tariffs were estimated from the 1990 input–

output data, US tariffs were estimated from the USDOC data, Mexican tariffs were estimated from data presented in the General Agreement on Tariffs and Trade (1993), and Chilean tariffs were estimated from data provided by UNCTAD and Chilean official sources.

2.3 SIMULATION RESULTS

This section presents a detailed interpretation of two of the many simulation experiments conducted with the NAFTA+ model described in the previous section. The policy scenarios presented here contrast two cases: original NAFTA implementation (the full results of which can still only be estimated), and a four-country liberalization. In both cases, the removal of nominal protection as well as NTB-induced price distortions are considered. In both liberalizations, each trading partner maintains its existing protection with respect to the rest of the world.[10] Our results indicate that all four countries could realize gains from more liberal trade relations, and that each economy would undergo significant shifts in its trade and domestic resource use patterns. The differences between NAFTA and NAFTA+, however, are most significant for the new entrant, Chile, indicating that all four economies have prior trade patterns which are complementary and minimize diversionary effects which would reduce incumbent advantages. We present the results in three stages: beginning with a description of the experiments, followed by a discussion of the aggregate results for several experiments and ending with a detailed sectoral discussion of the Chilean results.

NAFTA and incremental NAFTA+ effects: an overview

An empirical simulation model with this level of detail can generate results which defy detailed exposition. In this section, we provide an overview of the aggregate and main qualitative effects of Chilean accession. This first set of results contrasts our standard, three-country NAFTA liberalization estimates with the incremental effects of Chile's accession to the group.[11] The basic NAFTA scenario with which we begin is described elsewhere (see, for example, Reinert and Roland-Holst, 1995c). For the moment we simulate a very liberal base NAFTA convention, one which entails removal of all three-country bilateral tariff and non-tariff barriers observed in the base year. The second experiment, NAFTA+ or the inclusion of Chilean accession, is the same except that we include Chile's removal of existing tariff and non-tariff barriers.

Table 2.1 presents the basic NAFTA results, which again have been presented elsewhere and will not be discussed in detail here. Beyond the member countries in Experiment 1, note that Chile actually benefits from the formation of NAFTA even when it is excluded. This result is hardly surprising,

Table 2.1 Aggregate simulation results

Aggregates	Experiment 1: NAFTA				Experiment 2: NAFTA+				Differences			
	USA	Canada	Mexico	Chile	USA	Canada	Mexico	Chile	USA	Canada	Mexico	Chile
EV Income (%)	1.50	5.19	0.79	0.23	1.51	5.20	0.79	1.43	0.01	0.01	0.01	1.20
Real GDP	1.15	6.91	2.03	0.03	1.16	6.92	2.05	1.06	0.01	0.01	0.01	1.03
Imports	8.09	17.32	10.61	0.52	8.15	17.35	10.66	4.39	0.06	0.03	0.05	3.87
Exports	5.80	26.22	19.76	-0.04	5.87	26.24	19.87	3.37	0.06	0.03	0.11	3.41
Real ER	-0.48	1.30	5.38	-0.20	-0.48	1.30	5.46	-0.29	0.00	0.00	0.07	-0.09
Total	1643	980	307	1	1661	981	307	42	18.0	2.0	0	40.0
Prof. & mgmt	398	306	38	0	402	306	39	3	4.54	0.48	0.25	2.43
Sales, cler.	640	367	139	1	648	368	140	11	7.76	0.56	1.03	10.72
Agriculture	53	16	-23	0	53	16	-25	18	-0.04	0.12	-1.95	17.93
Crafts	221	213	107	0	223	213	108	7	2.04	0.31	0.65	6.57
Oper., lab.	331	79	46	0	334	79	46	3	3.31	0.11	0.28	2.82

Notes
Experiment 1: Bilateral tariff and NTB removal for the United States, Canada and Mexico
Experiment 2: Bilateral tariff and NTB removal, all four economies

given the magnitude of income effects among its three trading partners, but it provides some comfort for neighbours who choose to remain outside regional agreements, in that trade creation might generally be expected to outweigh trade diversion. Although Chile experiences a small real exchange rate appreciation and export decline when NAFTA is formed, the access to cheaper imported intermediates appears to stimulate domestic growth. The NAFTA results for Chile are very small in any case, and care should be taken about generalizing from them.

The two most salient features of the NAFTA+ aggregate results are the significant gains for Chile from accession and the negligible difference it implies for the incumbents, and both results are intuitive. Chile has a strong outward orientation and stands to gain appreciably from greater North American market access. The absolute and relative magnitudes of the gains are smaller than its three partners because of its smaller economy and North American trade shares. Chile's real GDP results are comparable to those of the US in percentage terms, not because of its self-sufficiency but because of its geographic isolation. Canada and Mexico have much higher levels of North American trade dependency than the other two, and thereby enjoy relatively greater stimulus from liberalization. Like the US, Chile experiences greater import than export growth, and this induces modest real exchange rate appreciation. Occupationally, Chile's employment adjustments are con-centrated in (export) agriculture and semi-skilled tertiary employment, which is likely to have a less dynamic benefit than the higher skill stimulus to US and Canadian employment.

Judging from these results, the benefits of NAFTA incumbency are robust against this new entrant, although this conclusion might not apply to econo-mies which are more proximate or structurally similar to the incumbents (particularly Mexico). Apparently, Chilean export and import patterns, with respect to the region are complementary with intra-regional bilateral trade, so relatively little net diversion occurs with Chilean accession. If account were taken of seasonality, it might even be found that Mexico and Chile are agricultural exporters with sufficiently strong complementarity to increase the gains of the latter and reverse the losses of the former.

Detailed results

In this sub-section, the effects on Chile of NAFTA accession are discussed in greater detail. From these adjustments, lessons can be drawn for aspirant members of such a regional agreement. Table 2.2 presents the four main sectoral components of supply and demand for NAFTA+, measured as changes in percentage and base real value terms.

The general pattern of structural adjustment which emerges is logical enough: stimulus to primary exports and imports of capital goods and chemicals. Both trends are consistent with intensification of prior trade

Table 2.2 Sectoral adjustments for Chile

	Percentage changes				Changes in real 1992 (US$m)			
	Domestic supply	Exports	Domestic demand	Imports	Domestic supply	Exports	Domestic demand	Imports
1 Agriculture	2.60	17.26	0.82	35.52	137	165	37	65
2 Mining	2.23	2.99	1.44	4.96	154	110	48	4
3 Petroleum	0.34	1.25	0.79	2.13	8	2	25	19
4 Food processing	1.54	3.43	1.27	5.20	92	47	63	17
5 Beverages	1.50	6.48	0.66	3.75	10	7	4	1
6 Tobacco	−0.10	4.65	−0.28	1.62	0	1	−1	0
7 Textiles	0.33	8.21	0.75	3.13	4	4	10	10
8 Apparel	0.37	1.70	0.55	2.15	3	1	5	3
9 Leather	0.69	2.32	0.77	2.33	4	1	4	1
10 Paper	−1.14	−2.53	0.75	10.33	−22	−13	12	21
11 Chemicals	0.24	1.39	1.42	3.63	5	3	41	39
12 Rubber	0.34	0.26	0.89	3.25	3	0	8	6
13 Non-metal minerals	0.48	10.40	0.63	2.93	3	2	5	3
14 Base metals	1.52	9.60	1.39	3.36	13	9	15	11
15 Wood & metal prods	0.13	−0.01	0.42	2.38	3	0	8	6
16 Non-elec. machinery	1.57	1.50	2.80	3.83	20	1	75	56
17 Electric machinery	0.12	0.25	1.38	2.91	1	0	21	20
18 Transport equipt	2.69	2.71	4.81	6.34	27	2	105	80
19 Other manufactures	1.81	5.33	2.26	3.24	8	2	16	10
20 Construction	0.52	0.00	0.52	1.45	18	0	18	0
21 Electricity	0.54	0.00	0.55	2.33	8	0	8	0
22 Commerce	0.56	−1.62	0.75	2.95	68	−8	90	13
23 Transport & comm.	0.02	−0.83	0.51	1.53	1	−9	18	8
24 Fin., Ins., and RE	0.17	−2.46	0.32	2.81	5	−2	9	2
25 Other services	0.59	−0.21	0.60	1.34	47	0	48	1

patterns for Chile, particularly with respect to the two larger partners. The rise in imports is more monotonic across sectors, largely because of net income gains and real exchange rate appreciation.

Export adjustments, on the other hand, are slightly more varied. Of particular interest is the decline of paper and wood exports, in which, conventional wisdom has it, Chile's comparative advantage lies. While this is surprising, however, it should be borne in mind that raw forestry products are included in agriculture in this aggregation and may contribute to the significant rise in exports for that sector. In any case, these results might justify further reflection on existing trade orientation in forestry products, particularly in light of the fragility of paper's competitiveness and the precedence for greater value-added capture which has been set elsewhere (e.g. the Indonesian log export ban).

The mining sector continues to be an engine of foreign exchange generation, and this is likely to continue well into the future on current domestic and regional trends, only accelerating with the advent of North American trade preferences.

Overall, the expansionary effects of NAFTA+ are concentrated in Chile's primary and tertiary sectors, where employment stimulus also focuses on unskilled and semi-skilled workers. One hopes that this can be augmented by the country's shifting emphasis towards higher average education levels and the endogenous growth externalities of accelerating technology imports.[12] Simply put, NAFTA accession confers upon Chile an intensification of its traditional patterns of comparative advantage, and these are unlikely to lead the country to the highest, most sustainable growth trajectories without coordination with policies which foster greater human capital development and broad-based economic modernisation. This is a lesson which is probably of relevance to a large group of NAFTA aspirants.

2.4 CONCLUSIONS AND EXTENSIONS

The more articulated trade linkages embodied in the NAFTA agreement are now a fact of life. Implementation of the agreement, however, is still in progress, and its ultimate effects on the member economies and other economies in the region will take years to be fully discernible. Meanwhile, empirical studies such as the present one can elucidate the basic forces at work and provide a basis for analysing other North–South trade liberalization initiatives. Many economy-wide evaluations of North American trade liberalization have been undertaken, but this one seeks to embark on an appraisal of the larger implications of Latin American regionalism. Using Chile's NAFTA accession as a starting point, we have attempted to assess the effects of a NAFTA+ arrangement for both the incumbents and the new entrant.

Using a CGE model calibrated to a detailed four-country SAM, we obtained results which indicate that the North American trade relations are relatively robust to new membership in the trade compact by a relatively distant and structurally complementary economy like Chile. While Chile appears to enjoy substantial benefits from NAFTA+, most of the gains for the members of the original agreement are retained, and when they change it is usually for the better. In other words, Chilean accession appears to be more expansionary than contractionary for the North American incumbents.

There may be a downside to Chilean gains, however, in the sense that accession appears primarily to intensify this country's traditional patterns of comparative advantage. This is typical of passive outward orientation, but Chile has already demonstrated an understanding of this dilemma in its recent reformist experiments. It is still worth emphasizing, however, that opening markets alone is unlikely to get the country on the highest sustainable growth trajectories. These external reforms must be coordinated with domestic policies of human capital formation and investment which foster growth and modernisation externalities.

The latter conclusion applies with even more force to some other Latin American economies which might contemplate joining a regional initiative of this kind, particularly those which might enter into more direct competition with one of the incumbents or be at an earlier stage of modernisation and economic diversification. This policy challenge can best be overcome by appealing to the most general conclusion of this chapter: that complex external and domestic reforms require detailed empirical assessment and support for their successful implementation.

NOTES

1 This section draws upon Corbo (1985) and Tybout (1989), see these references for a more detailed account of this period.
2 Compare, e.g., Coeymans and Larraín (1994).
3 See, e.g., Reinert and Roland-Holst (1995b) and Reinert, Roland-Holst, and Shiells (1993, 1994a, b).
4 For an introduction to this type of trade specification, see de Melo and Robinson (1989). The presence of intra-industry trade can modify results of simple inter-industry models such as Stoper–Samuelson effects. See Reinert and Roland-Holst (1995) for an example.
5 ROW import supply and export demand elasticities have been estimated by the authors for the United States, and in every case, for the present sectoral aggrega-tion and magnitude of trade adjustments, the small-country assumption appears to be tenable. We extended this reasoning to Canada, Mexico and Chile and thus the ROW price systems are essentially exogenous.
6 For an introduction to the use of SAMs in trade policy analysis, see Reinert and Roland-Holst (forthcoming).
7 This detailed parametric information is available upon request from the authors.
8 The new Chilean SAM, much more detailed than the NAFTA+ database, is described in greater detail in Alonso and Roland-Holst (1995).
9 SECOFI is the acronym for Secretaría de Comercio y Fomento Industrial.
10 It is possible that harmonization of ROW protection would alter the results given here, but such policies are not presently under consideration.
11 For convenience, we assume that the latter event happens simultaneously with original NAFTA formation, thereby avoiding issues of sequencing and timing which are in any case not appropriate to this comparative static model.
12 See Collado et al. (1995) for a discussion of these human capital issues in a regional context.

REFERENCES

Alonso, E. and Roland-Holst, D.W. (1995), *A Detailed Social Accounting Matrix for Chile*, Working Paper, Department of Economics, Mills College, Oakland, Cal.

Banco de México (1993), *The Mexican Economy 1993*, Mexico City: Banco de México.

Brown, D.K, Deardorff, A.V. and Stern, R.M. (1992), 'A North American Free Trade Agreement: analytical issues and a computational assessment', *World Economy*, 15: 1, January, 11–30.

Coeymans A.J.E. and Larraín B.F. (1994), 'Efectos de un acuerdo de libre comercio entre Chile y Estados Unidos: un enfoque de equilibrio general,' *Cuaderno Económicos*, 31: 94, 357–99.

Collado, J.C., Roland-Holst, D.W. and van der Mensbrugghe, D. (1995), 'Latin American employment prospects in a more liberal trading environment,' in D. Turnham, C. Foy and G. Larrain (eds), *Social Tensions, Job Creation, and*

Economic Policy in Latin America, Paris and Washington, D.C.: OECD Development Centre and the Inter-American Development Bank.

Corbo, V. (1985), 'Reforms and macroeconomic adjustment in Chile during 1974–84,' *World Development*, 13: 8.

de Melo, J. and Robinson, S. (1989), 'Product differentiation and the treatment of foreign trade in computable general equilibrium models of small countries', *Journal of International Economics*, 27: 1/2, 47–67.

Delorme, F. and Lester, J. (1990), 'The structure of production in ten Canadian industries,' *Empirical Economics*, 15: 4, 315–46.

Francois, J.S. and Shiells, C.R. (eds) (1994), *Modeling Trade Policy: Applied General Equilibrium Assessments of NAFTA*, Cambridge: Cambridge University Press.

General Agreements on Tariffs and Trade (1993), *Trade Policy Review: Mexico, 1993*, vol. I, Geneva: GATT.

Hufbauer, G. and Schott, J. (1992), *North American Free Trade: Issues and Recommendations*, Washington, D.C.: Institute for International Economics.

Instituto Nacional de Estadística, Geographía e Informática (1992), *Sistema de Cuentas Nacionales de Mexico: Cálculo Preliminar*, Mexico City.

International Monetary Fund (1992), *Direction of Trade Statistics Yearbook 1992*, Washington, D.C.: IMF.

International Monetary Fund (1993), *International Financial Statistics*, Washington, D.C.: IMF.

Killingsworth, M.R. (1983), *Labor Supply*, Cambridge: Cambridge University Press.

Krugman, P. and Lawrence, R. (1994), *Trade, Jobs, and Wages*, NBER Working Paper no. 4478, New York, National Bureau of Economic Research.

Maechler, A.M. and Roland-Holst, D.W. (forthcoming), 'Labor market structure and conduct', in J.F. Francois and K.A. Reinert (eds), *Applied Methods for Trade Policy Analysis*, Cambridge: Cambridge University Press.

Organization for Economic Co-operation and Development (1992), *OECD Economic Surveys: Mexico*, Paris: OECD.

Reinert, K.A. and Roland-Holst, D.W. (1995a), *Parameter Estimates for US Trade Policy*, Working Paper 95-01, Kalamazoo College, Kalamazoo, Michigan.

Reinert, K.A. and Roland-Holst, D.W. (1995b), *The Impact of North–South Trade Liberalization on Occupational Wages and Employment: The Case of North America*, Working Paper 95-02, Kalamazoo College Department of Economics, Kalamazoo, Michigan.

Reinert, K.A. and Roland-Holst, D.W. (1995c), *Employment and Wage Patterns Arising from North–South Trade Liberalization: The Case of North America*, Technical Paper No. 110, OECD Development Centre, Paris.

Reinert, K.A. and Roland-Holst, D.W. (forthcoming), 'Social accounting matrices,' in J.F. Francois and K.A. Reinert (eds), *Applied Methods for Trade Policy Analysis*, Cambridge: Cambridge University Press.

Reinert, K.A., Roland-Holst, D.W. and Shiells, C.R. (1993), 'Social accounts and the structure of the North American economy', *Economic Systems Research*, 5: 3, 295–326.

Roland-Holst, D.W., Reinert, K.A. and Shiells, C.R. (1994a), 'A general equilibrium analysis of North American economic integration', in C.R. Shiells and J.F. Francois (eds), *Applied General Equilibrium Analysis of North American Free Trade*, Cambridge: Cambridge University Press.

Roland-Holst, D.W., Reinert, K.A. and Shiells, C.R. (1994b), 'North American trade liberalization and the role of nontariff barriers', *North American Journal of Economics and Finance*, 5: 2, 137–68.

Sachs, J.D. and Shatz, H.J. (1994), 'Trade and jobs in US manufacturing', *Brookings Papers on Economic Activity*, 1, 1–84.

Shiells, C.R. and Reinert, K.A. (1993), 'Armington models and terms-of-trade effects: some econometric evidence from North America', *Canadian Journal of Economics*, 26: 2, 299–316.

Shiells, C.R. and Shelburne, R.C. (1992), 'A summary of "industrial effects of a free-trade agreement between Mexico and the USA" by Interindustry Economic Research Fund, Inc.', in US International Trade Commission, *Economy-Wide Modeling of the Economic Implications of a FTA with Mexico and a NAFTA with Canada and Mexico*, USITC Publication 2508, May.

Sobarzo, H.E. (1992), 'A General Equilibrium analysis of the gains from trade for the Mexican economy of a North American Free Trade Agreement', *World Economy*, 15: 1, 83–100.

Statistics Canada (1993a), *National Income and Expenditure Accounts*, Ottawa.

Statistics Canada (1993b), *Canada's Balance of International Payments*, Ottawa.

Taylor, J.E. (1992), 'Remittances and inequality reconsidered: direct, indirect and intertemporal effects', *Journal of Policy Modeling*, 14: 2, 889–96.

Tybout, J.R. (1989), *Entry, Exit, Competition and Productivity in the Chilean Industrial Sector*, Working Paper, Trade Policy Division, Washington, D.C.: World Bank, May.

United States Department of Commerce (1992a), *Survey of Current Business*, 72: 6, June.

United States Department of Commerce (1992b), *Survey of Current Business*, 72: 7, July.

3

RESOURCE ALLOCATION EFFECTS OF THE 1992 CAP REFORM ON THE GREEK ECONOMY

Stella Balfoussias and Roberto A. De Santis

3.1 INTRODUCTION

Greece's accession to the European Union (EU) has had a significant impact on Greek agriculture. The removal of import controls for EU products along with the implementation of the Common Agricultural Policy (CAP) have initiated substantial changes in prices of agricultural products and, in effect, in output composition, trade of agricultural products and agricultural incomes. Greek farmers are increasingly dependent on the various price and income support mechanisms of the CAP at a time when agricultural output remains stagnant and technological change is very slow, due to lack of investment. A substantial CAP reform is expected to have significant welfare and allocative implications for the Greek agricultural sector and the economy at large, given the present share of the sector in output and employment.

The 1992 reform aims to improve market orientation of CAP with a view to tackling the growing problem of food surpluses and the associated demands on the EU budget. The most significant policy change, applied mainly to the arable sector and to a lesser extent to the milk and beef sectors, is the reduction in the levels of intervention prices combined with the introduction of direct payments to farmers. This change is expected to reduce supply, increase demand and thereby reduce or even eliminate surpluses, ultimately reducing budgetary costs.

This chapter attempts to evaluate the resource allocation effects of recent CAP reform on the Greek economy, with particular reference to the sectoral implications, using an Applied General Equilibrium (AGE) model. AGE models offer perhaps the most suitable vehicle for examining such issues since they are structured to represent sectoral interdependencies.

The effects of agricultural liberalisation policies have been the subject of a number of AGE studies. Models designed to address particular changes in specific support programmes require a detailed representation of agricultural and food industries. Such models are usually country specific (for example, Hertel *et al.*, 1989), but they may also encompass a multicountry structure when the focus is limited to a specific agricultural commodity. Examples of such studies are the models of Trela *et al.* (1987) and Rutherford *et al.* (1990), which are grain-specific models.

Most multicountry models address questions relating to broad policy reforms. These models involve a very aggregated structure of either countries or sectors, depending on whether they focus on intersectoral or welfare consequences of such reforms. The best-known model in the first category is the OECD WALRAS model (Burinaux *et al.*, 1990a, 1990b), a multicountry model in which the agricultural sector is disaggregated into seven subsectors but countries are defined as broad trading blocks, the EU being one of them. Studies investigating questions about the CAP fall mainly into the second category. Examples are Harrison *et al.* (1989, 1995) and Fehr and Wiegard (1996), all of which involve a multicountry context where the EU is dissaggregated into member states, with agricultural and food sectors aggregated into one or two categories. Harrison *et al.* (1989) compare the welfare importance of the CAP in relation to total effect of EU membership. In their 1995 paper they examine welfare and output effects of elimination of the CAP. Fehr and Wiegard (1996) examine welfare effects of world-wide agricultural liberalisation, including reform of the CAP. Although the last two studies include analytic modelling of particular CAP instruments, the aggregate representation of agricultural sectors does not allow for changes in specific support programmes, usually the content of the actual CAP reforms to be simulated. In addition, they cannot trace the intersectoral consequences of liberalisation between those agricultural sectors which are subject to reform and those which are not.

In the present study we develop a static, single-country, multisector model of the Greek economy benchmarked to data for 1990. Although it gives attention to all sectors of the Greek economy, it highlights agricultural and food sectors in a fairly detailed manner. It incorporates a number of CAP parameters important for Greek agriculture, mainly production and export subsidies, thus allowing simulation of both the actual package of recent CAP changes and a broad set of possible future ones.

The remainder of the chapter is organised as follows. Section 3.2 presents the basic characteristics of the Greek agricultural sector in relation to the CAP. In section 3.3 we present the AGE model with particular emphasis on the modelling of agricultural support. Section 3.4 describes the data and the calibration procedure. Section 3.5 reports the policy experiments, and section 3.6 concludes.

3.2 THE GREEK AGRICULTURAL SECTOR IN THE CONTEXT OF THE CAP

The Greek agriculture sector in the EU context

Greece's participation in the EU at beginning of the 1980s has brought the Greek agricultural sector under the CAP support regime, that is, under a system combining market price support provided through administered prices, with export subsidies and tariffs as well as direct payments to producers. During the period 1980–1990 agricultural output has been declining. At the same time a number of structural changes have taken place. Table 3.1 summarises some key developments in the Greek agricultural sector with reference to the situation in the European community.

Although the value of the final agricultural production measured in ECUs has increased with rates higher than the EU average, the volume of agricultural production, measured in terms of gross value added at constant prices, has remained roughly unchanged. As a result the share of agricultural value added in GDP has declined from 15.9 to 7.5 per cent.

Labour, capital and land inputs in agricultural production have been reduced. Most remarkably, private investment in agriculture has continued on a long-run declining trend, despite the implementation of the EU structural policy.

Owing to the above structural changes, labour productivity has increased modestly. The rate of change was, nevertheless, inadequate to lead to any real convergence of the productivity level of Greek agriculture to that of the EU average, which is not surprising considering the lack of capital investment.

The external agricultural balance, which was in surplus in the early 1980s, has moved into deficit due to a low rate of increase in exports and a rapid increase in imports, especially imports from the Community. Over the period 1985–94 the share of agricultural imports within total imports has increased by an average rate of 5.7 per cent, whereas the share of agricultural exports to total exports has increased by only 1.5 per cent.

Nevertheless, agricultural income per head, measured in terms of real net value added per annual work unit, has increased by an average of 1.9 per cent per year since 1980. Although reflecting to some extent changes in agricultural employment, this development represents mainly the impact of the CAP. Notwithstanding the fact that the composition of agricultural output in Greece is dominated by products not particularly favoured by the CAP system of support, agricultural income has increased at an average rate higher than the agricultural product, due to the substantial average increase in direct subsidies.

The stagnation of the aggregate agricultural output conceals some significant compositional changes. Table 3.2 depicts the compositional characteristics of agricultural output. The most important changes are the reduction

Table 3.1 Key agricultural statistics for Greece and the European Union

	1980 EUR10 average	1980 GREECE	1985 EUR12 average	1985 GREECE	1990 EUR12 average	1990 GREECE	1994 EUR12 average	1994 GREECE	Average rate of change (%) EUR12 94/85	GREECE 85/50	GREECE 94/85
Production inputs											
Number of persons employed ('000)	906	956	788	931	664	769	591.5	683	-3.14	-0.53	-3.38
Share in employed civilian working population (%)	9.5	30.3	8.6	28.9	6.5	23.9	5.5	21.3	-4.85	-0.94	-3.33
Number of holdings ('000)	9,103	959	8,947	952	8,171	924	7,264	819	-2.29	-0.15	-1.66
Utilised agricultural area per holding (ha)	12.7	4.1	8.9	4.3	14	4	16.4	4.3	7.03	0.96	0.00
Private gross fixed capital formation (80=100)	100	100		123.4		84.8		56.1		4.29	-8.39
Income and output											
Final production of agriculture (ECUm)	12,854	6,226	15,420	8,182	16,841	7,522	16,179	8,722	0.54	5.62	0.71
Gross value added at constant prices (85=100)		100.6	100	100		89	106.7	106	0.72	-0.12	0.65
Share in the GDP (GVA/GDP)(%)	3.7	15.9	3.5	16.6	2.9	13.9	1.8	7.5	-7.12	0.87	-8.45
Agricultural income per head (80=100)	100	100	107.1	110.1	119.4	115	112.7	129.9	0.57	1.94	1.85
Labour productivity (EU 80=100)	100.0	45.9	137.9	62.0	178.9	69.0	192.8	90.0	3.80	6.18	4.24
Trade											
Share of agricultural imports in total imports (%)	15.7	12.8	15.1	10.6	11.5	12.3	12	17.5	-2.52	-3.70	5.73
Share of agricultural exports in total exports (%)	9	27.7	9	29	8.5	28.3	8.4	33.2	-0.76	0.92	1.51
External agricultural trade balance (ECUm)	-2,269	345	-27,056	48	-20,842.	-143	-19,334	-577	-3.66	-32.60	-231.8
Household consumption											
Share in total household consumption expenditure (%)[b]	23.6	41.5	21.9	41.3	20.2	38.3	19.6	36.4	-1.23	-0.10	-1.39
EU support											
EAGGF expenditure per head of agricultural employment[c]	942	144	2,296.64	1,154.29	3,863.61	2,480.92	5,643.92	3,424.43	10.51	51.63	12.84

Source: Commission of the European Communities

Notes
[a] Net value added at constant price per hour work unit
[b] Household consumption on food and beverages
[c] The figures in the first column refer to 1981

Table 3.2 The structure of agricultural production in Greece: shares of products in final production

Products subject to EU market organisations	1980	1990
Wheat	7.7	6.9
Barley	0.9	0.4
Maize	2.5	3.4
Rice	0.3	0.3
Sugar beets	2.0	1.2
Tobacco	5.7	6.1
Olive oil	7.5	13.7
Fruits and vegetables	21.3	22.6
Wine and must	2.4	1.6
Textile fibres	4.4	7.6
Milk	8.3	8.5
Beef/veal	4.8	3.0
Pigmeat	4.7	3.0
Sheepmeat and goatmeat	9.3	6.7
Poultry and eggs	6.7	5.2
Rest	0.2	0.2
Other products	11.3	9.6
	100.0	100.0

Source: Commission of the European Communities

of the shares of meat sectors and the concentration of agricultural production in favour of traditional products such as olive oil, fruits and vegetables, tobacco, and textile fibres.

Changes in the composition of agricultural output are due to a number of reasons such as changes in technology and increased competition from other European countries brought about by the removal of import controls. Nevertheless, the CAP support mechanisms are thought to have played a very important role in bringing about the above changes.

The above stylised facts underline the vulnerability of Greek agriculture to changes in the CAP regime. Given the relation of output structure to the CAP support mechanisms, it follows that certain types of reforms, particularly those affecting products receiving high support and contributing significantly to total agricultural production, may have far-reaching consequences.

The main CAP features and the process of reform

The 'old' CAP regime

The Common Agricultural Policy of the European Union is a system of high fixed prices received by the producer and in many cases paid by the consumer. Every year the EU sets a target price (TP) for each major product under the CAP, which is then supported by various intervention mechanisms.

In the pre-reform situation, once the target price was set, a threshold price representing a port equivalent of the target price was also determined. A tax or 'levy' was thus imposed on imports to bring them up to the required threshold price. Given that the world price would fluctuate, this tax had to be variable. The system is thus known as one of variable import levies.

Another important instrumental price is the intervention price (IP). This is the price at which the EU is prepared to buy an agricultural product when the market price is below it. IP is usually a few percentage points below the target price.

Intervention activities aiming to support the system of administered prices generate demands on the EU budget. The only exception is the imposition of import levies, which generate revenue. The cost of intervention in the agricultural market is born by the European Agricultural Guidance and Guarantee Fund (EAGGF). Total cost is classified into three types of expenditures, coinciding with three types of intervention activities having distinct economic roles.[1]

The first type of intervention is the provision of export subsidies, which are intended to cover the differences between internal prices and world prices in order to enable the disposal of EU excess supplies in the rest of the world. The second type of intervention involves various types of producer subsidies, which aim to guarantee minimum prices to producers whilst enabling consumers to obtain agricultural products at prices lower than those paid to farmers. Finally, storage and withdrawal activities involve purchasing excess supplies for storage or withdrawal, and comprise all technical and financial costs plus the offsetting of losses incurred or profits made on the sale of the products stored. The cost of the above interventions was ECU 30553 million in 1991. Export subsidies represent 33 per cent, production subsidies 46.6 per cent and storage and withdrawal activities 20.4 per cent.

Table 3.3 shows the support received by the Greek agricultural sector under the above schemes. The table portrays the overriding importance of production subsidies in the Greek case since they represent 92 per cent of total EAGGF expenditure for Greece. Export subsidies have some significance, not so much in terms of expenditure level, but because they affect a variety of products. Storage and withdrawal activities relate to three products only, and they represent 3.4 per cent of total expenditure.

The 1992 reform

The main objectives of the 1992 CAP reforms were the improvement of market orientation through reduction in farm surpluses below what they would have been, the reduction in total EAGGF expenditure, and achievement of greater transparency of the support system through the shift of the cost from consumers to taxpayers.

The main feature of the reforms is the replacement of a significant part of

Table 3.3 EAGGF expenditure in Greece by intervention activity (Dr m)

	Export refunds		Storage and withdrawals		Production subsidies		Total
	1991	%	1991	%	1991	%	1991
Arable crops	2,260.5	11.1	0.0	0.0	18,149.9	88.9	20,410.4
Cereals	2,260.5	14.0			13,847.4	86.0	16,107.9
Oilseeds					4,017.0	100.0	4,017.0
Protein products					285.5	100.0	285.5
Sugar	20.0	1.0	2,069.0	99.0		0.0	2,089.0
Olive oil	1,214.0	2.4			49,609.0	97.6	50,823.0
Dried fodder and vegetables							
Textile plants					75,711.0	100.0	75,711.0
Fruits and vegetables	7,039.0	9.0	9,485.0	12.1	62,027.0	79.0	78,551.0
Wine	331.5	9.9	363.0	10.8	2,661.5	79.3	3,356.0
Tobacco	4,381.0	5.3			77,800.0	94.7	82,181.0
Other agriculture	38.6	20.3			274.0	100.0	312.6
Rice	38.6	20.3			151.5	79.7	190.1
Milk and milk products		0.0			1,771.0	100.0	1,771.0
Beef/veal	44.0	2.1			2,046.0	97.9	2,090.0
Sheepmeat–goatmeat		0.0			30,256.0	100.0	30,256.0
Pigmeat		0.0			1.7	100.0	1.7
Eggs and poultrymeat	11.0	100.0					11.0
Rest animal products							
Fishery							
Rest							
Total	15,339.6	4.4	11,917.0	3.4	320,307.1	92.2	347,563.7

Source: Greek Department of Agriculture

the market price support with a range of direct payments. More specifically the following measures were applied:

- substantial cuts in intervention prices, along with a corresponding cut in export subsidies: the price cuts would be phased in over the period 1993–1996 (the intervention prices would still, however, be somewhat above world prices);
- payment of full compensation to farmers for their resulting loss of income: since this income support would be based on past yields, it would be independent of any changes in production and the income support would thus provide no direct incentive to increase production;
- reduction in the utilised land through linkage of direct aid to set aside constraints: in order to receive the income support, all except small farmers would have to agree to set aside 10 per cent of their land;
- measures limiting the volume of production and in particular the tightening of production quotas for milk and sugar, where price support policies are operating in conjunction with such quotas.

The above changes applied mainly to the so-called arable sector, that is cereal, oilseed and protein crops and, to a lesser extent, to the beef sector.

Intervention prices in the arable sector were cut by 29 per cent and in the milk beef and sheep sectors by 12 per cent. For cereals and oilseeds, direct payments are based on historical areas and yields and are made in conjunction with a set-aside requirement. For livestock, payments are also based on fixed reference numbers of livestock, and for beef they are subject to limitations on stocking density. At the same time a set of 'accompanying measures' to the CAP reform was also implemented, according to which the EU and member states finance other policies with varying objectives, including the encouragement of diversification, early retirement, infrastructure improvement, and research and development. Finally, following the Uruguay Round agreement, measures affecting border prices and protection of the internal market have changed. Threshold prices were abolished and the system of variable import levies were replaced with fixed tariffs in 1995.

As the implementation of the 1992 CAP reform provisions was completed in 1995, the overall effect of the reform on budgetary expenditure can be assessed only when 1996 figures are final. However, on the basis of 1995 data it can be observed that, despite substantial savings in storage costs and export subsidies, the overall decrease in administered prices has been more than compensated by the increase in direct payments. As a result the overall expenditure has increased by 3.5 per cent. Even though the purpose of the budget reduction has been missed, the budget is now subject to less fluctuations due to changes in world markets, but most importantly income support expenditure is under direct control of the EU.

3.3 THE MODEL

The model presented in this section is built to analyse the resource allocation effects of CAP reform on the Greek economy. The model is a static multisector representation of the Greek economy with emphasis on detailed disaggregation of the agricultural sector. In what follows, we describe the main equations relating to the interaction of Greek economy with the CAP mechanisms. Following the discussion of the previous section, the policy instruments of interest are production and export subsidy rates. As the intervention prices would still be somewhat above the world prices, the common external tariff should not be affected.

It is assumed here that the setting of a particular intervention price by the EU is exogenous to the conditions in the Greek market. We therefore assume that producers face exogenous production and export subsidy rates. Similarly, the common import levy is modelled as an exogenously set tariff rate. The storage and withdrawal activity is not modelled due to its low importance for Greek agriculture.

The model assumes perfect competition and constant returns to scale.

Thus, the marginal cost (c_i) to produce one unit of output (Y_i) can be defined as follows:

$$c_i = \frac{w\text{AL}_i + r\text{AK}_i + l_i\bar{L}_i}{Y_i} + \sum_j a_{ji}p_j + t_i py_i \tag{3.1}$$

where, AL_i, AK_i and $\bar{L}_i$ denote labour, capital and sector specific land, respectively; w, r and l_i the respective factor inputs returns; a_{ji} the input–output coefficients; t_i the indirect tax rate; p_j the consumer price; and py_i the composite producer price.

The assumptions that the technology exhibits constant returns to scale and that there are no barriers to entry imply the equality between total costs and total revenues for the zero profit condition to hold. As total revenues originate from domestic and foreign sales, plus the agricultural subsidies on exports and on total production, then the zero profit condition can be written as:

$$c_iY_i = (pd_i \, D_i + \overline{pwe}_i^{EU} \, E_i^{EU} + pe_i^{RoW} \, E_i^{RoW})(1 + s_i) \tag{3.2}$$

where pd_i is the producer price for the domestic sale, D_i; $\overline{pwe}_i^{EU}$ is the fixed producer price for the export sale to the EU, E_i^{EU}; pe_i^{RoW} is the producer price for the export sale to the non-member states, E_i^{RoW}, gross of the export subsidy; and s_i denotes the subsidy rates on total agricultural production at sectoral level. Producers then equate the marginal cost with the market price gross of subsidies. With this specification, the subsidy on agricultural production directly affects the amount of output produced.

The agricultural subsidy rate on exports to the non-member states indirectly affects agricultural export production through changes in the price obtained by Greek firms for their agricultural exports towards this market:

$$pe_i^{RoW} = \overline{pwe}_i^{RoW} \, (1 + se_i^{RoW}) \tag{3.3}$$

where $\overline{pwe}_i^{RoW}$ is the fixed price of exports prevailing in the market of the non-member states and se_i^{RoW} the subsidy rate on these exports.

Import demand specification involves a two-stage nested separable CES function. Thus, it is assumed that buyers first decide between domestically produced goods (D_j) and the composite imported commodities (M_j^c) with a constant elasticity of substitution ε_j, and then choose between imports from the EU (M_j^{EU}) and imports from the non-member states (M_j^{RoW}) with elasticity of substitution μ_j, according to the Armington specification (Armington, 1969), which treats products of different countries competing in the same market as imperfect substitutes. On the supply side the *small-country* assumption is postulated:

$$M_j^{EU} = A_j^{\mu_j-1}\alpha_j^{\mu_j}\left(\frac{\overline{pwm_j}^{EU}}{pm_j^c}\right)^{-\mu_j} M_j^c \tag{3.4}$$

$$M_j^{RoW} = A_j^{\mu_j-1}(1-\alpha_j)^{\mu_j}\left(\frac{(1+tm_j^{RoW})\overline{pwm_j}^{RoW}}{pm_j^c}\right)^{-\mu_j} M_j^c \tag{3.5}$$

where pm_j^c is the composite domestic price of imports; $\overline{pwm_j}^{EU}$ and $\overline{pwm_j}^{RoW}$ denote the world price of commodities imported from the EU and the non-member states, respectively; tm_j^{RoW} is the effective European common external tariff; α_j is the share parameter in the second-nest Armington trade aggregation function, and A_j is the shift parameter of the CES import aggregation function.

The *small-country* assumption implies the export demand functions from both regions are infinitely elastic. Hence, Greek export production is totally absorbed by foreign trade partners at world prices. On the supply side, exports to the EU (E_i^{EU}) and the non-member states (E_i^{RoW}) are derived by maximising total export sale revenues subject to the composite export frontier, which is defined by a constant elasticity of transformation (CET) function:

$$E_i^{EU} = \Gamma_i^{-(\eta_i+1)}\beta_i^{-\eta_i}\left(\frac{\overline{pwe_i}^{EU}}{pe_i^c}\right)^{\eta_i} E_i^c \tag{3.6}$$

$$E_i^{RoW} = \Gamma_i^{-(\eta_i+1)}(1-\beta_i)^{-\eta_i}\left(\frac{pe_i^{RoW}}{pe_i^c}\right)^{\eta_i} E_i^c \tag{3.7}$$

where E_i^c is the composite export, pe_i^c the composite export price, β_i the share parameter in the second-nest CET function, η_i the elasticity of transformation, and Γ_i the CET export aggregation function shift parameter.

Since European subsidies to the Greek agricultural sector, in the form of either production or exports subsidies, represent inflows and import duties outflows (collected by Greek authorities and transferred to the European Commission), the balance of payment is in equilibrium if the following condition holds:

$$\sum_i \overline{pwe_i}^{EU} E_i^{EU} + \sum_i pe_i^{RoW} E_i^{RoW} + \sum_i s_i py_i Y_i \overline{CA} + \overline{THW} =$$
$$\sum_i \overline{pwm_j}^{EU} M_j^{EU} + \sum_i (1+tm_j^{RoW}) \overline{pwm_j}^{RoW} M_j^{RoW} + TWG \tag{3.8}$$

where $\overline{CA}$ denotes the current account deficit, $\overline{THW}$ the remittances from foreign institutions to the representative household, and $\overline{TWG}$ represents the government transfers to foreign institutions.

Another feature of the CAP reform is the direct control of the supply side, through the arable land set-aside policy. This aspect is straightforward to analyse as the arable land is a sector-specific factor input of the production function. Sectoral output is described by a three stage nested separable CES function:

$$Y_i = \min\left[\frac{x_{ji}}{a_{ji}}, \frac{V_i}{a_i^v}\right] \tag{3.9}$$

$$V_i = \Phi_i\left[\delta_i \bar{L}_i^{(\xi_i-1)/\xi_i} + (1 - \delta_i)LK_i^{(\xi_i-1)/\xi_i}\right]^{\xi_i/(\xi_i-1)} \tag{3.10}$$

$$LK_i = \Theta_i\left[\gamma_i AL_i^{(\sigma_i-1)/\sigma_i} + (1 - \gamma_i)AK_i^{(\sigma_i-1)/\sigma_i}\right]^{\sigma_i/(\sigma_i-1)} \tag{3.11}$$

where x_{ji} are the raw material inputs, i the value added, a_i^v the value added requirement per unit of sectoral output, Φ_i and δ_i the shift and the share parameters in the value added function, ξ_i the elasticity of substitution among the composite labour–capital input and land, Θ_i and γ_i the shift and the share parameter in the labour–capital aggregation function, σ_i the elasticity of substitution among labour and capital.

With this specification, a set-aside policy would determine a backwards shift of the isoquant towards the origin, bringing about the desired contraction of sectoral output. Producers behave competitively, hence the demand of factor inputs in each sector is determined by the equality between factor returns and their marginal revenue product.

On the demand side of the model, it is assumed that the representative consumer and the government spend fixed budget shares on composite commodity; the aggregate intermediate demand is a Leontief function of output; and the investment demand is a fixed proportion of exogenous aggregate investment. The aggregate demand of each commodity is a CES function describing the substitution possibilities between the domestically produced goods and the competing foreign products.

The government levies two taxes in order to finance its expenditures: a direct tax on household income and an indirect tax on production. Public expenditure consists of exogenous transfers to households and foreign institutions and of consumption of composite commodities.

As far as the macro balances are concerned, total demand for factors equal their supply, the balance of payments is always in equilibrium by exogenously fixing the current account deficit, and aggregate savings always equate to aggregate investment, set exogenously in the model. The numéraire is the Laspeyres index of the price of domestic commodities.

The EC periodically determines the target price for all EU members. Since the immediate effect of a reduction in the target price is a reduction in the subsidy rate on exports to the non-member states, we vary se_k^{RoW} simultaneously with s_k ($k \in cap$)), to simulate various policy scenarios for the Greek economy.

3.4 DATA AND CALIBRATION

The model is calibrated using a social accounting matrix (SAM) of the Greek economy for 1990.[2] The SAM comprises three institutions (one household, one government, one foreign institution), twenty-two sectors, twenty-two commodities, one labour and one capital. The commodities are distinguished in domestic commodities, imports and exports. In turn, imports and exports are further disaggregated in order to separate the trade flows with the EU from the trade flows with the non-member states.

The construction of the SAM was based mainly on data provided by the National Statistical Service. A variety of other sources was also used, mainly trade data at the three-digit SITC classification, data on the service flows from the Bank of Greece and data on the EU agricultural support from the Department of Agriculture. The major building blocks of the SAM are adjusted to match the 1990 national income and product accounts data on output consumption and tax revenue figures.

The level of aggregation was chosen to serve the particular purpose of the study. Emphasis is given to the detailed representation of the various agricultural and agribusiness sub-sectors. In particular we distinguish between thirteen agricultural and agribusiness sub-sectors and nine non-agricultural sub-sectors. Table 3.4 shows the correspondence of the SAM sectors to the NACE[3] classification.

Ex ante effective agricultural production, export subsidy rates and the *ex ante* external tariff have been calibrated within the model. The values of elasticities employed in the model have been selected from existing literature. When estimates were not available, estimates for other countries, modified by personal judgement, were applied. Calibration of other parameter values, such as shift and share parameters of different functional forms, direct tax rate on household income, marginal propensity to save and initial prices, were based on standard techniques used in AGE models.

3.5 SIMULATIONS OF POLICY SCENARIOS

The scenarios reported in this section explore the sensitivity of the Greek economy, and the agricultural sector in particular, to changes in the CAP's major policy instruments: intervention prices, direct payments to farmers and land set-aside schemes. The experiments aim to assess the sectoral

Table 3.4 Correspondence between the SAM sectors and NACE Revision 1 codes

NACE classification		Sectors
1	01A	Grains and related activities
2	01B	Vegetables
3	01C	Fruits
4	01D	Milk and other animal products
5	02A+05A	Forestry, fishing and related activities
6	15A	Processed meat
7	15C	Processed fruit and vegetables
8	15D	Oils and fats
9	15E	Dairy products
10	15H	Bread and sugar industry
11	15I	Beverages
12	16A	Tobacco industry
13	15B+15F+15G	Processed fish, processed cereals, animal food industry
14	10+11+13+14	Mining
15	17+18+19+22+25+36	Other consumer industries
16	20+21+23+24+26+27+37	Intermediate industries
17	28+29+30+31+32+33+34+35	Capital industries
18	45	Construction
19	40+41	Electricity, gas and water
20	50+51+52+55+60+61+62+63+64+65+ 66+67+71+70+72+73+74+92+93+95	Trade, tourism, transport, banking, and other market services
21	80+85	Health and education
22	75+90+91	Non-market services

effects of recent CAP reform. Furthermore, we simulate the economic implications of a price reduction policy not accompanied by income support measures, a scenario that may be considered as a medium-term possibility.

Any CAP reform will of course take effect in all member states. Hence, the prevailing prices in the EU markets (that is, $\overline{pwe_i}^{EU}$ and $\overline{pwm_j}^{EU}$ in terms of our model's notation) will also be affected as a consequence of the reduction in intervention prices. A given reduction in the target price of the commodities under the 1992 CAP protocol, implemented by a reduction in production and export subsidy rates, implies therefore an equal reduction in $\overline{pwe_i}^{EU}$ and $\overline{pwm_j}^{EU}$. As a consequence of that, the foreign trade equations (3.4)–(3.7) indicate that imports from the EU will increase with respect to the imports from the non-member states, whilst the ratio between exports to the EU and exports to the non-member states will remain constant. It is important to stress that an equal reduction in $\overline{pwe_i}^{EU}$ and $\overline{pwm_j}^{EU}$ implies that the sectoral terms of trade are not affected. Hence, the *small-country* assumption is not violated.

The above experiments are carried out in terms of three specific scenarios. In scenario 1, production and export subsidy rates to grains, milk and other animal products are eliminated. In scenario 2, Greek farmers set aside 10 per cent of their grain land. Scenario 3 reports the results of a combination of the previous two scenarios, and in effect the estimates of the 1992 CAP reform.

The policy scenarios are performed for two alternative regimes regarding income support expenditure. The first encompasses full direct compensations to farmers, whereas the second assumes abolition of income support schemes. We define the direct payments to farmers as the income loss due to changes in the price support policy, such that the EU budgetary expenditure to Greece remains constant.

The results of simulations are reported in Tables 3.5 and 3.6. Tables 3.5 shows the sectoral implications of CAP reform. Looking at the results of scenario 1 in the actual case involving direct payments to farmers, we can see that resources are reallocated, especially within the agribusiness industries. The production of milk and other animal products is not really affected, whereas grain output decreases by 7.9 per cent. On the other hand, fresh fruit, oil and fats, dairy products and the bread and sugar industries record a remarkable growth. Also sectoral exports are strongly affected by the policy change. The elimination of export subsidies in grains and related activities and in milk and other animal products causes a fall in the exports of these goods by 55 per cent and 32.5 per cent in real terms, respectively. As a consequence of this and despite the expansion in export volume of other agricultural commodities, the aggregate volume of agricultural exports decreases by 2.9 per cent (see Table 3.6). On the import side, the slight rise of imports from the EU is due to the lower prices facing the commodity under analysis in the EU market. In fact, agricultural imports rise by 2.3 per cent in nominal terms. As far as the European transfers are concerned, Table 3.6 indicates that production and export subsidies decrease by 35.9 per cent and 10.1 per cent, respectively; whereas the direct payments to farmers amount to around Dr121 billion. The latter direct transfer to farmers would keep the EU budgetary expenditure towards Greece constant. The policy move from the market price intervention to the income support scheme allows a positive reallocation of resources among sectors, thus increasing the welfare of the nation by 0.4 per cent. When the income support scheme is abandoned by the EU, resources are reallocated, especially within the agribusiness industries, thus increasing the value added in agriculture and agribusiness activities by 1 per cent. This counterintuitive result is due to the balance of payment response to the policy change. The European transfers are a positive component of the balance of payment; their reduction implies an improvement of the trade balance to restore the balance of payment equilibrium: in fact, the volume of exports rises by 6.3 per cent, whilst the volume of imports decreases by 0.1 per cent. The increase in agricultural export brings about a rise of EU budgetary expenditure in the form of export

Table 3.5 Sectoral effects of the 1992 CAP reform (base year = 100)

Sectors	Scenario 1 Effects of the price support reduction				Scenario 2 Effects of arable land set-aside				Scenario 3 Overall effects of the 1992 reform			
	Output		Exports		Output		Exports		Output		Exports	
	(a)	(b)	(a)	(b)	(a)	(b)	(a)	(b)	(a)	(b)	(a)	(b)
Grains and related activities	92.1	92.4	45	45.3	94	92.1	81.2	72.5	84.1	85.1	27.5	30.4
Vegetables	101.8	100.5	107.3	95.1	100.1	100.3	100	101.3	104.3	100.4	118.5	93.3
Fruits	103.5	116.7	107.7	148.9	101.8	102.4	106.5	111.5	105.9	118.5	119.9	159.5
Milk and animal products	99.9	100.4	67.5	67.4	95.2	95.4	81.5	74.6	92.5	96.6	33.6	43.9
Forestry and fishery	100.7	106.3	102.7	129.8	101.6	101	107.3	104.5	101.9	107.5	108	136.5
Processed meat	101.8	100	106.5	100.4	95.6	97.7	84.6	91.7	98.2	99.9	93.4	99.9
Processed fruits and vegetables	100.9	109.8	101.4	115.8	100.4	99.9	100.6	99.9	101.8	111.4	102.9	118.4
Oils and fats	105.4	116.4	112.1	137.8	101	99	102.4	98	103.9	114.1	109.1	132.7
Dairy products	102.4	112.1	108	146.2	95.7	93.6	86.4	79.9	99.2	108.5	97.6	131.6
Bread and sugar industry	102.5	97.3	110.3	89.2	98.4	98.5	93.7	94.1	98.2	93.5	92.8	75.7
Beverages	101.7	104.1	107.1	118.8	101	100.6	103.6	101.9	102.5	103.5	109.8	115.9
Tobacco industry	100	96.2	100	90.9	99.3	98.4	98.4	96	99.5	94.1	98.7	85.8
Other processed food	106.7	109.7	132	156	93.7	92.3	77.1	71.2	100.7	98.7	112.7	104.7
Mining	102	126.1	104.5	154.6	103	102.9	106.2	105.8	103	132.2	104.7	167.9
Other consumer industries	102.4	103.2	106	107.8	100.3	100.3	100.8	100.7	102.3	103.1	105.6	107.6
Intermediate industries	99.7	102.3	99.1	104.7	100.2	100.4	100.4	100.9	101.5	102.6	103.4	105.7
Capital industries	99.9	100.2	99.7	99.8	100.7	101.6	101.7	103.8	100	101.8	99.6	103.6
Construction	100.2	100.7	—	—	100.1	100.1	—	—	100.4	100.7	—	—
Electricity, gas and water	100.9	104.2	—	—	100.7	101.4	—	—	102.2	105.1	—	—
Transport, communication, etc.	99.9	98.4	99.3	93.5	100.2	100.2	100.8	100.9	100.2	98.7	100.4	94.4
Health and education	99.7	97.3	—	—	100.2	100.2	—	—	100.1	97.6	—	—
Non-market services	99.8	99.2	—	—	100.1	100	—	—	100	99.4	—	—

Notes
(a) reports the results of the policy scenarios in the case of the adoption of the income support scheme by the EU
(b) reports the results of the policy scenarios if the EU abandons the income support scheme

Table 3.6 Economic effects on other main variables of some agricultural policy reforms (base year = 100)

	Scenario 1		Scenario 2		Scenario 3	
	(a)	*(b)*	*(a)*	*(b)*	*(a)*	*(b)*
Hicksian equivalent variation index	100.4	99.9	99.8	99.9	100.2	99.7
Aggregate output in real terms	100.4	101.0	99.8	99.8	100.2	100.8
GDP in real terms	100.3	100.8	99.9	99.9	100.2	100.7
Value added in agriculture sectors	100.0	101.0	99.3	99.1	99.0	100.0
Value added in non-agricultural sectors	100.3	100.3	100.4	100.5	100.9	100.8
Aggregate volume of exports	100.4	106.3	100.1	100.0	101.3	106.6
Volume of exports to the EU	101.3	108.8	100.3	100.1	102.1	109.2
Volume of exports to the ROW	99.2	102.8	99.8	99.8	100.1	103.0
Volume of agricultural exports	97.1	110.0	97.4	95.5	95.4	106.7
Volume of non-agricultural exports	101.5	105.1	101.0	101.4	103.1	106.6
Aggregate volume of imports	100.3	99.9	100.0	100.0	100.6	100.0
Volume of imports from the EU	100.5	100.2	100.1	100.0	100.9	100.3
Volume of imports from the ROW	99.9	99.5	100.0	99.9	100.2	99.6
Volume of agricultural imports	102.3	101.3	101.7	102.4	106.0	104.4
Volume of non-agricultural imports	99.9	99.7	99.8	99.6	99.7	99.2
Total agricultural subsidies	100.0	68.0	100.0	99.9	100.0	67.7
Agricultural production subsidies	64.1	66.1	99.8	100.0	63.9	65.8
Agricultural export subsidies to the ROW	89.9	106.9	98.7	97.9	93.4	108.3
Direct transfers (Dr m)	121,215	—	833	—	121,262	—

Notes
(a) reports the results of the policy scenarios in the case of the adoption of the income support scheme by the EU
(b) reports the results of the policy scenarios if the EU abandons the income support scheme

subsidies by 6.9 per cent; however, overall agricultural subsidies to Greece decrease by 32 per cent.

Coming to the sectoral economic impact of the grain land set-aside policy we see that the immediate impact is a reduction of grain output by 6 per cent and a reduction of exports by 18.8 per cent, in real terms. In general, this policy affects negatively most agricultural sectors, thus causing a reduction of the value added in agriculture and agribusiness industries by 0.7 per cent. Thus, if the price support reduction policy favours a more efficient reallocation of resources, the arable set-aside policy depresses the agricultural economy. These negative effects would be reinforced if the direct payments to farmers were not provided.

The overall effect of the 1992 CAP reform on the Greek economy is seen in scenario 3. The main impact is a decrease in the output of grains, milk and other animal products by 15.9 per cent and 7.5 per cent, respectively. Exports in these two sectors fall dramatically. As a consequence of this, the volume of agricultural exports decreases by 4.6 per cent. Despite the reallocation of resources in favour of fresh and processed fruits and vegetables, oil and fats, and beverages, the value added in agriculture and agribusiness industries decreases by 1 per cent. Another interesting result of the CAP reform scenario is the reallocation of resources not only towards the agricultural sectors not affected by the reform, but also in favour of the mining and industrial sectors. In fact, the value added in non-agricultural sectors increases by 0.9 per cent in real terms. As far as the Community transfers to Greek farmers are concerned, the volume of agricultural production subsidies and the volume of export subsidies decrease by 36.1 per cent and 6.6 per cent, respectively; whereas the estimate of direct payments to farmers is around Dr121 billion. Since the core of the CAP reform aims to reduce the surpluses in cereals and livestock commodities and to cut the Community budgetary expenditure in the form of market price support to farmers, we can argue that the 1992 CAP reform seems to fulfil both targets for the Greek economy. In addition, as a consequence of the resource reallocation gain, welfare and GDP rise by 0.2 per cent every year.

The resource allocation effects obtained in the case of no direct payments supporting farmers' incomes are modified due to the positive trade balance effect described earlier and represented by an increase in the volume of exports by 6.6 per cent, in real terms. Both the industrial sector and the agricultural sectors not subject to the CAP reform expand and as a result GDP rises by 0.7 per cent. However, overall welfare decreases by 0.3 per cent, due to uncompensated income losses suffered by farmers. It is important to stress that the welfare measure concerns the economy as a whole. Obviously, farmers would be worse off when the income support scheme is abandoned but a multihousehold model is necessary in order to assess welfare implications of the CAP reform for particular sections of the population.

3.6 SUMMARY AND CONCLUSIONS

The structure of Greek agriculture over recent years has been decisively affected by the CAP support mechanisms. It is therefore expected that any substantial CAP reform will have significant welfare and allocative implications for the Greek agricultural sector and the economy as a whole. The model developed in this chapter attempts to assess the above effects.

Looked at from the point of view of EU strategy, the results obtained here show that the reform achieves its objectives in the case of Greece. It causes a substantial reduction in the production of grains, milk and other animal products and it modifies the composition of the agricultural transfers towards the Greek economy, since a great part of those transfers is not output related and comes under the direct control of the EU. If direct payments compensating Greek farmers for income losses were abandoned, agricultural transfers to Greece would decrease by 32.3 per cent.

The main impact the 1992 CAP reform on the Greek economy is a reallocation of resources not only towards the agricultural sectors not affected by the reform, but also in favour of the mining and industrial sectors. The decrease in production of grains, milk and other animal products is quite significant, but even more significant is the respective fall in exports. As a result, the volume of total agricultural exports decreases by 4.6 per cent. Despite the reallocation of resources in favour of fresh and processed fruits and vegetables, oil and fats, and beverages, the value added in agriculture and agribusiness industries decreases by 1 per cent whereas the value added in non-agricultural sectors increases by 0.9 per cent, in real terms.

The above allocative effects of CAP reform are somewhat modified in the case of there being no direct payments by the EU to compensate farmers for income losses. The positive trade balance effect, necessary to restore balance of payment equilibrium after the contraction of EU transfers, leads to the expansion of the industrial sector as well as the agricultural sectors not subject to the CAP reform. This effect raises GDP by 0.7 per cent in real terms.

The welfare implications are somewhat mixed. The 1992 reform has a rather modest welfare gain due to resource allocation effects which turns into a modest loss if price reductions are not offset by income support schemes. It is nevertheless important to stress that the welfare measure concerns the economy as a whole. Farmers are, obviously, worse off when the income support schemes are abandoned. To allow for distributional implications of the CAP reform a multihousehold model is necessary.

The results presented in this chapter are obtained under the assumption of fully employed production factors and fully mobile capital and labour between agricultural sectors and the rest of the economy. Obviously the results would change to a certain extent if we allow for unemployment in the agricultural sector. The latter is a task currently being pursued by the authors.

NOTES

1 For a detailed discussion of the role of specific intervention activities, see Commission of the European Union Communities (1987a, p. 47).
2 The SAM was constructed by J.N. Anastassakou, S. Balfoussias and R.A. De Santis.
3 NACE is the French acronym for 'Nomenclature of Activities in European Communities'.

REFERENCES

Armington, P.S. (1969), 'A theory of demand for products distinguished by place of production', *IMF Staff Papers*, 16: 159–76.

Burinaux, J.M., Delorme, F., Lienert, I. and Martin, J.P. (1990a), WALRAS – A *Multi-sector, Multi-country Applied General Equilibrium Model for Quantifying the Economy-wide Effects of Agricultural Policies: A Technical Manual*, Working Paper No. 84, Paris: OECD.

Burinaux, J.M., Martin, J.P., Delorme, F., Lienert, I. and van der Mensbrugghe, D. (1990b), 'Economy-wide effects of agricultural policies in OECD countries: simulation results with WALRAS', *OECD Economic Studies*, 13: 131–72.

Commission of the European Communities (various years), *The Agricultural Situation in the Community*: 1981, 1985, 1992, 1995 Reports, Luxembourg: Office for Official Publications of the European Communities.

Commission of the European Communities (1987a), *The Agricultural Situation in the Community: 1986 Report*, Luxembourg: Office for Official Publications of the European Communities.

Commission of the European Communities (1987b), *Twentieth General Report on the Activities of the European Communities: 1986*, Luxembourg: Office for Official Publications of the European Communities.

Fehr, H. and Wiegard W. (1996), 'A CGE examination of world-wide agricultural liberalisation policies: model structure and preliminary results' in A. Fossati (ed.), *Economic Modelling Under the Applied General Equilibrium Approach*, Aldershot, Hants: Avebury.

Harrison, G., Rutherford, T.F. and Wooton, I. (1989), 'The economic impact of the European Community', *American Economic Review Papers and Proceedings*, 79: 288–94.

Harrison, G., Rutherford, T.F. and I. Wooton, I. (1995), 'Liberalising agriculture in European Union', *Journal of Policy Modelling*, 17: 223–55.

Hertel, T.W., Thompson, R.L. and Tsigas, M.E. (1989) 'Economy wide effects of unilateral policy liberalising in US agriculture', in A.B. Stoeckel, D. Vincent and S. Cuthbertson (eds), *Macroeconomic Consequences of Farm Support*, Durham, N.C.: Duke University Press.

Rutherford, T.F., Whalley, J. and Wigle, R. (1990), 'Capitalisation, conditionality and dilution: land prices and the US wheat program', *Journal of Policy Modelling*, 12: 605–22.

Trela, I., Whalley, J. and Wigle, R. (1987), 'International trade in grains: domestic policies and trade impacts', *Scandinavian Journal of Economics*, 89: 271–83.

Part II

POLICY SIMULATIONS WITH ALTERNATIVE TREATMENTS OF FACTOR MARKETS

4

THE LABOUR MARKET EFFECTS OF VAT HARMONISATION IN A MULTICOUNTRY AGE MODEL

Alan Duncan, John Hutton, Fouad Laroui and Anna Ruocco

4.1 INTRODUCTION

This chapter addresses the question of the sensitivity of policy analysis to the specification of the labour market. We compare the results of a specific reform of the value-added tax system in the European Union, according to a series of alternative specifications of a multicountry applied general equilibrium (AGE) model. Each specification introduces a different degree of detail into the labour market, with the general objective of achieving a greater degree of realism and hence policy relevance and credibility in the model. The model design allows for the presence of unemployment, which opens up a set of choices over model closure, and we show how these choices affect the policy recommendations.

Our model is derived from that developed by Fehr *et al.* (1995) (the FRW model), explicitly designed to consider issues of VAT reform. We take one of the simplest questions in this area, the effects of complete harmonisation of all VAT rates in the EU at a uniform rate across all goods and all countries; the particular uniform rate chosen is 15 per cent. We do not consider other vexed issues of VAT reform, such as the choice between origin and destination principles, or some hybrid: in our simulations the destination principle remains in force. Nevertheless, the simple issue we confront is still topical, and harmonisation of VAT around a single rate is high on the current political agenda.

In our simulation experiments, we find there to be significant incentive effects in the labour market following a change in the direct/indirect tax balance, with participation rates among part-time workers being especially affected.

4.2 TAX REFORM, UNEMPLOYMENT AND GENERAL EQUILIBRIUM ANALYSIS

Harmonising indirect taxes in Europe

In 1987 the EU Commission set the agenda for the redesign of VAT and the realignment of rates in the Union, as part of the programme of measures to complete the Internal Market by 1992 (see Commission, 1987). At the time of writing, the proposed reforms have still to be finally agreed and implemented, a 'transitional' system is in force and 1997 is the new target date for agreement on the 'definitive system'. It seems likely, however, that a minimum 15 per cent VAT rate may be proposed to limit tax competition, with some limited provision for reduced rates on a list of 'basic' goods and services.[1] The welfare consequences of these proposals are, not surprisingly, ambiguous. As Bliss (1994) points out, the Diamond–Mirrlees Theorem can be extended to recommend differentiated national indirect tax rates to gain the full benefits of trade creation in a customs union. To fund the change, each country will adjust its marginal rate of income tax. For most countries, the effect will be a switch from direct to indirect taxation. Part of the fiscal impact of such a change would be any change in the social security bill arising from changes in unemployment, so we accommodate this within the budget provision: in so far as unemployment rises, there will therefore be less scope for direct tax cuts.

In designing models purposes such as the study of EU VAT harmonisation, choices must be made as to which features are essential within a model of given size and 'solvability'. The model must be a multicountry one and must contain a sufficient number of 'commodities' to reflect the variety of VAT practice pre-reform. In the case of Fehr *et al.* (1995), eight countries and fourteen sectors, most giving rise to two-way trade flows, dictate a large minimum size, and rule out intertemporal considerations. The role of the model here is to illustrate and quantify an essentially theoretical discussion.

Features of the new model

Clearly, it is not hard to find possible 'improvements', and we have chosen to modify the FRW model, by making one market less than perfect, and to introduce some minor differentiation of labour. The reason for starting with the labour market is that the existence of unemployment has major fiscal consequences, so that any change on the revenue side of the budget which affects unemployment will generate important social security expenditure effects: this is the sort of knock-on effect that general equilibrium models are designed to analyse. Our model is calibrated for the early 1980s, when unemployment in Europe was typically running at around 10 per cent and social security expenditure amounted to about 20–30 per cent of GDP. In this context, tax reform can in principle yield larger gains if the waste from unemployment is somehow reduced or the burden of supporting the social security budget is redistributed.

The introduction of unemployment into general equilibrium models is not new: an early example is Kehoe and Serra-Puche (1983), who analyse the unemployment consequences of the 1980 fiscal reform in Mexico, and Kehoe et al. (1995), who analyse the effects on a range of macro indicators of Spain's introduction of VAT in 1986. Recently Gelauff et al. (1991) and Gelauff (1993) have developed sophisticated models of the Dutch labour market, incorporating a detailed treatment of the tax and benefit system, including a distribution of household types, and explicit modelling of the wage-bargaining system and employment effects. The scale and complexity of their models, however, rule them out as candidates for our purpose, which is to operate within a multicountry model. The 'curse of dimensionality' would be apparent.

We also investigate the feasibility and effects of distinguishing full-time and part-time labour, recognising that part-time labour has become a larger fraction of the labour force within recent decades, and that the degree of unionisation and legal protection of these workers is such that their participation in the labour market should be modelled differently from that of full-time workers. In the 1980s between 5 per cent and 25 per cent of all workers were part-time, and the fraction has risen again in the 1990s; further, many part-time workers are female. The idea here is that a 'competitive fringe' in the labour market may alter the predictions from those of a model of homogeneous unionised labour, and may pick up interesting consequences of the switch to or from direct to indirect taxation implied by VAT reform.

Why focus on the labour market?

It could legitimately be asked how such adjustments to the structure of the FRW model might affect the simulated general equilibrium consequences of a move towards European indirect tax harmonisation, particularly since such a move would seem quite naturally to impact most on the goods market rather than the labour market. Our response to this is threefold.

First, there has been some suggestion in the literature (see Mercenier, 1995, for example) that when the economy is located away from the efficiency frontier (with labour fully employed), the magnitude of any welfare change that one might expect from a given policy reform may be greater. Mercenier's example, considering the effect of the 1992 Single Market exercise, illustrated a distinctly Keynesian response to a demand shock in the presence of a fixed real wage.

Second, the production sector in a country typically draws on heterogeneous labour resources, with potentially different responses to wage rate movements, shifts in policy and the like. In the United Kingdom, for example, there is strong evidence of a move towards increased utilisation of part-time or flexible labour. Such a change in the character of the labour market has clear behavioural implications. Since part-time employees are typically more flexible in their labour supply and more responsive to changes in their economic circumstances, any shift in policy may induce a differentiated ultimate behavioural (and welfare) response among the various elements of the actual and potential labour force.

Third, the specific formulation of a policy of indirect tax harmonisation will have quite direct implications for other sectors of the economy. For example, the initial knock-on effects of adjustments to indirect tax rates within each country following harmonisation will be to push the domestic budget in each country out of balance. Given the need to maintain Government budget balances within each country, another tax instrument would typically be set endogenously to compensate for the indirect tax shock. If, for example, direct taxes were floated within an AGE framework, it might be expected that this too would have distributional, behavioural and hence welfare consequences also. The budgetary consequences of VAT harmonisation would be trivial or major, depending on the revenue effects of the switch to the uniform VAT rate: in Germany, for example, with low VAT rates, harmonisation would reduce the relative importance of direct taxation, while the opposite would be true of Denmark.

Taken together, there seem strong *a priori* grounds for a move away from simple market-clearing characterisation of the labour market, towards a model which admits labour supply heterogeneity and involuntary unemployment. In doing so, the potential of the model to reveal more realistic welfare responses to policy change is enhanced.

4.3 THEORETICAL FRAMEWORK

The basic model

The FRW model is a multicountry, multisector general equilibrium model typical in structure of the class of CGE models reviewed in Shoven and Whalley (1984). It is fully described in Fehr *et al.* (1995), and we need note only modifications here.

Specification of non-clearing market structures

The solution strategy in the basic model is common to the majority of AGE models in the literature. n commodity markets generate a system of excess demand functions $\xi_i(p)$ for $i = 1, \ldots n$ conditional on some price vector

$p = (p_1, \ldots, p_n)'$. Under conditions of Walrasian equilibrium, prices adjust to force zero excess demands in all markets, whereby the equilibrium vector $\tilde{p}$ satisfies:

$$\xi_i (\tilde{p}) = 0, \forall i \tag{4.1}$$

Behind these conditions is the tautology that if all agents satisfy their *ex ante* budget constraints whether at equilibrium prices or not, simple aggregation of these budget constraints in each market yields the result that the price-weighted sum of excess demands is zero. Thus, Walras's Law states that:

$$\sum_{i=1}^{n} p_i \xi_i(p) = 0 \tag{4.2}$$

where p_i denotes the unit price in the ith market and $\xi_i(p)$ denotes the ith excess demand as a function of prices. Whilst Walras's Law holds for any price vector, conditions (4.1) move prices and wages to a point where each $\xi_i(p) = 0$. In terms of solution strategy, a Walrasian equilibrium can be brought about either by imposing zero excess demands in all n markets (in which case Walras's Law is simply a confirmation of internal consistency), or by forcing zero excess demands in $n - 1$ markets and relying on (4.2) to clear the nth market. Under either strategy, the solution mechanism might be characterised as one of 'unconstrained price-adjustment', whereby prices and wages are adjusted to bring about a Walrasian equilibrium. Notably, since (4.2) is a homogeneous system, one good must be taken as numéraire with, say, $p_n = 1$.

We adopt the proposition that equilibrium condition (4.1) is not sustainable in the labour market, which forces us to adjust the solution strategy slightly. In fact, the adjustment is not too severe. One characterisation we might adopt for such an AGE model is one of 'constrained price-adjustment', a technique which closely mirrors the standard Walrasian solution, but which includes an additional set of constraints on a subset of excess demands.[2] Consider, for example, the introduction of an additional quantity constraint on the first market (the labour market, say) whereby $\bar{U} = \xi_i(p) > 0$ for some (fixed) positive $\bar{U}$. That is, the first market is forced to a position of excess supply at a level $\bar{U}$. If we again aggregate budget constraints for a given price vector, we find that:

$$p_1[\xi_1(p) + \bar{U}] + \sum_{i=2}^{n} p_i \xi_i p = 0 \tag{4.3}$$

which requires our constrained equilibrium at prices $\hat{p}_i > 0$ to be such that:

$$- \xi_1(\hat{p}) = \bar{U}$$
$$\xi_i(\hat{p}) = 0, \, i = 2, \ldots, n \tag{4.4}$$

For a price vector identical to the unconstrained equilibrium levels, the quantity constraint forces the representative household to consume more leisure and fewer goods. However, the equilibrium solution to the constrained Walrasian equilibrium will typically be different from the unconstrained solution.

The quantity constraint described above has been expressed in terms of some fixed level $\bar{U}$ below which excess demand $- \xi_1(p)$ is not permitted to fall. However, this is not the only possibility. We might instead parameterise the constraining level U to be dependent upon prices, such that $U = U(p)$, giving a 'price-dependent quantity constraint' of the form $- \xi_1(p) = U(p)$. By Walras's Law:

$$p_1[\xi_1(p) + U(p)] + \sum_{i=2}^{n} p_i \xi_i(p) = 0 \tag{4.5}$$

A set of constrained equilibrium conditions may then be written as:[3]

$$- \xi_1(\hat{p}) = U(\hat{p})$$
$$\xi_i(\hat{p}) = 0, \, i = 2, \ldots, n \tag{4.6}$$

In the context of a model in which labour markets do not clear, this equilibrium would relate directly to the imposition of some 'surrogate' labour supply schedule; specific parameterisations of a price-dependent quantity-constrained labour market can be derived from a variety of models of wage determination (for example, a wage curve derived from an efficiency wage or an insider–outsider model).

As a third alternative, we might consider a 'price-constrained' AGE model which includes a constraint not on the level of excess demand in the first market, but on the *price* of the first market good. This constraint would take the form $p_1 = \bar{p}_1$. To force excess supply in the first market, we would set $\bar{p}_1$ at a level which exceeds the market-clearing price. Let $p_{-1} = (p_2, \ldots, p_n)'$ represent an $(n - 1)$ vector of unconstrained prices in the remaining markets. Then the solution to our price-constrained equilibrium would be of the form:

$$- \xi_1(\bar{p}_1, \hat{p}_{-1}) > 0$$
$$\xi_i(\bar{p}_1, \hat{p}_{-1}) = 0, \, i = 2, \ldots, n \tag{4.7}$$

In this world of, say, an administered wage, labour is again in excess supply; the system is solved using only equations 2 to n, for which a reduced Walras's Law holds:

$$\sum_{i=2}^{n} \hat{p}_i \xi_i(\bar{p}_1, \hat{p}_{-1}) = 0 \qquad (4.8)$$

4.4 LABOUR MARKET VARIANTS

Heterogeneous labour supply

The basic model has a single representative consumer as the sole supplier of homogeneous labour. The richness of the labour sector can, however, be enhanced at relatively low computational cost. If the representative consumer can be interpreted more as a kind of consumer 'aggregate', then there is every justification for that consumer to supply elements of labour of different skill types. For the purposes of this study we choose to disaggregate labour into elements which might loosely be interpreted as part-time and full-time work. This is by no means the only interpretation, and the mechanism by which we introduce labour skill heterogeneity into the model is equally consistent with socio-demographic heterogeneity.

In order to have different labour supplies in the model, we modify the representative consumer utility maximisation, adding an additional nest to the production side and consequently modifying the clearing condition in the labour market and in the government budget constraint. Given two labour types we can specify tax structures for each. We also divide the labour market so that just one is subject to involuntary unemployment in equilibrium.

Household sector

A simple way of modelling two types of labour is to imagine that the household comprises two individuals, each with a specific time endowment, but having the same leisure consumption preferences. The household first decides its total leisure demand and aggregate consumption. Then, it decides how to share the leisure between two types by minimising its expenditure function, defined over the two types of leisure.

From the solution of that problem we obtain the conditional leisure demands and as usual we determine the two different labour supplies by taking the difference between the total time endowment and leisure demand.

More formally (suppressing country-specific subscripts), the representative consumer solves the following optimisation problem:

$$\text{max UT} = \left[cc^{\frac{1}{\delta_1}} \cdot \text{UT2}^{\frac{\delta_1 - 1}{\delta_1}} + cl^{\frac{1}{\delta_1}} \cdot \text{LL}^{\frac{\delta_1 - 1}{\delta_1}} \right]^{\frac{\delta_1}{\delta_1 - 1}} \tag{4.9}$$

subject to the budget constraint

$$\text{PUT2} \cdot \text{UT2} + w(1 - T) \cdot \text{LL} = M \tag{4.10}$$

where full disposable income M is determined by:

$$M = [r \cdot KS + w_1 \cdot E_1 + w_2 \cdot E_2](1 - T) + A \cdot T + TR \cdot QL$$

We use the following notation:

UT	top utility level	w_2	gross wage for labour type 2
UT2	second utility level	E_1	time endowment of labour type 1
LL	aggregate leisure demand	E_2	time endowment of labour type 2
cc, cl	share parameters	T	marginal income tax rate
δ_1	elasticity of substitution	A	income tax allowance
PUT2	price index of UT2	TR	transfer payments by government
w	net aggregate wage index	QL	Laspeyres price index
w_1	gross wage for labour type 1		

To guarantee the equivalence of Hicksian and Marshallian demand the following equation must hold:

$$\text{UT} \cdot \text{PUT1} = M$$

where

$$\text{PUT1} = \left\{ cc \cdot \text{PUT2}^{1 - \delta_1} + cl \cdot [w(1 - T)]^{1 - \delta_1} \right\}^{\frac{1}{1 - \delta_1}}$$

$$\text{UT2} = cc \cdot \text{UT} \cdot \left[\frac{\text{PUT1}}{\text{PUT2}} \right]^{\delta_1}$$

Using the definition of M in (4.10) we can rewrite the budget constraint as:

$$\text{UT} \cdot \text{PUT1} = [r \cdot KS + w_1 \cdot E_1 + w_2 \cdot E_2](1 - T) + A \cdot T + TR \cdot QL$$

Demand for aggregate leisure is given by:

$$\text{LL} = cl \cdot \text{UT} \cdot \left[\frac{\text{PUT1}}{w(1 - T)} \right]^{\delta_1}$$

This gives us total leisure demand. The consumer must now choose which type of leisure to demand, given that the cost per unit of aggregate leisure is:

$$w = \left\{ \alpha_1 \cdot [w_1(1 - T)]^{1 - \delta_5} + \alpha_2 \cdot [w_2(1 - T)]^{1 - \delta_5} \right\}^{\frac{1}{1 - \delta_5}}$$

Using Shephard's Lemma, we may derive the two optimal leisure demands:

$$LL_1 = \alpha_1 \cdot LL \cdot \left[\frac{w}{w_1(1 - T)} \right]^{\delta_5}$$

$$LL_2 = \alpha_2 \cdot LL \cdot \left[\frac{w}{w_2(1 - T)} \right]^{\delta_5}$$

The two labour supplies LS_1 and LS_2 simply constitute the difference between total endowments and leisure demands:

$$LS_1 = E_1 - LL_1$$

$$LS_2 = E_2 - LL_2$$

Production sector

We now consider the production side, where each firm chooses a labour aggregate and capital as inputs into the production process. Value added is derived from aggregate labour and capital through a CES function of the form:

$$VA = \left[\delta_2^{\frac{1}{\sigma_2}} \cdot LD^{\frac{\sigma_2 - 1}{\sigma_2}} + (1 - \delta_2)^{\frac{1}{\sigma_2}} \cdot KD^{\frac{\sigma_2 - 1}{\sigma_2}} \right]^{\frac{\sigma_2}{\sigma_2 - 1}}$$

where

LD aggregate labour demand
KD capital demand
δ_2 share parameter
σ_2 elasticity of substitution.

We may now define the cost function as

$$CVA = [\delta_2 \cdot w^{1-\sigma_2} + (1 - \delta_2) \cdot r^{1-\sigma_2}]^{\frac{1}{1-\sigma_2}} \cdot VA = PVA \cdot VA$$

where the aggregate production wage index is defined as:

$$w = w_1^{t_1} \cdot w_2^{1-t_1}$$

and where r is the rental cost of capital (uniform across sectors and countries) and t is a share parameter. Hence the price of value-added is:

$$PVA = [\delta_2 \cdot w^{1-\sigma_2} + (1 - \delta_2) \cdot r^{1-\sigma_2}]^{\frac{1}{1-\sigma_2}}$$

Demand for aggregate labour and capital, respectively, are given by:

$$LD = \delta_2 \cdot VA \cdot \left[\frac{PVA}{w} \right]^{\sigma_2}$$

$$KD = (1 - \delta_2) \cdot VA \cdot \left[\frac{PVA}{r} \right]^{\sigma_2}$$

Given the demand for aggregate labour the firm must choose between labour types. We therefore add an additional nest to the production function, using a Cobb–Douglas cost function to determine the choice between demand LD_1 and LD_2 for labour types 1 and 2 respectively. The conditional demands are therefore:

$$LD_1 = t_1 LD \cdot w/w_1$$

$$LD_2 = (1 - t_1) LD \cdot w/w_2$$

The labour market equilibrium conditions are, summing over production sectors,

$$\sum LD_1 - LS_1 = 0$$

$$\sum LD_2 - LS_2 = 0$$

In the presence of unemployment, care must be taken to relate household income and tax revenues to labour demand rather than labour supply. Hence, for example, income tax revenue in the government budget constraint should be expressed as:

$$[r \cdot KS + w_1 LD_1 + w_2 LD_2] \cdot T - AT$$

Full-time labour market non-clearing

To gain some insight into the structure of a non-clearing labour market, consider the scenario described in Figure 4.1.

The representative individual is modelled with preferences over consumption and leisure (consistent with the indifference map $\{U_0, U_1, U_2\}$ in 4.1. In the absence of taxes, firms are able to achieve efficiency by producing at the boundary of the production possibility frontier AB. In the absence of price or wage rigidities and of taxes, a competitive equilibrium would be achieved with zero excess demand for labour at real wages set at a level defined by the tangency of U_1 and the PPF (at point C). However, by introducing additional price or quantity constraints into the AGE model of the form described above, a benchmarked equilibrium can be obtained which includes an element of 'involuntary' unemployment. Consider, for example, a constraint which forces the real wage rate to a level above that which would have been achieved at competitive equilibrium. The slope of chord DE describes such a position. Then firms would demand less labour (or equivalently demand more leisure) by producing at point D. The consumer, on the other hand, would prefer less leisure (point E in Figure 4.1). Under these circumstances the actual consumption of leisure will exceed that which is desired, leaving

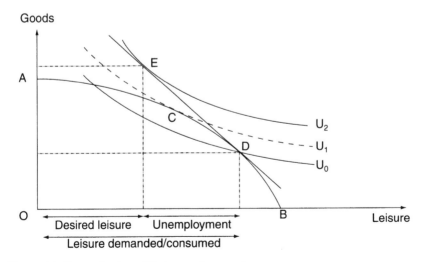

Figure 4.1 Constrained equilibrium and unemployment

the consumer on the lower indifference curve U_0 at point D. The horizontal difference between D and E represents the level of involuntary unemployment in the market.

The calibration of consumer preferences in such a constrained equilibrium requires some care. It is clear that the calibrated equilibrium at point D in Figure 4.1 does not correspond to the consumer's maximum attainable utility for a given real wage. Instead, consumer preferences are calibrated at point E to take account of an amount of 'excess' leisure consumption equivalent to the horizontal distance between D and E.[4]

This demonstrates how a given level of involuntary unemployment can feature in a benchmarked general equilibrium by introducing some form of constraining labour market imperfection. However, we have yet to discuss the precise nature of the constraint. The question is an important one, since the nature of the constraint will impact on any counterfactual equilibrium outcome following either a policy reform or some technological change.

Wage curve

One can appeal to a number of theories of wage determination to rationalise a labour market model where real wages are set at a level other than the competitive equilibrium rate. One rationalisation stems from the 'efficiency wage' hypothesis; a second characterises wage determination as the outcome of a bargaining process between firms and unions as monopoly suppliers of labour; a third relies on the 'insiders–outsiders' model.[5]

Whatever the economic rationale, there is a good degree of empirical support for the use of a wage curve as a model of wage determination. Blanchflower and Oswald (1994) have demonstrated the empirical robustness of a wage curve with an elasticity of -0.1 across a wide cross-section of countries: we use this value. In general terms, the wage curve relationship typically takes the form:

$$\frac{w}{p} = f(U); \ f'(U) < 0 \tag{4.11}$$

where U represents the level of unemployment. In the operation of the labour market, the wage curve effectively becomes a 'surrogate' aggregate labour supply schedule which interacts with labour demand to determine the level of real wages. Figure 4.2 describes one such equilibrium in which wages are set to a level above the competitive equilibrium, creating involuntary unemployment in the labour market.

Naturally, there are general equilibrium aspects to the introduction of a wage–unemployment trade-off in the labour market. Upward pressure on wage rates will feed through to the operation of the remaining commodity

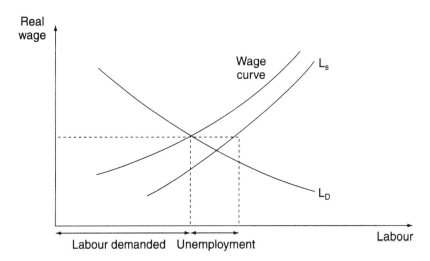

Figure 4.2 Unemployment and the wage curve

markets, forcing prices and quantities away from the competitive (uncon-strained) equilibrium. By expressing equation (4.11) in its inverse form $U = f^{-1}(w/p)$, we can relate the equilibrium outcome in the presence of a wage curve directly to the price-dependent quantity constrained equilibrium (equation (4.6)).

Fixed wage

By fixing wages through a constraint of the form $(w/p) = \overline{(w/p)}$ where $\overline{(w/p)}$ exceeds the market-clearing rate, we would generate a price-constrained equilibrium of the form (4.8). This is an approach that Mercenier (1995) adopts in his analysis of the impact of European single market integration. There are a number of economic rationales for such a rigidity (of which fixed real wages are an extreme form).

Fixed unemployment

Finally, instead of solving out for a solution with $U = 0$ for full employment, we can solve for $U = \bar{U}$, some fixed level of unemployment. This might be the 'natural rate' or the NAIRU (non-accelerating inflation rate of unemploy-ment) appropriate for the economy. Estimates of these rates can be derived from most macro-econometric models, but must be regarded with scepticism as highly dependent on model specification. Nevertheless, such estimates tend to be quite close to prevailing levels of unemployment, which is not surpris-ing when the model's data-set covers a period of roughly stable inflation. Accordingly, as one of our model variants we take 1981 (the benchmark year) rates of unemployment as the values of $\bar{U}$.

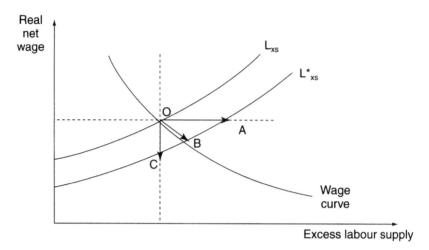

Figure 4.3 Wage and employment effects in constrained equilibrium.

Suppose that we observe a labour market with a given level of unemployment. The same equilibrium outcome can be achieved by fixing unemployment directly, by fixing wage rates to generate the required level of unemployment, or by calibrating a wage curve to cross the labour demand schedule at the required distance from the supply schedule. Consider the relationship between excess supply of labour (i.e. unemployment) and real wage rates as described in Figure (4.3).

Point O represents the benchmarked equilibrium for a given level of observed unemployment. Now, consider a policy shock which forces excess demand from L_{xs} to L_{xs}^*. The direction and scale of wage and employment effects depend directly on the means by which unemployment is factored into the AGE model. Under a fixed real net wage scenario, unemployment increases in the direction OA. At the other extreme, a fixed unemployment assumption forces wage rates to decrease along OC. And if a wage curve is used to generate the benchmarked equilibrium, wages fall and unemployment rises along OB.

4.5 IMPLICATIONS FOR COUNTERFACTUAL SIMULATIONS

Theoretical considerations

Making use of a simple one-good closed economy model, let us anticipate the effects of the VAT reform under the three closure rules: fixed real net wage, wage curve and fixed unemployment. The real net wage can be defined as $rnw = (w/p^*)(1 - a)/(1 + v)$ where p^* is the pre-tax price of value-added,

w/p^* is the real product wage, a is the average income tax rate and v is the value-added tax rate. The first-round, partial equilibrium effect of a revenue-neutral switch from direct to indirect tax would leave $(1 - a)/(1 + v)$ and rnw unchanged (conditional on unchanged employment and output). However, by reducing the marginal tax rate by more than the average tax rate the reform would raise the supply of labour by raising the opportunity cost of leisure. The resulting rise in unemployment would induce a rise in transfers, requiring a higher value of a. To maintain rnw constant, w/p^* must increase, with the effect of reducing output and the demand for labour. We can therefore expect the VAT reform to be welfare-reducing under this closure rule, since households are moved further from their preferred consumption and leisure choices.

If instead the closure rule is constant unemployment, no change in transfers will be induced, and the increased labour supply must be matched by increased labour demand: this is achieved by reducing w/p^* and hence rnw. Consumption and employment are closer to households' preferred values and welfare will increase. Full employment is a special case of the fixed-unemployment rule, with welfare increases also expected.

In the case of the wage curve, the results will be intermediate to the two cases just discussed, so we can expect unemployment to rise for most countries, more moderately than under the fixed rnw rule, but we cannot predict the welfare effects. Simulation is necessary to yield determinate results. For countries (like Denmark) for which the reform would amount to a switch towards direct taxes, we can predict the opposite results on the basis of this analysis: reduced unemployment for the wage curve, but ambiguous welfare effects. It is notable that in these examples there is a strong negative correlation between the real product wage and welfare.

4.6 RESULTS

The design of the tax harmonisation counterfactuals

The set of models for analysis is:

(a) The original FRW model;
(b) A model with homogeneous labour, but with unemployment;
(c) A model with full-time and part-time labour, with unemployment of full-timers.

Both (b) and (c) were simulated subject to the three alternative closure rules discussed above.

Numerical results

I   Table 4.1 shows the welfare effects of the VAT harmonisation for the various scenarios. The first feature to note is that, for groups a, b and c, the pattern of gains and losses across closure rules is much as we predicted in section 4.5, with welfare losses and higher unemployment for the fixed wage case, welfare gains for the fixed unemployment case, and intermediate values with mixed signs for the wage curve. The size of the welfare gains for the fixed positive unemployment case are, with one exception (Denmark), greater than for the fixed zero unemployment case of the FRW model: this is also in line with expectations, although the difference is very small indeed. The presence of heterogeneity in c is associated with small positive welfare gains relative to b for all cases (except Denmark with fixed U). Thus introducing heterogeneity in labour supply appears to have provided households with the means to mitigate the welfare impact of VAT reform when real net wages are fixed or sticky.

II   Tables 4.2a, 4.2b, 4.3a, 4.3b and 4.4 illustrate how heterogeneity works with VAT reform. With real net wages fixed, and VAT reform pushing up prices only partially offset by reduced income tax, the rise in the real product wage reduces the demand for full-time labour. Households respond by increasing their supply of part-time labour, reducing the w_p/w_f ratio (by between 1 per cent and 3 per cent) and offsetting the output fall. The fall in full-time employment is still substantial at 2 or 3 per cent, but part-time employment increases (by less than 1 per cent) and unemployment rates of full-timers rise quite sharply (by 1–4 per cent). Another feature of the heterogeneous case is that the income tax rate for most countries falls further below the benchmark except, of course, for Denmark (see Table 4.5).

III   When the closure rule is fixed unemployment, welfare and real consumption effects are much the same for all cases (i.e. (a) full employment, (b)

Table 4.1 Consumer welfare (percentage variation from benchmark)

Country:	FF	BL	NL	DD	II	UK	DK
(a) **Homogeneous labour, 0% unemployment**							
	0.408	0.401	0.235	0.210	0.383	0.187	0.376
(b) **Homogeneous labour, with unemployment**							
Fixed wage	−0.547	−0.837	−0.816	−0.265	−0.374	−0.707	−1.313
Wage curve	0.148	0.091	−0.041	0.059	0.198	−0.003	−0.143
Fixed U	0.429	0.436	0.232	0.255	0.420	0.266	0.330
(c) **Heterogeneous labour with unemployment**							
Fixed wage	−0.389	−0.593	−0.641	−0.263	−0.265	−0.574	−1.133
Wage curve	0.188	0.161	−0.005	0.079	0.230	0.026	−0.098
Fixed U	0.436	0.452	0.237	0.273	0.436	0.274	0.323

Table 4.2a Full-time wage (percentage variation from benchmark)

Country:	FF	BL	NL	DD	II	UK	DK
(c) Heterogeneous labour with unemployment							
Fixed wage	2.17	4.63	4.35	4.66	4.50	5.26	1.43
Wage curve	0.49	0.71	0.08	−0.53	1.17	0.08	−0.57
Fixed U	0.33	−1.18	−2.24	−1.81	−0.70	−2.52	0.52

Table 4.2b Part-time wage (percentage variation from benchmark)

Country:	FF	BL	NL	DD	II	UK	DK
(c) Heterogeneous labour with unemployment							
Fixed wage	1.14	2.43	1.52	2.42	2.22	2.20	0.78
Wage curve	0.33	0.01	−0.87	−0.99	0.37	−0.92	−0.37
Fixed U	0.33	−1.18	−2.24	−1.81	−0.70	−2.52	0.52

Table 4.3a Full-time employment (percentage variation from benchmark)

Country:	FF	BL	NL	DD	II	UK	DK
(a) Homogeneous labour, 0% unemployment							
	0.48	0.56	0.08	1.22	0.73	1.18	−0.62
(b) Homogeneous labour with unemployment							
Fixed wage	−1.40	−2.24	−3.16	−2.31	−1.78	−2.81	−2.11
Wage curve	0.20	−0.30	−1.02	0.47	−0.15	−0.17	−0.40
Fixed U	0.47	0.55	0.08	1.21	0.72	1.14	−0.61
(c) Heterogeneous labour with unemployment							
Fixed wage	−0.61	−2.01	−2.98	−1.55	−1.55	−2.16	−1.55
Wage curve	0.30	−0.28	−1.00	0.60	−0.10	0.00	−0.39
Fixed U	0.47	0.55	0.08	1.21	0.72	1.15	−0.61

Table 4.3b Part-time employment (percentage variation from benchmark)

Country:	FF	BL	NL	DD	II	UK	DK
(c) Heterogeneous labour with unemployment							
Fixed wage	0.40	0.08	−0.28	0.59	0.63	0.76	−0.92
Wage curve	0.48	0.47	0.01	1.11	0.71	1.06	−0.62
Fixed U	0.47	0.55	0.08	1.21	0.72	1.15	−0.61

Table 4.4 Unemployment rate[a]

Country:	FF	BL	NL	DD	II	UK	DK
(b) Homogeneous labour, with unemployment							
Fixed wage	9.5	14.2	12.6	8.0	11.1	13.3	9.9
Wage curve	7.9	12.0	10.1	5.4	9.1	10.5	8.4
Fixed U	7.7	11.1	8.8	4.8	8.0	9.2	8.7
(c) Heterogeneous labour with unemployment							
Fixed wage	9.1	13.9	12.5	7.8	11.0	13.1	9.5
Wage curve	7.9	12.0	10.1	5.4	9.0	10.5	8.4
Fixed U	7.7	11.1	8.8	4.8	8.0	9.2	8.7

Note
a   Full-time unemployment rate in the heterogeneous case.

Table 4.5 Income tax rate

Country:	FF	BL	NL	DD	II	UK	DK
Benchmark	5.10	16.70	9.80	17.80	10.70	18.20	27.10
(a) Homogeneous labour, 0% unemployment							
	0.50	10.90	3.80	9.90	1.30	9.10	30.10
(b) Homogeneous labour, with unemployment							
Fixed wage	3.80	12.85	6.16	13.94	2.71	12.40	32.75
Wage curve	1.02	11.51	4.61	10.82	1.80	10.24	29.99
Fixed U	0.51	10.94	3.82	9.97	1.31	9.18	30.16
(c) Heterogeneous labour with unemployment							
Fixed wage	1.24	12.97	5.78	11.95	2.22	10.63	31.47
Wage curve	0.65	11.59	4.50	10.42	1.64	9.67	30.10
Fixed U	0.51	10.94	3.82	9.97	1.31	9.18	30.16

benchmark unemployment with homogeneous or (c) heterogeneous labour): this is not the case for real net wage effects (see Table 4.6), which in the cases of France, Italy and Denmark depend considerably on the level of unemployment. Clearly, aggregate employment effects in these countries offset the wage effects, so that household real income is stabilised. Thus similar welfare indicators may conceal compositional differences.

Overall, introducing alternative closure rules, and some labour market differentiation, does yield different signs for welfare and other indicators and does change the distribution of effects across countries. The general nature of these effects can be predicted quite easily, using simple partial equilibrium and closed economy arguments, for both the homogeneous and heterogeneous labour cases. Policy recommendation for VAT reform therefore depends crucially on the closure rule, with results consistent with economic intuition.

Table 4.6 Full-time real net wage (percentage variation from benchmark)

Country:	FF	'BL	NL	DD	Il	UK	DK
(a) Homogeneous labour, 0% unemployment							
	0.33	−1.21	−2.23	−1.85	−0.73	−2.61	0.57
(b) Homogeneous labour, with unemployment							
Fixed wage	—	—	—	—	—	—	—
Wage curve	−0.35	−0.96	−1.60	−1.56	−1.48	−1.67	0.30
Fixed U	−0.07	−1.47	−2.62	−1.74	−2.38	−2.57	1.52
(c) Heterogeneous labour with unemployment							
Fixed wage	—	—	—	—	—	—	—
Wage curve	−0.30	−0.91	−1.59	−1.51	−1.45	−1.64	0.37
Fixed U	−0.07	−1.47	−2.62	−1.74	−2.38	−2.57	1.53

4.7 CONCLUSIONS

In this chapter we have studied the economic consequences of VAT harmonisation to a common rate in the presence of unemployment and when the income tax is used to offset revenue changes. We show that model closure rules, reflecting alternative approaches to modelling unemployment, and the incentive effects of the switch between direct and indirect taxation, have major impacts on the outcomes. In summary, we find that:

- changes in the direct/indirect tax balance have significant incentive effects on labour markets;
- participation rates among part-time workers are especially affected;
- policy recommendations and welfare gains/losses are sensitive to the choice of fixed unemployment, sticky wages or a wage curve as the closure rule;
- admitting unemployment into the applied general equilibrium framework has major budgetary effects since transfer payments depend on the level of unemployment: this means that harmonisation policy raises quite complex issues when a switch between direct and indirect taxation is envisaged, and applied general equilibrium analysis is well-suited to explore these issues.

NOTES

1 See Smith (1993) for a discussion of the issues and the policy options.
2 For rigorous demonstrations of the existence of constrained equilibria, see Dreze (1975).

3 We use p for all constrained equilibrium price vectors, though the vectors will differ for each case considered.

4 To operationalise this setup in an AGE model, the benchmark data set should therefore include information on the level of employment of labour ('labour consumed') and the rate of involuntary unemployment.

5 A useful survey of the empirical evidence can be found in Booth (1995).

REFERENCES

Blanchflower, D.G. and Oswald, A.J. (1994), *The Wage Curve*, Cambridge: Mass.: MIT Press.

Bliss, C. (1994), *Economic Theory and Policy for Trading Blocks*, Manchester: Manchester University Press.

Booth, A.L. (1995), *The Economics of the Trade Union*, Cambridge: Cambridge University Press.

Commission of the European Communities (1987), *Completion of the Internal Market: Approximation of Indirect Tax Rates and Harmonisation of Indirect Tax Structure. Global Communication from the Commission*, COM(87)320, Brussels: Commission of the European Communities.

Diamond, P.S. and Mirrlees, J.A. (1971), 'Optimal taxation and public production', *American Economic Review*, 61: 261–78.

Dreze, J. (1975), 'Existence of an exchange equilibrium under price rigidities', *International Economic Review*, 16: 301–20.

Fehr, H., Rosenberg, C. and Wiegard, W. (1995), *Welfare Effects of Value-added Tax Harmonization in Europe*, Berlin: Springer.

Gelauff, G.M.M. (1993), 'Taxation and employment', *Public Finance – Finances publiques* 48(3): 387–405.

Gelauff, G.M.M., Erp, F.V., Graafland, J., Hien, A.V. and Nibbelink, A. (1991), 'Towards an analysis of tax effects on labour market and allocation: a micro/macro approach', *De Economist*. 139: 243–71.

Kehoe, T, Polo, C and Sancho, F (1995), 'An evaluation of the performance of an applied general equilibrium model of the Spanish economy', *Economic Theory* 6: 114–41.

Kehoe, T.J. and Serra-Puche, J. (1983), 'A computational general equilibrium model with endogenous unemployment: an analysis of the 1980 fiscal reform in Mexico', *Journal of Public Economics*, 22: 1–26.

Mercenier, J. (1995), 'Can "1992" reduce unemployment in Europe? On welfare and employment effects of Europe's move to a single market', *Journal of Policy Modelling* 17: 1–37.

Shoven, J.B. and Whalley, J. (1984), 'Applied general equilibrium models of taxation and international trade: an introduction and survy', *Journal of Economic Literature* 22: 1007–51.

Smith, S. (1993), '"Subsidiarity" and the co-ordination of indirect taxes in the European Community', *Oxford Review of Economic Policy* 9: 67–94.

5

WAGE CURVES AND CAPITAL MOBILITY IN A GENERAL EQUILIBRIUM MODEL OF ITALY

*Roberto Roson**

5.1 INTRODUCTION

Macroeconomic implications of market imperfections, especially of imperfections in labour and capital markets, are widely recognised and extensively analysed in economic theory. Yet these issues have received little attention in Applied General Equilibrium Models (AGE/CGE), probably because these models stem from a theoretical paradigm which postulates perfect competion, closed economies and fixed endowments of primary resources.

It is often felt that more realistic assumptions about the functioning of primary markets require a significant increase in a model's complexity, hampering the mathematical tractability of large-scale, disaggregated models. By contrast, we shall show here that fairly simple non-neoclassical assumptions can be easily introduced in a general equilibrium model. We shall demonstrate this by using a CGE model of the Italian economy.

Other authors have discussed the introduction of alternative hypotheses about primary markets in CGE models. Imperfect labour markets are considered, for example, in Maechler and Roland-Holst (1995) and Harrigan *et al.* (1992). Issues of non-fixed capital supply are mostly related to dynamic, multiperiod models (e.g. Dixon *et al.*, 1992; Hutton and Kenc, 1996; Ruocco, 1996).

Here, we retain instead a single-period, comparative static framework, but we allow for the existence of a variable capital stock through the possibility of exporting and importing capital. We combine hypotheses of capital mobility with hypotheses of real wage rigidity. For this purpose, we draw on

* This research work has been partly supported by the Italian National Research Council (PFT2 project).

recent labour economics literature, in which issues of long-term disequilibrium wage rates are addressed, both theoretically and empirically.

We start by recalling the notion of a wage curve, presenting some estimates of real wage elasticity for Italy. The structure of an applied general equilibrium model, in which alternative hypotheses about labour and capital markets are adopted, is subsequently illustrated in section 5.3. In section 5.4 we present some results from numerical experiments in which the imposition of a trade balance constraint is simulated in the model. These are compared with data regarding the Italian economy, measuring the actual impact of a trade shock which occurred in the early 1990s. Section 5.5 analyses how well the model reproduces the actual performance of the real economy, shedding some light on the realism of the alternative assumptions.

5.2 WAGE CURVES: DEFINITION AND ESTIMATION

Wage rigidity models of the labour market are aimed at providing an explanation of the fact that often firms do not offer and/or workers do not accept lower wages in the presence of non-frictional unemployment and excess supply in labour market. Several models of this type have been presented in the labour economics literature. Among the various models, two main types of models can be distinguished:

- *efficiency wage models*, aimed at explaining why firms do not lower wages while minimising production costs. The class of efficiency wage models includes alternative approaches like monitoring models (Shapiro and Stiglitz, 1984), sociological models (Akerlof, 1982), turnover models (Stiglitz, 1985), and adverse selection models (Weiss, 1991);
- *bargaining models*, recognising that workers' associations influence the determination of labour costs. Within this model, sub-categories can be identified, like optimal bargaining models, starting with Leontief (1946), and trade unions models.

All these theoretical approaches support the existence of a positive long-term relationship between employment levels and the real wage. This relationship is often referred to as the *wage curve*. In models of imperfect competition, a wage curve replaces the traditional labour supply function in the determination of market equilibrium. Consequently, demand and supply are not equalised and involuntary unemployment is not eliminated by market forces in the long run.

In Blanchflower and Oswald (1994), estimates of the unemployment elasticities of a wage curve are presented for a large group of countries, including Italy.[1] Estimations have been obtained using data at the individual level.[2] The authors use a 'panel' of regional data, including annual dummies to control for short-term perturbations affecting the national economic system.[3] Other dummy variables have been introduced to account for factors like education, sex, age and other personal characteristics.

The function adopted has this general form:

$$\ln \frac{w_i^t}{p^t} = \alpha + \beta \ln U^t + \sum_t \gamma_t d^t + \sum_s \lambda_s d_i^s \qquad (5.0)$$

where w is the wage of an individual i at time t, p is a consumption price index, U is a regional or national index of unemployment and d are dummy variables referred to the reference year or to personal characteristics. Other explanatory variables have been taken into account in specific circumstances.

Estimates obtained for the unemployment elasticity parameter are shown in Table 5.1. Blanchflower and Oswald (1994) stress that estimated parameter values are quite similar, despite profound institutional differences among countries. In other words, results show no clear evidence of significant differences in the degree of wage flexibility, at least in relation to variations in employment levels.[4] The central value is around −0.1.

In the Blanchflower–Oswald model the possibility that real wages react in a differentiated way at the industrial level is not considered, although sometimes additional explanatory variables related to industries do appear in the estimated functions. The possibility of differentiated wage elasticities may emerge whenever some factors influencing the wage-setting process, such as monitoring, selection costs, informative asymmetries, etc., are industry specific.

In this chapter we try to roughly measure industrial elasticities via econometric estimation of parameters of a function similar to (2.1). In our

Table 5.1 Estimated elasticities for various countries

	Elasticity	t-stat
US	−0.1	>25.0
UK	−0.08	6.23
Canada	−0.09	6.1
South Korea	−0.04	25.7
Austria	−0.09	1.59
Italy	−0.1	0.63
The Netherlands	−0.17	2.35
Switzerland	−0.12	3.6
Norway	−0.08	2.19
Ireland	−0.36	1.92
Australia	−0.19	5.8
Germany	−0.13	1.75

Source: Blanchflower and Oswald (1994)

estimate we use aggregate data on average industrial wages by region and industry, but personal characteristics are not considered. This of course makes our estimates less reliable than those obtainable with microdata, especially because the size of the estimation sample is not large. None the less, we believe that these estimates can be used to get a first assessment of possible differences among industries in the degree of wage flexibility.

Average real wages by industry are regressed against a constant term, an index of regional unemployment level and a set of annual dummy variables. Table 5.2 shows our estimates of industrial real wage elasticities with respect to regional unemployment levels. Three regions are considered (North, Centre, South) and seventeen industries.[5]

Even if the size of our data base is quite limited, parameter values appear to be statistically significant, most of them have the correct sign (with two exceptions), and can be found around the reference value of −0.1 suggested by Blanchflower and Oswald (1994). Remarkably, differences between industries are quite significant. The most flexible industries in terms of wage setting are textiles, building and commerce. 'Rigid' industries are energy, banking and non-market services.

5.3 THE STRUCTURE OF AN APPLIED GENERAL EQUILIBRIUM MODEL

The industrial 'wage curves' described above have been inserted into an applied general equilibrium model of the Italian economy. Seventeen indus-

Table 5.2 Industrial real wage elasticities in Italy

	Elasticity	t-stat
Agriculture	−0.07	7.29
Energy	0.04	5.00
Metallic minerals	−0.09	7.64
Non-metallic minerals	−0.14	13.92
Chemicals	−0.05	3.39
Metal goods	−0.10	13.80
Vehicles	−0.01	1.71
Food	−0.16	14.63
Textiles	−0.30	17.81
Paper	−0.20	4.05
Wood and other products	−0.18	17.57
Building	−0.20	11.43
Commerce	−0.19	14.87
Transport	−0.02	1.23
Banking and insurance	−0.00	0.28
Market services	−0.13	5.56
Non-market services	0.06	5.56

tries are considered in this model, two primary factors (labour and capital), a representative consumer, a public and a foreign sector. Labour and capital are homogeneous and mobile between industries, although wages are differentiated. Labour is not internationally mobile, whereas capital is perfectly mobile or immobile in international markets, according to the simulation scenarios. All industries are modelled by a representative firm adopting a constant return to scale technology and operating under perfect competition. Following the traditional approach of AGE/CGE models, the structural parameters of the model are estimated by assuming that the economy is in equilibrium at a certain base calibration year (1988). Non-calibrated parameters include elasticities of substitution, which have been econometrically estimated (see appendix).

Production inputs are chosen by minimising production costs, on the basis of the available technology. The latter is described by means of a set of 'nested' production functions, in which intermediate inputs and value added are combined in fixed proportions. Intermediate factors are composite goods including domestic and imported products, whose (imperfect) substitution process is modelled through CES-type functions. In turn, labour and capital contribute to the formation of value added, also on the basis of CES relationships:

$$X_j = \min \left(\frac{VA_j}{a_j^0}, \frac{X_j^1}{a_j^1}, \frac{X_j^2}{a_j^2}, \ldots, \frac{X_j^n}{a_j^n} \right)$$

$$X_j^i = A_j^i \left(\alpha_j^{i,d} X_j^{i,d-\tau^i} + \alpha_j^{i,m} X_j^{i,m-\tau^i} \right)^{-1/\tau^i}$$

$$\frac{X_j^{i,d}}{X_j^{i,m}} = \left(\frac{p^{i,m}}{p^{i,d}} \cdot \frac{\alpha_j^{i,d}}{\alpha_j^{i,m}} \right)^{\frac{1}{\tau^i+1}}$$

$$VA_j = A_j \left(\alpha_j^L L_j^{-\tau_j} + \alpha_j^K K_j^{-\tau_j} \right)^{-1/\tau_j}$$

$$\frac{L_j}{K_j} = \left(\frac{r}{w_j} \cdot \frac{\alpha_j^L}{\alpha_j^K} \right)^{\frac{1}{\tau_j+1}} \tag{5.1}$$

where i and j are industry indexes, d and m identify the origin of flows (domestic or import), X stands for production levels, p are equilibrium prices in national currency, VA stands for value added, L and K represent labour and capital employed on the basis of the wage w and on the interest rate r. Remaining symbols are estimated parameters. Elasticity parameters for the substitution between domestic and imported goods depend on the goods considered, but do not vary among industries, households, and other demand components.

The hypothesis of imperfect substitution between imports and domestic products is a standard one in this class of models. This accounts for the fact that industries produce large sets of differentiated products, so it is possible that goods produced by the same industry are both imported and exported. Since there is no fixed partition between internationally traded and non-traded goods, and imports and exports are associated with different demand elasticities, variations in the exchange rate usually imply variations in the terms of trade (no purchasing power parity).

Demand for exports is given by:

$$E_j = \varepsilon_j \left(\frac{p^{j,d}}{e p_w^{j,m}} \right)^{-\phi_j}$$

(5.2)

where p are prices, domestic (d) and import in foreign currency (m), and e is the exchange rate.

A general equilibrium state is not compatible with a situation of permanent debt, so the absence of a foreign trade deficit is an equilibrium condition for the system, unless the deficit is financed by income transfers from abroad. Transfers may also be negative and possibly include interest payments on foreign capital investments.

The trade balance constraint is formulated as:

$$e \cdot B = e \cdot \sum_j p^{j,m} \left(\sum_i a_{ji}^m X_i + c_j^m \gamma_j^m + G_j^m + I_j^m V_j^m \right) + \sum_j p^{j,d} E_j$$

(5.3)

where m stands for the import share in input–output coefficients, in household consumption (c and γ), and in other final demand components. These include public expenditure (G), gross investments (I), and stock variations (V). The variable B is the exogenous level of allowed deficit, which can be interpreted as foreign net income transfers.

The hypothesis of calibration of the model for the estimation of parameters (see appendix), namely that the economic system is in equilibrium at the year 1988, associated with the fact that the Italian foreign trade balance was in deficit, implies an assumption of the existence of positive income transfers in the base year.[6]

The imposition of a strict trade balance constraint can be simulated in the model by setting the variable B to zero. This generates a macroeconomic shock that tends to reduce real wages and interest rates. If capital is internationally mobile, part of the Italian capital stock will be invested abroad, leaving Italian interest rates unchanged. Since interest payments are included in B, a certain amount of deficit will be maintained under perfect capital mobility, thereby reducing the magnitude of the negative shock.

Equilibrium prices for labour and capital are determined by equalising demand and supply in the markets for primary resources, where 'supply' means a long-term relationship between resource price and employed quantity.

In the capital market, domestic mobility implies a uniqueness of the equilibrium interest rate. Under the closed economy assumption, the capital stock is fixed, and the interest rate is implicitly determined by:

$$\sum_j K_j = \bar{K} \tag{5.4}$$

On the other hand, when capital can be freely exchanged on international markets and the country is small, the interest rate is a given. Demand for capital in this case is determined on the basis of marginal real productivity, but total demand for capital may not match total capital endowments.

In the labour market, a series of alternative specifications are adopted. First, wage curves are considered by inserting the elasticity values which have been estimated for each industry into:

$$w_j = pc \cdot \omega_j \left(\bar{L} - \sum_j L_j \right)^{-\theta_j} \tag{5.5a}$$

where pc is a consumption price index.

Results of simulations based on (5.5a) are compared with those obtained under alternative assumptions. To make our results comparable with those of Blanchflower and Oswald (1994), we begin by using the single value of -0.1 for all elasticity parameters in (5.5a). A 'classic' closure is then considered, with perfect inter-industrial labour mobility and 'pseudo' full employment. We say 'pseudo' because total labour demand is constrained to be equal to total demand in calibration, disregarding unemployment in the base year:

$$\sum_j L_j = \bar{L} \tag{5.5b}$$

Finally, a case of complete real wage rigidity is also considered:

$$w_j = pc \cdot (\bar{w}_j / \bar{pc}) \tag{5.5c}$$

Figure 5.1 shows how different assumptions about wage setting influences the model's results. Point A represents the initial calibration state with observable levels of employment (L) and real wage (w/p). Initially, the system is assumed to be in equilibrium, so all calibrated supply curves intersect the negatively sloped demand curve in A. When a negative shock, which shifts

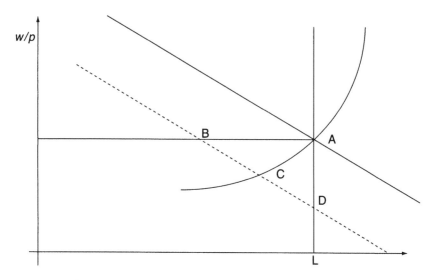

Figure 5.1 Labour market equilibria

the labour demand function backwards, is simulated, new equilibrium points are found in B, C or D, according to the assumptions adopted to determine the real wage. Point B is associated with constant real wage but lower employment. At point D employment levels are unchanged, but the real wage is reduced. Point C is an intermediate one, and it is found along a wage curve function.[7]

The demand for consumption goods by households stems from a two-stage optimisation process. At the lower level, domestic and imported products are combined in a way analogous to that of other sectors. At the higher level, the demand for composite goods is determined on the basis of:

$$\max U = \prod_j c_j^{\varepsilon_j}$$

$$\text{s.t. } \bar{c}\sum_j (rK_j + w_j L_j) = \sum_j p^{j,c}(c_j + \gamma_j)$$

(5.6)

where c is the consumption levels of the different goods, exceeding a minimum threshold level γ which does not affect the utility function, and p^c is a minimum cost index of the aggregated import/domestic goods or services. The marginal consumption propensity is constant.

Equation (5.6) defines the well-known linear expenditure system (LES). This is basically a Cobb–Douglas function computed in terms of non-basic consumption. Price demand elasticities converge to one for very high levels of available income, but γ parameters allow us to account for different income elasticities when the system does not deviate too much from the initial equilibrium state.

The model is mono-periodic, so there is no explicit intertemporal consumption choice. A fixed part of the nominal value added is assigned to households' consumption in the period under consideration. There is no explicit public sector balance constraint, and in equilibrium gross savings equalise public expenditure and investments when capital is not internationally mobile. Elements of final demand different from consumption vary in their levels but do not vary in their internal composition (no substitution among goods and services used for public expenditure and investments). Within each class of goods, however, it is possible to substitute imports and domestic products.

Figure 5.2 shows a graphical representation of the model described so far, highlighting the links between consumption and production blocks.

The general equilibrium state for the model is identified by a vector of price variables (e, r, w_j), which are equilibrium values in the markets for primary resources. From these price variables, prices for all goods and services produced in the seventeen industries are computed on the basis of

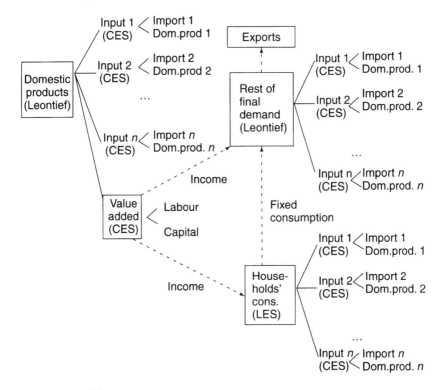

Figure 5.2 Model structure

industrial cost functions. Prices do not depend on production levels, because of the constant returns to scale assumption. These, in turn, equalise demand and supply:

$$\frac{VA_j}{a_j^0} = X_j = \sum_j a_{ji}^d X_i + c_j^d + \gamma_j^d + G_j^d + I_j^d + V_j^d + E_j \qquad (5.7)$$

It is interesting to note that, given the existence of distortions in the primary markets, the general equilibrium is not a Pareto optimum, and the utility of the representative consumer (5.6) is not maximised in the system.

5.4 SIMULATING THE IMPACT OF AN EXTERNAL SHOCK

As already mentioned, the general equilibrium model of the Italian economy has been used to simulate the effects of a trade balance constraint. A trade deficit is supported in the initial calibration state by the existence of positive income transfers from abroad. The elimination of these transfers is a nega-tive shock for the economy, causing a reduction of domestic absorption and a redistribution of resources towards export production.

A larger but similar shock affected the Italian economy in the early 1990s. The Italian balance of trade, after a small surplus in 1986, steadily deterio-rated until a significant deficit was reached in 1992 (Figure 5.3). The primary reason for this deterioration was an excessive over-valuation of the Italian lira in the European Monetary System, supported by expectations. These

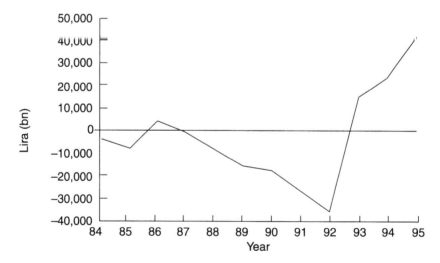

Figure 5.3 The Italian balance of trade 1984–95

changed dramatically during the summer of 1992, causing a monetary crisis in September that year, the exit of the lira from the EMS, and a large and rapid devaluation of the Italian currency (as well as of other 'weak' European currencies). This devaluation, however, markedly improved the competitiveness of Italian exporting industries. Correspondingly, the balance of trade switched from a large deficit to a large and growing surplus.

The elimination of the initial trade deficit can be simulated in the general equilibrium model simply by setting the exogenous parameter B to zero in equation (5.3). This has been done with eight different versions of the model, corresponding to the hypotheses adopted for the labour and capital markets:

- industrial wage curves with estimated elasticities without international capital mobility (BASE scenario), and with capital mobility and interest payments in the balance of trade (BASE2);
- single wage curve with identical elasticity for all industries, again with and without capital mobility (SING and SING2);
- classic closure with unchanged employment (CLASS, CLASS2);
- full real wage rigidity (FXWG, FXWG2).

The impact of the external shock can be first analysed by looking at the percentage variations in some aggregate macro variables, reported in Table 5.3. The negative shock is summarised by a reduction of the GDP, ranging from -1.34 per cent (CLASS2) to -2.35 per cent (FXWG).

Since the exchange rate (e) is chosen in the model as numéraire, the model simulates a devaluation through a reduction in nominal price variables: wages, interest rates and consumer price index (CPI). In general, the reduction in the cost of labour is larger than the reduction in the capital cost, making possible a substitution of capital with labour. Apart from the classic closure, this is, however, not sufficient to compensate for the decline in labour demand due to the average reduction in production levels.

In general, the reduction in the consumer price index is smaller than the average reduction of wages. This means that real wages are generally

Table 5.3 Changes in macro variables (%)

	BASE	SING	CLASS	FXWG	BASE2	SING2	CLASS2	FXWG2
Employment	-0.37	-0.46	0.00	-1.83	-0.22	-0.25	0.00	-1.78
Nominal wage	-1.99	-2.10	-2.30	-1.50	-0.36	-0.40	-0.80	0.00
Nom. cap. cost	-1.80	-1.80	-1.80	-1.90	0.00	0.00	0.00	0.00
L/K rel. price	0.998	0.997	0.995	1.004	0.996	0.996	0.992	1.00
CPI	-1.60	-1.60	-1.60	-1.50	-0.10	-0.10	-0.20	0.00
Real wage	-0.39	-0.50	-0.70	0.00	-0.26	-0.30	-0.60	0.00
GDP	-2.01	-2.06	-1.97	-2.35	-1.39	-1.42	-1.34	-1.7

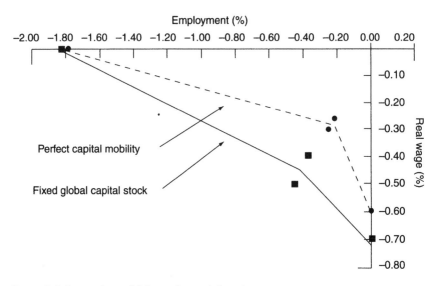

Figure 5.4 Approximated labour demand functions

reduced. Figure 5.4 plots the points corresponding to the eight versions of the model in the real wage/employment space. Two curves, interpolating the points, are added in the figure to approximate the estimated labour demand functions (as in Figure 5.1). We draw two different curves, according to the hypotheses adopted for the capital market. Under capital mobility, the curve lies on the right because a certain amount of income transfers, due to interest payments on the Italian capital invested abroad, makes the external shock smaller, thereby reducing the leftward shift of the demand function. Notice that, in both regimes, industry-specific wage curves make average real wages *and* employment levels higher than in the case of a single wage curve with homogeneous elasticities in all industries.

Tables 5.4 and 5.5 present the percentage variations which have been simulated for industrial production and employment levels. Quite different pictures emerge in the two cases of fixed and variable capital stock. To understand where these differences come from, consider first the case of the FXWG2 scenario. In this scenario, the capital cost is fixed because of capital mobility, labour costs (real) are fixed by assumption, and foreign prices are fixed because the exchange rate has been chosen as numéraire. Since all prices are determined on the basis of direct and indirect costs of primary resources and imported inputs, all prices remain unchanged in the new equilibrium state and no substitution process takes place at any level. In this case, the elimination of the trade deficit cannot be achieved through a devaluation, but only through a reduction of imports, of final demand and of activity levels.

On the other hand, when the capital cost is endogenous, larger variations

Table 5.4 Percentage variations in industrial production levels

	BASE	SING	CLASS	FXWG	BASE2	SING2	CLASS2	FXWG2
1 Agriculture	2.65	2.64	2.83	2.07	−0.88	−0.88	−0.71	−1.58
2 Energy	0.25	0.27	0.41	−0.16	−1.08	−1.05	−0.97	−1.59
3 Metallic minerals	1.38	1.42	1.59	0.92	−0.36	−0.23	−0.52	−1.25
4 Non-metallic minerals	0.03	0.02	0.19	−0.46	−0.97	−0.67	−0.93	−1.58
5 Chemicals	1.69	1.72	1.89	1.22	−0.7	−0.67	−0.58	−1.34
6 Metal goods	−0.34	−0.31	−0.17	−0.73	−0.31	−0.24	−0.8	−1.37
7 Vehicles	0.31	0.45	0.62	−0.07	−0.43	−0.31	−0.7	−1.44
8 Food	1.89	1.81	1.99	1.27	−0.89	−0.94	−0.82	−1.65
9 Textiles	1.16	0.9	1.03	0.5	−0.59	−0.74	−0.59	−1.18
10 Paper	1.02	0.92	1.08	0.44	−0.89	−0.95	−0.81	−1.53
11 Other manuf.	0.28	0.24	0.36	−0.13	−0.75	−0.72	−0.83	−1.36
12 Building	−2.03	−2.03	−1.87	−2.51	−1.9	−1.27	−1.54	−2.07
13 Commerce	0.1	0.02	0.16	−0.38	−1.06	−1.09	−1.12	−1.69
14 Transport	0.51	0.55	0.7	0.11	−0.85	−0.8	−0.78	−1.42
15 Banking	2.15	2.15	2.32	1.65	−0.98	−0.96	−0.72	−2.06
16 Market services	1.07	1.01	1.15	0.58	−3.22	−3.61	−1.06	−1.7
17 Non-market services	−3.74	−3.69	−3.54	−4.15	−0.05	−0.04	−1.71	−2.27

Table 5.5 Percentage variations in industrial employment levels

	BASE	SING	CLASS	FXWG	BASE2	SING2	CLASS2	FXWG2
1 Agriculture	2.73	2.94	3.36	1.68	−0.55	−0.44	0.15	−1.58
2 Energy	0.01	0.64	1.08	−0.66	−0.86	−0.49	0.13	−1.59
3 Metallic minerals	1.76	2.1	2.8	0.01	0.51	0.79	1.47	−1.25
4 Non-metallic minerals	1.08	0.83	1.61	−1.52	0.42	0.54	1.44	−1.58
5 Chemicals	1.66	2.36	3.02	0.38	−0.12	0.28	1.27	−1.34
6 Metal goods	−0.12	−0.01	0.37	−1.13	0.11	0.22	0.1	−1.37
7 Vehicles	−0.45	1.64	2.73	−1.64	0.27	1.48	2.79	−1.44
8 Food	2.24	2.03	2.38	0.98	−0.49	−0.62	−0.2	−1.65
9 Textiles	2.42	1.24	1.63	0.05	0.46	−0.24	0.4	−1.18
10 Paper	1.84	1.3	1.75	−0.06	−0.05	−0.39	0.28	−1.53
11 Other manuf.	1.2	0.72	1.22	−0.77	0.25	0.01	0.59	−1.36
12 Building	−0.19	−1.2	−0.4	−3.61	0	0	0.96	−2.07
13 Commerce	1.29	0.6	1.18	−1.14	0.19	−0.22	0.58	−1.69
14 Transport	0.36	0.82	1.17	−0.24	−0.68	−0.4	−0.01	−1.42
15 Banking	1.78	2.73	3.35	0.88	−0.65	−0.1	0.96	−2.06
16 Market services	2.23	1.8	2.56	−0.46	−1.82	−2.46	1.26	−1.7
17 Non-market services	−3.77	−3.66	−3.48	−4.2	−0.03	0.02	−1.6	−2.27

in relative prices are observed, especially in the CLASS scenario. Larger differences can also be observed among industries, with growing production levels in export-oriented industries (e.g. agriculture, textiles) and declining production in industries whose products are mainly absorbed domestically (non-market services, building).

Variations in employment levels follow quite closely those of production levels, with differences among industries and scenarios mainly due to differences in elasticities of the real wage and of substitution between capital and labour.

5.5 COMPARING SIMULATION RESULTS
WITH REAL DATA

General equilibrium models simulate the structural adjustments which are induced in an economic system by macroeconomic shocks. The analysis is a comparative static one, so the effects are evaluated, *ceteris paribus*, by keeping fixed all other factors that may affect the performance of an economic system in a given period. A validation of a model of this kind, based on a comparison of the model results with real data, is clearly limited by the fact that real economies are actually affected by several simultaneous adjustment processes, due to technological change, changes in consumer behaviour, interdependencies between economies, etc. However, when a shock is sufficiently large, its effects may outweigh those of other phenomena, and changes in the economic structure can be mainly explained in terms of the impact of the most important shock.

In this respect, the large external shock which affected the Italian economy after the monetary crisis of 1992 is a good candidate to use to test the simulation results illustrated in the previous section. Therefore, in this section we compare results of the model with data about the Italian economy describing structural changes that occurred in the period 1993–5.[8] We focus on the industrial composition of production and employment levels and, to disentangle the marginal effects due to the devaluation of the Italian lira, we consider percentage changes in industrial production[9] and employment with respect to the linear trend computed for each industry in the period 1984–95 (see Table 5.6).

The 'goodness of fit' of each version of the model is evaluated here by a set of indices, based on the absolute value of the difference between estimated and observed variations in industrial production and labour demand variables. Each index is computed as a weighted mean of 'errors' measured at the industrial level. Therefore, a lower index indicates a better model performance.

Table 5.7 shows the index values for each version of the model when simulation results are compared with real data regarding the structure of production and employment. Changes in the industrial composition of domestic production seem to be best described by the version with industrial wage curves and fixed costs of capital, followed by the variant with a single wage curve.

To analyse the composition of employment, we used two different criteria. First (case A), we compared model results with real data in a way analogous to that of production levels. In this case, the version of the model which performs better is FXWG2 with fixed prices. This outcome, however, does not seem to be due to a better estimate of structural changes occurring among industries, but to the fact that employment levels decline for all

Table 5.6 Percentage variations in industrial production and employment levels (1993–5) from the linear trend 1984–95 (%)

	Production	Employment
1 Agriculture	0.45	−1.53
2 Energy	−0.39	−3.08
3 Metallic minerals	4.09	−1.39
4 Non-metallic minerals	−2.31	−4.25
5 Chemicals	−4.65	−4.55
6 Metal goods	−2.22	−2.89
7 Vehicles	−11.11	−3.90
8 Food	−1.19	−1.27
9 Textiles	−0.96	−1.37
10 Paper	5.00	−2.22
11 Other manuf.	5.39	−2.28
12 Building	−4.59	−0.57
13 Commerce	−1.34	−1.72
14 Transport	0.61	−2.73
15 Banking	1.52	−1.11
16 Market services	−3.29	−3.57
17 Non-market services	−0.45	−1.09

Table 5.7 Evaluation indices for alternative model versions

	BASE	SING	CLASS	FXWG	BASE2	SING2	CLASS2	FXWG2
Production	2.56(7)	2.51(6)	2.61(8)	2.28(5)	1.38(1)	1.44(2)	1.71(3)	1.86(4)
Employment A	3.11(7)	2.94(6)	3.24(8)	2.09(4)	1.48(3)	1.34(2)	2.15(5)	0.86(1)
Employment B	1.92(5)	2.05(7)	2.12(8)	1.88(6)	0.51(1)	0.67(2)	1.29(4)	0.94(3)

Note: Figures in parentheses are rankings.

industries in the period 1993–5 and the FXWG2 is the only version exhibiting negative changes in employment in all industries.

In other words, data on the structural changes of employment in Italy seem to highlight the existence of a productivity shock affecting all industries, which overlaps with the main external shock. This can also be seen at the aggregate level, as in Figure 5.5, depicting total employment in Italy in the period 1984–95. The dotted line shows estimated values based on the trend.

To focus on the industrial composition of employment, we used an alternative criterion (case B). Rather than comparing absolute variations (Tables 5.5 and 5.6), we considered simulated and real deviations from the average, at the industry level. Although this implies some loss of information, it also allows us to eliminate potential effects of productivity shocks uniformly affecting all industries in the economy.[10] Using this criterion, the ranking of the different versions of the model is quite similar to that

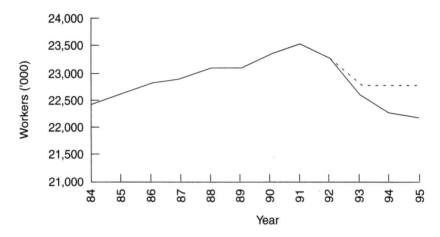

Figure 5.5 Aggregate employment in Italy 1984–95

obtained with a comparison of production levels. Again, the best models are those with wage curves and capital mobility. Observe also that models with fixed capital endowment are never found among the best versions.

5.6 CONCLUDING REMARKS

Some caution is necessary when assessing the results illustrated in the previous section, because several factors can make the comparison of real data with model results ambiguous. This can only provide some 'clues' about the seeming goodness of fit of alternative hypotheses. Nevertheless, empirical evidence does support some conclusions, since a clear picture seems to emerge from the numerical experiments.

It has been shown that non-standard assumptions about the functioning of labour and capital markets can be easily introduced in applied general equilibrium models, improving the model's realism without extra mathematical complexity. It is hoped that even models which do not focus on primary markets may adopt more realistic assumptions about labour and capital markets, especially when these models are applied to small, open economies.

Our results clearly support the hypothesis of invariance of capital cost with respect to the overall conditions of the (open) economy. This has been justified here by an hypothesis of international capital mobility, but other arguments could be put forward.

Real wages appear to be neither fixed nor perfectly flexible, and the process of wage setting is best described by means of 'wage curves'. More accurate results seem to be obtainable when the real wage elasticity of unemployment is differentiated by industry. The introduction of wage curves in a general equilibrium model poses no technical difficulty, since wage curves simply replace the conventional labour supply functions in the determination of equilibrium wages.

APPENDIX: ESTIMATION OF MODEL PARAMETERS

Calibration

The equilibrium conditions of the model can be represented as a set of equations of the following type:

$$F_i(x_j \ldots, x_n, y_k, \ldots, y_m, e_i) = 0 \qquad (A5.1)$$

where x are endogenous variables (e.g., prices and quantities), y are parameters, and e is an error term accounting for dynamic biases, measurement error, etc. The calibration method amounts to setting $e = 0$, and to solve for parameters y, given observed values of variables x. This allows one to estimate n parameters. Usually $m > n$, so $m - n$ parameters must be estimated with other methods (Bergman, 1990).

Basic consumption LES parameters

Parameters in equation (5.6) have been estimated in a study for Italy by Levaggi and Ruocco (1991). Their estimates have been adapted and included in the model described in this work.

Substitution elasticities for labour and capital

Parameters for the following equation have been estimated (Berndt, 1991):

$$\ln\left(\frac{Y}{L}\right) = a + b \ln\left(\frac{w}{p_y}\right) + \varepsilon \qquad (A5.2)$$

We considered 21 industries, using annual series 1970–90 for value added, employee units and wages. Results are shown in Table A5.1.

Substitution elasticities for imports and exports

We used the 1959–80 series of input–output tables at constant and current prices (Bertoletti et al., 1987), and more recent tables. For imports, the regressions were based on:

Table A5.1 Substitution elasticities for labour and capital

Industry	Elasticity (b)	R^2
Agriculture	1.56	0.20
Energy	1.83	0.71
Metallic minerals	3.87	0.75
Non-metallic minerals	4.37	0.80
Chemicals	3.47	0.77
Metal goods	2.42	0.61
Industrial machines	2.19	0.31
Office machines	5.43	0.74
Electrical appliance	3.93	0.89
Transport means	7.71	0.82
Food	0.65	0.58
Textiles	1.86	0.70
Wood and other products	3.45	0.70
Building	4.55	0.79
Commerce	2.43	0.39
Hotels, restaurants	(−0.45)	0.15
Transport	3.31	0.68
Communications	1.53	0.44
Banking and insurance	3.32	0.66
Market services	3.29	0.74
Non-market services	0.63	0.14

Table A5.2 Substitution elasticities for imports and exports

	Import elast.	CES R^2	Import elast.	(aut.) R^2	Export elast.	(aut.) R^2
Agriculture	5.13	0.77	1.50	0.57	2.28	0.53
Energy	1.54	0.74	0.84	0.31	1.17	0.37
Metallic minerals	3.58	0.62	1.89	0.48	3.16	0.63
Non-metallic minerals	3.43	0.70	1.84	0.57	2.57	0.62
Chemicals	3.70	0.61	1.35	0.27	2.81	0.56
Metal goods	2.78	0.60	1.25	0.37	0.97	0.19
Vehicles	3.76	0.57	1.57	0.63	1.73	0.58
Food	8.55	0.78	3.33	0.71	4.28	0.42
Textiles	5.10	0.67	1.47	0.62	0.90	0.22
Paper	3.21	0.75	2.95	0.44	2.82	0.67
Wood and other products	1.82	0.75	2.77	0.78	1.84	0.51
Building	—	—	—	—	—	—
Commerce	5.25	0.44	2.23	0.50	4.05	0.65
Transport	4.03	0.50	0.50	0.47	1.81	0.32
Banking and insurance	20.90	0.20	7.18	0.55	—	0.74
Market services	18.82	0.20	7.03	0.40	9.27	0.24
Non-market services	—	—	—	—	—	—

$$\Delta \ln \frac{X_t^{i,d}}{X_t^{i,m}} = \alpha + \sum_{\nu=t}^{t-4} \beta_t \ \Delta \ln\frac{p_t^{i,d}}{p_t^{i,m}} + \varepsilon_t \tag{A5.3}$$

Long-run elasticities have been obtained by summing all b parameters. For exports, the regressed equation is (5.2), with explanatory variables also lagged for five years. In order to make export elasticities comparable with those for imports, we regressed a similar additional equation for imports, obtaining the elasticities which are shown in the second column of Table A5.2.

NOTES

1 Observe, however, that the t statistic obtained by Blanchflower and Oswald for Italy does not allow the rejection of the hypothesis of real wages unaffected by unemployment levels.

2 In some cases the sample size exceeds one million observations (unfortunately, not in the Italian case).

3 This is because the function to be estimated is referred to the long term. It should not be confused with a Phillips curve, which refers instead to the short term and accounts for dynamic adjustments.

4 Of course, a higher or lower variability may exist in relation to time or personal characteristics.

5 Gross wages and labour units are drawn from *Conti economici regionali* ISTAT (1980–93), and wage levels are aggregated with a weighted average within each industry. The regional unemployment levels are drawn from *Statistiche del lavoro* (1980–6) and *Annuario di contabilità nazionale* (1986–93).

6 This is a working assumption, introduced to account for the existence of a trade deficit in a hypothetical equilibrium state. Actually, no relationship exists between these hypothetical transfers and real income transfers which may have occurred in Italy in 1988. Their introduction simply means that the trade balance constraint was not active in the Italian economy in that year.

7 If the wage curve is not the same for all industries, it is possible that industrial employment and the real wage move in opposite directions after a shock. This is because the industrial wage is only affected by aggregate unemployment.

8 However, whereas the model simulates a long-run equilibrium, data on the period 1993–5 are also affected by short-run adjustment processes.

9 Data refer to industrial value added at constant prices which, in the model, is assumed to be proportional to gross production levels.

10 Changes in productivity may be linked to changes in employment levels. Using other specifications of the labour market, productivity may be made (at least partially) endogenous.

REFERENCES

Akerlof, G.A. (1982), 'Labor contracts as partial gift exchange', *Quarterly Journal of Economics*, 97(4): 543–69.

Bergman, L. (1990), 'The development of a computable general equilibrium modelling', in L. Bergman, D.W. Jorgenson, and E. Zalai, (eds), *General Equilibrium and Economic Policy Analysis*, Oxford: Basil Blackwell.

Berndt, E.R. (1991), *The Practice of Econometrics*, Reading, Mass.: Addison-Wesley.

Bertoletti, P., Rampa, G. and Silva, V. (1987), *Serie annuale di tavole delle transazioni dell'economia italiana a prezzi correnti e a prezzi costanti*, Working Paper CNR – Progetto Finalizzato Economia, Università di Pavia.

Blanchflower, D.G. and Oswald, A.J. (1994), *The Wage Curve*, Cambridge, Mass.: MIT Press.

Dixon, P.B., Parmenter, B.R., Powell, A.A. and Wilcoxen, P.J. (1992), *Notes and Problems in Applied General Equilibrium Economics*, Amsterdam: North-Holland.

Harrigan, F., McGregor, P.G., Swales, J.K. and Dourmashkin, N. (1992), 'Imperfect competition in regional labour markets: a computable general equilibrium analysis', *Environment and Planning A*, 24: 1463–81.

Hutton, J. and Kenc, T. (1996), 'Replacing the UK income tax', in A. Fossati (ed.), *Economic Modelling Under the Applied General Equilibrium Approach*, Aldershot, Hants: Avebury.

Leontief, W. (1946), 'The pure theory of the guaranteed annual wage contract', *Journal of Political Economy*, 54: 76–9.

Levaggi, R. and Ruocco, A. (1991), 'La calibrazione di benchmark', in A. Fossati (ed.), *Equilibrio Generale e Simulazioni*, Milan: Franco Angeli.

Maechler, A.M. and Roland-Holst, D.W. (1995), 'Empirical specification of labor market structure and conduct in a general equilibrium framework', in J.F. Francois, and K.A. Reinert (eds), *Applied Trade Policy Modeling: A Handbook*, Cambridge: Cambridge University Press.

Ruocco, A. (1996), 'Savings and investment fiscal policies: a quantitative analysis for the Italian economy', in A. Fossati, (ed.), *Economic Modelling Under the Applied General Equilibrium Approach*, Aldershot, Hants: Avebury.

Shapiro, C. and Stiglitz, J.E. (1984), 'Equilibrium unemployment as a worker discipline device', *American Economic Review*, 75(4): 433–44.

Stiglitz, J.E. (1985), 'Equilibrium wage distribution', *Economic Journal*, 95(379): 595–618.

Weiss, A. (1991), *Efficiency Wages Models of Unemployment, Layoffs and Wage Dispersion*, Oxford: Clarendon Press.

6

DEVELOPMENT AND APPLICATION OF AN AGE MODEL WITH A VARIABLE POPULATION

Eckhard Lübke

6.1 INTRODUCTION

For a long time the problems associated with an ageing population were considered to be primarily due to the financial charges entailed by provision for old age. In order to represent these problems and quantify their economic repercussions, static partial models of social security were set up and used to work out the contribution rate required to balance the social security budget in a system with a changing demographic structure.

Provision for old age, however, is probably not the most serious of the problems that arise within an economy which is developing under the influence of an ageing population.[1] The future development of the economy is determined to a large extent not only by the size of the workforce, but also by the stock of capital accumulated within a society. Both of these elements are strongly influenced by demographic processes.

Over the past decade, the dynamic Applied General Equilibrium model has shown itself to be a suitable instrument for analysing these problems.[2] When this kind of model is employed,[3] a fairly simple population model is often combined with a life-cycle model with overlapping generations. In addition to a corporate sector, the state and a social security system are integrated into the Applied General Equilibrium model. Taking account of the state and social security ensures that the model is a more accurate reflection of reality. What is more, some other parameters are integrated into the model – parameters which can be varied in order to simulate the effects of politico-economic measures.

The models of this type discussed in the literature are already quite well developed in regard to the modelling of the corporate, state and social security sectors. Their main deficiency, however, resides in the fact that they fail to incorporate a population model in a sufficiently precise and detailed manner. Thus Auerbach and Kotlikoff (1987: 167) point out that, in their model, special measures have to be taken in order to ensure a return to a stable demographic structure following a change in the birth rate.

Keuschnigg *et al.* (1991) complain that owing to the current state of modelling techniques it is not yet possible 'to take account of stochastic phenomena and introduce insurance benefits in the ordinary sense of the term'.[4] Moreover, the types of inheritance process that can be observed in real life are not depicted in a satisfactory manner.

Real-life demographic processes have a momentum of their own. This momentum is transmitted to the economic system. Population models, constructed with the aid of the cohort-component projection method,[5] take account of the mortality rate within individual age brackets as well as age-specific fertility. These models enable us to comprehend the momentum of demographic processes. If this type of population model is integrated into an Applied General Equilibrium model, it is possible to represent the way in which the economy is affected by the momentum of demographic processes.

It follows therefore that mortality within individual age brackets must perforce be taken into account in the life-cycle model. Individuals who act in accordance with the life-cycle hypothesis will plan their entire life cycles in the best possible way, i.e. with a view to utility maximisation. This means that they will take account of the fact that they are likely to reach a certain age, thereby maximising the expected value of their utility. Individuals do not know when they will die. However, we shall proceed on the assumption that they know the age they are likely to reach. Moreover, in their economically active phase, individuals must acquire personal assets which will enable them to support themselves from the beginning of retirement until the maximum attainable age. This being so, they will bequeath their assets if they die before reaching the maximum attainable age. In this kind of life-cycle model, there is no need for an inheritance motive to account for the existence of inheritances.

In a model which has been extended in the aforementioned manner, an individual's estate has to be divided up among his or her progeny. This means that we must begin by expanding the population model in such a way as to take account of family relationships. Such relationships come about through births and have to be corrected in the course of time to take account of deaths among the descendants. On the basis of these family relationships, inheritances can be divided up among the progeny by means of an inheritance model. The inheritances received by the descendants affect their life-cycle decisions. The inheritance model takes account of inheritance variations caused by demographic fluctuations, economic malfunctions or politico-economic measures. Thus, for instance, it is possible to reproduce waves of inheritances due to increased life expectancy or a fall in the birth rate.

In what now follows, we shall attempt to improve on the model discussed in the literature. Using the procedure described above, we shall expand this model in a consistent manner by incorporating a population model (section 6.2). Then we shall discuss the results of the simulation run for an ageing population (section 6.3).[6]

6.2 THE MODEL

An outline of the model

Figure 6.1 is a simplified representation of the interaction of the elements that constitute the model. In the figure, the 100 life spans taken into account in the model are reduced to five.

The population model expanded to take account of family relationships represents the demographic development of the model population. The

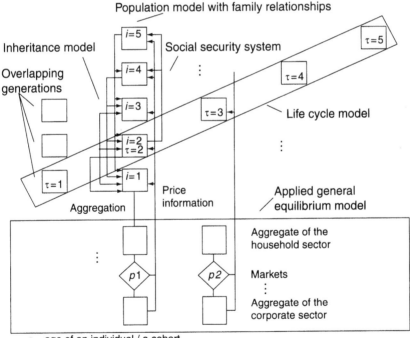

Figure 6.1 Schematic diagram showing the interaction of the elements constituting the model

inheritance model reproduces the transfer of the assets of deceased individuals to their descendants. The behaviour of the individuals in the model population is defined by the life-cycle model. An individual who is representative of a cohort plans all his or her future decisions immediately after birth. Since the representative individual has complete information, he or she does not need to revise plans later on. The aggregate supply and demand variables in the household sector result from the aggregation of individual decisions. There is a certain amount of overlapping between the generations or age cohorts. The model is expanded by incorporating a corporate sector, the state and social security. In the present instance, social security is a pay-as-you-go system of provision for old age. It effects transfers from the working population to old-age pensioners.

To come now to the economic interaction between individuals, we may draw a distinction between market and non-market transactions. Market transactions are conducted in the commodity, labour and capital markets, while non-market transactions are effected as inheritance transfers or as social security transfers within the context of the pay-as-you-go system of provision for old age.

The population model with family relationships and the inheritance model

The population model is based on the cohort-component projection method. With the aid of the fertility and mortality components, the future development of the initial population is represented by means of forward projections. No allowance is made for migratory movements in the model described here. When forward projections are made, distinctions are drawn between age cohorts, and males are normally distinguished from females. In this model, however, no sex distinctions are made. The population model under discussion is unisexual.

Mortality, i.e. the evolution of the death rate, is represented in the form of life tables in statistical publications. The appropriate mortality function can easily be determined from a life table. The mortality function $l(\tau,j)$ for year j indicates the likelihood that a newborn child will reach the age τ. In the model, the mortality function is represented as follows by a logistic function (Dinkel 1989: 365ff.):

$$l'(\tau) = 1 - \frac{1}{1 + e^{b(a-\tau)}}$$

$$l(\tau,j) = \begin{cases} 1.0 & \tau \leq 0 \\ 0.0 & \tau > T \\ \frac{l'(\tau)}{l'(0)} \cdot (1-c) & \text{misc.} \end{cases}$$

T = maximum age that can be reached; e.g. T = 100.

Parameter a influences the average age, parameter b the slope of the mortality function in old age, and parameter c indicates the likelihood that a child will die in the first year of life (infant mortality).

Turning now to the question of mortality variations over a given period, it is important to draw a distinction between the period and cohort mortality function (Bomsdorf and Trimborn 1992: 458). The period mortality function is valid for one calendar year, while the cohort mortality function is valid for the entire life span of a cohort. For an age cohort born in period j the relationship between the period mortality function (l) and the cohort mortality function (lk) is as follows:

$$lk(\tau,j) = \begin{cases} l(\tau,j) & \tau = 0 \\ lk(\tau - 1,j) \cdot \dfrac{l(\tau,j+\tau)}{l(\tau-1,j+\tau)} & \text{misc.} \end{cases}$$

In Figure 6.2 the mortality functions in the model are contrasted with those calculated on the basis of the life tables. Fertility is represented in virtually the same way as mortality. In this case, however, a distinction is made between the development and the level of fertility. In statistical publications, the development of fertility is represented in the form of age-specific fertility tables which can be used to calculate the fertility function and can indicate

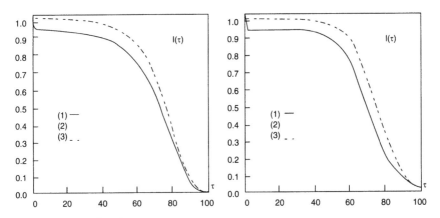

Figure 6.2 Mortality function
(a) Germany's male population
(b) Population model
Sources
(a) Plots (1) and (2) calculated on the basis of data from Statistisches Bundesamt, *Annual Abstract of Statistics*, (1991: 38ff, Table 1); plot (3) Bomsdorf and Trimborn (1992: 480ff, Table 4), with (1) mortality function, 1949–51; (2) mortality function, 1986–8; (3) mortality function 2010.
(b) Author's computations with the following parameter settings:
(1) $a = 70$, $b = 0.13$, $c = 0.08$
(2) $a = 74$, $b = 0.14$, $c = 0.02$
(3) $a = 76$, $b = 0.15$, $c = 0.01$

the likelihood that a woman will give birth to a child when she has reached a certain age. The development of the fertility function is reproduced as follows by means of a modified function of the normal distribution (Lübke forthcoming):

$$m'(\tau) = \begin{cases} f(z(\tau)) & 15 \leq \tau \leq 44 \\ 0 & \text{misc.} \end{cases}$$

$$f(z(\tau)) = \frac{1}{\sqrt{2.\pi}} \, e^{\frac{-z(\tau)}{2}}$$

$$z(\tau) = -\frac{I}{2} + \frac{I}{44 - 14} \cdot (\tau - 15) \qquad \text{for} \quad \tau = 1, \ldots, T.$$

I = range of values of the normal distribution used as a basis for model-building.

Figure 6.3 reproduces the fertility function of the model as well as the fertility functions derived from the statistically established age-specific fertility tables. The level of fertility is determined with the aid of the net reproductive rate (NRR) concept. The net reproductive rate indicates the total number of female live births that can be expected from a woman when she herself is born.[7] If the net reproductive rate is equal to one, a generation of women will be exactly reproduced by their daughters. If we have the net reproductive rate for one year, the previously modelled fertility function can be converted to this birth level:[8]

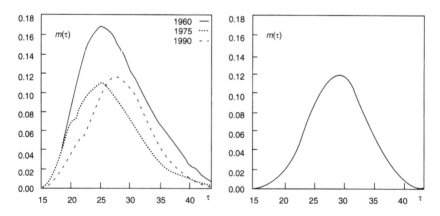

Figure 6.3 Age-specific fertility function
(a) Germany's female population
(b) Population model
Sources
(a) Calculated on the basis of the Statistisches Bundesamt, *Annual Abstract of Statistics*, various years
(b) Author's computations

$$m\ (\tau, j) = m'\ (\tau) \cdot \frac{NRR}{NRR(m',\ l)} \qquad \text{for} \quad \tau = 1, \ldots, T.$$

NRR = net reproductive rate to which the fertility function is to be converted:

$$NRR(m',\ l) = \sum_{\tau = 1}^{T} l(\tau, j) \cdot m'(\tau)$$

Figure 6.4 shows how the net reproductive rate has evolved over the past forty years.

Once the components of the population model we have considered have been reproduced, we can look at the evolution of an initial population. In the model to be developed here, the initial population is the population represented in the life table. In the long run, this age pattern of the population will be established in a population which neither grows nor dwindles, i.e. a stationary population (Dinkel 1989: 85). By contrast, a stable population is one that grows or dwindles at a constant rate. If an economy is to remain in a steady state, a stable population is a prerequisite. Since the model economy is assumed to be in a steady state at the outset, there must be a stable population in the initial phase. In order to simplify model-building, we proceed on the assumption that the population is stable. The stationary initial population is given directly by the mortality function:

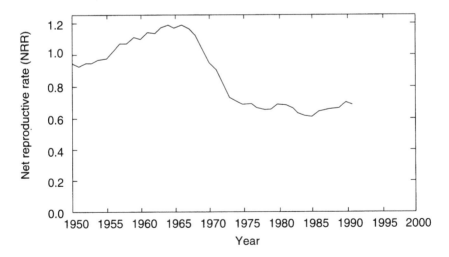

Figure 6.4 Evolution of the net productive rate in Germany, 1950–91
Source: Calculated on the basis of the Statistisches Bundesamt, *Annual Abstract of Statistics*, various years

$$P(\tau, 1) = \frac{l(\tau, 1)}{\sum\limits_{t=0}^{T} l(t, 1)} \cdot \text{Pop} \qquad \text{for} \quad \tau = 0, \ldots, T.$$

$P(\tau, 1)$ represents the number of persons aged τ, and Pop the total number of persons in the population. For year one the family relationships in the stationary initial population are determined as follows:[9]

$$E(\tau_1, \tau, 1) = P(\tau, 1) \cdot \frac{l(\tau - \tau_1, 1)}{l(\tau, 1)} \cdot m(\tau - \tau_1, 1) \cdot l(\tau_1, 1)$$

for $\tau = 0, \ldots, T$ and $\tau_1 = 0, \ldots, \tau - 1$.

$E(\tau, \tau1, 1)$ = number of $\tau1$-year old children in the parent cohort τ in year one. $P(\tau, 1) \cdot \frac{l(\tau - \tau_1, 1)}{l(\tau, 1)}$ is the number of individuals in a parent cohort τ when their children (aged $\tau1$ in the initial situation) are born. $P(\tau, 1) \cdot \frac{l(\tau - \tau_1, 1)}{l(\tau, 1)} \cdot m(\tau - \tau_1, 1)$ represents the number of children procreated by the parent cohort τ and aged $\tau1$ in the initial situation. Finally, $P(\tau, 1) \cdot \frac{l(\tau - \tau_1, 1)}{l(\tau, 1)} \cdot m(\tau - \tau_1, 1) \cdot l(\tau_1, 1)$ is the number of $\tau1$-year-old children who were still alive in the initial situation after the decease of their coevals.

Starting with the population in year one, the population in year two and all the following years in the simulation period can be calculated successively. The number of newborn babies in year j is given by the sum of the products from the number of persons in an age group and the fertility value for that age group:

$$P(0, j) - \sum_{\tau=1}^{T} P(\iota, j) \cdot m(\iota, j).$$

The number of deaths that have occurred in the meantime is corrected as follows:

$$P(\tau, j) = P(\tau - 1, j - 1) \cdot \frac{l(\tau, j)}{l(\tau - 1, j)} \qquad \text{for} \quad \tau = 1, \ldots, T.$$

New births result in new family relationships:

$$E(0, \tau, j) = P(\tau, j) \cdot m(\tau, j) \qquad \text{for} \quad \tau = 1, \ldots, T.$$

The figures representing existing family relationships are corrected to take account of deaths:

$$E(\tau_1, \tau, j) = E(\tau_1 - 1, \tau - 1, j - 1) \cdot \frac{l(\tau, j)}{l(\tau - 1, j)}$$

for $\tau = 0, \ldots, T$ and $\tau_1 = 0, \ldots, \tau - 1$.

When dealing with family relationships, we do not assign individuals straightforwardly to their children. Instead, we record the number of children for an entire cohort as a frequency distribution.

Figure 6.5 represents the result of the demographic projection for an ageing population.[10] The variations in the parameters of the population model (a, b, c and NRR) are reproduced in Figure 6b.[11]

In the inheritance model, inheritance transfers are made on the basis of family relationships (Lübke forthcoming). The inheritance bequeathed to the representative individual in period j is given by the sum of the inheritances bequeathed to him or her by the individual parent cohorts. Thus:

$$WE_{i,j} = \sum_{i1=i+1}^{T} WEI_{i,\,i1,j} \qquad \text{for } i = 0, \ldots, T.$$

If a cohort has children $\left(\sum_{i2=0}^{i-1} E(i2, i, j) \neq 0 \right)$, the assets of the deceased members of the cohort $(WI_{i-1,j-1} \cdot (P(i - 1, j - 1) - P(i, j)))$ are divided up equally among the children. However, if a cohort has no children, the inheritances are divided up among the other members of the cohort in order to simplify model-building:[12]

$$WEI_{i,i1,j} = \begin{cases} WI_{i-1,\,j-1} \cdot (P(i-1,j-1) - P(i,j)) \cdot \frac{E(i1,i,j)}{\sum_{i2=0}^{i-1} E(i2,i,j)} \cdot \frac{1}{P(i1,j)} & \text{if } \sum_{i2=0}^{i-1} E(i2,i,j) \neq 0 \\[2ex] \frac{WI_{i-1,j-1} \cdot (P(i-1,j-1) - P(i,j))}{P(i,j)}. \end{cases}$$

The life-cycle model with overlapping generations and uncertainty regarding mortality

In conformity with the assumptions underlying the population model, the model describing individual behaviour[13] is based on the assumption that when individuals plan their lives they take account of the likelihood that they will still be alive at a certain point in time. They weight their utility in particular years of their lives with the likelihood that they will still be alive in the years in question.[14]

The conditional probability in respect to life expectancy for an age cohort born in period j (LP) can be derived directly from the cohort mortality function:

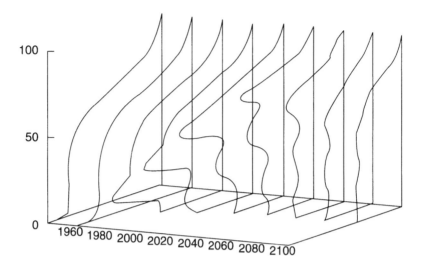

Figure 6.5*a* Simulation of demographic trends with an ageing population. Age structure
Source: Author's computations

$$LP(\tau|t,j) = \frac{lk(\tau,j)}{lk(t,j)}.$$

This indicates the likelihood that an individual who has reached age t will
also reach age τ. Since the model individual maps out his or her plans in the
first year of life, in what follows $t = 1$. The individual decides how much to
consume (CI) each year. During the economically active phase which extends
from age $t1 + 1$ to age $t2$, the individual also has to make decisions
concerning the allocation of time (LT), i.e. the amount of time to be
allocated to work and leisure (FI) in a given period.

The individual maximises his or her expected lifetime utility:

$$\max \rightarrow E(U) = \prod_{\tau=1}^{T} CI_{\tau,j+\tau}^{\beta c.LP(\tau|1,j)} \cdot \prod_{\tau=t1+1}^{t2} FI_{\tau,j+\tau}^{\beta f.LP(\tau|1,j)}.$$

This maximisation, however, is subject to constraints imposed by the limitations of the lifetime budget:

$$0 = - \sum_{\tau=t1+1}^{t2} (LT - FI_{\tau,j+\tau}) \cdot w_{j+\tau} \cdot \frac{1}{\prod_{\tau1=1}^{\tau} (1 + rW_{\tau1,j})}$$

$$+ \sum_{\tau=1}^{T} WE_{\tau,j+\tau} \cdot q_{j+\tau} \cdot (1+r_{j+\tau}) \frac{1}{\prod_{\tau1=1}^{\tau} (1 + rW_{\tau1,j})}$$

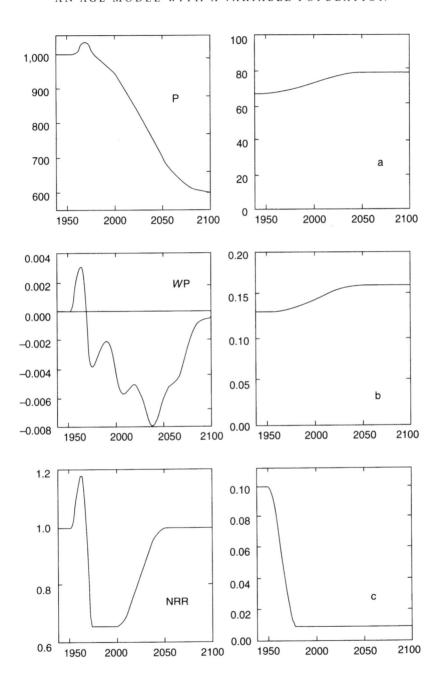

Figure 6.5b. Simulation of demographic trends with an ageing population. Parameter
(a, b, c and NRR), total population (P), population growth rate (WP)
Source: Author's computations

109

$$- \sum_{\tau=1}^{T} CI_{\tau,j+\tau} \cdot P_{j+\tau} \cdot \frac{1}{\prod_{\tau1=1}^{\tau} (1 + rW_{\tau1,j})}$$

In this context, βc and βf are preference parameters, w is the nominal wage rate, q the price of capital goods, r the capital-market interest rate, and p the price of consumer goods. rW is a mixed profit rate which depends on an exogenous portfolio decision (qV) and which results from the yield of an investment in the capital market and the yield of an investment in a private pension insurance (Lübke forthcoming):

$$rW_{\tau,j} = (1 + r_{j+\tau}) \cdot (1 - qV_{j+\tau}) + (1 + r_{j+\tau}) \cdot (1 + rV_{\tau,j}) \cdot qV_{j+\tau} - 1.$$

qV is the share of assets invested in a private pension insurance. In addition to the yield in the capital market (r), private pension insurance returns an additional profit ($rV\tau$) owing to the fact that the assets of deceased members paid into the private pension insurance scheme are divided up among the remaining members.

Since private pension insurance yields an additional profit, an individual who acts rationally would opt for $qV = 1$. In reality, however, there are certain reasons for not keeping some of the assets in private pension insurance. Thus there are consumer durables, jewellery and real estate which all count as assets. In addition to uncertainty concerning the time of death, there are other risks which may lead to precautionary saving. No attempt is made to account for these and other reasons in the model. This is why an exogenous portfolio quota is incorporated in it.

If the members of a cohort are assigned to a separate category as a risk group (they all incur the same mortality risk), and if the insurance is fairly calculated in actuarial terms, the additional profit is given directly by the mortality function. Thus:

$$rV_{\tau,j} = \frac{lk(\tau - 1, j)}{lk(\tau, j)} - 1.$$

The additional profit may be interpreted as follows. At the beginning of a period, all the members of a cohort pay part of their assets (the part fixed by qV) into a pool, which then has a volume of $WI_{\tau-1,j+\tau-1} \cdot P(\tau-1, j+\tau-1)$. At the end of this period, the fund is divided up equally among the survivors. Each survivor receives ($WI_{\tau-1,j+\tau-1} \cdot P(\tau-1, j+\tau-1)/P(\tau, j+\tau)$ or – expressed as a profit –

$$rV_{\tau,j} = \frac{WI_{\tau-1,j+\tau-1} \cdot P(\tau - 1, j + \tau - 1)}{WI_{\tau-1,j+\tau-1} \cdot P(\tau, j + \tau)} - 1.$$

With

$$P(\tau, j + \tau) = P(\tau - 1, j + \tau - 1). \frac{lk(\tau, j)}{lk(\tau - 1, j)}$$

we get

$$rV_{\tau,j} = \frac{lk(\tau - 1, j)}{lk(\tau, j)} - 1.$$

Figure 6.6 shows the life cycle model result for the parameters fixed in Table 6.1.

The total accumulated assets are divided equally ($qV = 0.5$) between capital market investments and private pension insurance. Unintentional inheritances result from the assets invested in the capital market.

In their youth, the individuals are not supported by their parents. Instead, maintenance is provided by borrowing in the capital market or by an insurance. In return for the maintenance credit it grants, the insurance, in addition to capital market interest, demands an extra charge to cover the risk of default.[15] If the assets are negative, the inheritances are negative too. The credit contracted in the pre-employment phase is repaid during the first few years of gainful employment.

Owing to the individual's low regard for future utility,[16] the consumption curve is shaped like a hill. After the age of sixty, there is a rapid decline in conditional probability in respect to life expectancy. Accordingly, consumption within this age bracket is considered to be less important. This is counteracted, however, by the additional profit of private pension insurance – a profit which increases as the insured individual grows older. If the individual keeps his assets exclusively in private pension insurance, the two variables cancel each other exactly (Lübke forthcoming). In the course of the individual's life, consumption then increases with the rate of interest in the capital market. Throughout life, the individual's mortality has no influence on consumption, and there are no unintentional inheritances either.

The beginning and end of the individual's economically active phase are determined exogenously, but the utility-maximising individual decides when to begin and end his or her gainful activity within a given period.

For a given population we can now form macroeconomic aggregates for period j:

Consumption demand $\quad C_j = \sum_{i=1}^{T} CI_{i,j} \cdot P(i, j)$

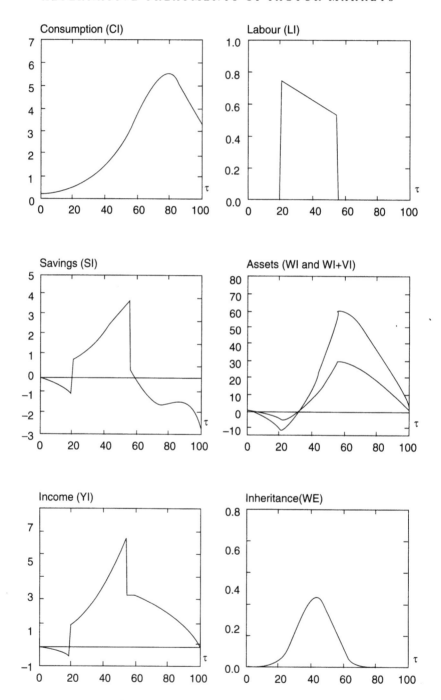

Figure 6.6 Optimum life paths in the life-cycle model
Source: Author's computations

Table 6.1 Fixing parameters for the simulation of the life-cycle model in a steady state

Parameter	Variable	Values
End of pre-employment phase	t1	20.00
End of gainful employment	t2	55.00
Available time	LT	1.00
Preference for consumption	βc	1.00
Preference for leisure	βf	1.00
Output elasticity of labour	α	0.75
Rate of technological progress	m	0.03
Life expectancy	a	75.00
Slope of the mortality function	b	0.17
Infant mortality	c	0.00
Portfolio quota	qV	0.50

Labour supply
$$L_j^s = \sum_{i=1}^{T} LI_{i,j} \cdot P(i, j)$$

Savings
$$S_j = \sum_{i=1}^{T} SI_{i,j} \cdot P(i, j)$$

Assets
$$W_j = \sum_{i=1}^{T} (WI_{i,j} + VI_{i,j}) \cdot P(i, j)$$

Inheritance volume
$$E_j = \sum_{i=1}^{T} WE_{i,j} \cdot P(i, j).$$

The applied general equilibrium model with the corporate sector, the state and social security

The corporate sector is represented by a linear homogeneous Cobb–Douglas production function. A homogeneous good (Yr) is produced with the factors labour (L) and capital (K); the labour factor is subject to technical progress whose rate is m:

$$Y_j^r = (1 + m)^{j \cdot \alpha} \cdot L_j^\alpha \cdot K_j^{1-\alpha} .$$

α is the output elasticity of the labour factor.

Social security is modelled on the German scheme and is therefore presented in the form of a statutory pension insurance fund with a pay-as-you-go system. If the social security receives a subsidy from the state (ZG) and the pension level is linked to earned income before deductions (rn_j^{br}), the pension fund's budget equation will be as follows:

$$E_j = A_j$$

$$b_j \cdot w_j \cdot L_j^S + ZG_j = rn_j^{br} \cdot \frac{w_j \cdot L_j^S}{EP_j} \cdot RP_j.$$

In this equilibrium model without unemployment the economically active population (EP) and the number of old-age pensioners (RP) will be as follows:

$$EP_j = \sum_{i=t_1+1}^{t2} P(i, j) \quad \text{and} \quad RP_j = \sum_{i=t2+1}^{T} P(i, j).$$

Isolating the contribution rate (b), we can solve the budget equation as follows:

$$b_j = rn_j^{br} \cdot \frac{RP_j}{EP_j} - \frac{ZG_j}{w_j \cdot L_j^s}.$$

The 1992 pension reform in Germany brought a transition to a net wage-related pension.[17] In the pension fund's budget equation, the pension payment is now calculated on the basis of the net pension level (rn_j^{ne}) and the net wage or the gross wage after deduction of contributions to the pension fund and wage tax payments (tw). Since 1992, the pension fund's budget equation has therefore been modified as follows:

$$b_j \cdot w_j \cdot L_j^s + ZG_j = rn_j^{ne} \cdot \frac{w_j \cdot L_j^s \cdot (1 - tw_j - b_j)}{EP_j} \cdot RP_j.$$

This gives us the following contribution rate:

$$b_j = \frac{rn_j^{ne} \cdot \frac{RP_j}{EP_j} \cdot w_j \cdot L_j^s \cdot \left(1 - tw_j\right) - ZG_j}{w_j \cdot L_j^s \cdot \left(1 + rn_j^{ne} \cdot \frac{RP_j}{EP_j}\right)}.$$

The changeover took place in such a way that the pension payments worked out with the two pension formulae were identical in the transition year. In that year, the net pension level was fixed accordingly.

The national budget looks like this:

Public goods $\quad G_j \cdot p_j = gg_j \cdot Y_j^r \cdot p_j$ Wages tax $\quad L_j \cdot w_j \cdot tw_j$

Social security subsidy $\quad ZG_j$ Capital gains tax $\quad W_j \cdot q_j \cdot r_j \cdot tr_j$

Interest payments $\quad Z_j$ Value added tax $\quad C_j \cdot p_j \cdot tp_j$

                                                  Inheritance tax $\quad E_j \cdot q_j \cdot te_j$

                                                  Budget deficit $\quad BD_j \cdot q_j$

The goods provided by the state (G) represent a fixed percentage (gg) of the volume of goods in real terms. The interest payments (Z) are made on the national debt of the previous period (D_{j-1}). The national debt in real terms is supposed to stand in a fixed relation to the volume of goods for the period $(D_j = dg_j \cdot Y_j^r)$ under discussion. The state's social security subsidy represents a fixed percentage (zg) of the value of the goods volume $(ZG_j = zg_j \cdot Y_j^r \cdot p_j)$. The parameters tw, tr, tp and te are the tax rates for wages, capital gains, value added and inheritance. The national budget equation is solved by isolating the wage-tax rate. This variable balances the national budget.

In order to obtain a solution from the Applied General Equilibrium model, the constituent elements of the model are fitted together to produce a general model of a closed economy, and values are attached to the parameters. The solution obtained from the general model is characterised by market equilibria in all markets and in all periods. The national and social security budgets are always balanced. Individuals have no false expectations about present or future data (Auerbach and Kotlikoff 1987: 41). However, they do not know when they will die; they merely know whether they are likely to be alive at a later point in time. The values from Table 6.2 are attached to the parameters (Lübke forthcoming). They are supposed to give an approximate idea of conditions in Germany.

The state subsidy to pension schemes is fixed at $rg = 0$, the implication being that non-insurance payments not included among pension fund expenditures in this model are equivalent to the state subsidy.

For the general model the initial steady state is first established iteratively. After that, the adjustment path of the economy is determined by means of the Gauss–Seidel method (Keuschnigg 1989: 39). This path is ascertained on the basis of the demographic processes which can be observed as an economy evolves with an ageing population. When the malfunctions associated with

Table 6.2 Fixing parameters for the simulation of the model

Simulation period					
T1	T2				
1850	2350				
Parameters of representative individuals					
$t1$	$t2$	LT	βc	βf	qV
20	55	1.0	6.0	1.0	1/3
Parameters of the corporate sector					
α	m				
0.75	0.02				
Parameters of social security					
$rnbr$					
0.40					
Parameters of the state					
gg	dg	zg	tp	te	tr
0.30	0.40	0.00	0.15	0.03	0.20

the adjustment process have virtually disappeared, a final steady state is established (Auerbach and Kotlikoff 1987: 46).

In what now follows, we shall attempt to explain the results of a simulation for Germany.

6.3 SIMULATION RESULTS FOR GERMANY

The model simulation is carried out with the parameters from Table 6.2 and the demographic process of an ageing population represented in Figure 6.5.

All in all, the macroeconomic results reveal a fairly strong and lasting influence of the demographic process on macroeconomic ratios (see Figure 6.7). In the initial phase, the percentage of savings in disposable income (the savings rate) rises from the steady state level of approximately 0.09 to 0.14 in 1990. After that, it begins to fall, moving downwards at a fairly moderate pace at first, but then plummeting to somewhere in the region of zero in the year 2030. The increase in the savings rate can be explained by the rise in life expectancy: individuals have to make provisions for a longer retirement phase. The subsequent sharp decline in the savings rate until the year 2030 is due to the fact that there is a drop in the birth rate from 1970 onwards. Until the year 2030, that fall in the birth rate is the main reason for the change in the ratio of savings-accumulating active persons to dissaving retirees.

Since in this simulation the net reproduction rate is assumed to rise again to NRR = 1.0, the savings rate eventually increases until it reaches its steady state level. The saving rate level in the final steady state is higher than the level observed in the initial steady state. This is because there has been an increase in life expectancy in the meantime.

The growth rate of output is determined by the development of factor inputs. Capital input and labour input display more or less the same basic pattern in the development of their growth rates. However, the growth rate of capital input lags behind the growth rate of labour input by about ten years.

The basic pattern displayed by the growth of labour input and capital input is transmitted to the growth rate of output. The growth rate of output or the national product rises from its steady-state level of 2 per cent to approximately 2.73 per cent until 1987, then it drops to somewhere in the region of 1.4 per cent in the year 2000. After that it falls again, levelling out at slightly less than 0 per cent in the year 2025.

If the net reproduction rate is assumed to rise to NRR = 1 at some time in the future (as was the case in this simulation), the growth rate of the national product rises again and fluctuates before returning to its initial level in the steady state.

The growth rate of output is mainly determined by the development of the growth rate of labour input. The development of the growth rate of capital,

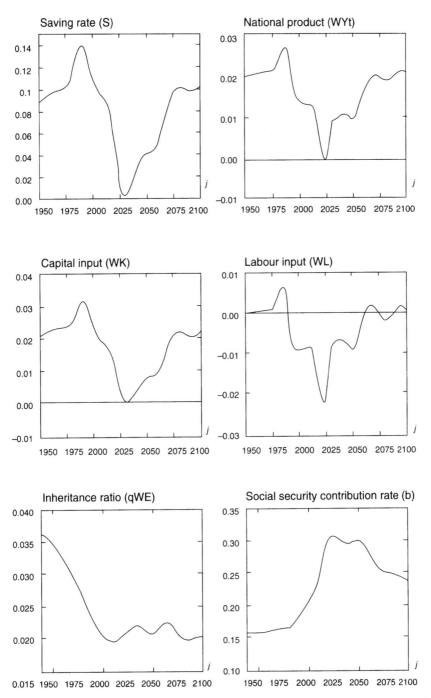

Figure 6.7   Savings rate (S), growth rate of national product (WYt), capital input (WK) and
labour input (WL), inheritance ratio (qWE) and social security contribution rate (b)

Source: Author's computations

by contrast, is only to a slight extent reflected in output. This is due to the value selected for the output elasticity of the labour factor ($\alpha = 0.75$). This parameter fixes the relative importance of the production factors. Towards the end of the simulation period, the growth rates are subject to fluctuations, but as these fluctuations decrease in amplitude, they edge towards their steady state values. The fluctuations are due to the petering out of the demographic waves in the age structure of the model population (see Figure 6.5).

In the initial steady state, the level of inheritances, considered in relation to hereditable assets (the inheritance ratio), is about 3.7 per cent. As life expectancy increases (parameter a of the mortality function rises from $a = 67$ to $a = 79$), assets are passed on less frequently by inheritance. The inheritance ratio drops to 2 per cent.

The contribution rate for statutory pension insurance rises steadily from 15.5 per cent to approximately 30.6 per cent in the year 2030 and remains at this high level for about thirty years. The 24 per cent contribution rate in the final steady state is higher than in the initial steady state since there is an increase in life expectancy between the two states in question.

6.4 CONCLUSION

Applied General Equilibrium models with a variable population were first developed more than a decade ago, yet the possibilities of such models have by no means been exhausted. They are by nature quite intricate, hard to set up as simulation programmes, and hard to use. None the less, these models are becoming increasingly popular with more and more economists, and they are now used in various forms with different kinds of extensions.

In this chapter, we have presented some extensions to this kind of model. One extension concerns the integration of a population model with the aid of the cohort-component projection method. Earlier AGE models with a variable population comprise only very rudimentary population models which fail to take account of age-specific fertility or age-specific mortality. By using a population model constructed with the aid of the cohort-component projection method, we can reproduce real-life demographic processes in detail. If this kind of population model is integrated in an AGE model, it becomes possible to show how the momentum of demographic processes is transmitted to the macroeconomic system. These demographic processes include the one under discussion here, namely that of an ageing population.

Moreover, the population model is expanded to include first-degree family relationships. This makes it possible to divide up an individual's assets among his or her children in an inheritance model. Inheritance waves which occur in the demographic process are reproduced in this way.

Inheritances need not be intentional. They may also result from individuals' uncertainty about the date of their own death. If individuals keep part of their wealth in the form of personal assets instead of investing in an insurance policy, death will result in involuntary inheritances. The third extension consists in the fact that the problems posed by uncertain death dates in the individual's life-cycle model are taken into account in the general model. It is only within such a model that the existence and effects of private pension insurance can be properly accounted for.

There is no contradiction between the simulation results of this model and those obtained from its predecessors.[18] To this extent, there is a perfectly smooth transition from these earlier models to the one outlined here. The results show up the macroeconomic effects of demographic processes in much more detail than was possible with previous models.

NOTES

1 Cf. Bös and von Weizsäcker (1989), who give an overview of the macroeconomic consequences of an ageing population. They note that much more research needs to be done in this field of investigation.

2 The prototype of these models was developed by Scarf (1973). Auerbach and Kotlikoff (1985) subsequently integrated a variable population into their model, which has been adopted by several other authors such as Keuschnigg (1989), Neusser (1993) and Lübke (forthcoming).

3 Cf., for instance, Auerbach and Kotlikoff (1987).

4 See Keuschnigg et al. (1991: 138): 'Beim gegenwärtigen Stand der Modellierungstechnik ist es allerdings noch nicht möglich, stochastische Phänomene zu berücksichtigen und dadurch Versicherungsleistungen im üblichen Sinn einzuführen.' (With the current state of the modelling technique, however, it is not yet possible to consider stochastic phenomena, and so to introduce insurance coverage in the usual sense.)

5 For a description of this method, see, for instance, Feichtinger (1979), Hauser (1982) or Dinkel (1989).

6 For further details, see Lübke (forthcoming).

7 See, for instance, Dinkel (1989: 83) or Statistisches Bundesamt (1994: 48ff.).

8 See, for instance, Dinkel (1989: 83) and Anderson et al. (1983: 249).

9 Cf. Lübke (forthcoming) on the integration of family relationships into a population model with the aid of the cohort-component projection method.

10 Cf. Hauser (1982: 169ff.) for this way of presenting the results of demographic simulations.

11 A Spline interpolation procedure was used in order to smooth out fluctuations in the parameters. For further details, see, for instance, Bronstein and Sementjajew (1981: 796).

12 The mortality rate for young people is very low. Moreover, individuals' (negative) assets are very limited in comparison with the assets they will accumulate in later life. By and large, the error entailed by this simplification is insignificant.

13 Seminal studies on the life-cycle hypothesis include Brumberg and Modigliani (1979) and Ando and Modigliani (1963). On the concept of overlapping generations, see Samuelson (1958).

14 This approach was developed by Yaari (1965).

15 The 'actuarial note' considered by Yaari corresponds, to a large extent, to the

private pension insurance introduced here. The insurance considered by Yaari is such that it can only be taken out on positive assets. Cf. Yaari (1965: 146).

16 On the interpretation of the mortality risk in the utility function as a subjective rate of time preference, see Hurd (1989: 779).

17 Cf. Bundesminister für Arbeit und Sozialordnung (Federal Minister of Labour and Social Order) (1990) for details of the 1992 pension reform in Germany.

18 Cf. Lübke (forthcoming) for a comparison of the results obtained from various models and those obtained from the model presented here.

REFERENCES

Anderson, O., Schaffranek, M., Stenger, H. and Szameitat, K. (1983), *Bevölkerungs- und Wirtschaftsstatistik: Aufgaben, Probleme und beschreibende Methoden*, Berlin: Springer.

Ando, A. and Modigliani, F. (1963), 'The "life cycle" hypothesis of saving: aggregate implications and tests', *American Economic Review*, 53: 55–84.

Auerbach, A.J. and Kotlikoff, L.J. (1985), 'Simulating alternative social security responses to the demographic transition', *National Tax Journal*, XXXVIII: 153–68.

Auerbach, A.J. and Kotlikoff, L.J. (1987), *Dynamic Fiscal Policy*, Cambridge: Cambridge University Press.

Bomsdorf, E. and Trimborn, M. (1992), 'Sterbetafel 2000 – Modellrechnung der Sterbetafel', *Zeitschrift für die gesamte Versicherungswirtschaft*, 81: 457–85.

Bös, D. and Weizsäcker, R.K. von (1989), 'Economic consequences of an ageing population', *European Economic Review*, 33: 345–54.

Bronstein, I.N. and Sementjajew, K.A. (1981), *Taschenbuch der Mathematik*, Frankfurt and Zurich: Harri Deutsch.

Brumberg, R. and Modigliani, F. (1979), 'Utility analysis and aggregate consumption function: an attempt at integration', in A. Abel, (ed.), *Collected Papers of Franco Modigliani*, vol. 2, Cambridge, Mass.: MIT Press.

Bundesminister für Arbeit und Sozialordnung, Referat für Öffentlichkeitsarbeit (ed.) (1990), *Rentenreform '92*, Bonn.

Dinkel, R.H. (1989), *Demographie*, Band 1: *Bevölkerungsdynamik*, Munich: Vahlen.

Feichtinger, G. (1979), *Demographische Analyse und populationsdynamische Modelle: Grundzüge der Bevölkerungsmathematik*, Vienna and New York: Springer.

Hauser, J.A. (1982), *Bevölkerungslehre für Politik, Wirtschaft und Verwaltung*, Bern and Stuttgart: Paul Haupt.

Hurd, M.D. (1989), 'Mortality risk and bequests', *Econometrica*, 57: 779–813.

Keuschnigg, C. (1989), 'Tax incentives for investment: a dynamic general equilibrium perspective', *Empirica*, 16: 31–51.

Keuschnigg, C., Kunst, R. and Wörgötter, A. (1991), 'Bevölkerungsentwicklung und Pensionsfinanzierung – Analyse von Problemfeldern mit einem angewandten allgemeinen Gleichgewichtsmodell mit privater und gesetzlicher Altersvorsorge', in S. Fickl, (ed.), *Bevölkerungsentwicklung und öffentliche Haushalte*, Frankfurt: Campus, 135–68.

Lübke, E. (forthcoming), *Private Ersparnis und wirtschaftliche Entwicklung bei einer alternden Bevölkerung – Eine theoretische Analyse mit Hilfe von Simulationsmodellen*, Heidelberg and Berlin: Physica.

Neusser K. (1993), 'Savings, social security, and bequests in an OLG model: A simulation exercise for Austria', *Supplement to Journal of Economics*, 7: 133–55.

Samuelson, P.A. (1958), 'An exact consumption-loan model of interest with or without the social contrivance of money', *Journal of Political Economy*, 66: 467–82.

Scarf, H. (1973), *The Computation of Economic Equilibria*, New Haven, Conn.: Yale University Press.

Statistisches Bundesamt (ed.) (1991), *Bevölkerung und Erwerbstätigkeit, Fachserie 1, Reihe 1.S.2 Allgemeine Sterbetafel für die Bundesrepublik Deutschland* (Gebietsstand vor dem 3.10.1990) 1986/88, Stuttgart: Metzler-Poeschel.

Statistisches Bundesamt (ed.) (1994), *Statistisches Jahrbuch 1994 für die Bundesrepublik Deutschland*, Stuttgart: Metzler-Poeschel.

Statistisches Bundesamt (ed.) (various years), *Statistisches Jahrbuch für die Bundesrepublik Deutschland*, Stuttgart: Metzler-Poeschel.

Yaari, M.E. (1965), 'Uncertain lifetime, life insurance, and the theory of the consumer', *Review of Economic Studies*, 32: 137–50.

Part III

POLICIES FOR CARBON DIOXIDE ABATEMENT

7

INTRA- AND INTERGENERATIONAL EFFECTS OF GLOBAL CARBON LIMITS

A five-region analysis

Gunter Stephan, Georg Müller-Fürstenberger
and Pascal Previdoli

7.1 INTRODUCTION

Today, the economic analysis of global warming is primarily concentrated on the costs and benefits of greenhouse gas abatement (for an overview, see Nordhaus and Yang, 1996). Obviously, there are simple but important reasons for being so concerned about efficiency in greenhouse gas reduction. Global change defines a public good problem and, since we need to proceed beyond 'no regrets' policies, there must be some arrangement for abatement and for burden-sharing between regions and over time. Economic efficiency ensures that potential exists for each participant to gain from an international agreement.

From a political economy point of view, however, fairness in burden-sharing is at least as important as efficiency. On the one hand, there is the problem of intergenerational equity. The greenhouse debate typically focuses on carbon dioxide; its annual emissions are small relative to the existing stock of atmospheric carbon. Hence, abatement costs are borne early, but benefits do not accrue until the distant future. This is why it is generally expected that future generations are likely to be wealthier in terms of conventional capital, but to be poorer in terms of natural resources, unless there is agreement in global greenhouse policy.

On the other hand, there is the problem of finding an equitable arrangement for intragenerational cost sharing between regions. Wealth is unequally distributed across regions. Costs of reducing greenhouse gas emissions differ quite significantly from region to region, and participation in greenhouse gas abatement is completely voluntary. Of course, interregional wealth transfers could be designed to support the willingness to participate voluntarily in sharing the burden of greenhouse gas abatement. But they cannot be viewed as a substitute for foreign aid from wealthier to poorer nations, nor as a substitute for transfers from wealthier to poorer generations. Implicit in all negotiations is the idea that no major changes are proposed in the ownership of labour, capital and other conventional resources.

Given these circumstances, it will not be easy to reach agreement on cooperative carbon abatement unless it were feasible to separate the issue of efficiency from that of equity. A commonsense way to describe equity-efficiency separability conditions is that the economic impact of global climate change is limited sufficiently such that there are no significant effects upon the productivity of capital and/or the willingness to pay of each group. In the latter case, the time path of global emissions could be determined independently of the contentious issue of the specific arrangements for abatement cost sharing. An expert group could recommend a global total of carbon dioxide emissions while a political group negotiates on how that total might be divided up (see Manne, 1996).

To be more precise, a new international institution such as a global environmental bank might sell carbon emission permits on an annual or five-year basis which in turn would be tradable on an international market. The bank's worldwide rate of permit sales could be based on principles of intertemporal economic efficiency. The equity issues could be focused on the debate over the ownership shares of individual nations in the net revenues of such a bank.

This chapter considers the following questions in more detail: (a) Do equity-efficiency separability conditions apply in greenhouse gas abatement? (b) If not, what are the economic effects of different allocations of ownership shares in carbon rights among regions and across generations? In order to compare the costs and benefits of alternative cost-sharing rules in greenhouse gas abatement, some type of model for the integrated assessment of global climate change is required. Key features of our model are: it has an explicit age structure; it is regionally disaggregated; basic materials and carbon dioxide emission rights are traded internationally on open markets; international capital markets are imperfect. Section 7.2 contains the formal representation of our Computable Overlapping Generations model. Results of computational experiments are presented and interpreted in section 7.3. Finally, conclusions are drawn in section 7.4.

7.2 MODELLING

Consider a simple intertemporal model of an international market economy. Time is taken as discrete, and commodities of different periods are viewed as distinct. Agents behave as price takers with consumers maximising utilities and producers maximising profits.

The world is divided into five geopolitical regions: US; other members of OECD (OOECD); former Soviet Union (FSU); China; and Rest of the World (ROW). In each region there is a sequence of overlapping age cohorts. Just as in Stephan *et al.*, (1997), each regional generation is represented by a single consumer who lives for three periods. During childhood there are no expenses and no income. During working life capital is accumulated from labour income. During retirement there are consumption expenditures but no labour income. For convenience, the first period of life is not considered explicitly and age cohorts are indexed by date of entering working life.

Interactions between regions are kept as simple as possible (see Figure 7.1) and production is highly aggregated. In each region there is a macro-sector which produces a specific regional gross product. Macro outputs can be used as inputs into the production of basic materials which in turn enter into regional macro-production. As in Perroni and Rutherford (1993), basic materials are traded internationally, but there are only regional markets for the other factors of production such as labour and capital.

Welfare of future generations is viewed as a public good. Agents do not provide for the climate of their offspring by acting individually. Physical capital stocks are passed on to the succeeding generation without any

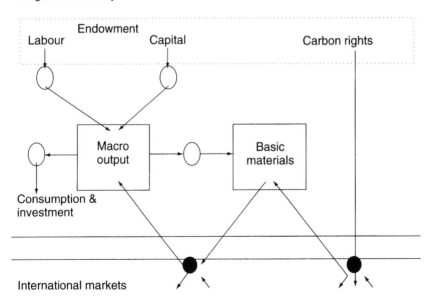

Figure 7.1 Commodity and factor flows

bequest motive. Intergenerational altruism occurs through an international climate convention.

Among the various greenhouse gases, carbon dioxide (CO_2) is considered as the only relevant one. Increased atmospheric CO_2 concentration causes global warming and directly affects regional production, but not utilities. Climate policy is based on the institutional arrangement of internationally tradable emission permits. For example, there could be a new institution such as a global environmental bank which would issue carbon emission permits on an annual basis and these permits would in turn be traded on an open international market.

Carbon rights, consumption and investment

This chapter elaborates the following thought experiment. It supposes that an expert group has recommended a global total of carbon dioxide emissions and has determined the time path of global emissions. A political group has negotiated how these totals are to be divided up into single regional emissions. A global environmental bank has been installed which issues carbon emission permits on an annual basis and trades these permits on an open competitive market (for details, see Stephan and Müller-Fürstenberger 1996b).

Let $a_R(t)$ denote the carbon rights assigned to region R during period t. Let $p_R(t)$, $w_R(t)$ and $r_R(t)$ be the spot-market prices for regional output, labour and service of capital goods respectively. $q(t)$ is the international spot-market price of emission permits.

If $^1a_R(t)$ is the fraction of region R's carbon rights which age cohort t holds in its first period of economic life, and if $l_R(t)$ denotes its labour endowment, then income:

$$w_R(t)l_R(t) + q(t)^1a_R(t) \tag{7.1}$$

is divided into consumption $^1c_R(t)$ and savings $b_R(t)$ such that (period-related) utilities are maximised. As in Howarth and Norgaard (1992), the preferences of the young are expressed by a Cobb–Douglas utility function $^1U_R(^1c_R(t),b_R(t))$.

$K_R(t)$ is region R's physical capital stock at date t. As mentioned above, the consumers' saving decisions can be viewed as investment in the society's future capital stock. Therefore, the young generation's decision to buy property rights $b_R(t)$ on future capital determines, together with the depreciation rate λ, the capital stock $K_R(t + 1)$ of region R in the following period:

$$b_R(t) + (1 - \lambda)K_R(t) = K_R(t + 1). \tag{7.2}$$

The old generation holds the region's capital endowment $K_R(t + 1)$ and some of the carbon emission rights $^2a_R(t + 1)$. Given their budget constraint:

$$p_R(t + 1)^2 c_R(t + 1) \leq r_R(t + 1)K_R(t + 1) + q(t + 1)^2 a_R(t + 1), \qquad (7.1a)$$

they choose a utility maximising consumption bundle $^2c_R(t + 1)$.

Production, emissions and abatement

For each region R gross production $y_R(t)$ is characterised by constant elasticity of substitution (CES) between two aggregates of inputs: value added on the one hand and basic materials $m_R(t)$ on the other.

$$y_R(t) = [\beta_1(1_R(t)^\gamma K_R(t)^{1-\gamma})^\varepsilon + \beta_2 m_R(t)^\varepsilon]^{1/\varepsilon}. \qquad (7.3)$$

Value added is produced by capital $K_R(t)$ and labour $l_R(t)$; γ is the corresponding Cobb–Douglas parameter; ε is the CES elasticity of substitution parameter, and the coefficients β_1 and β_2 are derived from base year data.

Producing basic materials in region R requires both regional macro inputs and fossil fuels. Rather than considering greenhouse resources directly, carbon dioxide emissions are viewed as inputs into basic material production.[1] Their production possibilities are characterised by a Cobb–Douglas formulation:

$$n_R(t) = \beta_3 e_R(t)^\tau o_R(t)^{1-\tau}, \qquad (7.4)$$

where $n_R(t)$ and $o_R(t)$ denote outputs of basic materials and the macro-inputs, respectively; $e_R(t)$ is the 'consumption' of carbon dioxide emissions in regional basic materials production.

Global climate and green output

To model the relationship between carbon dioxide emissions and economic damage it is necessary (a) to specify the accumulation of CO_2 in the atmosphere, or alternatively the time profile of the atmospheric CO_2 concentration, (b) to evaluate the relationship between increasing the atmospheric CO_2 concentration and feedback on gross production.

Based on historical data, Nordhaus (1991) estimated the correlation between global carbon dioxide emissions and the atmospheric concentration of CO_2. According to that, the actual stock $Q(t)$ of atmospheric carbon dioxide is a linear function of the lagged stock $Q(t - 1)$ and past-period global CO_2 emissions $e(t - 1)$:

$$Q(t) = \Psi [Q(t - 1) + \Theta e(t - 1)]. \qquad (7.5)$$

Equation (7.5) takes the following considerations into account: (a) only a fraction Θ of past emissions will rest in the atmosphere: the other part is subject to oceanic uptake; (b) due to a long-run transfer of CO_2 from the rapid mixing surface layers into the deep ocean, the stock of atmospheric CO_2 is reduced by factor Ψ.

Global CO_2 emissions are given by:

$$e(t - 1) = \Sigma_R e_R(t - 1). \tag{7.6}$$

Note, if global climate policy is in force through tradable quotas, then at any point of time t:

$$\Sigma_R e_R(t) \leq \Sigma_R a_R(t) \tag{7.6a}$$

has to be obeyed: that is, global CO_2 emissions are limited by the total amount of carbon rights issued by the global environmental bank during this period.

Estimates on the economic impact change are based on case studies, educated guesswork and extrapolation (see Tol, 1995). The most speculative feature is the specification of a damage function which relates economic losses to atmospheric CO_2 concentration. As in the MERGE model (see Manne et al., 1995) the quadratic form:

$$\Phi(t) = 1 - [(Q(t) - Q^*)/\Omega]^2 \tag{7.7}$$

is used to estimate the loss factor $\Phi(t)$ in gross production. Q^* denotes pre-industrial atmospheric CO_2 concentration, and Ω marks the critical value for CO_2 stocks. Beyond this concentration, production is reduced to zero.

Due to climate change only a fraction $\Phi(t)$, $0 < \Phi(t) < 1$, of the regional conventional gross output $y_R(t)$ is actually at the agent's disposal:

$$\Phi(t)y_R(t) = {}^1c_R(t) + {}^2c_R(t) + b_R(t) + o_R(t). \tag{7.8}$$

As (7.8) indicates the 'green output', $\Phi(t)y_R(t)$, can be: invested, $b_R(t)$; consumed by the young, ${}^1c_R(t)$, and old, ${}^2c_R(t)$; or used to produce basic materials, $o_R(t)$, at any point in time.

7.3 NUMERICAL RESULTS

The model is benchmarked against 1990 data (see Appendix 1 for details). The numerical results are computed with MPS/GE (see Rutherford, 1995).

Business-as-usual simulations

Under business-as-usual (BAU) assumptions economic growth is mainly driven by the development of the labour force, technical progress and physical capital formation. Labour and exogenous technical progress are measured together in efficiency units and grow at 2.5 per cent in any region. No significant structural changes in the regional decomposition of world output are observed under BAU assumptions.

Business as usual development uses up environmental capital by increasing the atmospheric CO_2 concentration and implies notable economic damage in the long run. By the end of the next century, climate change could account for economic losses in gross production in a range between 1.1 per cent in the former Soviet Union (FSU) and 2.8 per cent in the Rest of the World (ROW).

Climate policy and alternative burden-sharing rules

For counterfactual analysis let us assume that the individual regions have agreed to implement jointly the Intergovernmental Panel on Climatic Change's (IPCC) S750 stabilisation policy (see Houghton *et al.*, 1995). This means that global CO_2 concentration is limited to 620 ppm by the end of the next century and should be stabilised at 750 ppm during 2200. In other words, by 2100 the stock of atmospheric carbon is double the size of pre-industrial concentration, but is still allowed to grow.

Compared to other climate policy scenarios (for a reference, see ibid.) this is a rather weak requirement. Nevertheless it requires a sharp slow-down of emissions in comparison to business as usual (see Figure 7.2) Under BAU assumptions atmospheric carbon dioxide concentration would reach 1,100 ppm: this is twice as much as in the S750 policy case. As is well known from the literature, greenhouse gas emissions can be reduced efficiently if climate policy is based on a system of internationally tradable carbon rights. Since

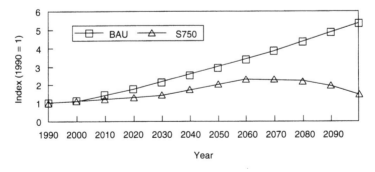

Figure 7.2 Carbon dioxide emissions with (S750) and without (business-as-usual) climate policy

we are interested in the issue of equity and fairness, we contrast three cases of an initial interregional allocation of carbon rights:

1   *Grandfathering*: carbon rights are initially issued according to 1990 regional emission shares.
2   *Equity*: carbon rights are issued on a constant per capita basis, and regional shares are determined according to the region's share in world population. This rule is based on the principle: equal men–equal CO_2 emission rights.
3   *Traverse*: the allocation of carbon rights linearly moves from 'grandfathering' to 'equality' over the time horizon considered.

Table 7.1 summarises the three options of an initial interregional distribution of carbon rights. It furthermore shows that intergenerational distribution can typically follow two polar rules: either the young or the old generation obtains all of the regional carbon rights.

Counterfactual analysis

Effects on green output

Figures 7.3, 7.4 and 7.5 illustrate the impact of an S750 climate policy on green output as a function of different initial allocations of carbon rights to the single regions. If green output is viewed as a measure of welfare, then our simulations suggest that an S750 climate policy will not improve overall welfare. This result is due to the low damages of climate change in relation to the total economic costs of climate policy (see also Tol, 1995).

Nevertheless, the regional effects of such policy might be quite different. As Figure 7.3 reports, independent of the initial allocation of carbon rights, OECD countries are losers under a S750 climate policy. Since the same holds true for the former Soviet Union (FSU) virtually all industrialised countries are welfare losers. For example, if grandfathering is used as the interregional sharing rule, then OECD countries' green output is reduced by 3 per cent in 2100 (see Figure 7.3); if carbon rights are issued on a constant per capita

Table 7.1 Climate policy scenarios

Scenario	Distribution rule	Ownership
GF-Y	Grandfathering	Young
GF-O	Grandfathering	Old
P-Y	Equity	Young
P-O	Equity	Old
GF-P-Y	Traverse	Young
GF-P-O	Traverse	Old

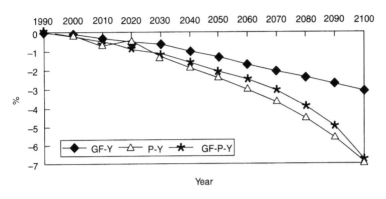

Figure 7.3 Deviation from business-as-usual (OECD)

basis, then the economic costs of the climate policy are even higher. There-fore, if the most industrialised countries were to agree on the S750 policy, they could do best by insisting on grandfathering with the young generation as owner of the carbon rights.

In contrast to the most industrialised countries, China and the Rest of the World (ROW) can gain from a climate convention, provided the distribution of carbon rights follows an 'equity' regime. On a traverse from grandfather-ing to equity, China will break even in the middle of the next century. ROW can gain from this policy even earlier (see Figures 7.4 and 7.5).

What is an explanation for the fact that OECD countries will lose welfare under any, even a weak, climate convention such as IPCC's S750 policy, whereas China and ROW can gain, provided carbon rights are initialised on a constant per capita basis? How can it be explained that regional effects of greenhouse gas abatement will be smaller, if the young, working genera-tions hold the regional endowment of carbon rights?

An answer to the second question is the topic of a paper by Stephan and Müller-Fürstenberger (1996a). However, given the model formulation used in the present chapter, the explanation is quite obvious. Age cohorts save and hence invest during the working phase of their lives. During retirement they use their income for consumption only. Hence, if additional income is given to the young, this has a positive effect both on consumption and capital formation, whereas the allocation of carbon rights to the old only increases the demand for consumption. Therefore, a positive effect can be observed over the long term only if the young hold society's endowment of carbon rights.

Effects on international trade

To answer the initial question, let us consider first the case that carbon rights are assigned to the single regions on a constant per capita basis. Given the

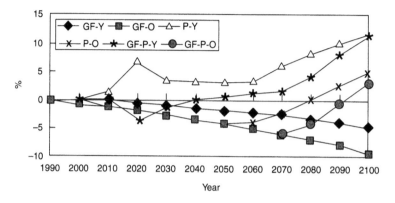

Figure 7.4 Deviation from business as usual (China)

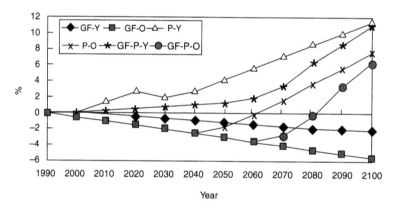

Figure 7.5 Deviation from business as usual (Rest of World)

equity assumption it is obvious that the most industrialised countries will suffer from an under-supply of carbon rights. This can lead to two different reactions. On the one hand, heavily emitting industries, such as production of basic materials, are relocated to regions where a sufficient endowment of carbon rights exists. On the other hand, highly industrialised countries buy carbon rights on international markets. Both effects can be observed if we analyse the imports of basic materials through the single regions.

Figure 7.6 shows how imports in basic materials will deviate from BAU, if CO_2 emissions are restricted by an S750 policy and carbon rights are initialised on a constant per capita basis. Recall that with our model formulation, carbon rights and basic materials are the only internationally traded commodities.[2] Since trade must be balanced at each date (see Appendix 2), imports of carbon rights induce exports of basic materials and vice versa. If carbon rights are issued according to the equity rule, the highly industria-

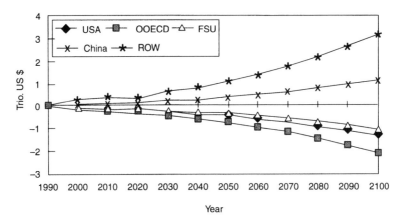

Figure 7.6 Imports of basic materials (P−Y): deviation from business-as-usual

lised countries aim to compensate for the shortage in their initial carbon rights endowment. They try to buy carbon rights on the international markets which can be financed only through exports of basic materials. Therefore imports of basic materials through the developing regions such as China and ROW increase compared to BAU.

If grandfathering is used as the initial distribution rule, then the results obviously change. As Figure 7.7 indicates, OECD countries are now net importers of basic materials. Only FSU exports basic materials, hence imports carbon rights, under both distribution schemes. Note that Figures 7.6 and 7.7 exhibit significant differences in the order of magnitude in the deviation of imports from BAU. However, the reason for these differences becomes quite obvious if we look at the price of carbon rights. Under grandfathering they are significantly higher than under equity assumptions (see Figure 7.8).

7.4 CONCLUSIONS

This chapter started from the assumption that policy makers have agreed on a weak CO_2 concentration stabilising policy. To ensure cost-efficiency, internationally tradable emission rights are issued according to the politically mandated CO_2 concentration target. It hardly comes as a surprise that changes in regional welfare strongly depend on the initial endowment of carbon rights.

In short, our simulations suggest that stabilising concentration at 750 ppm will not improve global welfare. Regional welfare gains or losses depend on the initial distribution of carbon rights. With grandfathering, where the initial distribution is based on base year emission shares, none of the regions

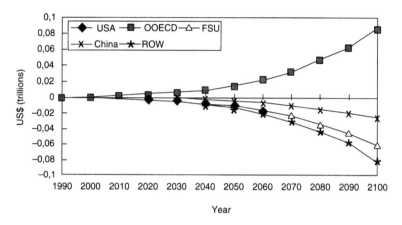

Figure 7.7 Imports of basic materials (GF−Y): deviation from business-as-usual

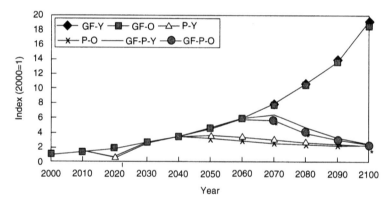

Figure 7.8 Price of carbon rights

will encounter welfare gains compared to the 'business as usual' scenario. This holds true even with an optimal intergenerational distribution rule. Indeed, in any region, abatement costs are higher than prevented climate damages. Only if the distribution of carbon rights is issued on an equity rule, i.e. on a constant per-capita basis, will the welfare of China and ROW be improved, while the other regions will still suffer losses under this regime. Even a smooth traverse from grandfathering to equalising does not provide welfare gains in regions other than China and ROW.

These results depend on two crucial assumptions. First, the estimated damage is very optimistic and global climate policy calls for weak interventions only. Second, international capital markets are imperfect such that no major changes in the ownership of produced capital can occur. This assumption is, however, in line with the modelling of capital markets by Perroni and

Rutherford (1993) and Nordhaus and Yang (1996). Nevertheless, if international agreements on climate policy are required to provide welfare gains for all participants, then our results are discouraging. In fact, we observe some kind of distribution paradox: since China and ROW will gain significantly from an agreement on a per-capita basis, they would have to offer other regions side-payments. Otherwise, the other regions would not participate voluntarily as long as individual rationality prevails.

APPENDIX 1: BENCHMARK DATA

	US	OOECD	FSU	China	ROW	Total
GDP (trillion US$)	5.6	10.2	2.7	1.1	3.4	23
Labour value share (%)	76	72	70	70	70	
Basic materials input share on total output (%)	8.3	7.8	13.8	12.6	9.6	
Energy input share on basic materials (%)	14	14	14	14	14	
Capital (trillion US$)	13.44	28.56	8.1	3.3	10.2	63.6
Growth rate labour (%)	2.5	2.5	2.5	2.5	2.5	
Depreciation rate (%)	5	5	5	5	5	5
Investments (trillion US$)	1.008	2.142	0.6075	0.2475	0.765	4.77
Elasticity of substitution (Value-added/basic material)	0.4	0.4	0.4	0.4	0.4	
Elasticity of substitution (Macro input/carbon input)	1	1	1	1	1	
Population (million)	250.4	490.0	289.3	1133.7	3102.7	5266.1
Emissions (GtC)	1.43	1.375	1.055	0.641	1.502	6.003
Diffusion coefficient, per decade Ψ						0.9
Short-run oceanic uptake, per decade Θ						0.5
Economic damage 550 ppm (%)	1.1	1.1	0.8	1.5	2.1	

APPENDIX 2: TRADE BALANCES

Market equilibrium implies that the value of exports equals the value of imports in each region and in any period. This is a consequence of individual budget constraints, as the following reasoning shows.

Consider the young and the old generations' budget constraint at date t in region R:

$$p_R(t)[{}^1c_R(t) + b_R(t)] = w_R(t)l_R(t) + q(t){}^1a_R(t), \qquad (A7.1)$$

$$p_R(t)[{}^1c_R(t) + {}^2c_R(t) + b_R(t)] = r_R(t)K_R(t) + q(t)^2a_R(t). \tag{A7.2}$$

Utility functions are strictly increasing in their arguments, hence both budget constraints hold with equality. Note that (A7.1) and (A7.2) are incomplete, since profits from producing macro outputs and basic materials do not appear as income. This incompleteness does not matter as long as technologies exhibit constant returns to scale, which in turn imply zero profits in equilibrium. Taking profits into consideration explicitly, and adding up (A7.1) and (A7.2) yields:

$$p_R(t)[{}^1c_R(t) + {}^2c_R(t)] = w_R(t)l_R(t) + r_R(t)K_R(t) + \\ q(t)[{}^1a_R(t){}^2a_R(t)] + \Pi^R{}_M(t) + \Pi^R{}_{BM}(t), \tag{A7.3}$$

where $\Pi^R{}_M(t)$ and $\Pi^R{}_{BM}(t)$ denote short-run profits in the 'macro output' and 'basic materials' sectors respectively. These profits are given by:

$$\Pi^R{}_M(t) = p_R(t)y_R(t) - w_R(t)l_R(t) - r_R(t)K_R(t) - v(t)m_R(t), \tag{A7.4}$$

and

$$\Pi^R{}_{BM}(t) = v(t)n_R(t) - q(t)e_R(t) - p_R(t)o_R(t), \tag{A7.5}$$

with $v(t)$ as the international spot-market price of basic materials.

Market clearing for macro-outputs requires at any date t:

$$y_R(t) = {}^1c_R(t) + {}^2c_R(t) + o_R(t) + b_R(t). \tag{A7.6}$$

Market clearing for capital and labour are already anticipated in (A7.3) and (A7.4).

Inserting (A7.4)–(A7.6) in (A7.3) gives

$$q(t)[a_R(t) - e_R(t)] + v(t)[n_R(t) - m_R(t)] = 0, \text{ with } {}^1a_R(t) + \\ {}^2a_R(t) = a_R(t). \tag{A7.7}$$

Equation (A7.7) says that net exports of carbon rights equal net imports of basic materials, both denoted in value terms. Therefore trade is balanced for each region at any date t.

NOTES

1 Direct proportionality of CO_2 emissions and fossil fuel use allows us to treat carbon rights and fossil fuels as a single composite 'carbon' input.

2 Note that this assumption is consistent with the models developed by Perroni and Rutherford (1993) and Nordhaus and Yang (1996). It implies in particular that international capital markets are imperfect.

REFERENCES

Houghton, J.T., Meira Filho, L.G., Bruce, J., Hoesung Lee, B., Callander, A., Haites, E., Harris, N. and Maskell, K. (eds) (1995), *Climate Change 1994: Radiative Forcing of Climate Change and an Evaluation of the IPCC IS92 Emission Scenarios*, published for the Intergovernmental Panel on Climate Change, Cambridge: Cambridge University Press.

Howarth, R.B., and Norgaard, R.B. (1992). 'Environmental valuation under sustainable development', *American Economic Review*, 82, 2: 473–7.

Manne, A.S. (1996), 'Intergenerational Altruism, Discounting and the Greenhouse Effect', Department of Operations Research, Stanford University, mimeo.

Manne, A.S., Mendelsohn, R. and Richels, R. (1995), 'MERGE: a model for evaluating regional and global effects of GHG reduction policies', *Energy Policy*, 23: 17–34.

Nordhaus, W.D. (1991), 'To slow or not to slow: the economics of the greenhouse effect', *Economic Journal*, 101, 407: 920–37.

Nordhaus, W.D. and Yang, Z. (1996) 'A regional dynamic general-equilibrium model of alternative climate-change strategies', *American Economic Review*, 86, 4: 741–64.

Perroni, C. and Rutherford, T.F. (1993), 'International trade in carbon emission rights and basic materials: general equilibrium calculations for 2020', *Scandinavian Journal of Economics*, 95, 3: 257–78.

Rutherford, T.F. (1995), *General Equilibrium Modeling using MPS/GE as a GAMS Subsystem*, Working Paper 92–15, Department of Economics, University of Colorado.

Stephan, G. and Müller-Fürstenberger, G. (1996a), '*The double dividend of carbon rights*', Department of Applied Micro-economics, University of Bern, mimeo.

Stephan, G. and Müller-Fürstenberger, G. (1996b), 'Economic incentives, intergenerational altruism and sustainability', in John Weyant (ed.), *Essays in Honor of Alan S. Mann*, Dordrecht: Kluwer.

Stephan, G., Müller-Fürstenberger, G. and Previdoli, P. (1997), 'Overlapping generations or infinitely lived agents: intergenerational altruism and the economics of global warming', *Environmental and Resource Economics*, 10: 27–40.

Tol, R.J. (1995), 'The damage costs of climate change toward more comprehensive calculations', *Environmental and Resource Economics*, 5: 353–74.

8

UNILATERAL TAXATION OF INTERNATIONAL ENVIRONMENTAL EXTERNALITIES AND SECTORAL EXEMPTIONS

Christoph Böhringer

8.1 INTRODUCTION: UNILATERAL ABATEMENT, LEAKAGE AND EXEMPTIONS

In response to the greenhouse gas problem, the European Union decided in 1991 to stabilize its CO_2 emissions by the year 2000 at the level of 1990 (CEC, 1991). Subsequent efforts to introduce a joint European carbon tax have been abandoned, because other major economic actors such as Japan or the US refused to take similar steps (Rio, 1992) and the EU feared adverse impacts of unilateral action on the international competitiveness of its member countries. Recent negotiations on concerted global action have revealed serious problems in identifying concrete abatement targets and timetables for reducing global CO_2 emissions (Berlin, 1995). There is no consensus on 'quantified emission limitation and reduction objectives for specific time-frames' (so-called QELROS) as the issue of fair burden sharing remains unresolved. It is likely that any concrete steps towards emission abatement in the near future will take the form of unilateral actions, in which single countries will commit themselves to emission abatement policies. At the EU level, the EU Council of Environmental Ministers has left it to the member states to introduce carbon abatement measures on a national basis. Several northern member countries, where domestic voters stress the need for taking a leading role, have implemented some kind of carbon tax (OECD, 1995), in the hope that unilateral action will provide an incentive to other countries to join through an 'example or credibility effect'.

The problem with unilateral abatement of a global externality (such as carbon emissions) is that leakage can significantly decrease efficiency. Leak-

140

age occurs when emission reduction in the abating country is partially offset by increased emissions in non-abating countries through the relocation of emission-intensive industries, international energy market effects, exchange rate effects or changes in the levels of savings and investment (see Hoel, 1991; Rutherford, 1992; McKibbin and Wilcoxen, 1995; Rutherford, 1995). As the cost of unilateral action to combat global carbon emissions must be related to the net global emission changes (and not only to the domestic reduction), leakage increases the unilateral cost for meeting a given global reduction target. In extreme cases, leakage could even lead to a perverse outcome, such that a country acting unilaterally faces economic costs of abatement while global emissions are increased.[1] To avoid leakage and ensure the global efficiency of unilateral action, exemptions or tax-breaks for energy- and export-intensive industries are a commonly adopted strategy (CEC, 1992; TemaNord, 1994). However, an efficient exemption (tax-break) scheme requires careful accounting of the emissions embodied in imports and exports. Otherwise (consider, for example, the case of wide-ranging exemptions), carbon relocation due to unilateral action may be negligible but the cost of meeting a specific reduction target would increase significantly because the marginal cost of emission reduction would no longer be equalized across sectors. At the political level, the risks involved in costly exemptions are obvious when considering the lobbying power of energy- and export-intensive sectors such as the iron and steel industry or the chemical industry. Managers of these politically influential industries use the leakage argument to push forward wide-ranging exemptions.[2]

This chapter investigates the implications of sectoral exemptions from unilateral carbon taxes on leakage and abatement costs within the EU. The analysis is based on numerical computations with a large-scale general equilibrium model for the EU, which includes a detailed description of twenty-three production sectors and final demand in six major EU member countries. Our key finding is that leakage rates are not high enough to justify exemptions on global efficiency grounds. For a given domestic reduction target exemptions reduce leakage but induce significant excess costs when compared to uniform taxes. Not surprisingly, exemptions lower the adjustment costs for export- and carbon-intensive industries but this occurs at the expense of society as a whole. Our numerical results support the single-country analysis by Böhringer and Rutherford (1997) who identify the substantial excess costs of tax exemptions predicated on the assumption that leakage effects are of a second-order magnitude.

The remainder of this chapter is organized as follows: section 8.2 reviews important sources of leakage and discusses implications for the design of an analytical framework suited to the estimation of leakage rates. Section 8.3 presents policy scenarios for unilateral carbon abatement and reports numerical results. Section 8.4 summarizes and concludes.

8.2 LEAKAGE AND IMPLICATIONS FOR MODEL DESIGN

There are various channels through which carbon leakage can occur (for a summary, see Rutherford, 1995). Unilateral carbon taxes increase domestic fossil energy prices and cause the domestic carbon-intensive industries to relocate their activities abroad. A large region acting unilaterally cuts back fossil energy demands, which could induce a significant drop in world energy prices with a subsequent increase of demand in other regions. Other determinants of leakage include macro-economic effects operating through exchange rates, rates of return on investment and international capital flows.

It is hardly possible to account for all potential determinants of carbon leakage within a single analytical framework. A practical modelling approach is to focus on those determinants which are most important for the actual policy question. For the policy scenarios considered in this chapter (see section 8.3 below), we assume trade in carbon-intensive goods to be the key source of leakage and neglect energy market effects[3] as well as macro-economic effects. The scope for CO_2 leakage then crucially depends on the pattern of carbon intensity in the production of traded goods across different regions and the trade volumes of specific goods. This has at least three important implications for the design of the model used to analyse leakage effects. First, the regional disaggregation of the model should include all major trading partners of the unilaterally acting country. Second, the sectoral disaggregation of the model must cover those production sectors which exhibit significant total (i.e. direct and indirect) emissions as well as non-negligible trade volumes. And third, the choice of elasticities to indicate substitution possibilities across traded goods requires careful analysis in terms of empirical evidence.

These considerations have been incorporated in the development of a static multisector, multiregion general equilibrium model for the European Union, designed to investigate the implications of grandfathered permit systems on leakage and efficiency of unilateral carbon abatement within the EU (Böhringer et al., 1997). The model includes a detailed description of twenty-three production sectors and final demand as well as bilateral trade, for six EU member countries which together account for the largest part of the overall EU trade volume, production output and carbon emissions: Germany, France, the United Kingdom, Spain, Italy and Denmark. We use this model to analyse the efficiency implications of sectoral exemptions. Table 8.1 provides an overview of the sectoral disaggregation which has been chosen on the basis of the sector-specific potential for carbon leakage exhibited in the benchmark production and trade pattern. The appendix provides a brief algebraic summary of the model's structure and the baseline parameterisation.

Table 8.1 Production sectors in the model

Sector	Description*
COA	Coal, including 031 hard coal, 033 lignite, 050 coke
REF	Oil, including 071 crude oil and 073 refined petroleum products
GAS	Gas, including 075 natural gas and 098 manufactured gas
ELE	Electricity, including 097 electricity and 099 steam
ORE	135 Iron ore ECSC iron and steel products
NFM	137 Non-ferrous metals
CHM	170 Chemical products
CEM	151 Cement lime and plaster
CER	155 Earthenware and ceramic products
GLS	153 Glass
OMN	157 Other mineral and derived products
PLP	471 Pulp and paper and board
TRA	570 Wholesale and retail trade
CON	530 Building and civil engineering works
AGR	010 Agricultural, forestry, fishery
AIR	633 Air transport services
INL	617 Inland waterway services
ROD	613 Road transport
TRS	631 Maritime and coastal transport services
RLW	611 Railway transport services
MAN	Manufactured products aggregate, including 095 Water, 110 Nuclear fuels, 190 Metal products, 136 Non-ECSC iron and steel products, 210 Agricultural and industrial machinery, 230 Office machines, 250 Electrical goods, 270 Motor vehicles and engines, 290 Other transport equipment, 490 Rubber and plastic products, 473 Paper goods and products of printing, 410 Textiles and clothing, 430 Leather and footwear, 450 Timber and wooden furniture, 510 Other manufacturing products
FOO	Food products aggregate, including 310 Meat and meat products, 330 Milk and dairy products, 350 Other food products, 370 Beverages, 390 Tobacco products
SRV	Services aggregate, including 550 Recovery and repair services, 590 Lodging and catering services, 650 Auxiliary transport services, 670 Communications, 690 Credit and insurance, 710 Business services provided to enterprises, 730 Renting of immovable goods, 750 Market services of education and research, 770 Market services of health, 790 Other market services, 810 General public services, 850 Non-market services of education and research, 890 Non-market services of health, 930 Other non-market services

* Digits indicate R59 index of Eurostat classification.

8.3 SCENARIOS AND COMPUTATIONAL RESULTS

In our simulations we compare two different policy designs for CO_2 abatement in a single EU member country:

Uniform tax: The country acting unilaterally levies carbon taxes sufficient to reduce the domestic CO_2 emissions by 10%, 20% and 30% as compared to base year levels. The uniform carbon tax applies to all industrial sectors and final (household) demand.

Tax exemptions: The country acting unilaterally levies carbon taxes sufficient to reduce the domestic CO_2 emissions by 10%, 20% and 30%, but exempts selected export- and energy-intensive sectors from paying the tax.

The EU member country considered for unilateral action is Germany. This choice was made for two reasons: first, Germany is the main emitter of CO_2 within the EU and has a high level of intra-EU trade, such that leakage is potentially important.[4] Second, the advisory board of the German government suggested exemptions for energy- and export-intensive industries if Germany levied a unilateral carbon tax without similar steps being taken by other EU regions. Exemptions are discussed for sectors whose energy cost share of the gross production value is greater than 3.75% and whose export share of turnover is greater than 15% (Enquete, 1994). Based on these criteria the following five sectors are potentially exempted from carbon taxes: chemical products (CHM), earthenware and ceramic products (CER), glass (GLS), iron and steel (ORE) and pulp and paper (PLP). It should be noted that the share of exempted sectors in gross output and carbon emission is rather small.

Efficiency of abatement

Figure 8.1 illustrates the welfare cost[5] for a representative agent in Germany for reducing EU carbon emissions either by a unilateral uniform carbon tax or by a unilateral tax with exemptions.[6]

Our results suggest that exemptions significantly magnify the costs of EU-wide emission abatement, even when the exempted sectors have a small share in overall economic activity and carbon emissions. For a given domestic reduction target, exemptions decrease leakage (for the numerical results, see Table 8.2 below) but increase the costs of abatement: Exemptions for carbon-intensive industries impose a higher burden of cut-backs to non-exempted sectors, which typically exhibit lower, i.e. more expensive, carbon mitigation possibilities as compared to carbon-intensive sectors. The efficiency gains through reduced leakage are more than offset by efficiency losses through sub-optimal domestic carbon substitution. The excess cost of exemptions increase with the target level of emission reduction. Table 8.3 reports the marginal costs of abatement which reflect the higher infra-marginal cost of

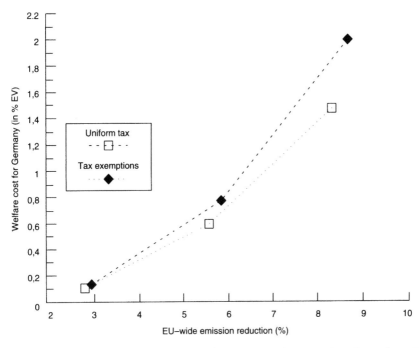

Figure 8.1 Welfare cost for Germany of reducing EU carbon emissions by unilateral action

Table 8.2 Leakage rates (%) due to unilateral abatement by Germany

	Uniform tax			Tax exemptions		
	10%	20%	30%	10%	20%	30%
France	2.9	3.1	3.1	0.6	0.7	0.9
Spain	0.5	0.5	0.6	0.3	0.3	0.4
Italy	1.4	1.5	1.6	0.5	0.6	0.7
UK	1.9	2.1	2.3	0.8	0.9	1.1
Denmark	0.1	0.1	0.1	0.2	0.2	0.2
EU total	6.8	7.3	7.7	2.4	2.7	3.3

Table 8.3 Marginal abatement costs: carbon taxes (in DM_{85} per ton CO_2)

	Uniform tax			Tax exemptions		
	10%	20%	30%	10%	20%	30%
Germany	43	105	196	75	190	367

exemptions as compared to uniform taxes. Exempting carbon-intensive sectors requires a higher carbon tax rate to meet a given domestic reduction target. Higher carbon tax rates indicate less potential for cheap carbon substitution possibilities and a stronger welfare-worsening resource reallocation (substitution) effect.

Sectoral effects: output, employment and exports

Tables 8.4–8.6 report the effects of both abatement policies on sectoral production, employment and export performance (note: sector ROI summarises all sectors except the exempted ones). We can see why managers and workers in carbon- and export-intensive industries would resist uniform taxes and lobby for tax exemptions. Uniform carbon taxes induce a severe decline in production, employment and exports in carbon- and export-intensive industries. Exemptions significantly lower the adjustment costs for these industries. However, the benefits for exempted sectors work at the expense of the non-exempted sectors (and of society as a whole: recall Figure 8.1).

Under uniform taxation, carbon- and export-intensive industries face a

Table 8.4 Output (% change from benchmark)

	Uniform tax			Tax exemptions		
	10%	20%	30%	10%	20%	30%
ORE	−26.7	−51.4	−71.7	−2.3	−5.9	−11.0
GLS	−2.8	−7.0	−13.3	−0.8	−1.9	−3.4
CER	−4.3	−10.2	−18.0	−1.0	−2.5	−4.5
CHM	3.0	9.3	17.0	0.7	1.6	3.1
PLP	−5.0	−11.7	−20.6	−3.9	−8.8	−15.1
ROI	−0.3	−0.7	−1.4	−0.8	−1.8	−3.3

Table 8.5 Exports (% change from benchmark)

	Uniform tax			Tax exemptions		
	10%	20%	30%	10%	20%	30%
ORE	−34.5	−61.0	−78.9	−3.0	−7.7	−14.2
GLS	−5.4	−13.2	−23.7	−1.3	−2.9	−4.6
CER	−4.9	−12.5	−23.3	−1.7	−4.1	−7.0
CHM	−4.9	−11.8	−21.2	−0.6	−1.4	−2.5
PLP	−7.5	−17.3	−29.3	−5.6	−12.5	−21.0
ROI	1.3	2.8	4.6	−0.7	1.4	−2.1

Table 8.6 Employment (% change from benchmark)

	Uniform tax			Tax exemptions		
	10%	*20%*	*30%*	*10%*	*20%*	*30%*
ORE	−25.37	−49.49	−69.91	−1.79	−4.74	−8.89
GLS	−1.91	−5.13	−10.21	−0.28	−0.64	−1.07
CER	−3.68	−8.74	−15.64	−0.53	−1.41	−2.65
CHM	−3.06	−7.69	−14.45	−0.23	−0.50	−1.02
PLP	−4.13	−10.01	−18.13	−3.43	−7.79	−13.25
ROI	0.39	0.86	1.39	0.07	0.15	0.27

sharp decline in sectoral production and exports because domestic carbon taxes increase the cost of carbon-intensive production and unilateral action implies a loss of comparative advantage. Due to the change in relative prices, domestic consumers substitute domestically produced carbon-intensive goods with carbon-extensive goods or cheaper imports; likewise, consumers from abroad reduce demands for relatively expensive carbon-intensive exports. Changes in sectoral employment involve the composition of output and substitution effects. The output effect on employment is generally negative (carbon taxes cause a reduction in output which decreases labour demand). The substitution effect of carbon taxes on employment is generally positive as carbon taxes reduce the marginal productivity of labour, i.e. the relative price for labour inputs. A positive substitution effect lowers the decrease in employment in the case of a negative output effect and strengthens the increase in employment in the case of a positive output effect. The larger the value share of labour, the larger the substitution effect and the more likely it becomes that carbon taxes will produce an increase rather than a decrease in sectoral employment. In our case, Tables 8.4 and 8.6 indicate that the negative output effect dominates the positive substitution effect for all sectors.

Tax incidence

In the present model we do not distinguish households with different factor endowments and different preferences. As a consequence, we cannot identify winners and losers in alternative abatement schemes at the household level. Nevertheless, Table 8.7 provides some insights into the effects of tax exemptions on factor earnings.

Carbon taxes decrease fossil energy demands in sectoral production and drive down the marginal productivity of labour and sector-specific capital, which implies a fall in the real wage and sector-specific rental rates. As expected, exemptions represent a windfall gain for stock holders in exempted sectors in comparison with the uniform tax case. These gains are at the

Table 8.7 Effect on specific factor earnings (% change from benchmark)

	Uniform tax			Tax exemptions		
	10%	*20%*	*30%*	*10%*	*20%*	*30%*
Wage	−2.1	−4.8	−8.3	−2.7	−6.4	−11.3
Rents						
AGR	−1.6	−4.1	−7.9	−3.7	−9.1	−16.4
COA	−18.1	−33.0	−45.5	−16.3	−30.1	−42.9
REF	−5.4	−12.0	−19.9	−7.3	−16.0	−25.5
GAS	−22.0	−47.2	−72.7	−35.2	−70.1	−93.5
ELE	−2.4	−5.4	−9.2	−1.5	−4.0	−7.7
ORE	−26.7	−51.5	−72.0	−3.4	−8.5	−15.4
NFM	−4.0	−9.5	−16.8	−9.2	−20.3	−33.2
CEM	−2.9	−6.3	−10.4	−2.3	−5.5	−11.2
GLS	−3.7	−9.0	−16.4	−1.9	−4.6	−8.2
CER	−5.4	−12.4	−21.4	−2.2	−5.3	−9.6
OMN	−1.9	−4.5	−7.9	−2.3	−5.5	−9.9
CHM	−4.8	−11.4	−20.3	−1.9	−4.5	−8.1
PLP	−5.8	−13.6	−23.7	−5.0	−11.5	−19.5
CON	−0.9	−2.3	−4.1	−0.2	−1.0	−2.5
TRA	−1.1	−2.7	−5.0	−1.2	−3.2	−6.2
RLW	−3.5	−7.6	−12.3	−3.3	−7.6	−13.3
ROD	−2.1	−5.0	−8.8	−3.2	−7.6	13.3
INL	−6.1	−13.4	−22.2	−8.4	−18.8	−30.9
TRS	−1.9		−4.7		−8.0	

expense of capital owners in non-exempted industries as well as the representative worker who receives lower factor earnings due to higher marginal costs of abatement.

8.4 CONCLUSIONS

In this study, we have investigated the implications of sector-specific exemptions from unilateral carbon taxes on leakage and welfare costs. We find that tax exemptions for carbon- and export-intensive industries decrease leakage but increase the costs of EU-wide carbon abatement. Even though the share of exempted sectors in overall economic activity and carbon emission may be small, leakage rates are not high enough to justify exemptions on global efficiency grounds. At the sectoral level, exemptions significantly lower the adjustment cost for exempted sectors but these concessions are costly to society as a whole. Policy makers considering exemptions as a means of saving jobs in politically influential sectors should be aware that there might be more-efficient sectoral employment policies (see Böhringer and Ruther-ford, 1997).

The analysis presented here has neglected several issues which could be important for the robustness of our conclusions:

1   We adopted the Armington trade specification in which goods are differ-entiated by region of origin. It is well known that the magnitude of leakage and thus the justification for exemptions depends on the assump-tions regarding the substitutability of traded (carbon-intensive) goods. In a world where traded goods are perfect substitutes (the Heckscher–Ohlin assumption) leakage rates tend to be very high, which justifies the special treatment of carbon- and export-intensive sectors on global efficiency grounds. Böhringer *et al.* (1997) illustrate this point in the context of grandfathered CO_2 permits. Empirical evidence on trade elasticities is ambiguous. Different assumptions on determinants such as the time-horizon (short-run versus long-run) or the level of aggregation seem to be the main reasons for diverging values or trade paradigms (Heckscher–Ohlin versus Armington). In this study, we followed the proposition of Armington and used uniform values of substitution elasticities for groups of traded goods across regions and sectors. To test the robustness of our results it would be useful to perform an extensive literature review and numerical sensitivity analysis on alternative empirical values for trade elasticities.

2   Leakage estimates depend crucially on the differences in the carbon/energy-intensities of sectors within and across regions. It is therefore important to employ good estimates on energy and emission flows associated with benchmark monetary flows, as provided by national input–output tables. The complementary use of physical flow data and economic input–output data reveals severe consistency problems and a thorough reconciliation of both data sources would be an important, yet very tedious task.

3   Our simplistic treatment of savings and investment is hardly suited to an investigation of the macroeconomic impacts of unilateral action on the level and location of investment (savings) as a further determinant of leakage.

4   The static model structure is less than perfectly suited to analysing the adjustment of physical and human capital stocks to carbon emission constraints. Another shortcoming in this context is the assumption of long-run perfect labour market mechanisms with flexible wages and frictionless labour movement between sectors within each region.

APPENDIX: ALGEBRAIC SUMMARY AND KEY ELASTICITIES

Summary of prices determining an equilibrium

P_{ir} Output price of good i produced in region r

P_{ir}^M Import price aggregate for good i imported to region r

P_{ir}^E Composite price for aggregate energy inputs into sector i in region r (i = C for final consumption)

P_r^C Composite price for aggregate household demand in region r

P_r^G Composite price for government demand in region r

P_r^I Composite price for investment demand in region r

w_r Economy-wide wage rate in region r

r_{jr} Rate of return for sector-specific capital inputs, sector j in region r

R Rate of return for mobile capital (interregional and intersectoral)

PCO   Price of carbon emission rights

Summary of quantity indices determining an equilibrium

Y_{jr} Level of production, sector j in region r

C_R Aggregate household consumption, region r

I_r Aggregate investment, region r

Key benchmark shares, endowment parameters and elasticities

$\theta_{i'jr}^M$ Benchmark value share of good i imports to sector j in region r

α_{jr}^E Benchmark value share of energy inputs, sector j in region r

β_{jr}^E Value shares for k = L (labour), S (sector-specific capital) and K (interregionally mobile capital) in sector j of region r

α_{jr}^{KLE} Benchmark value share of capital, labour and energy composite, sector j of region r

α_{ijr} Benchmark value share of non-energy input i in sector j of region r

$\theta_{irr'}^{MM}$ *Benchmark value share of region r exports in aggregate imports of good i into region r'*

ε_{ijr} Carbon emission coefficient for energy input i into sector j in region r

α_{ir}^C Benchmark value share of good i in aggregate non-energy household demand, region r

θ_{ijr}^E Benchmark value share of energy good i in energy demand by sector j in region r

$\bar{L}_r$ Aggregate labour endowment for region r

$\bar{K}_r$ Aggregate endowment of interregionally mobile capital, region r

$\bar{K}_{jr}^S$ Sector-specific capital for sector j in region r

$CRTS_r$ Carbon emission rights endowment, region r

$\bar{G}_r$ Exogenously specified demand for public output, region r

$\bar{B}_r$ Benchmark balance of payment deficit/surplus

σ_{MM} Elasticity of substitution between imports from different foreign countries

σ_{DM} Elasticity of substitution between domestic and imported inputs or demands

σ_E Elasticity of substitution between energy inputs

Exhaustion of product conditions

1 Production:

$$\Pi_{jr}^Y = P_{jr} - \sum_{i \notin EG} a_{ijr} \left(\theta_{ijr}^M \, P_{ir}^{M\,1-\sigma_{DM}} + (1 - \theta_{ijr}^M) \, P_{ir}^{1-\sigma_{DM}} \right)^{\frac{1}{1-\sigma_{DM}}}$$

$$- a_{jr}^{KLE} \left[\alpha_{jr}^E \, P_{jr}^{E\,1-\sigma_{KLE}} + (1 - \alpha_{jr}^E) \left(w_r^{\beta^L} \, r_{jr}^{\beta^S} \, R_{jr}^{\beta^K} \right)^{1-\sigma_{KLE}} \right]^{\frac{1}{1-\sigma_{KLE}}} = 0$$

2 Sector-specific energy demand:

$$\Pi_{jr}^E = P_{jr}^E - \left\{ \sum_{i \in EG} \theta_{ijr}^E \left[(\theta_{ijr}^M \, P_{ir}^{M\,1-\sigma_{DM}} + (1 - \theta_{ijr}^M) P_{ir}^{1-\sigma_{DM}}) \, \frac{1}{1-\sigma_{DM}} \right. \right.$$
$$\left. \left. + \varepsilon_{ijr} \, PCO \right]^{1-\sigma_E} \right\}^{\frac{1}{1-\sigma_E}} = 0$$

3 Import demand:

$$\Pi_{jr}^M = P_{jr}^M - \left(\sum_{r' \neq r} \theta_{j'rr}^{MM} \, P_{j'r}^{1-\sigma_{MM}} + \theta_{jROWr}^{MM} \, P_{jROW}^{M1-\sigma_{MM}} \right)^{\frac{1}{1-\sigma_{MM}}} = 0$$

4 Investment demand:

$$\Pi_r^I = P_r^I - \sum_i a_{ir}^I \left(\theta_{ilr}^M \, P_{ir}^{M1-\sigma_{DM}} + (1 - \theta_{ilr}^M) \, P_{ir}^{1-\sigma_{DM}} \right)^{\frac{1}{1-\sigma_{DM}}} = 0$$

5 Public output:

$$\Pi_r^G = P_r^G - \prod_i \left(\theta_{iGr}^M \; P_{ir}^{M\,1-\sigma_{DM}} + (1 - \theta_{iGr}^M) \; P_{ir}^{1-\sigma_{DM}} \right)^{\frac{\alpha_{ir}^G}{1-\sigma_{DM}}} = 0$$

6 Household consumption demand:

$$\Pi_r^C = P_r^C - \left[\theta_{Cr}^E \; P_{Cr}^{E\,1-\sigma_{EC}} + (1 - \theta_{Cr}^E) \right.$$
$$\left. (\prod_{i \notin EG} (\theta_{iCr}^M \; P_{ir}^{M\,1-\sigma_{DM}} + (1 - \theta_{iCr}^M) \; P_{ir}^{1-\sigma_{DM}}) \; \frac{\alpha_{ir}^C}{1-\sigma_{DM}})^{1-\sigma_{EC}} \right]^{\frac{1}{1-\sigma_{EC}}} = 0$$

7 Household energy demand:

$$\Pi_{Cr}^E = P_{Cr}^E - \left[\sum_{i \in EG} \theta_{iCr}^E \; ((\theta_{iCr}^M \; P_{ir}^{M\,1-\sigma_M} \right.$$

$$\left. + (1 - \theta_{iCr}^M) \; P_{ir}^{1-\sigma_M})^{1-\sigma_M} + \varepsilon_{iCr} \; PCO)^{1-\sigma_E} \right]^{\frac{1}{1-\sigma_E}} = 0$$

Market clearance conditions

8 Labour:

$$\bar{L}_r = \sum_j Y_{jr} \; \frac{\partial \Pi_{jr}^Y}{\partial w_r}$$

9 Sector-specific capital:

$$\sum_r \bar{K}_r = \sum_{j,r} Y_{jr} \; \frac{\partial \Pi_{jr}^Y}{\partial R}$$

10 Interregionally mobile capital:

$$\bar{K}_{jr}^S = Y_{jr} \; \frac{\partial \Pi_{jr}^Y}{\partial r_{jr}}$$

11 Output:

$$Y_{ir} = \sum_j Y_{jr} \; \frac{\partial \Pi_{jr}^Y}{\partial P_{ir}} + C_r \; \frac{\partial \Pi_r^C}{\partial P_{ir}} + I_r \; \frac{\partial \Pi_r^I}{\partial P_{ir}}$$

$$+ G_r \; \frac{\partial \Pi_r^G}{\partial P_{ir}} + \sum_{r'} M_{i'r} \; \frac{\partial \Pi_r^M}{\partial P_{ir}} + M_{ir\text{ROW}}$$

12 Imports:

$$M_{ir} = \sum_j Y_{jr} \ \frac{\partial \Pi_{jr}^Y}{\partial P_{ir}^M} + C_r \ \frac{\partial \Pi_r^C}{\partial P_{ir}^M} + I_r \ \frac{\partial \Pi_r^I}{\partial P_{ir}^M} + G_r \ \frac{\partial \Pi_r^G}{\partial P_{ir}^M}$$

13 Balance of payments:

$$\sum_{i,r} \bar{P}_i^x M_{irROW} = \sum_{i,r} \bar{P}_i^M M_{iROWr} + \sum_r \bar{B}_r$$

14 Supply-demand balance for carbon emission rights:

$$\sum_r CRTS_r = \sum_{j,r} Y_{jr} \ \frac{\partial \Pi_{jr}^Y}{\partial PCO}$$

Income and aggregate demand

15 Final consumption demand:

$$C_r = (1 - mps_r)(w_r \ \bar{L}_r + R \ \bar{K}_r + \sum_j r_{jr} \ K_{jr}^S$$

$$+ PCO \ CRTS_r - P_r^G \ \bar{G}_r - \bar{B}_r)/P_r^C$$

16 Savings:

$$I_r = mps_r \ (w_r \ \bar{L}_r + R \ \bar{K}_r + \sum_j r_{jr} \ K_{jr}^S$$

$$+ PCO \ CRTS_r - P_r^G \ \bar{G}_r - \bar{B}_r)/P_r^C$$

Index	Description	Value
σ_{KLEM}	Elasticity of substitution between the Leontief material input aggregate M and other inputs (capital K, labour L and energy E)	0
σ_{KLE}	Elasticity of substitution between energy inputs and value-added	0.5
σ_{KL}	Elasticity of substitution between labour, sector-specific capital and mobile capital	1
σ_{E_ELE}[a]	Elasticity of substitution between the aggregate of electricity and different fossil inputs in the energy aggregate of sectoral production and household demand	0.3
σ_{E_FOS}[a]	Elasticity of substitution between fossil energy inputs in the aggregate of fossil energy inputs at the level of sectoral production and household demand	0.5
σ_{NC}	Elasticity of substitution between different non-energy inputs into the non-energy bundle of household demand	1
σ_{DM}	Elasticity of substitution between domestic and imported inputs or demands in the Armington model	4
σ_{MM}	Elasticity of substitution between imports from different foreign countries in the Armington model	4
σ_{XROW}	Elasticity of export demand of ROW for imports from EU countries	4

Notes
[a] Instead of trading off different energy inputs in the energy aggregate of sectoral production and final demand with a uniform substitution elasticity of σ_E an additional nesting is introduced to account for differences of substitution between electricity inputs and non-electric (fossil) energy inputs.

NOTES

1 Assume, for example, that the energy efficiency level of the abating country is very high relative to other countries and unilateral action induces strong substitution of energy-intensive goods produced in the abating country through goods from abroad.

2 Obviously, they are less concerned with global efficiency but try to minimise adverse effects of carbon taxes on CO_2-intensive industries. Full exemptions to these industries could on balance even lower their production costs and provide a competitive edge over competing non-exempted industries.

3 The abstraction from energy market effects is a reasonable assumption for unilateral action of a single EU country because it has a relative small share in worldwide energy supply and demand.

4 At 1990 levels West Germany accounted for roughly 25% of the overall EU emissions (EU without East Germany); East Germany's emissions amounted to an additional 11% of the EU emissions (EU without East Germany).

5 Welfare costs are reported as Hicksian equivalent variations in income.

6 The empty squares and solid rhombs in Figure 8.1 indicate CO_2 emission abatement of Germany by 10%, 20% and 30% either by a uniform tax (squares) or by a tax with exemptions (rhombs).

REFERENCES

Böhringer, C. and Rutherford, T.F. (1997), 'Carbon taxes with exemptions in an open economy: a general equilibrium analysis of the German tax initiative', *Journal of Environmental and Economic Management*, 32(2): 189–203.

Böhringer, C., Ferris, M. and Rutherford, T.F. (1997), 'Alternative CO_2 abatement strategies for the European Union', in J. Braden and S. Proost, *Climate Change, Transport and Environmental Policy – Empirical Applications in a Federal System*, Aldershot, Hants: Edward Elgar.

Commission of the European Communities (CEC) (1991), *A Community Strategy to Limit Carbon Dioxide Emissions and to Improve Energy Efficiency*, SEC(91), 1744 final, Brussels: CEC.

Commission of the European Communities (CEC) (1992), 'The climate challenge', *European Economy*, 51: 45–8.

Enquete (1994), 'Vorsorge zum Schutz der Erdatmosphaere' des Deutschen Bundestages, Arbeitspaper: Michaelis-Vorschlag-Steuerbefreiung von export- und energieintensiven Industrien, Bonn: Economica Verlag.

Hoel, M. (1991), 'Global environment problems: the effects of unilateral actions taken by one country', *Journal of Environmental Economics and Management*, 20(1): 55–70.

McKibbin, W. and Wilcoxen, P.J. (1995), 'Environmental policy and international trade', Department of Economics, University of Texas at Austin, mimeo.

Organization for Economic Cooperation and Development (OECD) (1995), *Environmental Taxes in OECD Countries*, Paris: OECD.

Rio (1992), *United Nations Earth Summit: Convention on Climate Change*, June, UN Conference on Environment and Development, Rio de Janeiro, Brazil.

Rutherford, T. (1992), 'The welfare effects of fossil carbon restrictions: results from a recursively dynamic trade model', in OECD, *The Costs of Cutting Carbon Emissions: Results from Global Models*, Paris: OECD, pp. 95–106.

Rutherford, T. (1995), 'Carbon dioxide emission restrictions in the global economy', Department of Economics, University of Colorado at Boulder, mimeo.

TemaNord (1994), *The Use of Economic Instruments in Nordic Environmental Policy*, Copenhagen: TemaNord.

9

MODELLING THE EFFECTS OF ENERGY MARKET DISTORTIONS ON THE COSTS OF CARBON ABATEMENT

Computable general equilibrium and partial equilibrium assessment

T. Huw Edwards

9.1 INTRODUCTION

The issue of the economic costs of potential measures to reduce emissions of carbon dioxide and other greenhouse gases can be approached using different modelling approaches (Clarke *et al.*, 1991). As there are limits to complexity, any model is effectively a simplification of economic reality, chosen to focus on certain aspects of the questions of how greenhouse gases are best abated and what the cost would be.

Even if measures are only taken by individual nations, not specifically affecting world fossil fuel prices, the costs can vary greatly, depending upon the make-up of that country's energy sector and upon overall industrial and trade structure, market imperfections in the energy markets, such as taxes, subsidies, monopolistic cartels, import restrictions, quantitative restraints or the presence of sizeable externalities.

This study focuses on these country-specific issues, and more particularly on the effects of energy market structure and distortions on the cost of carbon abatement in two of the major OECD energy consuming nations: Japan and Germany. The model used can be taken either to represent the base year, 1990, as it would have been had carbon abatement measures been in force, or alternatively as representing the 'long-term' effect of such abatement compared with a non-abatement 'business as usual' scenario. The study is a continuation of the approach used in the Clarke and Winters (1995) study of China, and the Japanese studies of Edwards (1996) and Clarke and

156

Edwards (1996). The model computable general equilibrium is a relatively simple (CGE) model, covering just one country in a static model, and with a great deal of aggregation of non-energy sectors, not least of government and private consumer expenditure (avoiding 'double-dividend' issues of the benefits of carbon tax revenue cutting other forms of taxation), but it is relatively detailed in its treatment of the energy sector and energy market distortions.

This chapter attempts to link the results of the CGE modelling with more traditional partial equilibrium microeconomic analysis, to explain the results of the 'black box' model for economic welfare using a series of simpler calculations based on the model's results. One issue raised is how well the CGE results can be reconciled with simpler methods.

9.2 OTHER STUDIES OF JAPAN AND GERMANY

Amano (1992) contains a number of studies of Japanese carbon abatement, but as Edwards (1996) points out, these are largely based on extrapolation into the long run of relatively short-term macroeconomic models, and tend to give higher estimates of costs than might be expected from a longer-term equilibrium model where greater adjustment takes place at the microeconomic level. Those studies which are more microeconomic in their basis (notable Goto, 1992) give lower abatement costs, at 0.22 per cent of GDP in 2000 rising to 0.99 per cent by 2030. This study, however, did not take specific account of the effects of existing distortions in Japanese energy markets or of terms-of-trade effects.

In the case of Germany, Böhringer and Rutherford (1995) utilised a static CGE approach broadly similar to this study. They concentrated on a carbon tax with exemptions for some energy-intensive industries, with a 20 per cent abatement producing a welfare cost of 0.22–0.47 per cent of GDP in counterfactual studies for West Germany in 1990 (depending on elasticity) with exemptions, and 0.16–0.33 per cent of GDP with no exemptions. It is not clear whether this study took account of energy market distortions other than the sectoral exemptions in a carbon tax.

Another paper by Böhringer (1995) focused on the effect of distortions in the German coal industry, in particular the use of the coal pfennig tax (*Kohlepfennigsteuer*) on electricity sales to subsidise hard-coal producers. A 15 per cent carbon dioxide reduction would produce a welfare cost of 0.03 per cent of GDP in the case where hard-coal sales to power generators are fixed in quantity, and 0.01 per cent of GDP where the quantity was allowed to vary, but the cost of the subsidy was fixed.

9.3 OUTLINE OF THE BASIC MODEL

The basic model, initially developed by Clarke and Winters, is summarised in Edwards (1996). It uses a CGE structure, developed from input–output tables on the assumption that the observed 1990 data represent an economy in competitive equilibrium. However, compared with many CGE models it is relatively simple in the following senses:

1   The model is for only a single country, which is assumed to be small (it cannot affect world dollar prices of its imports), but produces differentiated exports, whose price it can affect.
2   The model is for a single time-period, assumed to represent 'long-run equilibrium'.
3   The model only has a single consumption sector, which includes the government. Only indirect taxes are modelled, which are assumed to be redistributed to consumers in a lump-sum fashion.
4   Labour supply is fixed, but completely mobile between sectors.
5   The economy is assumed to be in a static long-term equilibrium with zero net investment. Investment is split into its component inputs, and added to other intermediate inputs. Consequently, there is no capital, investment or profit line in the equation.
6   Stockbuild is included in consumption.
7   Rents are payments to a fixed factor, 'land', which is immobile between sectors, but can be withdrawn from use as its price falls towards zero.

This simplicity in certain respects allows for the model to be relatively detailed in its modelling of the energy sector and energy market imperfections, as outlined in the following sections.

The economy is split into the following sectors:

Energy: Hard coal, Soft coal (Germany only), Gas, Crude oil, Refined oil, Electricity, Nuclear/hydro/renewables.
Materials: Iron and steel (only separate for Germany), Energy-intensive industry, Other industry and commerce, Transport.
Value-added: Labour, Land.
Consumption: Final consumption.
Overseas: Exports, Imports.

The model uses a nested constant elasticity of substitution (CES) structure for its production function: first, imports and domestic produce are combined for each tradeable sector then for each sector inputs from other sectors are combined into aggregates for energy, materials and value added. Finally, energy, materials and value added are themselves combined to produce overall output for each sector.

Prices incorporate indirect taxes and subsidy from the government. Changes in government revenue are passed in lump-sum form to consumers. Consumers are assumed to maximise utility subject to a linear expenditure system (LES) consumption function. Exports depend on relative prices of home-produced goods and world prices, using a fixed elasticity. The exchange rate is flexible, moving to keep the trade balance constant.

9.4 DATA SOURCES

The nature of this study, with its rather distinctive sectoral breakdown and detailed modelling of the energy sectors, required the merging of data from a number of sources. Consequently, the input–output tables produced do not correspond exactly with any one published source.

For Japan, basic input–output data for 1990 from the Ministry of International Trade and Industry were combined with energy demand tables from the International Energy Agency's *Energy Statistics of OECD Countries* and *Energy Prices and Taxes*. A few further refinements were added, such as including the purchase of private motor cars as purchases by the transport sector, with a corresponding use value of motor cars included in transport sector sales to final consumers.

A similar method has been used for Germany: in this case merging input–output tables from the German Federal Statistical Office (kindly supplied us by the Stuttgart Energy Institute) with energy data from the International Energy Agency.

9.5 STRUCTURE OF THE ENERGY ECONOMY

As Table 9.1 shows, the Japanese economy is just over twice the size of that of pre-unification Germany in terms of measured GDP, though since investment forms a higher proportion of Japanese GDP, once this is netted out steady-state GDP in Japan is 68 per cent larger than Germany's. Final energy expenditure is just over 10 per cent of steady-state GDP in both countries, though electricity is markedly more important in Japan, while coal is more important in German final consumption.

Japanese primary energy consumption in million tonnes of oil equivalent (Mtoe) is 58 per cent larger than Germany's, indicating that Japan is slightly more energy-efficient (in terms of Mtoe/steady-state GDP) than Germany (Table 9.2). Coal (which in Germany includes soft coal or lignite) and gas are slightly more important in Germany than in Japan which has fewer coal reserves and cannot import gas by pipeline. Both countries are largely dependent on imports for oil supplies (which account for 50 per cent of

Table 9.1 Japan and Germany, 1990: key features of the energy sector of the economy

	Japan ($bn)	Germany ($bn)
GDP pre-adjustment	3,008	1,481
Steady state GDP	2,103	1,247
	per cent of steady-state GDP	per cent of steady-state GDP
Final energy		
Expenditure	10.69	10.41
of which: coal	0.29	0.79
gas	0.65	0.90
oil	4.12	4.86
elec	5.64	3.85
Imports	14.15	28.67
of which: energy	2.68	1.83
Exports	15.48	32.70
of which energy	0.08	

Source: Author's calculations. For original sources, see section 9.4

Table 9.2 Germany and Japan, 1990: primary energy consumption, imports and exports

Mtoe	Primary	Import (%)	Export (%)
Germany			
Hard coal	67.72	8.15	9.19
Soft coal	21.71	1.70	0.00
Gas	46.16	74.62	2.27
Crude oil	78.55	92.68	0.00
Refined oil	36.64		
Electricity	0.03		
Nuclear/renewable	14.48	0.00	0.00
Total	265.28	60.38	6.65
Fossil	250.78	63.14	6.32
Japan			
Coal	116.34	63.60	0.84
Gas	63.50	66.54	0.00
Crude oil	180.66	99.65	0.00
Refined oil	32.62		
Electricity	0.00		
Nuclear/renewable	26.12	0.00	0.00
Total	419.23	81.38	3.17
Fossil	393.12	86.79	3.38

Source: Author's calculations. For original sources, see section 9.4

Japan's primary energy and rather less in Germany), while Japan has a marginally higher proportion of non-fossil supplies.

Overall, Germany is largely self-sufficient in coal, which is an important source of power, but dependent on imports for oil and gas. Japan mostly depends on imports for all fossil fuels.

9.6 MODELLING ENERGY MARKET DISTORTIONS

Energy markets are distorted in a number of ways in both Germany and Japan, in the sense that prices do not accurately reflect marginal social opportunity costs. These include tax and subsidy policy, the effects of lack of competition (partly reflecting industrial and trade policies), the effects of imperfect competition between trading nations and the effects of externalities. It must be added that there are interactions between these effects, so one distortion can either offset or increase the costs of another. However, it is also important to bear in mind that the various fuels compete very closely in the long run, most notably as inputs in the power generation sector, so that relative prices of the various fuels are even more important than their absolute level.

This chapter is less concerned with the cost of the distortions *per se* than with their effect on the costs of carbon abatement by a carbon tax. The basic principles of this are outlined in Clarke (1993) and Clarke and Edwards (1996). Where there are no other distortions present, the deadweight welfare cost of a carbon tax can be approximated by the Harberger triangle: $\frac{1}{2} \times$ change in carbon emissions $\times$ tax rate. If the change in emissions is roughly proportional to the tax rate, this cost increases roughly in proportion to the square of the tax rate.

Pre-existing distortions can alter the marginal welfare cost of the tax significantly: some distortions increase it while others can reduce it. In some economies, for small to medium reductions in carbon emissions, it is conceivable that the carbon tax will actually benefit welfare even without taking account of the benefits of reduced pollution by offsetting the effects of existing distortionary subsidies. Eventually, however, the costs of a carbon tax will start to outweigh these benefits. For other economies, a carbon tax may reinforce existing distortions, and its cost may be high even for small amounts of carbon abatement.

For estimating welfare effects, a CGE approach is greatly to be preferred to partial equilibrium, both because it can handle fuel switching effects and because it can estimate terms-of-trade effects.

Market distortions in the German and Japanese models

Taxes and subsidies

Table 9.3 summarises a number of different categories of taxation, subsidies and monopolistic revenue in Germany and Japan in 1990. Indirect taxes (excluding the coal pfennig tax) amounted to 11.3 per cent of adjusted steady-state GDP in Germany, while in Japan they were 10.4 per cent. Taxes on energy amounted to 1.8 per cent of GDP in Germany against 1.6 per cent in Japan.

Ad valorem taxes are levied as a fixed proportion of sales price. The main example is VAT, which in Germany in 1990 was levied at 15 per cent on sales of energy and most non-energy products to final consumers, as well as on some sales to companies investing, and on some purchases by service sectors. The small (3 per cent) Japanese *ad valorem* consumption has simply been treated as specific taxation.

Specific taxes, shown in Table 9.3, are much more important in the energy sector, even in Germany, raising 1.5 per cent of GDP against 0.3 per cent. In both countries, taxes on motor fuels account for the bulk of this revenue. In the model these taxes vary by commodity and purchasing sector.

Table 9.3 Taxes, subsidies and monopolistic distortions in Japan and Germany, 1990 (% of steady-state GDP).

	Japan	Germany
Indirect taxes		
ad valorem		7.48
specific	10.37	3.79
import duty	0.55	0
total	10.92	11.27
Energy taxes		
ad valorem		0.27
specific	1.59	1.52
import duty	0.09	0
total	1.68	1.79
of which transport energy tax	0.92	1.33
In model, not a tax		
cross-subsidy: electricity–coal	0.07	0.27
Energy subsidies		
cross-subsidy: electricity–coal	0.07	0.27
Subsidy for coal to steel	0.00	0.18
Coal current subs	0.00	0.04
Total coal current subs	0.07	0.49
Nuc/rens	0.09	0
Monopoly revenue		
refined oil	0.64	0

Source: Author's calculations. For original sources, see section 9.4

Import duties are relatively small on energy products and have been ignored completely in the German model, being included for simplicity in specific duties. In the Japanese version, import duties amount to 0.6 per cent of steady-state GDP, while those on energy amount to 0.1 per cent of GDP. Duties vary between commodities.

Taxes on one industry to subsidise inputs from another were used in both countries in 1990: in the case of Germany, the coal pfennig tax taxes electricity sales to subsidise coal sales to power generators. In Japan, the Electric Power Resource Development Tax (EPRDT) taxes general electricity sales to fund the development of nuclear and renewable resources. In our model, neither is treated as a tax: instead they are treated as direct cross-subsidies from one industry to another, and the fact that the money is transferred by way of government coffers is ignored.

The basic calculation of the effect of taxation on the final price of commodity i to consumer j can be summarised:

$$P_{ij} = (Sh_{ij} \cdot Ph_{ij} + Sm_{ij}(Pm_i + Tm_i))(1 + TV_i) + T_{ij} + CTAX \cdot CARB_i \quad (9.1)$$

where Sh_{ij} and Sm_{ij} are home and imported shares in consumption of commodity I by j, Ph_{ij} and Pm_i are respective pre-tax prices, Tm_i is the import duty, Tv_i is *ad valorem* tax (VAT) if j is the final consumption sector, T_{ij} is specific tax and CTAX is carbon tax, while $CARB_i$ is the carbon content of the commodity per unit of sales.

A partial equilibrium analysis would estimate the economics of adding a carbon tax t_2 to a commodity supplied at a constant production cost S, already bearing a tax t_1 as follows: to the first-best Harberger triangle estimate of the deadweight welfare loss of $t_2 \cdot (q_1 - q_2)/2$ should be added the loss in revenue to the existing tax t_1 due to the fall in sales. This amounts to $t_2 \cdot (q_1 - q_2)$. This is the second-best effect of the existing taxes on the cost of a carbon tax. (For a diagrammatic explanation of this, see Clarke, 1993.)

Subsidies to industry come in three major forms:

1 *General state support to an industry*, which can in turn be split into support to current production and support to meet unavoidable expenditures. A high proportion of state support to the coal industry in both Germany and Japan is of this second sort, linked to past employment, past capital expenditure or land damage from mining. In the Japanese model this has been netted out, while in the more recent German model the hard-coal sector receives DM10bn ($6.2 billion) but spends the equivalent on unavoidable expenditures unrelated to current production.

   Only a relatively small proportion of direct general state aid in Germany to the hard-coal mining industry goes to aid current production (Heilemann and Hillebrand, 1992): about $0.5 billion. In Japan general direct subsidies to current production are negligible.

2   *Cross-subsidies from one industry to another.* The German coal pfennig
tax is treated as a cross-subsidy from German power generators to hard-
coal mines, amounting in 1990 to $3.4 billion, or 0.27 per cent of steady-
state GDP, while Japanese generators made an effective subsidy to coal
mines of $1.6 billion or 0.07 per cent of steady state GDP by buying at
above world prices.

   In addition, the Japanese steel industry (treated in Japan as part of the
energy-intensive industry sector), cross-subsidised coal mines to the tune
of $145 million by buying at above world prices.

3   *State subsidies to one industry's purchases from another.* In Germany the
state subsidises coal sales to the steel industry, to bring down the price
of German hard coal to steel producers to the level of imports. This
subsidy amounts to $2.2 billion or 0.18 per cent of steady state GDP. The
model currently assumes the subsidy will vary in proportion to sales of
coal to this sector.

The effect of subsidies in the model can be summarised in the following
equations:

$$Ph_i = UC_i - (LSUB_i/Q_i) + (_j \Sigma XSUB_{ij}/Q_i) \tag{9.2}$$

$$Ph_{ij} = Ph_i - XSUB_{ji}/Q_{ij} \tag{9.3}$$

where Ph_i is the basic selling price of I, UC_i is unit cost of producing I, $LSUB_i$
is the general subsidy industry I receives from the state, Q_i is output of I and
$XSUB_{ij}$ is subsidy from industry I to industry j. Ph_{ij} is the selling price of I to
industry j.

   As Böhringer (1995) notes, the precise way in which the subsidies to coal
vary as carbon abatement measures are introduced can have quite important
effects on the economic and environmental effects of a carbon tax. In
Germany up till 1994 subsidies to coal producers varied according to coal
use, according to a rather complicated system (though whether the policy
would have remained in the face of substantial demand shifts is debatable),
while since that date its total value has been fixed. Our model currently
assumes a fixed total. The effects are shown in Figure 9.1

   For simplicity, a constant marginal cost of production, MC, has been
assumed. A subsidy, SUB, is provided, which is of constant monetary value,
regardless of sales volume, q. Consequently, the commodity is sold according
to the supply curve SS, at a net-of-tax price p, where $p = MC - SUB/q$. The
less output, q, is supplied, the greater will be the unit subsidy and the lower
the supply price.

   In this figure, drawn from the point of view of the commodity producer, a
carbon tax shifts the demand curve down, from DD to D'D', causing output
to drop to q' and price to p'.

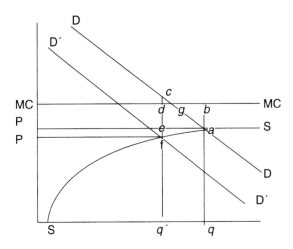

Figure 9.1 Interaction of a fixed value subsidy with a carbon tax

If SS represented the real marginal opportunity cost of supplying the commodity, the first-best welfare cost of the carbon tax would be given by the (approximately a) triangle *acf*. However, since in fact the real marginal cost is MC, additional resources above the curve SS are freed. The value of these is given by area *abdf*, approximately equal to $(q - q') \times (2 \times \text{SUB})/(q + q')$. Subtracting one area from another gives a net welfare change of *abg* − *gcd*, which in the figure is a gain.

Modelling the effects of trade restrictions and monopolistic mark-ups

Prior to reforms early in 1996 (see Clarke and Edwards, 1996), various non-tariff barriers allowed Japanese oil companies to keep imports to a very low level and maintain an effective cartel, pushing up refined oil prices.

While this situation was not quite a classical monopoly, our model assumes that the industry charges a fixed mark-up on marginal costs (which include indirect taxes), consistent with cartel behaviour. This mark-up varies between purchasing sectors, reflecting competition from other fuels or the different ability of various oil users to make direct imports. Total monopolistic mark-ups on oil products were assumed to amount in 1990 to $13.5 billion or 0.64 per cent of steady-state GDP, of which over 60 per cent came from sales to the transport sector.

The basic economic welfare effects of a monopolistic mark-up are analogous to an *ad valorem* tax such as VAT, except that the revenue accrues to shareholders rather than to the state.

Protection against imports is modelled by allowing the Japanese oil refining industry to apply (through its control of distribution) an even higher monopolistic mark-up to imports than to Japanese-refined oil. To allow detailed modelling of this, the model allowed for differences in the share of imports in refined oil sales to each purchasing sector, and different degrees of import restriction to each sector (with the greatest restriction on sales to transport). In addition, for sensitivity cases, it was assumed that the import mark-ups would be varied, so as to give extra cushioning to the Japanese industry when its costs rose relative to imports. The rationale for this is that the protection was partly to give security of demand and profits to Japanese manufacturers.

Costs not related to current production.

Both the German and Japanese models allow for an industry to employ fixed quantities of factors of production which are not linked to output at the margin. In Germany this is used to model costs in the coal industry of around 0.5 per cent of steady state German GDP in 1990, which Heilemann and Hillebrand (1992) identify as not linked to current production.

In Japan the oil industry contains a lot of old, small, inefficient plant both in refining and retail. It is assumed that, at the margin, the industry would install modern, efficient plant, so that the extra costs associated with the old plant can be treated as intramarginal. These were assumed to amount in 1990 to just under $7 billion or 0.33 per cent of steady state GDP.

If the crude input–output coefficient in the base case for units of input j in the output of sector I is a_{0ij}, total expenditure by sector I is q_{0i}, the input of j unrelated to marginal costs is L_{ij}, and total expenditure by I over and above that indicated by marginal costs is L_i (where $L_i = {}_j\Sigma\, L_{ij}$) then the model calculates a revised input–output coefficient:

$$a'_{0ij} = (a_{0ij} \cdot q_{0i} - L_{ij})/(q_{0i} - L_i) \tag{9.4}$$

The a' coefficients are assumed to represent the equilibrium of a CES production function. As taxes and prices are altered, so the a' coefficients alter to a'_{1ij}, and from that, the new versions of the crude input–output coefficients are calculated:

$$a_{1ij} = (a'_{1ij} \cdot (q_{1i} - L_i) + L_{ij})/q_{1i} \tag{9.5}$$

Modelling the terms-of-trade effects of a carbon tax.

Energy in 1990 was nearly 19 per cent of Japanese imports, against 5.7 per cent of German imports. However, Germany is a more open economy, so energy imports accounted for 1.6 per cent of German steady-state GDP, compared with 2.7 per cent in Japan.

166

In the model, neither Germany nor Japan is capable of altering dollar prices of their imports. However, as is standard practice in CGE trade models (see de Melo and Tarr, 1992), both face downward-sloping supply curves for their exports, and so possess a certain degree of potential power to force up real export prices. In the absence of 'optimal export taxes', both countries could gain up to a point by taxes which reduced their import demand, forcing up the real value of their currencies against the dollar.

The effect of a carbon tax on the terms of trade depends, first, on whether the commodities whose consumption falls when a tax is introduced have a higher proportion of imports at the margin than those whose consumption rises. As Table 9.2 shows, imports accounted for 63 per cent of primary energy consumption in Germany and 87 per cent in Japan. Against this, within energy a carbon tax falls particularly heavily on consumption of coal, which in Germany is 98 per cent home-produced for soft coal and 92 per cent for hard coal. In Japan, a much smaller proportion, 36 per cent, of coal is home-produced.

The effect of a carbon tax on the exchange rate will also tend to be greater the higher the share of energy in overall imports, as in Japan. Against this, however, the greater is the share of imports in overall GDP, the more a given change in exchange rate will affect overall welfare: the German economy is the more open of the two.

The higher are assumed trade elasticities, the smaller will be exchange rate movements needed to maintain trade balance, and the smaller will be the terms-of-trade effect. Our export elasticities are somewhere between the central and high estimates for the US in de Melo and Tarr (1992).

The assumption that Germany and Japan are too 'small' to affect world prices of their imports is a simplification: Japan is a sizeable importer of both oil and coal. In particular, Australian coal producers are highly dependent on Japan; this would give extra benefit to Japan from a carbon tax, at Australia's expense.

Germany is smaller than Japan in terms of global energy markets, but might be able to affect any new contract prices for Russian gas. Also, in practice, Germany would only take greenhouse gas abatement measures as part of an overall European Union environmental directive. But since a carbon tax would probably raise the real exchange rate of most participating countries, and since most of Germany's trade is with other EU members, the terms-of-trade benefit from a stronger German mark would be reduced. Against this, combined action by all EU members would be more likely to drive down world fossil fuel prices.

Benefits in terms of pollution abatement

The model estimates emissions of carbon dioxide (CO_2), sulphur dioxide (SO_2), nitrogen oxides/ozone (NOx) and particulates. For Japan the method

167

of estimating emission is that used in Edwards (1996). The basic assumption is that pollution is driven by the pollution content in tonnes or kilos of each type of pollutant k per Mtoe of each fossil fuel I. The calculation is done in the following steps:

1   For each sector j, pollution from primary fossil fuel inputs in the absence of abatement is calculated from the pollution content, PC_{ik}, the energy content of inputs of fuel I into sector j, $MTOEF_{ji}$, and a correction factor to account for certain peculiarities of the aggregate Japanese data.
2   For imported refined oil the pollutant content per Mtoe is then assumed to be the same as the initial value for Japanese refined oil.
3   Finally, a factor is applied to each type of pollution from each sector, to account for technological abatement and statistical differences (e.g. the use of lower sulphur fuel in certain sectors).

For Germany, the modelling approach has been made rather more sophisticated, to take better account of the substantial differences in pollution content between different types of refined oil products, which end up in different sectors.

The German model starts with UK Department of Environment (1992) estimates of pollution of each type per Mtoe of each fuel used by each sector. To these are applied abatement/correction factors to calibrate base-case pollution estimates to IEA estimates for West Germany in 1990.

The model still calculates the cruder pollution figures using the same method as for Japan. For sensitivity cases, the change in pollution for each sector and fuel is calculated by the old method, but applied to the new base pollution estimates.

9.7 SOME ILLUSTRATIVE RESULTS FOR THE WELFARE COST OF A CARBON TAX

In order to illustrate the effects of the various market distortions in Japan and Germany, this chapter looks at the potential cost of a 15 per cent carbon abatement, carried out unilaterally by the country concerned. The model concentrates on long-run effects, or rather on how the long-run equilibrium in 1990 would have been different had the countries been applying carbon abatement measures (assuming the actual input–output tables for 1990 represent equilibrium).

Table 9.4 shows the estimated welfare costs, before taking account of the benefit of reduced pollution. The required carbon tax is remarkably similar: $33.63 per tonne of carbon in Germany against $34.61 per tonne in Japan. This partly reflects the similar assumed elasticities, but must also be regarded as somewhat coincidental: these are not purchasing power parity figures and,

Table 9.4 Japan and Germany, 1990: CGE and partial equilibrium estimation of costs of 15 per cent abatement of carbon dioxide emissions

	Japan	Germany
Carbon tax ($/tonne)	34.61	33.63
	% of steady-state GDP	*% of steady-state GDP*
First-best Harberger triangle	0.034	0.038
Interaction with other industrial tax		
energy taxes	0.056	0.041
non-energy taxes	0.002	0.009
effect of GDP on tax revenue	0.008	−0.004
Total tax effect	0.066	0.046
Interaction with subsidies		
hard coal	−0.011	−0.100
electricity	0.000	0.006
nuclear/renewables	0.015	0.000
steel	0.000	0.000
transport	−0.001	−0.003
Total subsidy effect	0.004	−0.097
Loss of monopoly revenue	0.030	0.000
Exchange rate effect	−0.056	−0.058
Total estimated	0.077	−0.071
Sector-specific rents and residual/combined effects	0.004	0.032
Equivalent variation cost	0.073	−0.038

given the large relative exchange rate movements in subsequent years, it is unlikely that the tax rates would always be as close.

The next line is the Harberger triangle, which is an approximate estimate of what a carbon tax would cost if there were no other market distortions. For a 15 per cent carbon reduction this is small: 0.034 per cent of steady-state GDP in Japan and 0.038 per cent in Germany. The German figure is slightly higher, reflecting the higher initial carbon intensity of the German economy.

The final line represents the estimated equivalent variation in welfare cost of carbon abatement. For Japan, the carbon reduction would imply a welfare reduction of 0.073 per cent of steady-state GDP, while for Germany there would actually be a gain of 0.038 per cent of steady-state GDP. Since the Harberger triangle in both countries was similar, this implies that the reaction with energy market distortions is different: *in Japan the carbon tax tends to increase the cost of existing energy market distortions, while in Germany it tends to reduce it.*

For an explanation of this, the lines between show partial equilibrium estimates of the effects of various distortions. First, the reduction in energy tax revenues produces a rather higher cost in Japan (0.056 per cent of steady-state GDP) than in Germany (0.041per cent). At first sight this might seem rather odd, since, as Table 9.3 showed, Germany generally has higher indirect taxes than Japan. However, the difference in energy taxes is much smaller, dominated in both countries by transport fuel duties. Moreover, the reduction in transport sector oil demand caused by the carbon tax is higher in Japan (3.1 per cent) than in Germany (2.2 per cent). This reflects the fact that oil accounts for a higher share of transport sector output in Japan and, according to the CES formulae applied, is consequently more affected by price changes. Perhaps a bit surprisingly, when corrected for GDP change, non-energy tax take is also slightly lower in both countries, reflecting falling tax take on the transport sector. Since GDP is reduced in Japan this also lowers tax take (producing a welfare cost), while in Germany slightly higher GDP raises tax take (a benefit).

The major assumed distortion of the German energy market is the degree of subsidy and cross-subsidy to the hard-coal sector. On our critical assumption that the real term amount of these subsidies is fixed, a carbon tax causes a reduction in hard-coal output of 11.5 per cent in our model and hence a reduction in the cost of these subsidies (see Figure 9.1 above). A partial equilibrium estimation suggests that the economic cost of subsidies and cross-subsidies in Germany is reduced by 0.1 per cent of GDP following the introduction of a carbon tax. By contrast, in Japan subsidies are generally smaller relative to the size of the economy, and the economic cost of one of the most important subsidies – that to nuclear and renewable energies – is increased as a carbon tax causes a switch to non-fossil fuels.

The other major cost in Japan (pre-1996) is the addition of a carbon tax to oil products already bearing high monopolistic margins, producing an estimated extra cost of 0.03 per cent of GDP.

The estimated terms-of-trade effect of the carbon tax is very similar in both countries, reducing the cost of a carbon tax by 0.056 per cent of steady-state GDP in Japan and 0.058 per cent in Germany. The greater importance of energy in Japan's imports, and hence the greater effect of a carbon tax on the yen (0.4 per cent against 0.21 per cent for the Mark) is offset by the greater overall importance of trade in Germany.

The total estimated cost of 15 per cent CO_2 reduction using the partial equilibrium approximation is 0.077 per cent of steady-state GDP in Japan, but a benefit of 0.071 per cent of GDP in Germany. This differs from the equivalent variation estimated by CGE methods: the difference being just -0.004 per cent of GDP in Japan but 0.038 per cent in Germany. This difference is mainly accounted for by rents on land and other sector-specific factors. Since 'land' is immobile in our model, rents do not reflect its potential use value once output in that sector changes substantially: hence the cost of tax and subsidy distortions are generally overestimated by the simpler partial equilibrium methods used. This effect is more marked in Germany because of the large assumed effect of a carbon tax on coal production, and also because in Japan a carbon tax produces an offsetting rise in sector-specific factor values in the nuclear industry.

One caveat on the above figures is that they represent the effect of the distortions on a given level of carbon tax. If the German coal industry were not cross-subsidised, or if the value of the subsidy were kept fixed per unit sales rather than in total (see Figure 9.1), the elasticity of supply of German coal would be greater, and a given carbon abatement could be achieved with a lower tax rate.

9.8 POLLUTANT EMISSIONS

Calculation of the benefit of reductions in pollution depends not only on the pollutant but also on the country (as climate conditions, incomes and factors such as population density vary), and the sector in which they are emitted (and whether they are emitted near dense population or fragile ecosystems, and whether they are dispersed using tall chimneys). For these reasons, no effort has been made here to estimate monetary values. Nevertheless, these values can be quite significant, in some cases outweighing other purely economic costs (see Clarke and Edwards, 1996).

Table 9.5 shows our estimates of the changes in the four main pollutants for the various scenarios in Japan and Germany. In most cases sulphur dioxide emissions move roughly in line with carbon dioxide. Nitrogen oxide/ozone, which comes mainly from oil use in the transport sector and is less price elastic, is less affected by a carbon tax. For particulates (which are probably the most costly type of pollution, at least to human health), the position is more complicated. In Japan 73 per cent of particulates by volume come from coal and so are especially liable to be reduced by a carbon tax, which particularly affects coal consumption. This trend is less marked in Germany.

However, the particulates believed to be most harmful to human health are PM10s emitted largely by diesel road vehicles. For this reason total particulate figures may not accurately reflect the change in health and environmental costs.

Table 9.5 Japan and Germany, 1990: changes in various pollutant emissions in the various carbon reduction cases

		Carbon tax ($/t)	CO_2 (%)	SO_2 (%)	NOx (%)	Part (%)
Japan	Pre-reform	0	0	0	0	0
Japan		34.61	−15.00	−15.12	−12.72	−16.55
Germany	Pre-reform	0	0	0	0	0
Germany		33.47	−15.00	−15.03	−7.35	−11.94

9.9 CONCLUSION

This study has looked at the modelling of energy market distortions and at the effect these might have on the cost of introduction of a possible carbon tax in Japan and Germany. The basic modelling approach used is a single-country, static CGE model, in which treatment of government, household, investment and non-energy sectors is simplified, but where the modelling of the various energy sectors and of taxes, subsidies, monopolistic mark-ups and other distortions is relatively detailed.

While the chapter does not really focus on results or policy implications, it does attempt to combine the CGE modelling with a cruder disaggregation of costs, based upon a more traditional partial equilibrium approach, but using demand changes from the CGE model in order to explain how each assumed market distortion affects the cost of a hypothetical carbon tax. While this approach is of necessity rather rough (and does not take account, for example, of how a carbon tax would have to change in the absence of distortions in order to achieve the same target emission reduction), it does go some way to explaining why the costs of a carbon tax would be higher in some countries than in others.

On our assumptions, a 15 per cent reduction in CO_2 emissions in in 1990 would have required a very similar level of carbon taxes in Japan ($34.61) and in Germany ($33.47), though this may partly reflect the particular alignment of exchange rates at the time. This would reduce welfare in Japan by 0.073 per cent of steady-state GDP, before taking account of pollution, whereas in Germany there is actually a net benefit from abatement. The Japanese result reflects the large monopolistic margins on oil products, which produce a double-taxation effect when a carbon tax is introduced, as well as our assumption about the nature of the subsidies to German hard-coal producers and cross-subsidies from electricity, the economic cost of which would be partially offset by a carbon tax.

The partial equilibrium disaggregation proves successful at explaining the CGE cost estimates of a carbon tax in Japan, but is less good in the case of Germany, due to fixed factor costs: the fact that land is immobile between sectors means that rents do not reflect opportunity costs of land when taxes and subsidies are changed in a non-marginal way. This means that the simpler analysis tends to overestimate the potential costs or benefits of structural changes.

REFERENCES

Amano, A. (ed.) (1992), *Global Warming and Economic Growth*, Tsukuba, Japan: Centre for Global Economic Research, National Institute for Environmental Studies, Environmental Agency of Japan.

Böhringer, C. (1995), *Carbon Taxes and National Policy Constraints: The Case of German Coal Subsidies*, Universität Stuttgart, Institut für Energiewirtschaft und Razionelle Energieanwendung.

Böhringer, C. and Rutherford, T.F. (1995), *Carbon Taxes with Exemptions in an Open Economy: A General Equilibrium Analysis of the German Tax Initiative*, Universität Stuttgart, Institut für Energiewirtschaft und Razionelle Energieanwendung.

Clarke, R. (1993), 'Energy taxes and subsidies: their implications for CO_2 emissions and abatement costs', *International Journal of Environment and Pollution*, 3(1–3): 168–78.

Clarke, R. and Edwards, T.H. (1996), *The Welfare Effects of Japanese Energy and Environmental Policy*, University of Birmingham Department of Economics, Discussion Paper no. 96–103.

Clarke, R. and Winters, L.A. (1995), 'Energy pricing for sustainable development in China', in I. Goldin and L.A. Winters (eds), *The Economics of Sustainable Development*, Cambridge: Cambridge University Press.

Clarke, R., Boero, G. and Winters, L.A. (1996), 'Controlling greenhouse gases: a survey of global macroeconomic studies', *Bulletin of Economic Research*, 48(4): 269–308.

De Melo, J. and Tarr, D. (1992), *A General Equilibrium Analysis of US Foreign Trade Policy*, Cambridge, Mass.: MIT Press.

Edwards, T.H. (1996), 'A simplified CGE approach to modelling the welfare aspects of Japanese carbon abatement measures', in A. Fossati (ed.), *Economic Modelling Under the Applied General Equilibrium Approach*, Aldershot, Hants: Avebury.

Goto, N., (1992), 'Micro-economic costs of CO_2 emissions control policies in Japan', in A. Amano (ed.), *Global Warming and Economic Growth*, Tsukuba, Japan: Centre for Global Economic Research, National Institute for Environmental Studies, Environmental Agency of Japan.

Heilemann, U. and Hillebrand, B. (1992), 'The German coal market after 1992', *Energy Journal*, 13(3): 141–56.

International Energy Agency (1991), *Energy Statistics of OECD Countries*, Paris: OECD.

International Energy Agency (1992), *Energy Prices and Taxes*, Paris: OECD/IEA.

United Kingdom. Department of the Environment (1992), *Emissions of Air Pollutants, 1970–1990*, LR887(AP), London: HMSO.

Whalley, J. and Wigle, R. (1991), 'The international incidence of carbon taxes', *Energy Journal*, 12(1): 109–24.

10

EFFICIENCY AND DISTRIBUTIONAL EFFECTS OF ECOTAXES IN A CGE MODEL FOR ITALY

Alberto Pench

10.1 INTRODUCTION

This chapter represents another step in the development of the CGE model for Italy known as ITALIA/GE and shows the relative flexibility of a model aimed, basically, at the examination of fiscal policies. Within this model simulations have been performed concerning the substitution of indirect taxes for direct taxation (Fossati *et al.*, 1992) and value added tax reform (Fossati, 1991) among others; an extension of this model can be found in Pench (1996). The aim of the chapter is to examine the efficiency and distributional effects of two kinds of ecotaxes and to point out the effects on the emission levels of some of the most relevant pollutants.

This model is built with the aim of disaggregating, from the base version, transport activities. The motivation stems from the fact that, according to the OECD Environmental Performance Review for Italy (OECD, 1994), transport is responsible for 50 per cent of total emissions of NOx, 47 per cent of total emissions of volatile organic compounds (VOC), 79 per cent of total emissions of CO and 27 per cent of total emissions of CO_2.

Two kinds of simulations have been performed:

- the imposition of an exogenous tax on total output of oil products, compensated by an equiproportional reduction of personal income tax in order to keep public expenditure constant in real terms;
- an exogenous tax has been imposed on the same good, but only on purchases by households, with the same compensation as before.

Two variants have been tested within each simulation, in the replacement method; only the lump sum component of the tax function has been scaled

174

up or only the marginal rate has been scaled down. Details will be given in the section describing the modelling of the Italian tax system.

The effects of these taxes on emissions are computed in a very crude manner and can only give a rough idea of their real impact.

A complete description of the base version of the model can be found in Fossati (1991), but section 10.2 gives a summary of its main features. The present version of the model differs from the base version only by a disaggregation of production sectors. Section 10.3 describes the differences of this version from the base one, while section 10.4 presents the results of the simulations and a sensitivity analysis on some parameters which helps the understanding of the results; a final section summarises the lessons learned from this kind of simulation.

10.2 THE MODEL

The base version of the ITALIA/GE model includes seventeen production sectors and nine consumer groups; it is a standard CGE model in which all agents act as price takers and constant returns to scale are assumed on the production side. Firms maximise profits subject to technology constraints, while households maximize utility under their budget constraints.

It is a static model and this feature is a shortcoming in the analysis of the impact of ecotaxes, because effects connected with the adoption of cleaner technologies are ruled out. The equations in the model are determined through a calibration procedure[1] assuming that the Italian economy was in equilibrium in the benchmark (1982) year.

Production sectors

Fifteen of the seventeen production sectors in the base version produce consumer goods and services, the sixteenth produces a 'public good', while the last is the investment sector. Each sector produces a single output using intermediate inputs of other goods, imported goods and primary factors: capital and labour, divided into self-employed labour and employees. The supply of capital is fixed while labour is variable in supply. Depreciation is allowed in each sector, but it is simply modelled as an input of the investment good.

A two-stage nested structure is adopted. Intermediate inputs plus imported goods and depreciation are combined within a nest with elasticity of substitution equal to zero. The other nest produces 'value added' through the use of primary factors according to a Cobb–Douglas function; finally, the two nests are linked by means of a Leontief function (zero elasticity of substitution). Imported goods are demanded only as inputs by production sectors according to the corresponding row of the input–output table.

Furthermore, they have been considered as a homogeneous good so that there is a single price for (aggregate) imports. The Armington assumption holds, since imports are considered qualitatively different from domestic goods.[2]

Sector 16, the public sector, produces collective goods and services using intermediate inputs of other goods and labour services. Its output is demanded by the government. The investment sector uses only produced goods, in fixed proportions, to obtain a single homogeneous investment good demanded by all agents.

Data concerning production sectors is mainly derived from the input–output table for Italy in the year 1982. The allocation of self-employed labour and employees has been provided by the Central Bureau of Statistics (ISTAT) which also provided most of the data on production taxes.

Consumers and the government

The structure adopted to represent household preferences is a three-stage nested utility function. At the top level each household chooses between present and future consumption, the latter represented by savings which are modelled as a demand for the investment good; a Cobb–Douglas function is adopted. The second stage is represented by a CES function where present consumption is disaggregated into an aggregate of consumer goods and leisure: the elasticity of substitution is put equal to 0.5 and each household has a different endowment of time in order to give an elasticity of labour supply of 0.2. The overall labour supply from each household is further divided into the two kinds of labour through a Leontief-type transformation function (zero elasticity of transformation) replicating benchmark (1982) figures. At the bottom level the aggregate of consumer goods is disaggregated into its single components according to a CES function with an elasticity of substitution of 0.75. The choice of parameters, essentially the elasticities of substitution, reflects either the lack of data or the most plausible value; some of them have been subjected to sensitivity analysis, as shown below.

Households receive transfers from the government which are modelled, according to benchmark figures, as a fixed endowment of their aggregate 'utility good' whose price represents the expenditure function of the top-level utility function and may be interpreted as a measure of the cost of living, thus differentiated by households.

Households pay two main taxes: a progressive personal income tax (IRPEF) and a proportional tax on a part of their income from capital (interests from bank deposits and some type of private bonds[3]) at a rate of 20 per cent.

The major source of data is the annual consumer expenditure survey made by the Central Bureau of Statistics; the data concerning the disposable

176

incomes of consumers have been extensively rearranged, as have the data on taxes, mainly derived from statistics provided by the Ministry of Finance.

The public sector is represented very simply. Production activities are described by the sixteenth production sector. Tax collection and public expenditure are summarised in an additional consumer, which we may call a 'public household'; the output of sector 16, therefore, is an additional private good demanded by the public household and, negligibly, by some production sectors.

The public deficit, apart from the figure of public investment included as an input in the investment sector, is modelled as an endowment of the investment good for the public household.

Taxes

On the production side the most important tax, in terms of revenue, is social security contributions, which are modelled as an *ad valorem* tax on the use of each type of labour by sectors, at different rates. Value added tax is levied at different rates according to some broad categories of goods. It is collected by sectors on their sales and handed over to the government once the amount paid on intermediate inputs has been deducted. This mechanism has been, in a way, reproduced within the model, so that there is a different tax rate for each good. The only shortcoming is that our rates are fictitious because they incorporate tax evasion and are related to our sector classification.

Production taxes and subsidies are modelled as *ad valorem* taxes or subsidies on the total output of each sector.

On the consumer side of the economy there are two main taxes: the personal income tax and a tax levied on interest paid on private bonds and bank accounts, modelled as an *ad valorem* tax on capital income. The personal income tax is a progressive tax and its revenue has been approximated by a quadratic function of taxable income. Then it has been modelled through the resulting (linear) marginal tax rate applied to taxable income[4] and a compensatory transfer in order to give the government the correct tax revenue. The resulting transfer is a quadratic function of taxable income with a constant and a quadratic term. This transfer is given in terms of each household utility good, like other transfers from the government. In order to preserve the homogeneity of the demand functions, the tax function being quadratic, the taxable income is computed in real terms, being converted in terms of each household utility good. In this manner the doubling of all prices keeps taxable income and marginal personal income tax rates constant but doubles the compensatory transfer, and thus does not affect real variables.

The tax replacement scheme adopted in the base simulations consists of an equiproportional reduction of the entire tax function through a scaling parameter; the above-mentioned variants concern a scaling of the marginal tax rate function or a scaling (up in this case) of the constant term only in the compensatory transfer.

Transactions with the rest of the world are represented by constant elasticity import supply and export demand functions, which means that Italy is not a price taker on imports and on exports. Exports from each sector are demanded by an additional production sector which produces aggregate exports by means of a Leontief function. Thus constant elasticity export demand and import supply functions are formulated in terms of aggregate exports and imports. Consequently terms of trade are defined as the relative prices of these two goods and are very simply computed.

10.3 TRANSPORT VERSION

The version presented in this chapter differs from the base version only in the disaggregation of the production side, which encompasses three additional sectors. Within sector 2 of the base version, the energy sector has been disaggregated, sector 2*bis* is represented by branch 4 of the initial 44 branch input–output table. This branch encompasses crude oil, natural gas and products of refining: it plays the role of the tax base for the simulations. The second addition is sector 12*bis*, disaggregated from sector 12 of the base version (retail trade and hotels): it corresponds to branch 28 (repaired and used goods) of the initial table. Finally, communications, branch 34 of the 44 branch table, has been disaggregated from transports and represents sector 13*bis*.

The role of the additional sector 12*bis* and 'new' sector 13 (transports), together with sector 2*bis*, is to give a proxy of overall transport activities both on the production side and on the consumer side of the economy: following the classification adopted in the consumer expenditure surveys the category transports includes consumption of the output of these sectors. The aim is to give a rough estimate of the impact of the simulations on the emissions of the above mentioned pollutants: NOx, COV, CO and CO_2. Emissions are computed proportionally with respect to some base (1989) levels for each pollutant. The factor of proportionality, indicated by Δ, is a weighted average of the total output of sector 13 and the consumption by households of the product of sectors 2*bis*, 12*bis* and 7 (motor vehicles and relative motors). This way of modelling emissions is clearly crude for a number of reasons: first, it does not distinguish the effects of ecotaxes on different pollutants because they are all assumed to vary in the same proportion; second, sector 2*bis* includes some goods which are not connected with transports. None the less, parameter Δ may be thought to give a measure of the strength of the proposed tax reform in terms of reduction in that part of pollution due to transport activities.

10.4 RESULTS

Tax on total output

The first simulation consists of the imposition of an exogenous tax on the output of sector 2*bis*, compensated by an equiproportional reduction of personal income tax in order to keep public expenditure constant in real terms. Two exogenous tax rates have been tested: 20 per cent and 40 per cent, both modelled as additional *ad valorem* taxes. The results of this simulation are summarized in Table 10.1, where the two columns refer to tax rates. The effect on activity levels and prices are available on request; generally speaking, a tendency emerges towards a reinforcement of the results as the tax rate increases.

Table 10.1 shows the most important results for the policy-maker. Together with ML (which is the scaling parameter on personal income tax) the table shows parameter Δ, which gives an idea of the impact on emissions, the equivalent variation[5] for each household (rows EV*i*), their summation (row SUMEV) and the same summation with the exception of the top household (row SUMEV$_{-9}$).

The first observation concerns the distributive impact of the simulation proposed. An additional tax of 20 per cent generates a reduction in emissions of approximately 4.5 per cent, a welfare gain in the aggregate but a loss for households 1–4 and 6. This effect may be explained by the relative strength of the effects on the sources of income with respect to those on the uses of income; in both cases net factor prices increase for each household.

An additional tax of 40 per cent generates a greater welfare gain in the aggregate but gains accrue only to households 7, 8 and 9 for which the

Table 10.1 Equivalent variations and other parameters

	20% tax	40% tax
ML	0.713	0.236
Δ	0.956	0.906
EV1	−95.329	−385.831
EV2	−139.803	−485.527
EV3	−292.534	−914.896
EV4	−223.541	−719.776
EV5	12.952	−170.213
EV6	−70.993	−623.137
EV7	138.780	28.906
EV8	277.791	551.557
EV9	2,866.883	6,548.128
SUMEV	2,474.206	3,829.211
SUMEV$_{-9}$	392.677	2,754.917

increasing reduction in personal income tax rates reinforces the effect on the sources of income.

We can conclude that an additional tax on the output of sector 2*bis* has a regressive impact which is best illustrated by the last row of Table 10.1 where the welfare gains or losses of the first eight households are shown. It emerges that in both cases the welfare gains of the highest class of consumers more than offset the aggregate welfare losses of the first eight classes. From a theoretical point of view, this simulation consists of a substitution of a broad-based general tax (personal income tax) with a less-broad-based specific tax; indeed we should expect efficiency losses from this substitution. In a recent paper, Goulder (1994) performs similar simulations in a much more detailed and sophisticated dynamic model of the US economy; the presumable effect of each tax policy is first examined on theoretical grounds, considering the distortions generated by the proposed tax substitutions. In Goulder's paper the results confirm theoretical reasoning because welfare losses emerge.

In order to assess the apparently non-standard results of the present simulation it is worth taking a more careful look at the taxed sector. In this way we find that about 60 per cent of total output comes from imports, and this fact may give rise to significant terms-of-trade effects. Indeed, the terms of trade, measured by the relative price of exports with respect to imports, is equal to 1.024[6] and 1.052, respectively, in the case of a 20 per cent and 40 per cent tax. In addition the activity level of the sector producing aggregate exports falls to 0.968 and 0.933 and the trade deficit decreases from 14,441 to 13,357 and 12,290 billions of lira, respectively. These figures are not directly comparable with the equivalent variations, the rest of the world not being modelled as a consumer; none the less they may indicate that a significant part of the welfare gain may be attributable to terms-of-trade effects. In the sub-section devoted to sensitivity analysis this intuition will be confirmed and even reinforced.[7]

Other reasons may be invoked in order to explain the results:[8] first, personal income tax is far from being an optimal income tax[9] and may generate consistent distortions in consumers' choices; second, a possible explanation for the welfare gains of higher households may be found in labour supply, which increases for all households and increases more, in both cases, for household 9, thus reinforcing the above-mentioned effects on the sources of income.

Tax on consumers' purchases

The second simulation consists of a tax on consumer' purchases of good 2*bis*; the exogenous tax is levied at rates of 20 per cent and 30 per cent. Before turning to the analysis of the results a comment is in order: the present simulation is not strictly comparable with the previous one because it has a different tax base, different tax revenue and, consequently, a different scaling parameter on personal income tax rates. Nevertheless, the two simulations can be compared by their effects on emissions and their results in terms of welfare. From this point of view they may be regarded as different policies capable of achieving different target reductions in emissions.

As before, all results are available on request. Net factor prices increase as in the previous simulation; we have computed relative factor prices in the case of a 20 per cent tax for both simulations and we have found that for employees net price is greater for households 6–9 in the first simulation while the opposite holds for households 1–5. Net price for self-employed workers is greater for households 5–9 in the first simulation and net price of capital is greater for households 2–9 in the first simulation. As a consequence of these findings, and given the distribution of income across households, we can expect a greater positive effect on the sources of income for the first four households in the present simulation, when a 20 per cent tax is imposed. Besides, given the narrower tax base, we can also expect a 'softer' impact on the side of the uses of income.

These observations are confirmed by an analysis of the equivalent variations shown in rows EV1 to EV9 in Table 10.2, which also contains parameters Δ, ML, SUMEV and SUMEV$_{-9}$ as in Table 10.1. We have a welfare gain for each household, but the aggregate welfare gain is greater in the previous simulation than in both cases of the present one. If we consider that the value of parameter Δ in the second column of Table 10.2 is close to the value of a 20 per cent tax case in the previous simulation, we can conclude that a tax on consumer' purchases of good 2bis is preferable, on distributive grounds, to a tax on total output of the same good.

The difference in tax bases across simulations emerges clearly in the value of parameter ML, the scaling parameter on personal income tax. Finally, row

Table 10.2 Equivalent variations and other parameters

	20% tax	30% tax
ML	0.936	0.910
Δ	0.968	0.955
EV1	107.681	147.642
EV2	56.288	71.187
EV3	29.524	29.878
EV4	18.729	13.708
EV5	114.575	145.722
EV6	198.686	245.849
EV7	173.868	219.642
EV8	123.759	163.348
EV9	992.010	1,364.472
SUMEV	1,815.120	2,401.449
SUMEV$_{-9}$	823.11	1,036.977

SUMEV$_{-9}$ indicates that approximately one-half of aggregate welfare gain accrues to the highest household.

On theoretical grounds a tax on consumers' purchases is likely to generate fewer distortions than an equal yield tax on total output, while a comparison with an equal yield income tax would be dubious. Goulder (1994) argues in favour of the former, but his model is dynamic so an income tax distorts intertemporal choices. Actually a tax on consumers' purchases has a narrower tax base and it may be a source of excess costs. From another point of view, the introduction of this tax might be a welfare-improving tax reform following the well-known Corlett–Hague rule.[10] The matter is complicated, on the one hand, by the findings in Hatta (1986), where it is shown that tax reforms towards uniformity may be welfare improving[11] and, on the other, by a highly differentiated tax structure on production sectors. The comparison with an equal yield tax on output is not possible in the present simulations while the results seem to indicate a superiority with respect to income taxes. None the less, we note that there are still terms-of-trade effects which may be responsible for the positive welfare effect, even if they are, as expected, more relevant in the previous simulation by virtue of a larger effect on the taxed sector. The following sub-section will clarify the weight of these effects.

Sensitivity analysis

Sensitivity analysis has focused upon three parameters of the model and upon the 'closure rule' (see Whalley and Yeung, 1984) with the rest of the world. The parameters whose different values have been tested are: the elasticity of substitution between different goods in households' utility function; the elasticity of labour supply; and the elasticity of substitution between inputs in production sectors.

Before turning to this kind of sensitivity analysis, it is worth mentioning how previous results are affected by a change in the tax replacement scheme. As mentioned in the first section, both simulations have been repeated under the hypothesis that the scaling parameter (ML) is applied only to marginal personal income tax rates or only to the lump-sum component of the compensatory transfer. In order to save space we will present the results of the sensitivity analysis concerning only the most important variables; these are shown in a single table.

Table 10.3 shows the results of different replacement policies within the first simulation; the heading 'PIT rates' refers to the scaling (down) of marginal personal income tax rates only, while the heading 'lump-sum' refers to the scaling (up) of the constant term only for the transfer resulting from the tax function. As before, columns refer to the exogenous tax rates on total output of sector 2*bis* and rows show the equivalent variations, their sum and parameters ML and Δ; an additional row (TOT) is introduced with respect to former tables, giving the value of the terms of trade.

Table 10.3 Alternative replacement scheme (tax on total output)

| | PIT rates | | Lump-sum | |
	20% tax	40% tax	20% tax	40% tax
ML	0.818	0.518	3.456	7.084
Δ	0.954	0.902	0.952	0.896
TOT	1.027	1.060	1.032	1.073
EV1	−12.068	−154.913	1,459.073	3,481.067
EV2	−99.312	−369.304	1,051.588	2,472.058
EV3	−270.938	−840.450	820.372	1,865.222
EV4	−231.860	−728.443	486.590	1,051.712
EV5	−40.812	−299.365	399.645	779.575
EV6	−179.642	−888.223	47.140	−317.771
EV7	63.449	−163.453	−315.595	−1,088.270
EV8	251.736	482.822	−165.207	−540.004
EV9	3,014.229	6,908.272	−1,273.753	−3,636.642
SUMEV	2,494.782	3,946.944	2,509.852	4,066.947

As can be seen, the aggregate result in terms of welfare (row SUMEV) does not change dramatically even if a scaling of the lump-sum component reverses, almost exactly, the distribution of gains and losses among households.

Scaling only marginal personal income tax rates favours[12] households 1–3 (which still suffer a loss) and 9 (which increases its welfare gain), while the opposite holds for households 4 and 6 and for households 7 and 8 (which are still gaining); household 5 now suffers a loss while gaining in the base simulation. Scaling (up) only the lump-sum component reverses the previous results exactly since households 1–6 gain while the remaining households lose.

These results may suggest that for the first three households it is preferable to have an increase in the lump-sum component than a reduction in marginal rate, while the opposite holds for the last three households, with a qualification for the top household, which gains from a slight increase in the lump-sum component and marginal rate,[13] but is definitely damaged if the marginal rate is not scaled down. For the mid-income households the picture is mixed and shows an opposite tendency with respect to the highest household.

The value of Δ is not so different from the base simulation in the first case (column PIT rates), while a larger discrepancy emerges in the second.

The same sensitivity analysis has been performed for the second simulation, that is when the tax is levied on consumers' purchases of good *2bis*. The results are not shown but are available on request: the qualitative conclusions drawn from Table 10.3 are confirmed and parameter Δ is almost unaffected. In both cases, a better result in terms of aggregate welfare goes together with an increase in the terms of trade.

The second type of sensitivity analysis concerns the elasticity of substitution between different goods in households' utility functions. Starting from the base value of 0.75, it has been reduced to 0.5, 0.2 and 0.0; by narrowing the possibilities of substitution of the taxed good we expect a negative effect in terms of welfare.

The results, referring to the imposition on total output, are summarized in Table 10.4 and are computed for the base tax replacement scheme. The table shows a progressive deterioration in the welfare of each household such that, with an elasticity of substitution equal to zero, we have an aggregate welfare loss. The same findings also hold true in the case of a tax on consumers' purchases (results available on request). Thus we may conclude that the elasticity of substitution in consumption plays a crucial role and must be taken into account in assessing the most plausible results in the short run.

In both cases, as a result of narrower possibilities of substitution by households, the reduction in emissions achieved in the base case tends to vanish: with a zero elasticity of substitution, Δ is fairly constant in the case of a tax on consumers' purchases and increases in the case of a tax on total output. It is worth noting that in both cases the deterioration of the results in terms of welfare is combined with a decrease in the terms of trade, which is less than one when the aggregate result is negative.

Another parameter has been tested under sensitivity analysis, namely the elasticity of substitution between inputs in production. From the base value of 0.0 it has been increased to 0.5, 0.75 and 1.0.

The results for a tax on output, not shown but available on request, may be summarized as follows: the activity level of sector 2bis decreases, as expected, as the elasticity of substitution increases. The effect on households is somewhat mixed: households 1–4 gain as the parameter increases, while

Table 10.4 Alternative elasticity of substitution in consumption (tax on total output)

	$\sigma = 0.5$		$\sigma = 0.2$		$\sigma = 0.0$	
	20% tax	40% tax	20% tax	40% tax	20% tax	40% tax
ML	0.705	0.187	0.694	0.114	0.686	0.053
Δ	0.970	0.933	0.988	0.972	1.001	1.002
TOT	1.015	1.034	1.004	1.008	0.995	0.988
EV1	−152.497	−507.310	−231.052	−686.715	−290.789	−833.375
EV2	−196.236	−604.466	−274.031	−779.860	−333.373	−923.095
EV3	−374.169	−1,100.840	−487.523	−1,376.160	−574.497	−1,601.560
EV4	−297.613	−882.439	−400.319	−1,122.660	−479.041	−1,318.950
EV5	−78.903	−345.080	−205.893	−602.415	−302.993	−812.102
EV6	−255.778	−982.774	−511.637	−1,513.560	−707.559	−1,947.420
EV7	23.881	−171.686	−135.153	−467.858	−256.944	−710.442
EV8	230.514	483.447	165.217	382.772	115.293	300.027
EV9	2,751.323	6,561.705	2,587.933	6,572.306	2,460.470	6,572.317
SUMEV	1,650.522	2,450.555	507.541	405.856	−369.434	−1,274.600

the opposite holds for households 8 and 9; finally, households 5–7 gain as the elasticity of substitution increases to 0.75, but lose for a further increase to 1.0. A possible explanation for these results may be the increase in parameter ML,[14] since we have seen that higher households are relatively favoured by a smaller scaling factor.

Parameter Δ, as a consequence of the effect on sector 2bis, decreases as the elasticity of substitution increases.

In the case of a tax on consumers' purchases, welfare decreases for each household as the elasticity of substitution increases; this may be explained by an increase in the price of good 2bis with respect to the base simulation, generated by the decrease in the activity of the taxed sector. Parameter Δ is fairly unaffected by this sensitivity analysis.

The following sensitivity analysis aims at identifying the weight of terms-of-trade effects on the results of the base simulation. The exercise consists of a substitution of the tax base. Instead of sector 2bis, the taxed sector is sector 9 (textiles), which has been chosen because its output is close to that of sector 2bis but it does not depend on imports; on the contrary, it exports about one-third of its output. These last features make it a natural candidate for this kind of sensitivity analysis. The results are shown in Table 10.5 for both simulations. Parameter Δ, whose value is of no interest in this case, is not included.

In the first simulation a tax on the total output of sector 9 is levied at rates of 20 per cent and 40 per cent, with a compensatory scaling on the total personal income tax function. The value of the scaling parameter (ML) is comparable with that of the base simulation[15] but the results, in terms of welfare, are quite different and show an aggregate welfare loss as theoretically predicted. Due to

Table 10.5 Terms-of-trade effects of an alternative taxed sector (both tax bases)

Good 9	Tax bases			
	Total output		Consumers' purchases	
	20% tax	40% tax	20% tax	30% tax
ML	0.694	0.237	0.866	0.811
TOT	0.997	0.997	0.995	0.994
EV1	−330.292	−879.230	−146.919	−218.099
EV2	−337.696	−902.288	−152.302	−228.156
EV3	−537.328	−1,417.187	−240.137	−356.706
EV4	−462.183	−1,227.684	−219.961	−328.904
EV5	−314.666	−917.619	−150.086	−235.896
EV6	−981.565	−2,721.604	−525.915	−800.926
EV7	−480.237	−1,443.306	−277.315	−435.486
EV8	20.108	−100.673	−17.441	−44.489
EV9	2,097.800	4,210.078	935.675	1,241.514
SUMEV	−1,326.059	−5,399.511	−794.401	−1,407.146

the different tax base, the value of parameter ML is less comparable in the second simulation where the tax is levied on consumers' purchases at rates of 20 per cent and 30 per cent. Keeping in mind this caveat the results are, again, quite different from the base simulation and show an aggregate welfare loss.

Thus we may conclude that the cost structure of the taxed sector, in the base simulation, particularly its dependence on imports, may be responsible for an aggregate welfare gain not easily predictable by theoretical reasoning.

In order to confirm or reject the above conclusions, another kind of sensitivity analysis has been performed. The base simulations have been repeated under an alternative formulation for the transactions with the rest of the world; aggregate imports have been modelled as the output of an additional (internal) sector whose inputs are exports.[16] Again an aggregate welfare loss emerges in both simulations. This finding is robust since it is fairly unaffected by assuming different values for the elasticity of substitution between inputs.

Finally, sensitivity analysis has been performed with respect to the elasticity of labour supply and the structure of personal income tax. Setting the elasticity of labour supply equal to zero does not change the results of the base simulations in qualitative terms and yields very small discrepancies in quantitative terms.

In order to point out the weight of the distortive features of personal income tax, it has been imputed proportionally to the whole income of households, thus reproducing a first-best income tax. In fact, with households' utility functions being homothetic, with leisure separable from consumption, a proportional income tax is optimal.[17]

The somewhat surprising finding is that, despite the radical change in the personal income tax structure, the discrepancies are not dramatic, thus confirming that the key features of the model are the structure of the taxed sector and the modelling of the transactions with the rest of the world.

10.5 SUMMARY AND CONCLUSIONS

Some lessons can be drawn from the simulations proposed. The first is that the impact on emissions across simulations is not as different as, for example, the effect on prices or on individual welfare. The range for parameter Δ in the case of a 20 per cent tax on total output spans from 0.956, in the base simulation, to 0.940 when the elasticity of substitution in production is equal to 1.0; in the case of a 40 per cent tax the range is from 0.906 to 0.868. An even smaller range emerges in the second simulation when the tax is levied only on consumers' purchases. As a consequence it emerges that large reductions in emissions are not so easy to achieve. This conclusion must be qualified because the magnitude of parameter Δ gives an idea of the reduction in emissions due, roughly, to transport activities only. It is likely that taxing part of the energy sector could achieve reductions in emissions, so that globally pollution could be reduced by more than indicated by Δ, which is, therefore, an underestimate of the effective reduction.

The second lesson is that, from the point of view of aggregate welfare, both simulations yield a welfare gain. On the one hand, this result is surely reinforced by considering the external effects due to the emissions reduction, which is not computed in the households' utility function. On the other hand, sensitivity analysis has shown that positive welfare results are mainly due to terms-of-trade effects and are thus dependent on the modelling of transactions with the rest of the world. In addition, we must not forget that the simulations proposed, being focused on Italy, concern a unilateral taxation; the conclusions could be altered if we adopted a multicountry model and simulated a multilateral homogeneous taxation of the same good within the European Union.

The third lesson concerns the distributive impact of the simulations; given that they both tend to be regressive, at least adopting the base tax replacement scheme, we may conclude that, unless we aim at the largest reduction in emissions, a tax on consumers' purchases is preferable, on equity grounds, to a tax on total output. It is worth stressing this aspect because the detail on households permits a deeper assessment of the tax policies considered than an aggregated model. Indeed, due to homothetic utility functions, we can sum the equivalent variations and evaluate the policies on this aggregate indicator; however, this could be misleading since the aggregate result often covers sharp differences from a distributive perspective.[18]

Finally, sensitivity analysis helped in assessing and qualifying the results and in pointing out which parameters may alter the most important findings. Apart from the above-mentioned modelling of the transactions with the rest of the world, we have seen that increasing the elasticity of substitution in production may give rise to better results in terms of aggregate welfare and of emission reduction if the tax is levied upon total output, while the opposite holds for a tax on consumers' purchases. On the contrary, lowering the elasticity of substitution in consumption yields worse welfare effects and smaller reductions or even an increase in emissions.

These findings may be helpful to give a rough idea of the different impact of the simulations in the short and in the medium to long run. We cannot ignore the shortcomings of the model; first of all it is static so it cannot properly deal with the impact of the policies in the long run. Second, it does not encompass the possibility of adopting cleaner technologies which might be encouraged by such policies and, thus, seriously alter our findings. Third, the impact on emissions is modelled in a very crude manner since it does not discriminate among pollutants.

Another finding stemming from sensitivity analysis is the relatively light weight of some theoretical (or textbook theoretical) considerations in explaining aggregate results.

NOTES

1 Calibration is standard practice in this kind of model: for details, see Mansur and Whalley (1984).
2 See Armington (1969).
3 In 1982 public bonds were tax exempt.
4 Because consumer choice is affected by the marginal rate.
5 Expressed in billions of lire.
6 Like any other price, terms of trade are unitary in the benchmark.
7 On the importance of terms of trade effects, in a different context, see Fehr *et al.* (1995).
8 But their weight is surely less important, as will be confirmed by sensitivity analysis.
9 The substitution of which would surely result in a welfare loss.
10 There is only another tax on consumers' purchases of good 7.
11 For an excellent survey on commodity tax reform, see Bulckaen (1992).
12 With respect to the base simulation described on pp. 179–80.
13 Parameter ML in the first two columns of Table 10.3 is greater than ML in the corresponding columns of Table 10.1.
14 Which means a smaller scaling in the tax function.
15 It is 0.694 vs 0.713 in the case of a 20 per cent tax.
16 And the investment good which modelled the trade deficit in the base version.
17 Deaton (1979) and Auerbach (1985).
18 On the importance of distribution versus efficiency, the volume by Fehr *et al.* (1995) on value added tax reform in Europe is illuminating.

REFERENCES

Armington, P.J. (1969), 'A theory of demand for products distinguished by place of production', *IMF Staff Papers*, 16: 159–76.
Auerbach, A.J. (1985), 'The theory of excess burden and optimal taxation', in A.J. Auerbach and M. Feldstein (eds), *Handbook of Public Economics*, Amsterdam: North-Holland.
Bulckaen, F. (1992), 'The theory of commodity tax reform: a survey', in G. Galeotti and M. Marrelli (eds), *Design and Reform of Taxation Policy*, London: Kluwer.
Corlett, W.J. and Hague, D.C. (1953), 'Complementarity and the excess burden of taxation', *Review of Economic Studies*, 21: 21–30.
Deaton, A. (1979), 'The distance function in consumer behavior with applications to index numbers and optimal taxation', *Review of Economic Studies*, 391–405.
Fehr, H., Rosenberg, C. and Wiegard, W. (1995), *Welfare Effects of Value-added Tax Harmonization in Europe*, Berlin: Springer.
Fossati, A. (ed.) (1991), *Equilibrio Generale e Simulazioni*, Milan: Franco Angeli.
Fossati, A., Cavalletti, B. and Pench, A. (1992), 'From personal to indirect taxation: a general equilibrium approach', in G. Galeotti and M. Marrelli (eds), *Design and Reform of Taxation Policy*, London: Kluwer.

Goulder, L.H. (1994), 'Energy taxes: traditional efficiency effects and environmental implications', in J. Poterba (ed.), *Tax Policy and the Economy*, Cambridge, Mass.: MIT Press.

Hatta, T. (1986), 'Welfare effects of changing commodity tax rates toward uniformity', *Journal of Public Economics*, 29: 99–112.

Mansur, A. and Whalley, J. (1984), 'Numerical specification of applied general equilibrium models: estimation, calibration, and data', in H.E. Scarf and J.B. Shoven (eds), *Applied General Equilibrium Analysis*, New York: Cambridge University Press.

Organization for Economic Cooperation and Development (OECD) (1994), *Rapporti sulle performance ambientali: Italia*, Paris: OECD.

Pench, A. (1996), 'Preliminary results from the introduction of money and expectations in a CGE model for Italy', in A. Fossati (ed.), *Economic Modelling under the Applied General Equilibrium Approach*, Aldershot, Hants: Avebury.

Whalley, J. and Yeung B. (1984), 'External sector "closing" rules in applied general equilibrium models', *Review of International Economics*, 16: 123–38.

Part IV

COMPETITIVENESS AND CONVERGENCE

11

THE CONSEQUENCES OF TECHNOLOGICAL INNOVATION ON EMPLOYMENT IN THE EUROPEAN UNION USING AN AGE APPROACH

Hans Kremers

11.1 INTRODUCTION

In this chapter, we analyse the consequences of technological innovation occurring outside Europe on employment within the European Union. To this end, we use the multicountry model introduced in Fehr *et al.* (1995). Their model consists of seven countries constituting the European Union and one country representing the rest of the world, and was used to analyse the welfare effects of VAT harmonisation on the countries making up the European Union. Here we extend their model by including the existence of a minimum wage rate in each EU country in such a way that we can maintain the calibration of their original model. Consequently, we obtain the same benchmark equilibrium. Then, we assume that one of the producers in the rest of the world obtains a more efficient technology which allows it to lower its price level.

We consider three types of technological innovation. The first type considers a decrease in the use of labour and capital in production. The second considers a decrease in the use of certain intermediates in production, while the third considers a combination of the previous two. These three types of technological innovation lead to the computation of three counterfactual equilibria, which we discuss in section 11.3. We compute the consequences of each type of technological innovation on consumers' welfare by using the Hicksian equivalent variation, and on producers' output by using the change in gross national product.

Section 11.4 tries to explain the results obtained from the simulations by comparing the benchmark equilibrium with the counterfactuals. Usually this comparison implicitly assumes the existence of an underlying adjustment process linking the benchmark equilibrium with the counterfactual equilibrium under consideration. In section 11.4 we follow this habit by assuming the following adjustment process to generate the new counterfactual equilibrium. Given the benchmark equilibrium, technological innovation by one of the producers in the rest of the world allows it to decrease the price of its output commodity. The constant-returns-to-scale nature of each technology also allows the other producers in the rest of the world to lower their prices to the extent that they use this innovated product as an intermediate. The decrease in these prices causes a disequilibrium on the commodity markets which is cleared by adjusting the supply. The adjustment of the supplies of each commodity in the rest of the world causes a disequilibrium in its labour market due to the change in labour demand. The wage rate adjusts to clear the labour market.

The adjusted prices in the rest of the world, in turn, affect the markets in the EU countries, both through their influence on production costs inside the EU, on the one hand, and through substitution effects with the commodities in the rest of the world, on the other. Hence, technological innovation in the rest of the world disequilibrates the EU markets, leading to an adjustment of price levels, supply levels and wage rates. Ultimately, the wages, price levels and supply levels are assumed to settle on the values obtained in the counterfactual equilibrium under consideration. This counterfactual equilibrium involves unemployment in an EU country if the labour market in this EU country cannot be cleared because of the existence of a minimum wage rate level preventing the necessary decrease in the wage rate.

11.2 THE MODEL

The model underlying the simulations in this paper is given in Fehr *et al.* (1995), to which we refer for an extensive discussion on the details and underlying assumptions. In this section we provide only the most necessary information.

The Fehr–Rosenberg–Wiegard multicountry CGE model, to which we refer in short as the FRW model, consists of a set of countries I, indexed by i or ii. Each country i consists of a representative consumer i, n privately produced commodities 1, . . ., n, and a public good $n + 1$, indexed by j or h. The private good j is produced by producer j in each country i as his only output commodity. They are used for domestic as well as foreign consumption, and as intermediate inputs in domestic or foreign industries. The commodities produced in each country are substitutable, but not perfectly. This is known as the Armington assumption. The public good $n + 1$ is produced in each country i by the public sector of that country. As a non-traded good, it is either consumed by the country's representative consumer or used as an intermediate in domestic production.

The goods $1, \ldots, n + 1$ have prices $p_1^i, \ldots, p_{n+1}^i$ which we put into a vector $p^i \in \mathrm{IR}_+^{n+1} \backslash \{0\}$. The $(|\mathrm{I}|(n + 1))$-vector p then denotes the vector of all prices $p^1, \ldots, p^{|\mathrm{I}|}$, and p_{-j}^{-i}, the $(|\mathrm{I}|(n + 1) - 1)$-vector of prices which excludes p_j^i. The prices of the commodities are taken net of VAT taxes and tariffs imposed on them by the public sector, but include a production tax rate.

Each good j in country i is produced by producer j according to a constant returns to scale production function that consists of four nests, using labour and capital as its primary inputs, and domestically produced as well as imported commodities as intermediate inputs. The primary factors, labour and capital, are supplied by the consumers. Capital is homogeneous and mobile among producers and countries, while labour is only mobile among the production sectors within the country. The rental rate of capital is therefore the same in each country and is given by r, while the wage rate varies over the countries and is given by w_i in country i. The $|\mathrm{I}|$-vector w denotes the vector of all wage rates $(w_1, \ldots, w_{|\mathrm{I}|})^{\mathrm{T}}$.

Let the vector $y^i \in \mathrm{IR}_+^{n+1}$ denote the vector of all activity levels in country i, and let $y = (y^1, \ldots, y^{|\mathrm{I}|})$. Cost minimisation in each nest of the production function results in the following demand functions: labour, denoted by $l_j^i(w_i, r; y_j^i)$, capital, denoted by $k_j^i(w_i, r; y_j^i)$, the domestically produced intermediate commodity h, denoted by $a_{j,h}^i(p_h^{ii}|_{ii \in \mathrm{I}}; y_j^i)$; and the intermediate commodity h imported from country ii, denoted by $b_{ii,h}^{i,j}(p_h^{ii}|_{ii \in \mathrm{I}}; y_j^i)$, which produce y_j^i units of commodity j in country i.

The representative consumer in country i spends his or her income either on leisure or on domestically produced or imported commodities, so as to maximally satisfy his or her preferences, given the constraints imposed by income. Consumer i's preferences are given by a utility function U_i consisting of four nests, while income M_i is obtained from a capital endowment on which an interest rate r is received, from the hours actually spent on labour at an after-tax rate of $w_i(1 - v_i)$ per hour, v_i denoting the income tax rate in country i, and from the transfers T_i received from the public sector. Utility maximization in each nest results in consumer i's demand function for the domestically produced commodity j, denoted by $\xi_j^i(p_j^{ii}|_{ii \in \mathrm{I}}; M_i)$, in consumer i's demand function for commodity j imported from country ii, denoted by $\eta_{ii,j}^i(p_h^{ii}|_{ii \in \mathrm{I}}; M_i)$, and in consumer i's supply function for labour, denoted by $\Lambda^i(p, w_i; M_i)$. Contrary to Fehr et al. (1995), we assume that each country sets a minimum wage rate $\underline{w}_i$, thereby giving rise to possible unemployment of LU_i hours. Consumer i then actually works $\Lambda^i(p, w_i; M_i) - LU_i$ hours, from which his or her labour income is obtained.

The public sector in this model produces the public good $n + 1$ by using the constant-returns-to-scale technology described above and sets its price p_{n+1}^i according to a marginal cost pricing rule. The public sector is assumed to keep the expenses of transfers and public expenditure covered by the income it receives from collecting income taxes from the consumers, from tax revenues from the consumption of commodities by the consumer, production taxes from the producers and from tariffs levied on the imported commodities from countries $ii \neq i$ for final or intermediate consumption. The equality of these expenses and receipts is referred to as the budget constraint of the public sector. The amount of public expenditure is fixed as are the tariff and tax rates. Then, the public sector only has the transfer payment T_i to the consumer i to fulfil its budget constraint.

An equilibrium in this economy is defined by prices $p^* \in IR_+^{n+1} \backslash \{0\}$, $w^* \in IR_+^{|I|}$, and $r^* \in IR_+$, by activity levels $y^* \in IR_+^{|I|(n+1)} \backslash \{0\}$, by transfer payments $T^* \in IR_+^{|I|}$, and by the levels of unemployment $LU^* \in IR_+^{|I|}$, such that:

1 each price p_j^{i*} is determined by the per unit costs of producing country i's commodity j through the zero-profit condition imposed on its commodity's production technology;
2 the rental rate of capital r^* clears the capital market;
3 for each country i, either $w_i^* > \underline{w}_i$ and $LU_i^* = 0$, or $w_i^* = \underline{w}_i$ and $LU_i^* \geq 0$;
4 for each commodity j in country i, its market is cleared by the activity level y_j^{i*} of its production technology;
5 the transfer payment T_i^* to consumer i is such that the budget constraint of the public sector of country i is satisfied.

11.3 THE SIMULATIONS

The model we have described in the previous section is used in simulations to investigate the impact of technological change on employment in the EU countries. To this end we use the original dataset underlying the FRW model. Their model and simulations are based on a dataset containing the set of eight countries I: France (F), Belgium–Luxembourg (BL), the Netherlands (NL), Germany (D), Italy (I), United Kingdom (UK), Denmark (DK), Rest of the World (ROW), where each country i produces thirteen commodities, and one public good.

Fehr et al. (1995) calibrate their model on this dataset and obtain parameters ensuring the existence of a benchmark equilibrium with prices, wage rates and the rental rate all equal to one. The rental rate r is taken as the numéraire. We impose the minimum wage rates $\underline{w}_i$ in each country i, as given in Table 11.1. In this case, all the labour markets clear and there is no unemployment in the benchmark equilibrium, which is therefore the same as the original benchmark equilibrium calibrated in Fehr et al. (1995) (see 'Benchmark equilibrium' sub-section in the appendix to this chapter). We have limited ourselves to presenting only the most important results.

Table 11.1 The minimum wages $\underline{w}_i$.

Country:	F	BL	NL	D	I	UK	DK	ROW
$\underline{w}_i$	0.500	0.7500	1.000	1.000	0.500	0.500	0.500	0.000

In order to analyse the consequences of technological innovation on employment in the European Union, we suppose that producer 2 in ROW manages to obtain a new technology which allows it to produce its output commodity by using less of its inputs. In the FRW model, technological innovation can imply that ROW's producer 2 needs less value-added for the production of one unit of commodity 2, or that ROW's producer 2 needs less input of any commodity into the production of commodity 2. The first type of technological innovation results in a decreased demand for labour and capital by ROW's producer 2, while the second type of technological innovation results in a decreased demand by ROW's producer 2 for commodities h produced either domestically or abroad. In the first nest of the production function of ROW's producer 2, y_2^{ROW} units of ROW's commodity 2 are produced from va_2^{ROW} units of value-added and ci_h^{ROW} units of a composite intermediate commodity h, $h = 1, \ldots, n + 1$, which is a certain composite of the domestically produced commodity h and its foreign equivalents, according to the Leontief-type production function:

$$y_2^{ROW} = \min \left\{ \frac{va_2^{ROW}}{\alpha_2^{ROW}}, \frac{ci_{2,1}^{ROW}}{\beta_{2,1}^{ROW}}, \ldots, \frac{ci_{2,n+1}^{ROW}}{\beta_{2,n+1}^{ROW}} \right\}$$

where α_2^{ROW} and $\beta_{2,1}^{ROW}, \ldots, \beta_{2,n+1}^{ROW}$ are the share parameters of value added and the composite intermediate commodities $1, \ldots, n + 1$ respectively. Then, the first type of technological innovation can be represented by a decrease in the parameter α_2^{ROW} while the second type of technological innovation can be represented by a decrease in the parameters $\beta_{2,1}^{ROW}, \ldots, \beta_{2,n+1}^{ROW}$.

The benchmark values for the share parameters α_2^{ROW} and $\beta_{2,1}^{ROW}, \ldots, \beta_{2,n+1}^{ROW}$ in the production function of ROW's producer 2 are given in Table 11.2. In the first counterfactual, we consider a technological improvement in the value added by labour and capital to the production of one unit of commodity 2 in ROW. We therefore change the value of α_2^{ROW} to $\alpha_2^{ROW,C1} = 0.400$, while keeping all the other parameters at their benchmark values. We refer to this simulation as C1 (and the corresponding results can be found in the appendix labelled 'Counterfactual equilibrium C1').

In order to analyse the consequences of a change in the value of a parameter between the benchmark equilibrium and a counterfactual equilibrium on consumer welfare, we consider the Hicksian Equivalent Variation

Table 11.2 The benchmark values of the share parameters in the first nest of the production technology of producer 2 in country ROW

α_2^{ROW}	$\beta_{2,1}^{ROW}$	$\beta_{2,2}^{ROW}$	$\beta_{2,3}^{ROW}$	$\beta_{2,4}^{ROW}$	$\beta_{2,5}^{ROW}$	$\beta_{2,6}^{ROW}$	$\beta_{2,7}^{ROW}$
0.475	0.000	0.203	0.016	0.010	0.034	0.000	0 .000

$\beta_{2,8}^{ROW}$	$\beta_{2,9}^{ROW}$	$\beta_{2,10}^{ROW}$	$\beta_{2,11}^{ROW}$	$\beta_{2,12}^{ROW}$	$\beta_{2,12}^{ROW}$	$\beta_{2,14}^{ROW}$
0.000	0.000	0.000	0.000	0.006	0.167	0.000

Source: Ruocco (1996)

Table 11.3 The Hicksian equivalent variations and the changes in real gross national product for each country i under counterfactual C1

Country:	F	BL	NL	D	I	UK	DK	ROW
EV(i)	3,495.006	865.424	850.941	3,709.419	2,549.247	2,538.568	441.197	84,051.700
ΔGNP(i)	5,343.575	1,370.664	1,320.123	5,257.143	4,396.132	3,890.825	635.757	148,220.193

for every consumer. The Hicksian Equivalent Variation for consumer i is denoted by EV(i), and can be interpreted as the amount of money that is considered equivalent to the change in consumer i's utility due to the change that has taken place between the benchmark equilibrium B and the counterfactual equilibrium C, evaluated at benchmark equilibrium prices. Since utility functions are of the CES type, and therefore linear homogeneous, we can write EV(i) as:

$$EV(i) = \left(\frac{U_i^C - U_i^B}{U_i^B} \right) M^B(i).$$

The equivalent variations for counterfactual equilibrium C1 are given in Table 11.3.

The Hicksian Equivalent Variation is mainly used by economic theorists to measure a country's performance. In public debate the gross national product of a country is mainly used to this end. We therefore include the change in real gross national product into our simulations. Denote the change in real gross national product of country i by ΔGNP(i). Then ΔGNP(i) is calculated as:

$$\Delta GNP(i) = \sum_{j=1}^{14} \left(y_j^{iC} - y_j^{iB} \right).$$

Notice that we have evaluated this change at benchmark prices, which are all equal to one, in order to keep ΔGNP(i) comparable to EV(i). The results for counterfactual equilibrium C1 can also be found in Table 11.3.

Table 11.4 The Hicksian Equivalent Variations and the changes in real gross national product for each country i under counterfactual C2

Country: F	BL	NL	D	I	UK	DK	ROW
EV(i)	2,012.098	295.163	550.985	1,131.649	1,411.182	900.686	259.085	41,780.124
ΔGNP(i)	138.211	−485.227	−391.694	1,867.522	573.540	−1,438.475	95.624	3,069.968

Table 11.5 The Hicksian Equivalent Variations and the changes in real gross national product for each country i under counterfactual C3

Country: F	BL	NL	D	I	UK	DK	ROW
EV(i)	5,486.078	1,159.109	1,402.550	5,010.180	3,944.686	3,419.181	699.407	125,779.931
ΔGNP(i)	5,397.929	864.707	902.039	3,563.437	4,911.597	2,402.055	721.013	151,032.083

In the second counterfactual, to which we refer as C2, we only consider technological innovation in the use of the composite intermediate goods as inputs to the production of commodity 2 in ROW. We therefore have to lower the coefficients $\beta_{2,b}^{ROW}$ from their benchmark values. Recall from Table 11.2 that many of them are either zero or nearly zero. Only the composite intermediate commodities 2 and 13 exhibit reasonably large numbers. We therefore lower $\beta_{2,2}^{ROW}$ and $\beta_{2,13}^{ROW}$ from their benchmark values to obtain:

$$\beta_{2,2}^{ROW,C2} = 0.175 \text{ and } \beta_{2,13}^{ROW,C2} = 0.150$$

while leaving all the other parameters at their benchmark values. The results of this simulation can be found in the appendix labelled 'Counterfactual equilibrium C2'.

We have next calculated the corresponding Hicksian Equivalent Variations for every consumer and also the change in real gross national product in every country. The results are given in Table 11.4.

In the third counterfactual, to which we refer as C3, we combine C1 and C2 by lowering the parameter α_2^{ROW} as well as the parameters $\beta_{2,2}^{ROW}$ and $\beta_{2,13}^{ROW}$ from their benchmark values to obtain:

$$\alpha_2^{ROW,C1} = 0.400, \ \beta_{2,2}^{ROW,C2} = 0.175, \text{ and } \beta_{2,13}^{ROW,C2} = 0.150$$

while leaving all the other parameters at their benchmark values. The results from this simulation can be found in the appendix labelled 'Counterfactual equilibrium C3'. In Table 11.5 we have depicted the Hicksian Equivalent Variations and the changes in real gross national product with respect to C3.

11.4 AN ADJUSTMENT PROCESS

In the previous section we performed three simulations to study the impact of technological innovation on employment in the FRW model. Each simulation was based on a different assumption with respect to the type of technological innovation. This section seeks to explain the results of these simulations.

The consequences of technological innovation on employment follow from comparing the labour market equilibrium condition obtained in the counterfactual equilibrium with that in the benchmark equilibrium. The labour market equilibrium condition for each country i is given by the third condition defining an equilibrium in this economy. We represent the labour market equilibrium as the locus of points (w_i, p_j^i) where there exists full employment, i.e. the points (w_i, p_j^i) such that:

$$LU_i(p, w_i; M_i, y^i) = \Lambda^i(p, w_i; M_i) - \sum_{h=1}^{n+1} l_h^i(w_i, r; y_h^i)$$

and draw this locus of points as the $(LU_i = 0)$ curve or the full employment curve in the (w_i, p_j^i) space, with respect to each commodity j in country i.

In Figure 11.1 we have drawn the labour market supply curve Λ^i and the labour market demand curve $LD^i = \sum_{h=1}^{n+1} l_h^i$ as a function of the wage rate w_i of country i. We immediately notice that the labour market demand curve LD^i is a decreasing function of the wage rate w_i in the benchmark equilibrium, as:

$$\partial_{w_i} LD^i(w_i, r; y^i) \mid_B = \sum_{h=1}^{n+1} \partial_{w_i} l_h^i(w_i, r; y_h^i) \mid_B < 0.$$

This is more ambiguous with respect to the labour market supply curve as:

$$\partial_{w_i} \Lambda^i(p, w_i; M_i) \mid_B + \partial_{M_i} \Lambda^i(p, w_i; M_i) \mid_B (1 - v_i) L_i$$

contains two opposing effects, namely a price effect $\partial_{w_i} \Lambda^i(p, w_i; M_i) \mid_B > 0$ and an income effect $\partial_{w_i} \Lambda^i(p, w_i; M_i) \mid_B (1 - v_i) L_i < 0$. The derivatives of the labour demand functions in the benchmark equilibrium $\partial_{w_i} l_h^i(w_i, r; y_h^i) \mid_B$ are negative, since an increase in the wage rate w_i makes labour more expensive for producer j, which then decreases its demand for labour. In turn, the price effect $\partial_{w_i} \Lambda^i(p, w_i; M_i) \mid_B$ is positive as an increase in the wage rate makes leisure more expensive to consumer i, who therefore substitutes

Table 11.6 The values of the derivatives of the labour demand function LD^i, and the price and income effect of the labour supply function Λ^i in the benchmark equilibrium

Country:	F	BL	NL	D
$\partial_{w_i} LD^i(w_i, r; y^i) \mid_B$	$-64,423.436$	$-9,197.700$	$-18,924.608$	$-66,061.300$
$\partial_{w_i} \Lambda^i(p, w_i; M_i) \mid_B$	$111,542.749$	$27,897.776$	$41,582.108$	$235,676.819$
$\partial_{w_i} \Lambda^i(p, w_i; M_i) \mid_B$ $(1 - v_i) L_i$	$-75,555.363$	$-20,396.374$	$-29,673.202$	$-179,355.825$

Country:	I	UK	DK	ROW
$\partial_{w_i} LD^i(w_i, r; y^i) \mid_B$	$-43,102.922$	$-43,499.008$	$-6,244.953$	$-653,214.878$
$\partial_{w_i} \Lambda^i(p, w_i; M_i) \mid_B$	$93,025.768$	$185,364.138$	$16,387.126$	$2,619,028.910$
$\partial_{w_i} \Lambda^i(p, w_i; M_i) \mid_B$ $(1 - v_i) L_i$	$-66,073.490$	$-142,099.628$	$-11,210.116$	$-1,871,470.000$

consumption for leisure. In order to spend less on leisure, consumer i supplies more labour hours to country i's labour market. On the other hand, the income effect $\partial_{M_i} \Lambda^i(p, w_i; M_i) \mid_B (1 - v_i) L_i$ is negative as an increase in the wage rate gives consumer i the opportunity to spend more on, among other things, leisure, thereby decreasing his or her supply of labour hours to country i's labour market. Table 11.6 provides the values for the price effects, $\partial_{w_i} LD^i(w_i; r; y^i) \mid_B$ and $\partial_{w_i} \Lambda^i(p, w_i; M_i) \mid_B$, and the income effect $\partial_{M_i} \Lambda^i(p, w_i; M_i) \mid_B (1 - v_i) L_i$.

Table 11.6 indicates that we can draw the benchmark total labour demand curve of country i, $D^{i(B)}$, as a decreasing function of the wage rate w_i, and the benchmark labour supply curve $\Lambda^{i(B)}$ as an increasing function of the wage rate w_i. We have done so in the right-hand panel of Figure 11.1.

An increase in the price level of country i's commodity j, p_j^i, leaves the labour demand curve LD^i unchanged at $LD^{i(B)}$, but – as follows from Table 11.6 – this increases the amount of labour hours supplied to the labour market at the benchmark wage rate $w_i^B = 1.000$. This causes the labour supply curve Λ^i to shift to the right from its benchmark position $\Lambda^{i(B)}$ to $\bar{\Lambda}^i$ in Figure 11.1, so creating an excess supply of labour in country i's labour market at the benchmark wage rate $w_i^B = 1.000$. This forces country i's wage rate to decrease in order to restore equilibrium in its labour market. Hence, the benchmark full employment curve of country i is a decreasing function in (w_i, p_j^i)-space at the benchmark equilibrium.

In order to obtain the benchmark equilibrium $(w_i^B, p_j^{i(B)})$ in (w_i, p_j^i)-space, the benchmark full employment curve with the locus of points (w_i, p_j^i) should be intersected where country i's producer j makes zero profit. According to the first condition defining an equilibrium, this determines the price of country i's commodity j. Under constant returns to scale, the zero-profit condition determining the price of country i's commodity j entails p_j^i equalling the marginal

201

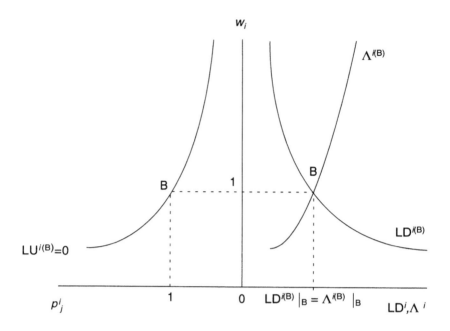

Figure 11.1 Right-hand panel: The benchmark labour market supply curve $\Lambda^{i(B)}$ and the benchmark labour market demand curve $LD^{i(B)}$ of country i as a function of wage rate w_i; *left-hand panel*: benchmark full-employment curve of country i in (w_i, p_j^i)-space

costs to produce one unit of country i's commodity j. Let $MC_j^i(p_j^{-i}, w_i, r; y_j^i)$ denote the marginal cost of country i's producer j to produce y_j^i units of commodity j under prices p_{-j}^{-i}, w_i and r.

The right-hand panel shows the benchmark labour market supply curve $\Lambda^{i(B)}$ and the benchmark labour market demand curve $LD^{i(B)}$ of country i as a function of the wage rate w_i. The left-hand panel shows the benchmark full employment curve of country i in (w_i, p_j^i)-space. Then, the benchmark locus of points (w_i, p_j^i) where country i's producer j makes zero profits is given by the set of points (w_i, p_j^i) such that:

$$p_j^i = MC_j^i(p_j^{-i(B)}, w_i, r^B; y_j^{i(B)}).$$

We denote this locus of points through the benchmark equilibrium B with the curve $MCP_j^{i(B)}$ in the left-hand panel of Figure 11.2. An increase in the wage rate w_i increases the marginal costs to produce y_j^i units of country i's commodity j. Therefore, p_j^i should rise to keep the profits of country i's producer j equal to zero. Consequently, the $MCP_j^{i(B)}$ curve is an increasing function of the wage rate w_i at the benchmark equilibrium B in (w_i, p_j^i)-space.

Total demand for country i's commodity j is given by:

202

$$\xi^i_j(p^{ii}_{j|_{iie1}};M_i)+\sum_{iie\,I\backslash\{i\}} \eta^{ii}_{i,j}(p^t_j|_{t\in 1};M_{ii})+\sum_{h=1}^{n+1}a^i_{h,j}(p^t_j|_{t\in 1};y^i_h)+\sum_{iie\,I\backslash\{i\}}\sum_{h=1}^{n+1}b^{ii,h}_{i,j}(p^t_j|_{t\in 1};y^{ii}_h).$$

The locus of points giving total demand at each price p^i_j is denoted by $D^i_j(p^i_j;\ p^{-i}_{-j},\ M_i,\ y)$. We have drawn the curve $D^{i(B)}_j = D^i_j(p^i_j;\ p^{-i(B)}_{-j},\ M^B_i,\ y^B)$ in the right-hand panel of Figure 11.2. This is a decreasing function of p^i_j. Given any point $(w_i,\ p^i_j)$ on the $\mathrm{MCP}^{i(B)}_j$ curve, supply of country i's commodity j is given by the horizontal line S^i_j at price level p^i_j. For the benchmark B, we have drawn the supply line $S^{i(B)}_j$ at benchmark price level $p^{i(B)}_j = 1$ in the right-hand panel of Figure 11.2. The supply level $y^{i(B)}_j$ clears the market for country i's commodity j. Technological innovation causes ROW's producer 2's per unit costs to decrease under all counterfactuals. This also occurs with respect to the per unit costs of producing commodity $j \neq 2$ in ROW, to the extent that ROW's producer $j \neq 2$ uses commodity 2 as an intermediate in its production process. Consequently, this implies a leftward shift of the $\mathrm{MCP}^{\mathrm{ROW}}_j$ curve in $(w_{\mathrm{ROW}},\ p^{\mathrm{ROW}}_j)$-space, thereby decreasing $p^{*\mathrm{ROW}}_j$ from its benchmark level of 1.000 at a given benchmark wage rate $w^*_{\mathrm{ROW}} = 1.000$.

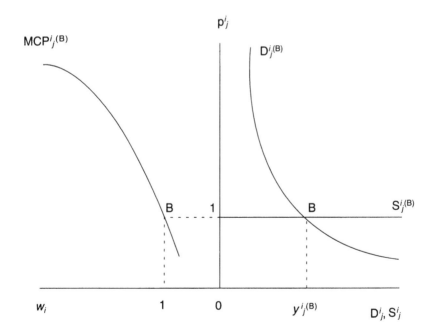

Figure 11.2 Right-hand panel: Supply curve $S^{i(B)}_j$ and the commodity j market demand curve $D^{i(B)}_j$ of country i as a function of the price level of country i's commodity j: *left-hand panel*: Marginal cost pricing curve $\mathrm{MCP}^{i(B)}_j$ for country i's commodity j in (w_i, p^i_j)-space.

The decrease in the price level p_j^{ROW} implies a downward shift of the S_j^{ROW}-line in Figure 11.2, so causing an excess demand for ROW's commodity j to occur at the benchmark supply $y_j^{ROW(B)}$. On the other hand, technological innovation under counterfactuals C2 and C3 implies less demand for the commodities 2 and 13, thereby inducing a leftward shift of the demand curves D_2^{ROW} and D_{13}^{ROW} in Figure 11.2. The simulation results show that these more than outweigh the initial increase in demand for ROW's commodities 2 and 13 under counterfactual C2 since, on balance, the supply of ROW's commodities 2 and 13 drops from its benchmark values to restore equilibrium in the ROW commodity markets 2 and 13 in C2. The right-hand panel shows the supply curve $S_j^{(B)}$ and the commodity j market demand curve $D_j^{i(B)}$ of country i as a function of the price level of country i's commodity j. The left-hand panel shows the marginal cost pricing curve $MCP_j^{i(B)}$ for country i's commodity j in (w_i, p_j^i)-space.

The consequences of technological innovation on ROW's labour market are caused by the effects of the change in supply in each of ROW's commodities on the demand for ROW's labour by ROW's producers. An increase in the supply of a commodity implies an increase in the demand for labour by the commodity's producer and vice versa. Under the counterfactuals C1 and C3 the supply of every commodity increases in ROW, thereby causing an increase in the demand for labour in ROW under these counterfactuals. This is more ambiguous under counterfactual C2 due to the decrease in supply of commodities 2 and 13. In Table 11.7, we provide the values for the change in labour demand in every country under every counterfactual. It follows from this table, that the decrease in labour by producers 2 and 13 is not sufficient to offset the increase in the demand for labour by the other producers in ROW. Hence, under all three counterfactuals, labour demand increases on ROW's labour market as a consequence of technological innovation.

The increase in labour demand on ROW's labour market shifts the LD^{ROW} curve to the right in the right-hand panel of Figure 11.1. At the benchmark wage rate, this creates an excess demand for labour on ROW's labour market which can only be offset by an increase in this wage rate from its benchmark level. Consequently, the full employment curve shifts upward in (w_{ROW}, p_j^{ROW})-space.

The upward shift of the full employment curve and the leftward shift of the MCP_j^{ROW}-curve in (w_{ROW}, p_j^{ROW})-space increase the wage rate under all counterfactuals. The consequences of technological innovation on the price levels in ROW seem to be more ambiguous, but the simulation results turn out to show an overall decrease in these prices under all counterfactuals.

The consequences of technological innovation on the wage rate and price levels of the commodities in the EU countries arrive through the effects of the decrease in the price level of ROW's commodities on the per unit costs to produce commodity j in EU country i. The decrease in the price level of ROW's commodities causes a decrease in the costs of producing EU country

Table 11.7 The change in demand for labour ΔLD^i in each country i under the different counterfactuals

Country:	F	BL	NL	D	I	UK	DK	ROW
C1	793.861	279.056	235.693	1,406.763	787.209	945.263	118.671	37,343.187
C2	42.227	−60.211	7.493	−242.784	150.427	−174.263	26.347	1,218.329
C3	823.803	214.794	239.565	1,214.599	927.006	759.245	142.124	38,222.857

i's commodity j to the extent that the respective producers use ROW's commodities as intermediates in their production process.

Instead of continuing with the same analysis as above, we now focus our attention on those EU countries where the full employment curve shifts downward as a consequence of falling labour demand in its labour market, in combination with the leftward shift of the MCP_j^i-curve.

Table 11.7 indicates that the full employment curve shifts downward in the EU countries of Belgium-Luxembourg (BL), Germany (D) and the United Kingdom (UK) under counterfactual C2. The simulation results under counterfactual C2 indicate that the full employment wage rate in these EU countries ultimately settles at a level below the benchmark level of 1.000. Notice, however, that we have set a minimum wage rate equal to 1.000 in Germany, prohibiting full employment from occurring there. In (w_D, p_j^D)-space, counterfactual equilibrium C2 can be found at the intersection of the $MCP_j^{D(C2)}$-curve and the line $w_D = \underline{w}_D$, where consumer D is unemployed for 313.110 hours. We have drawn this situation in Figure 11.3, where C is the full employment counterfactual equilibrium and C2 the unemployment equilibrium under counterfactual C2 for Germany (D).

Although Germany (D) faces unemployment under counterfactual C2, the simulation results show an increase in the labour supply from its benchmark value of 355,491 hours to 355,561 hours. While the wage rate w_D remains at its benchmark value of 1 under counterfactual C2, the prices of the commodities in Germany decrease, making leisure relatively more expensive. Consequently consumer D chooses a utility-maximising bundle containing less leisure, so increasing his or her labour supply.

We assume that technological innovation leads to the aforementioned adjustment process in prices and wages, starting in the benchmark equilibrium calibrated in Fehr *et al.* (1995), and ending in the appropriate counterfactual equilibrium C1, C2 or C3. The consequences of technological innovation on the welfare in the different EU countries under the different counterfactuals are measured by the Hicksian equivalent variations $EV(i)$, $i \in I$, and the changes in real gross national product, $\Delta GNP(i)$, $i \in I$, given in section 11.3. The Hicksian equivalent variation refers to the change in welfare of the representative consumer caused by technological innovation. As can be seen from the results in the previous section, technological

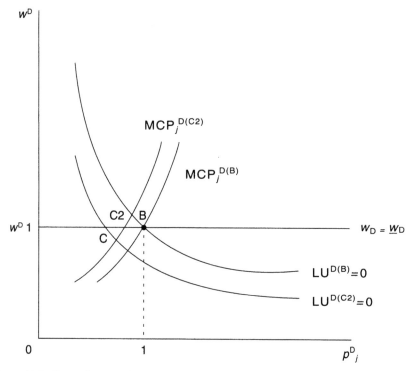

Figure 11.3 Unemployment in Germany (D) as a consequence of technological innovation under counterfactual C2

innovation leads to an improvement in the welfare of the representative consumer under all counterfactuals. The consumer obtains utility from consumption and leisure only. As the simulation results show, the consumer regularly chooses less leisure in his utility-maximizing bundle. This indicates that the main source of the welfare gain are the cheaper commodities in ROW, which enable the consumer to substitute more of ROW's commodities into his utility-maximizing bundle, thereby increasing his consumption. The utility increase caused by the extra consumption overtakes the possible decrease in utility due to the decrease in leisure.

Contrary to the Hicksian Equivalent Variation, the change in real gross national product is not unanimously positive concerning the consequences of technological innovation. As the results in section 11.3 show, the EU countries Belgium–Luxembourg (BL), the Netherlands (NL), Germany (D) and the United Kingdom (UK) show a decrease in real gross national product. Due to technological innovation under counterfactual C2 and the substitution of ROW's relatively cheaper commodities into each consumer's utility-maximizing bundle, the activity levels of the production sectors 2 and 13 in each country may fall. Then, in order for a country to have an increase in the real gross national product, this drop in activity levels should be more than compensated by an increase in the activity levels of the remaining sectors. Apparently, under counterfactual C2 this is not the case for the EU countries mentioned above.

REFERENCES

Fehr, H., Rosenberg, C. and Wiegard, W. (1995), *Welfare Effects of Value-added Tax Harmonization in Europe: A Computable Generable Equilibrium Analysis*, Berlin: Springer Verlag.

Ruocco, A. (1996), *A Multi-country General Equilibrium Model for the European Union: The Basic Features and Coding Structure*, Tübingen: Tübingen Diskussionsbeitrage Nr. 83, Wirtschaftswissenschaftliche Fakultät der Eberhard-Karls-Universität Tübingen.

Shoven, J.B. and Whalley, J. (1982), *Applying General Equilibrium*, Cambridge: Cambridge University Press.

APPENDIX: TABLES

The benchmark equilibrium

Table A11.1 The benchmark equilibrium: the level of production y

	1	2	3	4	5	6	7
F	69,648.000	139,250.000	40,953.000	44,065.000	32,613.000	11,401.000	32,283.000
BL	7,404.000	28,279.000	8,682.000	4,029.000	6,198.000	690.000	5,391.000
NL	17,301.000	48,044.000	13,298.000	6,529.000	6,624.000	1,347.000	10,301.000
D	37,689.000	160,169.000	53,379.000	49,462.000	61,275.000	15,307.000	51,639.000
I	47,885.000	93,227.000	29,817.000	21,633.000	26,380.000	4,949.000	18,614.000
UK	29,797.000	127,878.000	36,288.000	27,711.000	41,075.000	8,312.000	27,957.000
DK	8,541.000	7,836.000	2,440.000	2,355.000	4,472.000	561.000	1,841.000
ROW	349,314.000	39,117.000	348,786.000	339,172.000	329,172.000	113,779.000	479,751.000

	8	9	10	11	12	13	14
F	41,235.000	19,755.000	98,263.000	41,152.000	62,394.000	618,306.000	119,289.000
BL	6,442.000	1,354.000	16,125.000	8,336.000	10,119.000	69,939.000	18,044.000
NL	4,060.000	4,866.000	35,105.000	7,406.000	16,808.000	152,626.000	27,186.000
D	51,830.000	8,613.000	82,923.000	36,596.000	73,581.000	446,975.000	126,281.000
I	18,306.000	6,579.000	57,745.000	48,251.000	48,472.000	304,697.000	68,787.000
UK	27,371.000	16,535.000	77,926.000	31,050.000	53,877.000	371,718.000	25,035.000
DK		2,628.000	13,962.000	2,603.000	6,697.000	55,600.000	6,996.000
ROW	90,324.000	142,292.000	591,309.000	198,179.000	723,212.000	5,772,243.000	1,905,177.000

Table A11.2 The benchmark equilibrium: the commodity prices p

	1	2	3	4	5	6	7	8	9	10	11	12	13	14
F	1.000	1.000	1.000	1.000	1.000	1.000	1.000	1.000	1.000	1.000	1.000	1.000	1.000	1.000
BL	1.000	1.000	1.000	1.000	1.000	1.000	1.000	1.000	1.000	1.000	1.000	1.000	1.000	1.000
NL	1.000	1.000	1.000	1.000	1.000	1.000	1.000	1.000	1.000	1.000	1.000	1.000	1.000	1.000
D	1.000	1.000	1.000	1.000	1.000	1.000	1.000	1.000	1.000	1.000	1.000	1.000	1.000	1.000
I	1.000	1.000	1.000	1.000	1.000	1.000	1.000	1.000	1.000	1.000	1.000	1.000	1.000	1.000
UK	1.000	1.000	1.000	1.000	1.000	1.000	1.000	1.000	1.000	1.000	1.000	1.000	1.000	1.000
DK	1.000	1.000	1.000	1.000	1.000	1.000	1.000	1.000	1.000	1.000	1.000	1.000	1.000	1.000
ROW	1.000	1.000	1.000	1.000	1.000	1.000	1.000	1.000	1.000	1.000	1.000	1.000	1.000	1.000

Table A11.3 The benchmark equilibrium: wage rate, minimum wage, total labour time, leisure, labour supply and unemployment

	w_i	$\underline{w}_i$	L_i	LL_i	Λ^i	LU_i
F	1.000	0.500	410,527.250	175,940.250	234,587.000	0.0000
BL	1.000	0.750	81,571.000	34,959.000	46,612.000	0.0000
NL	1.000	1.000	133,113.750	57,048.750	76,065.000	0.0000
D	1.000	1.000	622,109.250	266,618.250	355,491.000	0.0000
I	1.000	0.500	299,878.250	128,519.250	171,359.000	0.0000
UK	1.000	0.500	480,156.250	205,781.250	274,375.000	0.0000
DK	1.000	0.500	52,414.250	22,463.250	29,951.000	0.0000
ROW	1.000	0.000	7,391,900.250	3,167,957.250	4,223,943.000	0.0000

Counterfactual equilibrium C1

Table A11.4 Counterfactual equilibrium C1: the level of production y

	1	2	3	4	5	6	7
F	69,972.829	140,026.234	41,196.742	44,317.409	32,835.301	11,444.714	32,449.055
BL	7,461.408	28,600.001	8,769.593	4,068.078	6,247.158	694.434	5,423.808
NL	17,395.988	48,210.321	13,402.840	6,564.378	6,666.402	1,352.159	10,357.903
D	37,916.300	160,412.929	53,618.976	49,769.341	61,634.553	15,381.110	51,902.717
I	48,098.371	94,104.579	30,078.094	21,849.496	26,683.956	4,980.619	18,758.778
UK	29,959.006	128,223.514	36,471.678	27,873.560	41,347.841	8,344.085	28,105.924
DK	8,597.509	7,917.800	2,455.036	2,372.523	4,506.993	563.062	1,852.646
ROW	353,260.336	1,083,470.866	355,200.519	343,494.256	333,732.368	114,849.687	485,302.831

	8	9	10	11	12	13	14
F	41,455.337	19,842.172	98,713.228	41,285.831	62,655.881	620,436.040	119,319.805
BL	6,490.648	1,361.773	16,253.817	8,371.281	10,171.218	70,440.359	18,049.088
NL	4,079.863	4,894.676	5,306.233	7,435.533	16,875.991	153,086.580	27,192.254
D	52,115.568	8,664.792	83,508.895	36,787.524	73,931.886	449,022.996	126,308.556
I	18,452.239	6,618.786	58,038.352	48,423.720	48,789.661	306,054.831	68,806.682
UK	27,548.827	16,583.415	78,415.815	31,194.399	54,108.803	373,181.276	125,062.682
DK		2,649.612	14,057.388	2,616.006	6,726.696	55,851.643	17,000.843
ROW	294,040.388	143,426.521	598,383.669	200,149.805	730,844.265	5,827,442.637	1,906,449.046

208

Table A11.5 Counterfactual equilibrium C1: the commodity prices p

	1	2	3	4	5	6	7	8	9	10	11	12	13	14
F	0.999	0.980	0.996	0.997	0.998	1.001	0.999	0.999	0.999	0.999	1.001	1.000	1.001	1.003
BL	0.998	0.960	0.992	0.994	1.001	1.002	1.001	1.000	1.002	1.000	1.003	1.002	1.001	1.010
NL	0.999	0.979	0.992	0.996	0.999	1.001	1.000	1.000	0.999	0.999	1.001	1.001	1.001	1.003
D	1.000	0.980	0.998	0.996	1.003	1.002	1.003	1.003	1.001	1.001	1.002	1.002	1.004	1.006
I	1.000	0.968	0.992	0.993	0.995	0.999	0.997	0.998	0.998	0.999	1.002	0.998	1.000	1.006
UK	1.002	0.988	0.999	0.999	1.002	1.003	1.002	1.001	1.003	1.001	1.003	1.003	1.004	1.007
DK	0.999	0.974	0.998	0.995	1.000	1.003	1.000	1.000	0.998	1.000	1.002	1.002	1.002	1.007
ROW	0.994	0.902	0.981	0.987	0.997	0.998	0.996	0.995	0.999	0.996	0.998	0.997	0.999	1.007

Table A11.6 Counterfactual equilibrium C1: wage rate, minimum wage, total labour time, leisure, labour supply, and unemployment

	w_i	$\underline{w}_i$	L_t	LL_t	Λ^i	LU_i
F	1.010	0.500	410,527.250	175,765.428	234,761.822	0.000
BL	1.018	0.750	81,571.000	34,848.603	46,722.397	0.000
NL	1.009	1.000	133,113.750	56,977.126	76,136.624	0.000
D	1.013	1.000	622,109.250	266,075.546	356,033.704	0.000
I	1.012	0.500	299,878.250	128,245.547	171,632.703	0.000
UK	1.012	0.500	480,156.250	205,372.233	274,784.017	0.000
DK	1.014	0.500	52,414.250	22,431.878	29,982.372	0.000
ROW	1.014	0.000	7,391,900.250	3,167,481.163	4,224,419.087	0.000

Counterfactual equilibrium C2

Table A11.7 Counterfactual equilibrium C2: the level of production y

	1	2	3	4	5	6	7
F	69,739.578	138,304.662	41,006.976	44,150.879	32,683.252	11,418.546	32,349.915
BL	7,414.003	27,561.944	8,707.757	4,039.313	6,211.551	690.482	5,412.334
NL	17,318.889	47,404.359	13,302.982	6,535.090	6,637.063	1,349.415	10,319.658
D	37,723.843	157,801.389	53,355.302	49,493.075	61,328.908	15,325.718	51,718.206
I	47,942.236	92,624.177	29,902.285	21,713.285	26,480.727	4,960.067	18,675.863
UK	29,819.044	126,016.425	36,284.193	27,721.009	41,121.844	8,324.788	28,003.187
DK	8,556.550	7,766.695	2,441.319	2,358.834	4,480.518	561.319	1,844.607
ROW	350,665.187	1,029,105.265	350,988.071	340,008.456	330,166.353	114,202.163	482,265.665

	8	9	10	11	12	13	14
F	41,328.379	19,791.703	98,409.178	41,208.800	62,457.911	618,606.225	119,289.209
BL	6,463.933	1,359.138	16,151.808	8,352.261	10,134.979	70,004.489	18,042.780
NL	4,071.963	4,880.530	35,157.023	7,420.269	16,817.205	152,708.491	27,186.368
D	51,940.139	8,634.993	83,043.900	36,650.319	73,611.827	446,950.891	126,272.968
I	18,377.382	6,600.224	57,859.312	31,091.393	53,899.958	305,101.865	125,026.784
UK	27,452.809	16,562.148	78,012.712	31,091.393	53,899.958	371,755.230	125,026.784
DK		2,638.988	13,990.498	2,608.041	6,702.468	55,680.747	16,997.042
ROW	292,158.847	142,883.687	594,024.689	199,011.794	725,294.687	5,768,929.491	1,905,192.615

Table A11.8 Counterfactual equilibrium C2: the commodity prices p

	1	2	3	4	5	6	7	8	9	10	11	12	13	14
F	0.998	0.987	0.996	0.997	0.997	0.998	0.997	0.998	0.997	0.998	0.999	0.998	0.999	0.999
BL	0.997	0.973	0.991	0.991	0.995	0.997	0.994	0.996	0.995	0.996	0.997	0.996	0.996	0.997
NL	0.998	0.987	0.994	0.996	0.997	0.998	0.997	0.997	0.997	0.998	0.998	0.998	0.999	0.999
D	0.998	0.985	0.995	0.994	0.998	0.998	0.997	0.997	0.996	0.997	0.998	0.997	0.998	0.998
I	0.999	0.980	0.993	0.994	0.996	0.998	0.996	0.996	0.997	0.998	0.999	0.997	0.999	1.000
UK	0.998	0.990	0.995	0.995	0.996	0.997	0.996	0.996	0.997	0.997	0.997	0.997	0.997	0.997
DK	0.998	0.983	0.997	0.995	0.998	1.000	0.998	1.000	0.996	0.998	0.999	0.999	0.999	1.001
ROW	0.995	0.942	0.987	0.990	0.995	0.996	0.995	0.994	0.996	0.995	0.996	0.995	0.997	1.000

Table A11.9 Counterfactual equilibrium C2: wage rate, minimum wage; total labour, time, leisure, labour supply and unemployment

	w_i	$\underline{w}_i$	L_i	LL_i	Λ^i	LU_i
F	1.002	0.500	410,527.250	176,012.678	234,514.572	0.000
BL	0.997	0.750	81,571.000	34,995.139	46,575.861	0.000
NL	1.001	1.000	133,113.750	57,069.361	76,044.389	0.000
D	1.000	1.000	622,109.250	266,547.957	355,561.293	313.110
I	1.003	0.500	299,878.250	128,495.168	171,383.082	0.000
UK	0.998	0.500	480,156.250	205,877.086	274,279.164	0.000
DK	1.004	0.500	52,414.250	22,464.560	29,949.690	0.000
ROW	1.003	0.000	7,391,900.250	3,168,740.639	4,223,159.611	0.000

Counterfactual equilibrium C3

Table A11.10 Counterfactual equilibrium C3: the level of production y

	1	2	3	4	5	6	7
F	70,059.712	139,064.440	41,248.726	44,400.756	32,904.438	11,461.587	32,513.914
BL	7,470.537	27,874.585	8,795.052	4,078.169	6,260.752	694.874	5,444.907
NL	17,412.170	47,559.551	13,407.379	6,570.084	6,679.434	1,354.547	10,376.272
D	37,952.710	158,061.776	53,606.930	49,811.704	61,708.941	15,403.005	51,994.788
I	48,152.461	93,490.957	30,161.314	21,927.997	26,782.610	4,991.214	18,818.788
UK	29,978.926	126,353.081	36,466.949	27,882.397	41,393.523	8,356.259	28,150.376
DK	8,612.085	7,846.876	2,456.244	2,376.183	4,515.248	563.325	1,856.056
ROW	354,534.203	1,075,460.935	357,348.579	344,283.740	334,721.261	115,249.670	487,713.172

	8	9	10	11	12	13	14
F	41,545.110	19,887.557	98,852.441	41,340.374	62,715.922	620,700.408	119,319.517
BL	6,512.756	1,366.813	16,278.512	8,386.907	10,186.435	70,498.617	18,047.790
NL	4,091.920	4,908.971	35,354.394	7,449.594	16,884.125	153,162.077	27,192.521
D	52,238.102	8,688.797	83,626.902	36,845.613	73,976.776	449,065.064	126,301.330
I	18,521.420	6,639.362	58,148.410	48,469.444	48,900.447	306,439.322	126,301.330
UK	27,628.097	16,609.831	78,496.029	31,233.696	54,128.758	373,200.028	125,054.106
DK		2,660.401	14,084.232	2,620.805	6,731.608	55,928.142	17,001.807
ROW	295,808.781	143,988.049	600,960.516	200,938.214	732,779.883	5,822,571.177	1,906,464.353

Table A11.11 Counterfactual equilibrium C3: the commodity prices *p*

	1	2	3	4	5	6	7	8	9	10	11	12	13	14
F	0.997	0.968	0.991	0.994	0.996	0.999	0.996	0.997	0.997	0.998	1.000	0.998	1.000	1.003
BL	0.995	0.934	0.983	0.985	0.996	0.999	0.995	0.996	0.996	0.996	0.999	0.998	0.997	1.007
NL	0.998	0.966	0.986	0.992	0.996	0.999	0.997	0.997	0.995	0.997	0.999	0.999	1.000	1.002
D	0.997	0.965	0.993	0.989	1.001	0.999	0.999	1.000	0.997	0.998	1.000	0.999	1.001	1.003
I	0.999	0.948	0.985	0.987	0.991	0.997	0.993	0.994	0.995	0.998	1.001	0.995	0.999	1.006
UK	0.999	0.978	0.994	0.993	0.998	1.000	0.998	0.997	0.999	0.998	1.000	1.000	1.001	1.004
DK	0.997	0.957	0.995	0.990	0.998	1.003	0.998	1.000	0.995	0.998	1.001	1.001	1.001	1.008
ROW	0.989	0.846	0.969	0.977	0.993	0.994	0.991	0.989	0.996	0.991	0.994	0.992	0.997	1.007

Table A11.12 Counterfactual equilibrium C3: wage rate, minimum wage, total labour, time, leisure, labour supply and unemployment

	w_i	$\underline{w}_i$	L_i	LL_i	Λ^i	LU_i
F	1.011	0.500	410,527.250	175,841.877	234,685.373	0.000
BL	1.016	0.750	81,571.000	34,886.702	46,684.298	0.000
NL	1.010	1.000	133,113.750	56,999.449	76,114.301	0.000
D	1.012	1.000	622,109.250	266,183.274	355,925.976	0.000
I	1.015	0.500	299,878.250	128,226.541	171,651.709	0.000
UK	1.010	0.500	480,156.250	205,472.820	274,683.430	0.000
DK	1.018	0.500	52,414.250	22,434.066	29,980.184	0.000
ROW	1.017	0.000	7,391,900.250	3,168,374.600	4,223,525.650	0.000

12

THE EFFECT OF DEFICIT IN A MULTICOUNTRY MODEL WITH PERFECT MOBILITY OF CAPITAL

Rosella Levaggi

12.1 INTRODUCTION

The public sector plays an important role in determining the growth of a nation, although that role is not clear. For the Keynesian school, for example, the public sector promotes the growth of the economy through a reduction of undesirable phenomena such as unemployment, while other schools of thought, such as the neoclassicals, see the public sector as a Leviathan which drains resources from private production.[1] At present, fiscal policies aimed at reducing deficit are a very topical issue for Europe, since all the governments are trying to modify their expenditure and debt structure in order to be able to meet the Maastricht requirements.

The models developed by this literature focus on the macroeconomic issues, taking the consumption side of the economy as a reference point. However, the public sector plays an important role in the determination of the cost of money in a way that, perhaps, has not yet received due attention. The effects on the cost of production of a high deficit are a topical issue within the European Union in view of the new stage of economic integration we are going to enter. In an integrated structure with internationally mobile capital, firms should be able to hire this factor at a uniform price, but this is not true if countries incur different risks of insolvency. The presence of these costs has important repercussions on the terms of trade, hence the effects on international competitiveness.

The traditional approach to modelling risk is through the use of portfolio analysis of investment. In this context, the price of capital varies according to the risk involved, so that the *expected* price of capital is equal in all regions. This approach is not well suited to examining the effects on international competitiveness of a different price for capital; a better instrument to analyse these effects is an AGE multicountry structure which explicitly models all the trade exchanges between the countries considered, and highlights the comparative advantage in trade derived from the ability to reduce costs. The model presented here focuses on the production side, and studies the effects of deficit reduction on this sector using a multicountry general equilibrium structure, similar to the one proposed by Fehr *et al.* (1995) (the FRW model).

The core assumption of the model is that the presence of a high deficit affects the degree of international competitiveness through a mark-up on the price of hiring capital. A wedge is inserted between the remuneration received by the owner of the capital and the price paid by the firm hiring this factor of production. This assumption ensures that capital is mobile across countries, and that it is perfectly indifferent for any agent to invest either in the country of residence or abroad. However, the producer's price to hire capital varies according to the deficit of the country in which it is located.

The model is used to simulate the effects on the economy of fiscal policies aimed at reducing the burden of the deficit of the public sector. The work is organized as follows: in section 12.2 the theoretical problems of the effects of deficit and debt on the other macroeconomic variables are described; section 12.3 describes the modifications to the FRW multicountry model which allow a consideration of the cost of locating in countries with a high deficit; section 12.4 presents the simulations of the policies aimed at reducing the deficit; and finally in section 12.5 some conclusions are drawn.

12.2 THE EFFECT OF DEBT AND DEFICIT ON THE REAL ECONOMY

The theoretical and empirical literature studying the relationship between deficit, debt and other variables offers quite controversial results about their effects on the economy. Most authors have studied the behaviour of consumers to determine whether deficit can be considered as net wealth,[2] leading the analysis to the (in)famous problem of testing for the Ricardian equivalence between deficit and future taxes. The literature has followed different approaches including: the study of interest rate differentials; the demand for money; and consumption determinants.[3] The results of the empirical literature are controversial, but the most recent estimations seem to confirm a link between deficit, debt and other variables.[4] As further evidence, we can also observe that interest rates vary across countries, evidence which contrasts with the assumption of a perfect market for capital. These differences could be explained by a consideration of the risk of investment in different sectors of the economy, and by the specific behaviour of politicians who use interest rates as an objective variable in their re-election campaigns,[5] but these explanation are only partially convincing.

Most of the literature studies the effects of debt and deficit on economic growth, taking as a reference point the consumer's side, with models based on financial and fiscal considerations. In doing so, it fails to consider the effects on the cost of hiring capital by private firms, a very topical issue for the next stage of European economic integration. Most European countries will have to reduce their deficit by a sensible amount to comply with the rules approved in Maastricht, which fixes 3 per cent of GDP as the criterion for entering the next stage of European economic integration. Although fixing a ceiling on the deficit has been interpreted by the literature as a way of avoiding the burden of the deficit in one country being spread abroad, the drastic reduction of the public deficit might have unexpected consequences on all EU countries through an alteration of the terms of trade caused by the reduction of the cost of capital in some areas. A structure like an AGE multicountry model, which considers simultaneously the production and the consumption sides of the economy, allows a consideration of all these aspects.

The model is oversimplified in order to focus on aspects of international competitiveness; for this reason, and due to the static nature of the model, I will assume that the consumer has no fiscal illusion in the perception of the burden of deficit. In very simple terms, capital is a perfectly mobile factor of production; the owner is indifferent between investing in any of the countries considered, since the remuneration that he or she receives is equal. However, firms hire capital for a price that varies according to the level of public deficit in the country where they locate. This mark-up reflects the fact that a higher level of deficit implies that in the future taxation will be higher, and that possibly the level of infrastructure and services offered by the government might be reduced.[6]

To simulate this situation, a fictitious market has been considered in which capital services are bought at a uniform price and sold in the various nations at a different price. This wedge is the income accruing to a fictitious consumer; it represents the cost for each nation, in terms of real income, of the burden of the public sector. In more practical terms, the wedge between the producer's price and the consumer's price causes a deadweight loss, hence the income of this fictitious consumer represents a measure of the market failure itself. In a multicountry model, input prices play a crucial role because they alter the relative competitiveness of the national industries. If, as a result of a decrease in the level of deficit, the cost of capital is reduced in a country, we can expect the national consumers to be better off because there should be a rise in national production and a reduction in the deadweight loss. The national industries should also increase their degree of competitiveness, since the cost of capital should decrease. If most nations apply the same policy at once it is also quite important to determine the comparative advantages. The countries with a high deficit ratio will have to make a bigger fiscal effort, but they will considerably increase their degree of competitiveness. To reduce public deficit, two main policies are available, namely: (a) reduction of the public expenditure and /or reduction of transfer to families keeping the tax rate constant; (b) increase in taxation keeping the level of public expenditure constant.

These possibilities and their implications for the consumer's welfare will be studied using a multicountry applied general equilibrium model with a fairly basic standard structure[7] which is the best instrument to take account of all the interdependencies among the countries and sectors considered.

12.3 THE MODEL

The analysis of the effects of the reduction of the deficit will be done using the basic structure of the Fehr *et al.* (1995) FRW model, with some important modifications. This structure is quite standard; it comprises eight countries – France, Belgium and Luxembourg, the Netherlands, Germany, Italy, United Kingdom, Denmark and Rest of the World – in which fourteen commodities are produced. Both the production sectors and the consumption side in each country behave according to the preferences of a representative agent, which is assumed to be a price taker. Each region has a set of preferences, technology of production and a specific endowment of primary factors; the Armington assumption regulates trade between different countries.

The behaviour of consumers is described by a four-nest CES utility function regarding the choice between leisure and aggregate consumption, with various goods available on the market: imported and domestic commodities and commodities imported from different countries. The consumption of public goods is compulsory, but is made free of charge at the point of use. Public production enters the utility function in a separable and additive form.

On the production side, all the technologies exhibit constant returns to scale, an assumption which allows the modelling of unit output, and which implies that, given the assumption of zero profits, marginal costs are equal to average costs, which in turn are equal to the market price. Within each country, the model specifies thirteen commodities and fourteen sectors; the last sector represents the production of the public commodity. The production function consists of a four-nest Leontief–CES technology: composite intermediate commodities and value added, labour and capital, domestic and foreign intermediate goods, and intermediate goods from various countries. There are two primary production factors, namely labour and capital, of which each country has a specific and distinctive endowment. Labour is mobile between sectors, but not internationally; capital is instead freely mobile between sectors and across countries. The government side is modelled in a very schematic way. From the expenditure side, central government mainly provides the consumer with net lump sum transfers,[8] and pays for the production of public goods; an activity mainly financed by direct and indirect taxation.[9] The model has been calibrated using data for the year 1982. Let us now examine the novel features introduced in this standard structure.

Defining deficit

First gross transfers from the state to consumers have been divided into two separate categories: net transfers and deficit, which are linked to net transfers by the following relationship:

GTRSF = NTRSF + DEFICIT

The benchmark results are presented in Table 12.1. Data for budget deficits have been obtained from OECD National Accounts. The Rest of the World is assumed to have a balanced budget because it is a heterogeneous aggregation of nations with quite different characteristics from the point of view of their budget deficit. Furthermore, the policies that are going to be analysed are focused on the European countries considered, hence the decision to assume that the ROW has no deficit. In the benchmark, the equation defining the budget for the national government can be written as:

$$\text{inctax} rb_i(\text{R KSB}_i + W_i(\text{EB}_i - \text{L L}_i) - \text{allow } b_i) + \Sigma_{subn} \Sigma_{ii} \text{XD3}_{i,subn,ii} \text{PG}_{ii,subn}(1 + \text{TARB}_{i,subn,ii}) \text{TTB}_{i,subn} +$$

$$+ \Sigma_{subn} \Sigma_{ii} \text{XD3}_{i,subn} \text{PG}_{ii,subn} \text{TARB}_{i,subn,ii} + \Sigma_{subn} \text{XD2}_{i,subn} \text{PG}_{i,subn} \text{TTB}_{i,subn}$$

$$+ \Sigma_n \Sigma_{subn} \Sigma_{ii} \text{CIX2}_{i,n,subn,ii} \text{PG}_{ii,subn} \text{TARPB}_{i,subn,ii} + \Sigma_n \text{YQ}_{i,n} \text{PG}_{i,n} \frac{\text{TPB}_{i,n}}{(1 + \text{TPB}_{i,n})} + \text{DEFICITB}_i \text{QL}_i$$

$$-\text{GTRSFB}_i \text{QL}_i - \text{pubexp} b_i \text{ PG}_{i,14}$$

The notation is that used in Fehr *et al.* (1995).

Estimating the cost of deficit

The relationship between the cost of capital, in terms of interest rates, has been widely studied in the literature using portfolio analysis considerations or from a macroeconomic perspective. In this second area, the literature has

Table 12.1 Gross and net transfers to consumers (ECU '000)

	Net transfers	Deficit	Gross transfers
France	114,195.48366	18,971.29	133,166.7736
Belgium–Luxembourg	4,795.69340	9,523.15	14,318.8434
The Netherlands	9,907.27740	10,725.35	20,632.6274
Germany	31,975.50640	13,470.76	45,446.2664
Italy	12,089.08670	55,001.51	67,090.5967
United Kingdom	19,692.25350	16,978.68	36,670.9335
Denmark	10,590.02760	4,601.19	15,191.2176
ROW	1,014,905.91100	0.0	18,971.29

studied the problem of the relationship between interest rates and debt to test for the existence of a Ricardian equivalence. Other models have dealt with political influences over the interest rate. A discussion of these models is beyond the scope of this chapter; for the purpose of estimating the cost to firms of a high deficit, it will be assumed that the interest rate follows the pattern:[10]

$$i = \alpha + \beta_1 \frac{D}{Y} + \beta_2\Delta Y + \beta_3 P + \beta_4 U + \varepsilon_t$$

where i is the nominal interest rate, D is the deficit, Y is the GDP, P is a measure of inflation and U is unemployment. The equation derives from the literature on political cycles and the models used to estimate the relationship between debt and the interest rate. In this scheme the interest rate is seen as a variable which central government does not completely control. Inflation, the growth of the economy, unemployment and the need to finance public expenditure have an important role in determining the fluctuations in the interest rate.

The link with inflation is self-explanatory: the nominal interest rate will have to rise if inflation is increasing in order to keep the real interest rate at an acceptable level. Both unemployment and the growth of the economy are important reference parameters for monetary policies and, in most cases, their behaviour can influence a decision on the timing of a change in the level of the interest rate. If the economy is in a phase of recession and inflation is not too high, the interest rate might have to be lowered to improve investment, independently of any other political consideration. At the same time, the need to finance the deficit through bonds might alter the policy related to interest rate setting. In order to make the bonds competitive the government might try to offer a higher interest on the new issues, which will finally make the interest rate rise.

On the other hand – and Italy is a good example – the government is asking for a reduction in the interest rate in order to reduce the burden of interest payments on its budget. This model has been estimated using a panel of data for the countries included in the AGE model, for the period 1980–5. The structure of the residuals is the one described in Kmenta (1986), which allows for the presence of cross-section heteroscedasticity and timewise autoregression.

The model has been estimated using SHAZAM; a first attempt to estimate the above equation has shown that unemployment was not an important variable in determining the variation in the interest rate; a new model was estimated without considering this variable, the results of which are presented in Table 12.2.

The process presented here represents a broad simplification of the determinants of the differences in the price of capital. The capital modelled in the

Table 12.2 Parameters of the interest rate equation

α	0.0568
	(9.369)
D/Y	0.0487
	(3.592)
DY	−0.082
	(2.076)
P	0.7889
	(12.94)
R^2	0.7123
LL	120.70

AGE structure is physical capital, and as such it comprises any durable commodity used in the production process. The type of technology used is of the putty-putty type, that is, it is implicitly assumed that capital can be reinvested without incurring any sunk cost. By this definition, capital is very similar to a commodity that is traded on a financial market and whose price is represented by the interest rate. However, the two concepts need to be carefully distinguished when their price is considered. On the financial market the interest rate reflects the remuneration that is due to the owner of the capital for the risk undertaken in lending it, and the sacrifice made by not consuming it today; on the capital market the price of this input reflects its productivity. To incorporate the results of Table 12.2 into the AGE structure presented above we need to assume that the differences in remuneration on the financial market and on the capital market are related by a one-to-one fixed relationship. It will also be assumed that the only factor that determines a difference in the price of capital is the D/Y ratio.

On the financial market, the mark-up on the interest rate paid by an indebted country can be defined as:

$$MUP_i = \frac{i_{d_i}}{i_{nd}}$$

where i_{di} and i_{nd} are the interest rate for country i and for a country with no debt respectively. With reference to the previous equation the two interest rates can be written as:

$$i_{nd} = \alpha$$

$$i_{d_i} = \alpha * \beta_1 \frac{D_i}{Y_i}$$

Table 12.3 Benchmark price on capital with mark-up

F	1.020
BB	1.088
N	1.056
DD	1.014
II	1.104
UK	1.029
DK	1.039
ROW	1.000

If D/Y is zero, the price of capital is one, as it is for the ROW, which is assumed to have a balanced budget.

For countries with a positive level of deficit, the cost of capital varies according to the D/Y ratio. In formal terms, the price of capital can be written as:

$$R_i = 1(1 + MUP_i)$$

The benchmark values for the cost of capital are presented in Table 12.3; they have been obtained using the intercept value of 0.0568 and 0.0487 as the value of the derivative of $\partial i/\partial(D/Y)$.

The production side

The introduction of the deficit alters the decisions of the firms about their shares of labour and capital. The functional relationship used at this level is of the CES type, and can be written as:

$$VA_{i,n} = \left[\delta_{2_{i,n}} LD_{i,n}^{(\sigma_2-1)/\sigma_2} + (1 - \delta_{2_{i,n}}) KD_{i,n}^{(\sigma_2-1)/\sigma_2}\right]^{\sigma_2/(\sigma_2-1)}$$

The cost function can be written as:

$$CVAD_{i,n} = \left[\delta_{2_{i,n}} W_i^{(\sigma_2-1)/\sigma_2} + (1 - \delta_{2_{i,n}}) R (1 + MUP_i)^{(\sigma_2-1)/\sigma_2}\right]^{\sigma_2/(\sigma_2-1)} VA_{i,n}$$

Defining PVAD as the unit cost of the output of this second nest, we can write that:

$$PVAD_{i,n} = \left[\delta_{2_{i,n}} W_i^{(\sigma_2-1)/\sigma_2} + (1 - \delta_{2i,n}) R (1 + MUP_i)^{(\sigma_2-1)/\sigma_2}\right]^{\sigma_2/(\sigma_2-1)}$$

so that the demand for capital can be written as:

$$KDD_{i,n} = (1 - \delta_{2_{i,n}})VA_{i,n} \left[\frac{PVAD_{i,n}}{R(1 + MUP_i)}\right]^{\sigma_2}$$

The consumer side

Consumers take their decisions on the basis of their current income, i.e. all the decisions are taken within a static context, an assumption that has important consequences for their perception of the deficit. Consumers, in deciding their consumption patterns and the hours they are devoting to work, take account of the net income that accrues to them from the state. Hence in their budget constraint consumers take account of net transfers. On the utility front, the static model does not take account of any intertemporal decision, so that a deficit does not affect the utility of the representative consumer. Another possible explanation for considering net transfers in the budget constraint is the acceptance of the Ricardian equivalence between the deficit and future taxation.

The second important modification to the consumer side is related to the introduction of a fictitious consumer in each country. This consumer receives the difference between the remuneration paid by the producers to hire capital and the income paid to the consumers that own it. The income YF_i of this agent can be written as:

$$YF_i = \Sigma_n MUP_i * KDD_{i,n}$$

This income is allocated following the rules of a Cobb–Douglas function to buy products from the different sectors in each country, that is, the fictitious consumer maximises the following utility function:

$$UF_i = \alpha_{i,n} \; \Sigma_i \; \ln \; (XD2_{i,n})$$

subject to the budget constraint:

$$\Sigma_n \; PG_{i,n} XD2_{i,n} = YF_i$$

where PG_i is the price of good i and $XD2_2$ is the demand for good i produced in the same country of origin.

The parameters of the Cobb–Douglas function have been calibrated to guarantee that the new benchmark exactly replicates the value of the original one. The use of a Cobb–Douglas function might give some distributional problems in simulation. For this reason, the parameters have been calibrated so as to avoid cross-country debt effects. The procedure used can be described as follows: (a) for each region the income derived from the countries risk has been summed up across sectors; (b) The consumption function of this sector has then been determined using a two-stage procedure. In the first procedure, the fixed coefficient terms for each production have been determined using the following expression:

$$\alpha_{i,n} = \frac{(a1D_{i,n} - a1_{i,n})}{Y_i}$$

where $a1D$ is the new benchmark value added after the mark-up on the cost of capital has been taken into account, and $a1$ is the original benchmark value added of the FRW model.

The demand for each good from this new sector can then be determined using the following formula:

$$PG_{i,n}XD2_{i,n} = \alpha_{i,n} * Y_i$$

12.4 SIMULATIONS

The model will now be used to study the likely effects of a series of counter-factual fiscal policies that could be applied by EU states to meet the Maastricht requirements. The focus of the modelling exercise is on the effects of deficit on the cost of hiring capital; the simulations will, accordingly, study the change in the cost associated with a reduction in the deficit. I will compare the effects of different fiscal policies aimed at reducing the deficit under two alternative situations in which (a) the mark-up on the cost of capital is fixed at its benchmark level; (b) the mark-up on the cost of capital decreases as deficit is reduced.

All the simulations have been performed using a target value equal to the limit set by the Maastricht agreement, i.e. 3 per cent of GDP. The values refer to the situation in 1982, and the targets for deficit in that year are presented in Table 12.4.

The starting points for the various countries are rather different. On one hand we have nations such as Germany which will not have to alter their deficit since they are already within the Maastricht limit. At the other end of the spectrum we have countries such as Italy, which will have to reduce its

Table 12.4 Actual level of deficit and its target (ECU '000)

	Deficit	Target
F	18,971.29	14,284.22
B	9,523.00	2,455.35
N	10,725.00	3,628.26
DD	13,470.00	13,470.76
II	55,001.51	10,467.82
UK	16,978.68	13,715.36
DK	4,601.19	1,313.76
ROW	0.00	0.00

deficit by about 70 per cent. Some countries will have to make a bigger fiscal effort to reach their target, but they will be better off in their trade terms with the other countries because their degree of international competitiveness will improve.

The fiscal effort that countries have to make might alter the relative prices of the goods they sell as well as the disposable income of their representative consumers. However, if, as in the model proposed here, deficit determines the price paid for capital by firms, the variations in the deficit level will also alter the terms of trade of the various nations and, as a consequence, the relative advantage gained by each country in producing or buying commodities abroad.

Reduction of the gross transfer

The first simulation considered is the reduction of the deficit through a decrease in the transfer to the private sector. In this case, the budget constraint for the public sector can be written as:

$$\text{inctax} rb_i(R\ KSB_i + W_i(EB_i - L\ L_i) - \text{allow } b_i) + \Sigma_{subn}\Sigma_{ii}\ XD3_{i,subn,ii}\ PG_{ii,subn}(1 + TARB_{i,subn,ii})TTB_{i,subn}$$

$$+ \Sigma_{subn}\Sigma_{ii}\ XD3_{i,subn}\ PG_{ii,subn}\ TARB_{i,subn,ii} + \Sigma_{subn}\ XD2_{i,subn}\ PG_{i,subn}\ TTB_{i,subn}$$

$$+ \Sigma_n\Sigma_{subn}\Sigma_{ii}\ CIX2_{i,n,subn,ii}\ PG_{ii,subn}\ TARPB_{i,subn,ii} + \Sigma_n\ YQ_{i,n}PG_{i,n}\frac{TPB_{i,n}}{(1 + TPB_{i,n})} + TARGET_iQL_i$$

$$-GTRSF_iQL_i - PUBEXPB_i\ PG_{i,14}$$

In the first simulation considered, in which it will be assumed that the risk is invariant, the equation determining the mark-up on the price of capital will be written as:

$$R_i = 1(1 + MUPB_i)$$

where $MUPB_i$ is the value of the mark-up in the benchmark position. In the model only one consumer in each country is considered, who takes decisions on the basis of the net transfer received by the state; hence, the final equilibrium will be invariant. In this case, in fact, the net transfer does not change since a simple substitution between gross transfer and deficit is operated.

This model is quite important as a reference point to compare the other results, since the fiscal policy applied is neutral, both from the producer and the consumer side. Let us now examine the case in which the cost of capital varies according to the level of public deficit. The results for this simulation are presented in Table 12.5.

Table 12.5 Results for the simulation with a reduction in gross transfer and a change in the cost of capital

	F	B	N	DD	II	UK	DK	ROW
W	1	0.987	1,001	0.999	0.992	1.001	0.996	0.998
R	0.998							
GTRSFB[a]	33,166	4,318	632	5,446	7,090	6,670	5,191	14,905
NTRSFB[a]	14,195	4,795	9,907	31,975	12,089	19,692	10,590	1,014,905
GTRSF[a]	138,082	11,876	21,791	48,078	59,030	40,943	14,551	1,013,236
NTRSF[a]	114,022	4,866	9,860	31,900	12,324	19,622	10,600	1,013,236
PUBEXPB[a]	98,500	16,200	22,600	110,000	58,700	106,600	14,300	1,658,768
PUBEXP[a]	98,500	16,200	22,600	110,000	58,700	106,600	14,300	1,658,768
INCTAXRB[a]	0.052	0.168	0.098	0.179	0.107	0.182	0.271	0.336
INCTAXR[a]	0.052	0.168	0.098	0.179	0.107	0.182	0.271	0.336
MUPB	0.020	0.088	0.056	0.014	0.104	0.029	0.039	0.000
MUP	0.016	0.023	0.019	0.014	0.020	0.023	0.011	0.000
QL	1.001	0.989	1.001	0.999	0.989	1.002	0.995	0.998
TOT	1.058	1.047	0.927	0.909	1.098	1.002	1.104	0.970
EV	−1,717.216	362.3	−435.041	−328.541	2,594.640	−723.901	102.080	−233.694

Notes

W = wage rate; R = price for capital; GTRSFB = gross transfer in benchmark; NTRSFB = net transfers in benchmark; GTRSF = gross transfer in simulation; NTRSF = net transfers in simulation; PUBEXPB = public expenditure in benchmark; PUBEXP = public expenditure in simulation; INCTAXRB = income tax rate in benchmark; INCTAXR = income tax rate in simulation; MUPB = mark-up on the price of capital in benchmark; MUPB = mark-up on the price of capital in simulation; QL = Laspeyere price index; TOT = terms of trade; EV = equivalent variation.

[a] In ECU '000.

As we can note, the situation has changed dramatically. As a general rule, the nations which had to reduce their deficit in a more drastic way are now better off, because their level of international competitiveness has improved. This simulation, which is neutral from the fiscal point of view, gives an idea of the comparative advantages of the various nations gained by reducing their deficits. The states with an initially high deficit will get most of the benefits; the reduction in the cost of capital means that the potential production is going to be less expensive, and this favours international competitiveness.

The cost of hiring capital in countries such as Italy is sensibly decreasing. In the benchmark situation, in fact, the mark-up was about 10 per cent of the cost of capital, while in the counterfactual equilibrium it will be reduced to about 2 per cent. Due to the reduction in the cost of capital, these nations will be able to hire a labour force at a relatively cheap price, and this will enhance their competitive advantage. The international price of capital is going to be slightly reduced, and this might be the effect of the reduction in the deadweight loss suffered by the economies.

The results of this simulation can be better interpreted if we look at the two indices QL and TOT. In particular, QL is the Laspeyere price index, i.e:

$$QL = \frac{\Sigma_{subn} \, \Sigma_{ii} \, A3_{subn,ii,i} \, PG_{ii,subn}}{\Sigma_{subn} \, \Sigma_{ii} \, A3_{subn,ii,i}}$$

where A3 is the quantity of each good that is bought by the consumer as a benchmark. Given the assumption of unit prices in benchmark, this index is equal to one in the initial situation.

The other important element to take into account when explaining the results of this simulation are TOT, or, more precisely, the change in the terms of trade. This index can be defined as:

$$TOT = \frac{\dfrac{PM_S}{PM_B}}{\dfrac{PX_S}{PX_B}}$$

where:

$$PM = \Sigma_n \, \Sigma_{subn} \, \Sigma_{ii} \, CIX2_{i,n,subn,ii} \, PG_{ii,subn} + \Sigma_{ii} \, \Sigma_{subn} \, XD3_{i,subn,ii} \, PG_{ii,subn}$$

$$PX = \Sigma_{ii} \, \Sigma_{subn} \, XD3_{i,n,subn,i} \, PG_{ii,subn} + \Sigma_{ii} \, \Sigma_n \, \Sigma_{subn} \, CIX2_{ii,n,subn,i} \, PG_{i,subn}$$

and the indices B and S represent the evaluation of PM and PX at benchmark and in the simulation respectively.

PM represents the money evaluation of the goods that have been imported, while PX is the corresponding value for export. TOT is then the ratio of the variation in the volume of imports, compared with the equivalent change in the volume of exports. If this index is above one, imports have increased more than exports, i.e. the country in the simulation is more dependent on other countries. If the value of TOT is greater than one, the terms of trade for the country considered have deteriorated, but this element alone might not be used to determine the sign of the equivalent variation for the consumer. It is, in fact, the joint effect of TOT and QL which ultimately determines the comparative advantage of the consumers in the various countries. The variation in QL represents a measure of the change in the purchasing power of income, and its value ultimately depends on the preferences of the consumer considered. Most countries with a negative equivalent variation experience an increase in the general level of prices.

A reduction in public expenditure

In this second simulation, a reduction in the quantity of public goods offered to the consumer is considered as a means to reduce public debt; the budget constraint can be written as:

$\text{inctax} rb_i (\text{R KSB}_i * W_i(\text{EB}_i - \text{L L}_i) - \text{allow } b_i) * \Sigma_{subn} \Sigma_{ii} \text{XD3}_{i,subn,ii} \text{PG}_{ii,subn}(1 + \text{TARB}_{i,subn,ii}) \text{TTB}_{i,subn}$

$+ \Sigma_{subn} \Sigma_{ii} \text{XD3}_{i,subn,ii} \text{PG}_{ii,subn} \text{TARB}_{i,subn,ii} + \Sigma_{subn} \text{XD2}_{i,subn} \text{PG}_{i,subn} \text{TTB}_{i,subn}$

$+ \Sigma_n \Sigma_{subn} \Sigma_{ii} \text{CIX2}_{i,n,subn,ii} \text{PG}_{ii,subn} \text{TARPB}_{i,subn,ii} + \Sigma_n \text{YQ}_{i,n} \text{PG}_{i,n} \dfrac{\text{TPB}_{i,n}}{(1 + \text{TPB}_{i,n})} + \text{TARGET}_i \text{QL}_i$

$-\text{GTRSFB}_i \text{QL}_i - \text{PUBEXP}_i \text{PG}_{i,14}$

In the first simulation considered, it will be assumed that the risk is fixed at its benchmark level. In this model PUBEXP is measured in real terms, and for this reason its reduction might be different from the corresponding reduction in the deficit. The first impression from Table 12.6, could be that all the countries but the ROW are better off when this policy is applied, but the equivalent variations are not a good measure of the change in consumer welfare in this model.

The commodity that is produced by the public sector is sold, for a marginal amount, to the private sector, and as such enters in the production function of the thirteen productive processes considered. The main bulk of real public expenditure is represented by the production of public goods in their traditional definition. They are offered to the consumer free of charge, and their consumption is compulsory.

The specific form of the utility function allows public goods to enter in the utility process in a separable and additive way. Thus, all the other consumption decisions are not affected by the level of public expenditure[11] and it might not be considered in the utility function of the consumer.

This assumption does not alter the interpretation of equivalent variations

Table 12.6 Results for the simulation with a reduction in public expenditure and no change in the cost of capital

	F	B	N	DD	II	UK	DK	ROW
W	1.000	0.930	0.970	1.004	0.876	1.001	0.971	0.995
R	1.006							
GTRSFB	133,166	14,318	20,632	45,446	67,090	36,670	15,191	1,014,905
NTRSFB	114,195	4,795	9,907	31,975	12,089	19,692	10,590	1,014,905
GTRSF	133,166	14,318	20,632	45,446	67,090	36,670	15,191	1,014,905
NTRSF	118,342	11,863	17,004	31,976	56,623	22,956	13,877	1,014,905
PUBEXPB	98,500	16,200	22,600	110,000	58,700	106,600	14,300	1,658,768
PUBEXP	94,921	8,970	15,797	110,234	14,110.6	103,462	11,087	1,652,457
D PUBEX	−3,579	−7,230	−6,803	234	−44,589	−3,138	−3,213	−6,311
MUPB	0.020	0.088	0.056	0.014	0.104	0.029	0.039	0.000
MUP	0.020	0.088	0.056	0.014	0.104	0.029	0.039	0.000
INCTAXRB	0.052	0.168	0.098	0.179	0.107	0.182	0.271	0.336
INCTAXR	0.052	0.168	0.098	0.179	0.107	0.182	0.271	0.336
QL	1.003	0.985	0.995	1.004	0.970	1.003	0.994	1.005
TOT	1.058	1.043	0.925	0.910	1.094	1.001	1.103	0.971
EV	4,428.970	5,906.630	6,523.443	362.959	39,777.371	3,183.460	3,093.041	−30,857.790

Note: For notation, see Table 12.5.

for simulations in which the real level of public expenditure is kept constant; when it is changed account should be taken of the variation in the utility level and the consumer be compensated for this loss. The money evaluation of this loss is an arbitrary operation, since its amount depends on the evaluation of the public good made by the consumer, but the model does not offer any element to make such a decision. For this reason, I have not included in the equivalent variation the change in public expenditure. However, it must be clear that the sign of the variation itself, in most cases, will be determined by the value attached to the public good. As we can note from Table 12.6, the wage rate tends to decrease in countries with a higher deficit. If we were to consider a one-to-one-correspondence in the utility received from public expenditure, we could conclude that the countries with high deficits are worse off in the simulations since they experience a bigger decrease in public expenditure than the increase in the equivalent variation.

Let us now turn to the discussion of the model in which the cost of capital varies according to the level of the deficit. The results of the simulation are presented in Table 12.7. When the mark-up on the cost of capital is reduced as a result of the reduction of the deficit, there is a comparative increase in the welfare of the countries considered. This advantage is more important for those nations for which the reduction in the deficit has been more sensible. This is partly due to the reduction in the deadweight loss and to an improvement in the price index. Wages in the nations that reduce their deficit in a more sensible way are decreasing comparatively more than in the previous simulation. If we adopt the same criterion to evaluate public expenditure, all the nations are better off. In this case, as with the model presented in the previous section, the countries with a high deficit experience a reduction in

Table 12.7 Results for the simulation with a reduction in public expenditure and a change in the cost of capital

	F	B	N	DD	II	UK	DK	ROW
W	1.000	0.926	0.958	1.008	1.010	1.001	0.964	1.006
R	1.004							
GTRSFB	133,166	14,318	20,632	45,446	67,090	36,670	15,191	1,014,905
NTRSFB	114,195	4,795	99,072	31,975	12,089	19,692	10,590	1,014,905
GTRSF	133,166	14,318	20,632	45,446	67,090	36,670	15,191	1,014,905
NTRSF	118,342	11,863	17,004	31,976	56,623	22,956	13,877	1,014,905
PUBEXPB	98,500	16,200	22,600	110,000	58,700	106,600	14,300	1,658,768
PUBEXP	95,182.449	9,720	16,059	110,448.09	35,220	103,554	11,222.892	1,663,625
D PUBEXP	−3,317.551	−6,480	−6,541	448.09	−23,480	−3,046	−3,077.108	4,857
INCTAXRB	0.052	0.168	0.098	0.179	0.107	0.182	0.271	0.336
INCTAXR	0.052	0.168	0.098	0.179	0.107	0.182	0.271	0.336
MUPB	0.020	0.088	0.056	0.014	0.104	0.029	0.039	0.000
MUP	0.016	0.023	0.019	0.014	0.020	0.023	0.011	0.000
QL	0.999	0.963	0.974	1.003	0.963	1.000	0.980	1.005
TOT	1.058	1.037	0.921	0.910	1.095	1.002	1.100	0.971
EV		6,325.119	7,502.846	9,139.959	1,448.340	61,450.026	4,207.280	3,623.050	671.048

Note: For notation, see Table 12.5.

the cost of labour, which is proportionally higher than in other countries. The cost of capital at international level is increasing slightly, but in general all countries are better off. As we can note, comparing Tables 12.6 and 12.7, the equivalent variations are higher in the second table and the reduction in public expenditure is considerably lower.

An increase in direct taxation

Finally, let us consider a reduction of the deficit through an increase in the general taxation. It could be important to remember here that a general tax on income and capital is levied at a constant rate. A minimum of progressivity in the system is guaranteed by the presence of an allowance on income, i.e. of a part of income which is not considered in the taxable income. The budget constraint in this case can be written as:

$$\text{inctax} r_i (R\ KSB_i * W_i (EB_i - L\ L_i) - \text{allow}\ b_i) * \Sigma_{subn}\ \Sigma_{ii}\ XD3_{i,subn,ii}\ PG_{ii,subn}(1 + TARB_{i,subn,ii})TTB_{i,subn}$$

$$+ \Sigma_{subn}\ \Sigma_{ii}\ XD3_{i,subn,ii}\ PG_{ii,subn}\ TARB_{i,subn,ii} + \Sigma_{subn}\ XD2_{i,subn}\ PG_{i,subn}\ TTB_{i,subn}$$

$$+ \Sigma_n\ \Sigma_{subn}\ \Sigma_{ii}\ CIX2_{i,n,subn,ii}\ PG_{ii,subn}\ TARPB_{i,subn,ii} + \Sigma_n\ YQ_{i,n}PG_{i,n}\frac{TPB_{i,n}}{(1 + TPB_{i,n})} + TARGET_iQL_i$$

$$-GTRSFB_iQL_i - PUBEXPB_i\ PG_{i,14}$$

In the first simulation considered, it will be assumed that the risk is fixed at its benchmark level; the results are presented in Table 12.8.

In this first model considered, the fiscal policy of reducing the deficit has important effects on the consumption side of the economy considered. The

Table 12.8 Results for the simulation with an increase in direct taxation and no change in the cost of capital

	F	B	N	DD	II	UK	DK	ROW
W	1.000	1.109	1.032	0.996	1.113	1.008	1.069	0.996
R	0.996							
GTRSFB	133,166	14,318	20,632	45,446	67,090	36,670	15,191	1,014,905
NTRSFB	114,195	4,795	99,072	31,975	12,089	19,692	10,590	1,014,905
GTRSF	133,166	14,318	20,632	45,446	67,090	36,670	15,191	1,014,905
NTRSF	118,342	11,863	17,004	31,976	56,623	22,956	13,877	1,014,905
PUBEXPB	98,500	16,200	22,600	110,000	58,700	106,600	14,300	1,658,768
PUBEXP	98,500	16,200	22,600	110,000	58,700	106,600	14,300	1,658,768
INCTAXRB	0.052	0.168	0.098	0.179	0.107	0.182	0.271	0.336
INCTAX	0.060	0.276	0.150	0.180	0.252	0.195	0.347	0.337
MUPB	0.020	0.088	0.056	0.014	0.104	0.029	0.039	0.000
MUP	0.020	0.088	0.056	0.014	0.104	0.029	0.039	0.000
QL	0.998	1.026	1.008	0.998	1.027	1.002	1.020	0.997
TOT	1.057	1.060	0.927	0.908	1.104	1.002	1.109	0.970
EV	−928.414	1,190.468	127.103	−1,080.387	1,510.655	−192.107	26.724	−4,467.600

Note: For notation, see Table 12.5.

Table 12.9 Results for the simulation with an increase in direct taxation and a change in the cost of capital

	F	B	N	DD	II	UK	DK	ROW
W	1.000	1.075	1.017	0.996	1.073	1.006	1.056	0.998
R	0.998							.
GTRSFB	133,166	14,318	20,632	45,446	67,090	36,670	15,191	1,014,905
NTRSFB	114,195	4,795	9,907	31,975	12,089	19,692	10,590	1,014,905
GTRSF	133,166	14,318	20,632	45,446	67,090	36,670	15,191	1,014,905
NTRSF	118,342	11,863	17,004	31,976	56,623	22,956	13,877	1,014,905
PUBEXPB	98,500	16,200	22,600	110,000	58,700	106,600	14,300	1,658,768
PUBEXP	98,500	16,200	22,600	110,000	58,700	106,600	14,300	1,658,768
INCTAXR	0.052	0.168	0.098	0.179	0.107	0.182	0.271	0.336
INCTAX	0.060	0.272	0.148	0.179	0.244	0.194	0.344	0.337
MUPB	0.020	0.088	0.056	0.014	0.104	0.029	0.039	0.000
MUP	0.016	0.023	0.019	0.014	0.020	0.023	0.011	0.000
QL	0.996	0.997	0.987	0.996	0.976	0.999	1.005	0.998
TOT	1.058	1.037	0.921	0.910	1.095	1.002	1.100	0.971
EV	1,731.580	2,676.595	3,077.031	304.095	18,190.290	914.884	674.873	40.027

Note: For notation, see Table 12.5.

substitution of deficit with higher taxation has, in fact, the effect of increasing the net lump sum transfer to the consumer, while at the same time his or her disposable income is reduced by the higher income tax. The wage rate usually increases, and this increase is proportional to the reduction in the deficit. This policy has important redistribution effects that cannot be considered in this model due to the schematic representation of the consumer side. In general, the countries which have to reduce their deficit less have a negative equivalent variation. The disposable income for these consumers is probably decreasing, since the level of wage rate in these states is decreasing more than the general price level.

When the cost of capital is made variable according to the level of the deficit, the counterfactual situation of the fiscal policy could be described as in Table 12.9. Also in this case, the results present an improvement in consumers' welfare. This is due to the reduction of the deadweight loss created by the wedge between the price of the capital paid by the firms and that received by the consumer. The wage rate is still increasing in the countries experiencing a sensible reduction in the deficit, but the difference is far less important than in the previous model.

In particular, in this last simulation, all the equivalent variations are positive, even if some are rather small. It seems, then, that this policy could be considered to improve the welfare of all the actors involved.

12.5 CONCLUSIONS

To explain the role of the government and its policies in influencing economic growth has been the objective of many theoretical and empirical studies, the results of which are quite controversial. The literature has, in particular, focused on research into the effects of budget deficits on the economy, examining the consumer side with particular reference to the fiscal illusion that deficit could create. However, budget deficits, especially when they are consolidated in debt, can also have important consequences for the productive side of the economy. The effects of deficits and of government policies aimed at reducing their size are very topical issues for Europe nowadays, in view of the new stage of the process of economic integration.

In this chapter, I have assumed that deficit can influence the cost of hiring capital; in this situation any fiscal policy aimed at reducing the level of the deficit will also have important consequences for the degree of international competitiveness of the countries considered. An AGE multicountry model is one of the most suitable instruments to analyse the effects of such policies, because it allows account to be taken of all the relationships between sectors and countries in the model.

I have presented the simulation results of counterfactual fiscal policies that could be put forth by EU nations to meet the Maastricht requirement of reducing their deficit to 3 per cent of GDP, using a standard multicountry AGE model. The fiscal policies analysed have been the reduction of gross transfers, a cutback in public expenditure and an increase in the rate of direct income taxation, in the two alternative situations in which the mark-up on the cost of capital is fixed at its benchmark level and the mark-up on the cost of capital decreases as deficit is reduced.

The comparison of these alternative simulations highlights the effects on production of the fiscal policies considered. The first simulation, namely a reduction in gross transfers, is, due to the structure of the model, neutral from the consumer's side and takes account of the effects of international competitiveness alone. In this case, those nations with a relatively high deficit will be better off when their deficit is reduced. A reduction in public expenditure has important effects on consumers and producers, but the welfare effects of these policies might be very difficult to evaluate, since the value attached to public expenditure can only be arbitrary.

Finally, an increase in direct income taxation might have positive effects on all the countries considered in the hypothesis that the mark-up on capital is reduced as a consequence of the reduction in public deficit. In conclusion, the model shows that, in evaluating fiscal policies, it might be very important to take account of the effects of government activity on the productive side of the economy.

NOTES

1 On this point, see Cullis and Jones (1983).
2 See Barro (1974, 1989), Bernheim (1989) and Feldstein (1982).
3 See Evans (1985), Gulley (1994). For a review of the different approaches, see Levaggi (1996).

4 See Levaggi (1996) and Damalagas (1994) for more details.
5 In this context there is positive evidence of the influence of a political monetary cycle on the demand for money and on interest rates. For a review of this literature, see Grieg (1989) and Ito and Park (1988).
6 The level of economic growth itself could also be severely impaired by public deficit, both because of the resources drained by this sector from the production side of the economy and for other reasons, such as having to pay for raw materials in foreign currency due to the continuous change in the rate of exchange.
7 The structure has been taken from the model developed by Fehr et al. (1995), but it differs in some important aspects, which will be explained at length in the next section.
8 The net lump-sum transfer is given by the difference between transfers to households and deficit.
9 And, marginally, by the sale to firms of a part of the public good produced.
10 The model derives from Ito and Park (1988).
11 At least in relative terms. The only effect that public goods can have on private consumption is through an exogenous change in the level of public goods produced, which is financed through a change in the disposable income of the consumer. If disposable income varies, so will the quantities of goods brought, but this is not a direct effect brought about by the level (or its change) of public goods produced.

REFERENCES

Barro, R.J. (1974), 'Are government bonds net wealth?', Journal of Political Economy, 82: 1095–117.
Barro, R.J. (1989), 'The Ricardian approach to budget deficits', Journal of Economic Perspectives, 3: 37–54.
Bernheim, B.D. (1989), 'A neoclassical perspective on budget deficits', Journal of Economic Perspectives, 3: 55–72.
Cullis, J. and Jones, P.R. (1983), Microeconomics and the Public Economy: A Defence of Leviathan, Oxford: Basil Blackwell.
Dalamagas, B. (1994), 'The tax versus debt controversy in a multivariate cointegrating system', Applied Economics, 26: 1197–1206.
Dornbush, R. and Fisher, S. (1985), Macroeconomia, Bologna: Il Mulino.
Evans, P. (1985), 'Do large deficits produce high interest rates?', American Economic Review, 75: 68–87.
Fehr, H., Rosenberg, C. and Wiegard, W. (1995), Welfare Effects of Value-added Tax Harmonization in Europe: A CGE Analysis, Berlin: Springer Verlag.
Feldstein, M. (1982), 'Government deficits and aggregate demand', Journal of Monetary Economics, 9: 1–20.
Grieg, K. (1989), 'On the existence of a political monetary cycle', American Journal of Political Science 33(2): 376–89.
Gulley, O.D. (1994) 'An empirical test of the effects of government deficits on money demand', Applied Economics, 26: 239–47.
Ito, T. and Park, J.H. (1988), 'Political business cycles in the parliamentary system', Economic Letters, 27: 233–8.
Kennedy, P. (1992), A Guide to Econometrics, Oxford: Basil Blackwell.

Kmenta, (1996), *Elements of Econometrics*, 2nd edn, London: Macmillan.

Levaggi, R. (1996), 'La relazione fra debito e tasso di interesse', *Studi Economici*, 58(1): 107–24.

Shazam (1993), *User's Reference Manual, version 7.0*, New York: McGraw-Hill.

Part V

VAT AND INCOME TAX REFORM

13

GERMAN INCOME
TAX REFORMS

Separating efficiency from redistribution

*Hans Fehr and Wolfgang Wiegard**

13.1 INTRODUCTION

In spring 1996, a very heated debate began about reforming the income tax system in Germany. Several committees of scientific and political experts were established; for more than six months, the newspapers were full of proposals, comments and rebuttals; at the time of writing this chapter, the discussion has not yet come to an end.

There are, indeed, good reasons for reforming the German income tax system. For example, marginal tax rates are rather high in Germany when compared with its main international competitors. Moreover, there are many allowances and deductions, making the tax system non-transparent and fostering misuse. Here we do not contribute to this discussion by adding an additional reform proposal: there are already too many kinds of proposals. Our concern, rather, is that the current debate almost exclusively focuses on efficiency effects and efficiency reasoning; (re)distributional issues are more or less neglected and do not seem to play any noticeable role in the final decisions to be made. We feel that the strong emphasis placed on efficiency is too narrow a point of view. We therefore wish to ask in this chapter what, on the one hand, are the efficiency effects of some recent tax reform proposals in Germany, and what are the redistributional ones, on the other. More precisely, in a computable general equilibrium (CGE) framework, we numerically compute the welfare effects of tax reforms for different generations and income classes within a generation and decompose these welfare effects into efficiency and redistributional components.

The main findings of our simulation exercises are:

* The authors wish to thank Volker Grzimek for his research assistance.

1   Redistributional effects dominate efficiency effects in almost all cases. Averaged over all simulation runs, about 70 per cent of total welfare changes are due to redistribution.

2   For the tax reform proposals considered in our chapter (and to be described later), the differences in aggregate efficiency effects are relatively small. Their main differences are with respect to intergenerational and intragenerational redistribution. Hence, when choosing between the different tax reform proposals, redistributional effects should count more than pure efficiency considerations.

Our general conclusion is that the time is ripe for a shift to a more balanced view when evaluating tax reforms, including efficiency and redistribution as two equally important policy goals.

To substantiate our claim, we proceed as follows: in section 13.2 we briefly describe the present income tax in Germany and outline three different tax reform proposals. We then sketch the economic model on which our numerical calculations are based. In section 13.4 we analytically decompose the total welfare changes of tax reforms into their efficiency and redistributional parts. After that we present the numerical results of our simulations and offer some economic explanations. We conclude by pointing out some limitations of our approach.

13.2 INCOME TAXATION AND RECENT TAX REFORM PROPOSALS IN GERMANY

Some main features of current income taxation

Personal income tax is the central element of the German tax system. In 1995, income tax revenue totalled DM326.4 billion, corresponding to 40 per cent of total tax receipts. In comparison, value added tax, as the second largest tax, generated a revenue of DM234.6 billion, which is about 29 per cent of total tax revenue.

The German income tax is comprehensive, taxing income from various sources including wages, capital income, income from agriculture and forestry, from trade or business, from self-employment, from rentals and royalties and from 'other' income such as parts of pensions or capital gains if realised within some limited periods of time. On the other hand, the allowances granted for different income sources are asymmetric. There is a special wage- or salary-earner's standard allowance of DM2,000 annually, unless the taxpayer has incurred higher expenses. Most notably, for capital yields in the form of interest income and dividends, there is a special tax exemption of DM6,100/12,200 annually for single persons/married couples. Due to this high exemption, the interest income of about 80 per cent of all savers remains untaxed in Germany. This is reflected in revenues from taxing the various sources of income. Whereas the wage income tax in 1995 amounted to DM282.7 billion and to about 87 per cent of total income tax, the tax on interest income totalled only DM12.8 billion, i.e. 4 per cent of total income tax revenue. As a final remark we note that, since 1993, the capital yields tax on interest income is provisionally withheld at source at a rate of 30 per cent (or 35 per cent in the case of over-the-counter transactions),[1] with the final tax liability being determined in the course of the annual tax assessment.

Turning to the tax rate schedule, the T 96 – the tax schedule valid in 1996 – divides taxable income into four different zones. The first consists of a basic personal allowance of DM12,095/24,191 annually for single persons/ married couples. If taxable income falls below this allowance, the tax liability is zero. In the second zone, marginal tax rates rise linearly from 25.9 per cent on taxable income in excess of the basic allowance, to 33.5 per cent on taxable income of DM55,727/111,455. This income range is called the first linear-progressive zone. The adjacent second linear-progressive zone includes taxable income up to DM120,041/240,083 and imposes marginal tax rates increasing linearly between 33.5 per cent and 53 per cent. In the fourth zone, the marginal tax rate on taxable income of above DM120.042/240,084 (single persons/married couples) is constant at the rate of 53 per cent. This fourth zone is sometimes called the upper proportional zone. Figure 13.1 illustrates the marginal and average tax rates for the T 96 for single persons.

Reforming the income tax: why and how

For most industrialized countries, the 1980s may be characterized as a decade of tax reform. Despite considerable differences in detail, tax reforms almost

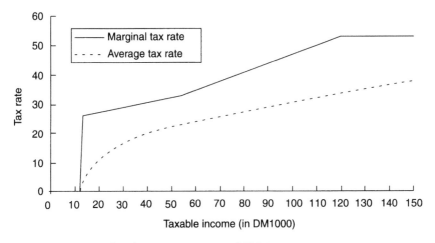

Figure 13.1 Marginal and average tax rates of T 96

all over the world shared two common features. One was the tendency to lower top marginal tax rates and to decrease the number of tax brackets, and the other was to broaden the tax base. To mention just a few examples, the top marginal income tax rates fell from 83 per cent in 1978 to 40 per cent in 1988 in the UK, from 50 per cent in 1981 to 31 per cent in 1992 in the US, and from 80 per cent in 1985 to 50 per cent in 1992 in Sweden. The major motivation for these tax changes was the concern that high marginal tax rates result in considerable distortions on product and factor markets and produce substantial welfare losses. One of the (few) basic lessons of optimal taxation theory tells us that the first-order approximation of the excess burdens of the tax system vary quadratically with marginal tax rates. Hence tax-cut-cum-base-broadening was considered to be the appropriate policy response.

In Germany, recent income tax reform concentrated on cutting marginal tax rates. An increase in unemployment rates and the fear of losing international competitiveness were the main impetuses for striving for a more efficient income tax with heavily reduced marginal tax rates. While the reduction in marginal tax rates was considered as the indispensable cornerstone of the envisaged tax reform, the exact form of the tax schedule remained unspecified. Soon after the government's announcement, a great range of different tax reform proposals was launched. All those made so far follow one of the following three reform patterns.

The first class of reform proposals is quite fundamental in nature: it abandons the linear-progessive form of the tax schedule. In addition to a reduction in marginal tax rates, the linear-progressive income tax schedule is replaced by a flat tax with very few tax brackets. This clearly mimics the basic structure of the UK and US tax codes. The most prominent proposal comes from the MP G. Uldall and features three constant marginal tax rates of 10, 20 and 30 per cent[2] for taxable incomes between DM12,096 and 20,000, DM20,000 and 30,000 and above DM30,000, respectively. Because the top marginal tax rate starts at a very low taxable income, this proposal basically amounts to a linear income tax. We will speak of TRP1 (tax reform proposal 1) when referring to the Uldall tax system.

The second class of proposals basically retains the linear-progressive structure of the T 96 but reduces the marginal tax rates at the beginning and at the end of the linear-progressive zones. Here we pick out the proposal made by the Bavarian Minister of Finance, E. Huber. His idea is to reduce the two linear-progressive zones of the T 96 to one, starting with a marginal tax rate of 20 per cent and ending at a top marginal tax rate of 40 per cent on taxable incomes of DM140,000 for single persons. In the following, we will refer to this proposal as TRP2.

In Figure 13.2, we compare the marginal tax schedules of TRP1 and TRP2 with the current T 96.

The third tax reform proposal is even more far-reaching in that it aban-

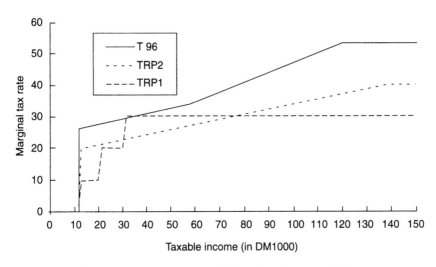

Figure 13.2 Reforming the income tax: TRP1 and TRP2 versus T 96

dons the comprehensive income tax and replaces it by a consumption or wage income tax. The background story is that a group of German tax experts[3] played a prominent part in restructuring the Croatian tax system after Croatia declared independence from the former Yugoslavia. One of the exceptional features of the new Croatian tax system is that it completely abandons the taxation of interest income. The central elements of the tax system are a 22 per cent value-added tax, a wage income tax with two flat tax rates of 25 per cent and 35 per cent and a neutral profits tax at a rate of 25 per cent.[4] Now the Croatian tax system is considered as a guideline for the German tax reform, not only by its German originators but also by some prominent and influential organizations in Germany.[5] In our context, the abolition of the taxation of interest income is the crucial feature of the reform. This is captured in our TRP3, which otherwise retains the current linear-progressive tax schedule on wage incomes. This allows us to concentrate on the efficiency and distributional effects of interest income taxation – even if it does only partly match the ambitious intention of the original reform plan.

All three tax reform proposals imply a more or less considerable loss of income tax revenue. In our chapter, we consider differential tax incidences only. Our assumption is that revenue losses are compensated for by either increasing the VAT rate or by some combination of broadening the tax base and increasing VAT. Due to space limitations, we can only present numerical results for the first of these cases. Results for the other are available upon request.

13.3 THE ECONOMIC MODEL:
AUERBACH–KOTLIKOFF EXTENDED

We are interested in the efficiency and redistributional effects of possible income tax reforms in Germany. Our chapter, therefore, is a contribution to tax incidence. In the literature, there are two different approaches to studying tax incidence.

The first is to classify households on the basis of their annual income and to evaluate changes in income following some tax reform. Income changes occur because relative factor and commodity prices differ before and after the reform and because of the behavioural reactions of taxpayers. For a long time, such annual incidence studies were the predominant approach in empirical public finance, and public debate about tax incidence still focuses exclusively on annual figures. In recent years, however, a second approach has come to the fore. Not annual but lifetime income is increasingly considered the appropriate characteristic for household classification and is used to measure the redistributional content of tax policy. And indeed, there is good reason to assume that lifetime income is a much better indicator of economic well-being than annual income. In tax incidence studies relying on the latter, completely different households are lumped together and treated the same. For example, in the lower income range, young people who are at the very beginning of their careers are lumped together with persons who are having a bad year due to unemployment, with retirees who made insufficient provision for old age during their working lives and, finally, with the perennially poor. Even if annual incomes are the same in some years, most economists would agree that these households are in fact rather different and, consequently, should be treated differently by tax policy. In contrast, one could be much more confident that households with identical (and appropriately measured) lifetime incomes face rather similar economic positions.

Relying on lifetime income in tax incidence studies requires a life-cycle model of economic behaviour. In addition, if tax-induced price changes are determined endogenously and not just assumed, the life-cycle model needs to be supplemented with a fully fledged and consistent intertemporal general equilibrium model. Finally, if the interest is in a quantitative measure of tax incidence, the appropriate approach is through a numerically specified overlapping generations (OLG) model of the Auerbach–Kotlikoff (AK, henceforth) variety. In our context, however, a major disadvantage of this model is that each generation or age cohort is represented by just one household (or a given number of identical households). Consequently, the traditional AK model is well suited to tackle problems of *inter*generational tax incidence but is not tailored to deal with *intra*generational redistribution between rich and poor households. We therefore extend the AK framework by considering two different types of households, rich ones and poor ones, within each age cohort.

We do not describe the AK model in detail. Over the last ten years it has become an indispensable methodological instrument in any applied general equilibrium modeller's toolbox. Even if this model is less well known outside the CGE community, space is too scarce to give a more satisfactory description of the AK model, so a few words must suffice. The interested reader is referred to Auerbach and Kotlikoff (1987) or to one of the many subsequent contributions.

The life cycle of each generation is divided into fifty-five periods. Consumption demand as well as labour supply and participation decisions are endogenous. Each household decides how many hours to work within each period and when to quit the workforce. For the latter decision, it compares its reservation wage with the market wage. Preferences over current and future consumption and over leisure are governed by a constant elasticity of substitution (CES) utility function, which is assumed to be the same for both poor and rich households. The distinction between rich and poor is attributed to differences in their productivity or earning capacity, not in utility functions. This reflects the belief that poor people would behave like rich people if they had the same income. It is assumed that within each generation there are four times as many poor as rich people.

The model's production sector is characterised by perfectly competitive firms operating under a Cobb–Douglas production function. Investment decisions result from maximizing the market value of firms. For the sake of simplicity, we neglect capital adjustment costs. The government supplies a given amount of public goods – which enters the utility functions in an additively separable manner – and levies progressive income taxes and a value-added tax. Note that we do not consider corporate income taxes or other business taxes. This is not as serious a restriction as it may appear. We want to concentrate on the reform of the personal income tax, leaving the taxation of the business sector unchanged. Given this restriction it seems permissible to neglect completely all business taxation.

There is another feature of our model which is far more restrictive. This is the assumption that households leave no bequests and give no gifts. This is particularly unrealistic because life-cycle saving was found to explain only about half of the economy's capital stock (Kotlikoff and Summers, 1981). In our model, the elderly dissave to finance consumption expenditures.

Even if measuring tax incidence in a lifetime context is an appealing idea, there are some conceptual and practical difficulties in determining lifetime income. Usually household income is used as the unit for categorising consumers. But household composition changes over the life cycle due to divorce, death or the moving out of children. An even more intricate question is how to define income if labour supply is endogenous. Consider two households with identical endowments and productivities. One prefers to work hard in order to earn high incomes and consumes lots of market goods, while the other prefers to consume plenty of leisure and spends little on market goods. In terms of consumption possibilities, including leisure, both households are identical, but they differ with respect to present-value lifetime wage income. Lifetime tax incidence studies usually classify households according to lifetime 'endowment income' as the value of total time endowment over the life cycle. Assuming that each household has an annual time endowment of 5,000 hours, the present value of lifetime income after taxes (LI) is given by:

$$\text{LI} = \sum_{t=1}^{55} \left[w^t \left(1 - \tau_w^t \right) \times 5{,}000 \right] \Big/ \left(1 + r_n^t \right)$$

Here w^t is the wage rate, τ_w^t the wage income tax rate and r_n^t the net-of-tax rate of return. We used the panel data of the German Socio-economic Panel to estimate the parameters of the age earnings profiles for poor and rich households. The steady states and the transitional paths between the two long-run equilibria are computed as a solution of the intertemporal equilibrium model. This requires the specification of a set of baseline parameters. To be in line with some recent, more-conservative estimates of savings and labour supply elasticities, 0.2 was chosen as the value of intratemporal and intertemporal elasticities of substitution. The population growth rate is 2.5 per cent and the rate of time preference is 1 per cent. The remaining parameters are taken from Auerbach and Kotlikoff (1987: 50f).

As a final remark, we want to emphasize that the combination of *inter*generational and *intra*generational income redistribution in applied tax incidence studies is not really new. In 1993, Fullerton and Rogers published an impressive study on the efficiency and (intra)distributional effects of taxes in a life-cycle framework. As a disadvantage of their approach one could mention that these authors use a sequenced dynamic equilibrium model, implying myopic, non-rational expectations. More recently, some efforts have been made to extend the AK model to include some intragenerational heterogeneity (Altig and Carlstrom 1995; Kotlikoff 1996). The distinctive feature of our chapter is not the combination of intergenerational and intragenerational tax incidence, but the separation of efficiency effects, on the one hand, from intergenerational as well as intragenerational redistribution effects, on the other. It is this decomposition of the total welfare effects of tax reforms into their efficiency and redistributional components which is new in applied work and to which we now turn.

13.4. DECOMPOSING THE WELFARE EFFECTS OF
TAX REFORMS IN EFFICIENCY AND
REDISTRIBUTIONAL EFFECTS

When evaluating tax reforms, neoclassical economists are principally interested in their welfare effects. Welfare changes must be due either to (re)distributional effects or otherwise to efficiency effects. Distributional effects alone can work through two different channels. On the one hand, a specific household may face different tax burdens before and after the tax reform. In general, some households will pay more and others will pay less taxes, even if the tax reform is revenue-neutral in the aggregate. A second reason for distributional changes is that tax reforms do not only change relative prices after taxes, but also gross-of-tax prices. Whereas from an efficiency point of view these price changes do no harm, they do cause some redistribution between agents. Efficiency effects of tax reforms are associated with behavioural reactions. Substitution effects may be isolated by compensating households for any distributional gains or losses.

To illustrate this decomposition of the total welfare effects of tax reforms, consider a simple two-period model and assume just one representative agent per generation with no population growth.[6] The utility of this generation, u^t, depends on its first and second periods' consumption, c_1^t and c_2^{t+1}, as well as on leisure demand in both periods, l_1^t and l_2^{t+1}. In period t a tax reform is implemented with the tax system consisting of a consumption tax, a wage income tax and an interest income tax at constant rates. The tax reform affects the welfare of the by now old members of the generation born in period $t-1$. Furthermore, it affects the utility of the generation born in period t as well as that of all future generations. Consider the old generation first. While its first period consumption and leisure demand decisions have been made, the second period's choices can be adjusted. Totally differentiating the utility function:

$$u^{t-1} = u(c_1^{t-1}, l_1^{t-1}, c_2^t, l_2^t) \qquad (13.1)$$

and the second period's budget constraint:

$$(1 + \tau_c^t)c_2^t = w^t (1 - \tau_w^t)(1 - l_2^t) + \left[1 + r^t(1 - \tau_r^t)\right]k^t \qquad (13.2)$$

or equivalently,

$$c_2^t = w^t (1 - l_2^t) + (1 + r^t)k^t - T_2^t \qquad (13.3a)$$

with

$$T_2^t = \tau_c^t c_2^t + \tau_w^t w^t(1 - l_2^t) + \tau_r^t r^t k^t \qquad (13.3b)$$

gives the utility change following a tax reform as:[7]

243

$$\frac{du^{t-1}}{\lambda^{t-1}} = \underbrace{-dT_2^t}_{\substack{\text{welfare} \\ \text{change}}} + \underbrace{\left[k^t\,dr^t + (1 - l_2^t)dw^t\right]}_{\text{redistribution (RD}_2^t)} + \underbrace{\left[\tau_c^t\,dc_2^t - \tau_w^t\,w^t\,dl_2^t\right]}_{\text{efficiency (EB}_2^t)} \quad (13.4)$$

Equation (13.4) reflects our above-mentioned decomposition of total welfare changes following a marginal tax reform. On the left-hand side we have the monetary equivalent of the old generation's utility change. The first two terms on the right-hand side (RHS) represent the (re)distributional content of the change in tax policy: the first term, $-dT_2^t$, gives the change in the tax payments of the elderly in period t, while the second term stands for the change in factor incomes due to gross-of-tax factor prices. RD_2^t defines the (re)distributional content of the tax reform in question as the sum of these two terms. The third term on the RHS gives the efficiency part of the utility change, provided the household is compensated for its distributional gains or losses.[8] In this case, dc_2^t and dl_2^t describe compensated behavioural reactions and the third term represents the marginal excess burdens (EB_2^t).

Turning to the generations born in periods $s \geq t$, the utility functions are:

$$u^s = u(c_1^s, l_1^s, c_2^{s+1}, l_2^{s+1}), \quad s \geq t \quad (13.5)$$

and the budget constraints are given by:

$$(1 + \tau_c^s)c_1^s + \frac{1 + \tau_c^{s+1}}{[1 + r^{s+1}(1 - \tau_r^{s+1})]}\,c_2^{s+1} = w^s(1 - \tau_w^s)(1 - l_1^s) + \frac{w^{s+1}(1-\tau_w^{s+1})}{[1 + r^{s+1}(1 - \tau_r^{s+1})]}\,(1 - l_2^{s+1}) \quad (13.6)$$

or equivalently·

$$c_1^s + \frac{c_2^{s+1}}{1 + r^{s+1}} = w^s\,(1 - l_1^s) + \frac{w^{s+1}}{1 + r^{s+1}}\,(1 - l_2^{s+1}) - T_1^s - \frac{T_2^{s+1}}{1 + r^{s+1}} \quad (13.7a)$$

with

$$T_1^s = \tau_c^s c_1^s + \tau_w^s w^s\,(1 - l_1^s) \quad (13.7b)$$

$$T_2^{s+1} = \tau_c^{s+1} c_2^{s+1} + \tau_w^{s+1}\,(1 - l_2^{s+1}) + \tau_r^{s+1} r^{s+1}$$
$$\left[w^s(1 - \tau_w^s)(1 - l_1^s) - (1 - \tau_c^s)c_1^s\right]$$

where
$$\left[w^s(1 - \tau_w^s)(1 - l_1^s) - (1 - \tau_c^s)c_1^s\right] =: k^{s+1}. \quad (13.7c)$$

Totally differentiating equations (13.5) and (13.7a) gives, after some tedious but not very exciting manipulations:

$$\frac{du^s}{\lambda^s} = \left[-dT_1^s - \frac{dT_2^{s+1}}{1 + r^{s+1}} \right] + \left[\left(1 - l_1^s\right)dw^s + \frac{1}{1 + r^{s+1}} \left(k^{s+1}dr^{s+1} + \left(1 - l_2^{s+1}\right)dw^{s+1}\right) \right]$$

$$+ \left[\tau_c^s dc_1^s - \tau_w^s w^s dl_1^s + \left(\frac{1 + \tau_c^{s+1}}{1 + r^{s+1}\left(1 - \tau_r^{s+1}\right)} - \frac{1}{1 + r^{s+1}} \right) dc_2^{s+1} \right.$$

$$\left. - \left(\frac{1 - \tau_w^{s+1}}{1 + r^{s+1}\left(1 - \tau_r^{s+1}\right)} - \frac{1}{1 + r^{s+1}} \right) w^{s+1}dl_2^{s+1} \right] \qquad (13.8)$$

As before, equation (13.8) decomposes the total welfare change following a tax reform into its redistributional and efficiency components. The first two bracketed terms on the RHS stand for the present value of changes in tax payments and in factor incomes due to gross-of-tax price variations, while the third one represents efficiency gains or losses, provided the household is compensated for real income changes. For later reference, we will define:

$$RD_1^s: = -dT_1^s + \left(1 - l_1^s\right)dw^s \qquad (13.9a)$$

and

$$RD_2^{s+1}: = -dT_2^{s+1} + k^{s+1}dr^{s+1} + \left(1 - l_2^{s+1}\right)dw^{s+1} \qquad (13.9b)$$

as the first and second period's change in real income and

$$RD^s: = RD_1^s + \left(1 + r^{s+1}\right)^{-1}RD_2^{s+1} \qquad (13.10)$$

as the present value redistributional content of the tax reform programme for generation s. The last bracketed term on the RHS of equation (13.8) gives the present value of excess burdens (EB^s) for this generation, if compensation for any income changes is assumed.

Finally, when adding the distinction between poor and rich households within one generation, we define the redistributional and efficiency components of the poor and the rich household's utility change by RD_P^s, RD_R^s and EB_P^s, EB_R^s.[9]

We can now compare the efficiency and redistributional effects of a given tax reform programme for different generations and for different households within each generation. Furthermore, we can evaluate excess burdens as well as aggregate intragenerational and intergenerational redistribution. Table 13.1 illustrates the basic structure of our presentation in the next section. For the sake of simplicity, a time-invariant interest rate is assumed in this table. The tax reform is implemented in period t.

For each generation, as well as for poor and rich households within each

Table 13.1 Separating efficiency from redistribution in tax reform

| Generation | Intragenerational redistribution | | | | | Intergenerational redistribution | | efficiency |
	efficiency poor households	redistribution poor households		redistribution rich households	efficiency rich households	losers	winners	
$t-1$	$EB_{2,P}^t$	$RD_{2,P}^t$	$\leftrightarrow$	$RD_{2,R}^t$	$EB_{2,R}^t$	$-RD_2^t \;\leftrightarrow$		EB_2^t
t	EB_P^t	RD_P^t	$\leftrightarrow$	RD_R^t	EB_R^t	$-RD^t \;\leftrightarrow$		EB_s^t
$t+1$ ...	EB_P^{t+1}	RD_P^{t+1}	$\leftrightarrow$	RD_R^{t+1}	EB_R^t	$-RD^{t+1}$		EB^{t+1}
$t+s$ ...	EB_P^{t+s}	RD_P^{t+s}	$\leftrightarrow$	RD_R^{t+s}	EB_R^{t+s}		$+RD^{t+s} \;\leftrightarrow$	EB^{t+s}
Σ	$EB_{2,P}^t + \sum\limits_{s=t}^{\infty} EB_P^s(1+r)^{t-s}$	$RD_{2,P}^t + \sum\limits_{s=t}^{\infty} RD_P^s(1+r)^{t-s}$		$RD_{2,R}^t + \sum\limits_{s=t}^{\infty} RD_R^s(1+r)^{t-s}$	$EB_{2,R}^t + \sum\limits_{s=t}^{\infty} EB_R^s(1+r)^{t-s}$	$-RD_{2s}^t - \sum\limits_{s\in L}^{\infty} RD^s(1+r)^{t-s}$	$\sum\limits_{s\in W}^{\infty} RD^s(1+r)^{t-s}$	$EB_{2s}^t + \sum\limits_{s=t}^{\infty} EB^s(1+r)^{t-s}$

Aggregate intragenerational redistribution

Aggregate intergenerational redistribution

generation, we compare the efficiency with the redistributional content of a tax reform. When evaluating the intergenerational redistribution we aggregate poor and rich households within one period and distinguish between loser and winner generations.[10] A generation s loses if the real income change RD^s is negative and it wins if it is positive (or zero). As an example, Table 13.1 depicts a situation in which the generations born in periods $t - 1$ to $t + 1$ lose, whereas all others gain.

In the last line of Table 13.1 we present aggregate figures for excess burdens and redistribution. That redistribution is indeed a zero-sum game can be shown by considering the present value of real income changes over all generations:

$$RD_2^t + RD^t + \sum_{s-t+1}^{\infty} RD^s \cdot R^s$$

$$= RD_2^t + \left[RD_1^t + \left(1 + r^{t+1} \right)^{-1} RD_2^{t+1} \right] + \sum_{s=t+1}^{\infty} \left[RD_1^s + \left(1 + r^{s+1} \right)^{-1} RD_2^{s+1} \right] R^s$$

$$= RD_2^t + RD_1^t + \sum_{s=t+1}^{\infty} RD_1^s \cdot R^s + RD_2^{t+1} \left(1 + r^{t+1} \right)^{-1} + \sum_{s=t+1}^{\infty} RD_2^{s+1} \left(1 + r^{s+1} \right)^{-1} R^s$$

$$= RD_2^t + RD_1^t + \sum_{s=t+1}^{\infty} RD_1^s \cdot R^s + \sum_{s=t+1}^{\infty} RD_2^s \cdot R^s$$

$$= \left(RD_2^t + RD_1^t \right) + \sum_{s=t+1}^{\infty} \left(RD_1^s + RD_2^s \right) R^s$$

$$= 0$$

where we have defined

$$R^s: = \prod_{j=t+1}^{s} \left(1 + r^j \right)^{-1}$$

The last transition follows from the fact that in each period $s = t, t + 1, \ldots$, it is true that

$$RD_1^s + RD_2^s = -\left(dT_1^s + dT_2^s \right) + k^s dr^s + \left[\left(1 - l_1^s \right) + \left(1 - l_2^s \right) \right] dw^s \quad (13.11)$$

If the tax reform is considered to be revenue-neutral in each period:

$$dT_1^s + dT_2^s = 0$$

holds.[11] Furthermore, from the constant-returns production function:

$$Y^s = F(K^s, L^s) = L^s f(K^s/L^s)$$

and the first-order conditions for profit maximisation:

$$r^s = f'(K^s/L^s); \quad w^s = f(K^s/L^s) - K^s/L^s f'(K^s/L^s)$$

we can derive the total differential of the factor-price frontier as:

$$K^s dr^s = -L^s dw^s$$

In our simple two-period model, k^s is the aggregate capital stock available in period t (hence $k^s = K^s$) and $\left[(1 - l^s_1) + (1 - l^s_2)\right]$ is aggregate labour supply L^s, so that

$$k^s dr^s + \left[(1 - l^s_1) + (1 - l^s_2)\right] dw^s = 0$$

holds. Hence, in equation (13.11) $RD^s_1 + RD^s_2 = 0$ holds for all periods $s = t$, $t + 1, \ldots$.

By partitioning the generational income changes into those of poor and rich households, or into losers and winners, we obtain the aggregate intra-generational or aggregate intergenerational redistribution, as shown in Table 13.1.

Once again, we will conclude this section by briefly relating our approach to the literature. Two papers by Keuschnigg (1992, 1994) are of special importance. Keuschnigg uses the same methodology in separating efficiency from redistribution in intergenerational tax incidence. His interest, however, is not in quantitatively comparing the importance of efficiency and redistribution, respectively, but in describing intergenerationally neutral tax reforms. The two papers mentioned are purely theoretical and do not contain any empirical applications.

Auerbach and Kotlikoff (1987) were the first to separate efficiency from purely redistributive effects numerically. They used lump-sum taxes and transfers to keep the utility of all cohorts born before the reform at the initial level, and to raise (or lower) the utility of all cohorts born in and after the reform year by a uniform amount. Older generations are therefore not affected and newborn and future generations share the efficiency gains or losses of the policy reform equally. While it is possible to measure the aggregate efficiency effects by doing this, we cannot isolate the generation-specific substitution effects. All efficiency gains (or losses) of the older generations are implicitly transferred to the newborn and future generations (see Gravelle, 1991). In contrast, our compensation method allows us to identify the efficiency components of the generational-specific utility changes. The lump-sum transfers in every period s exactly neutralise the income effects RD^s_1 and RD^s_2 so that the compensated utility change of each generation arises solely from the distortion of its economic choices, which is given in the last bracket of equations (13.4) and (13.8).

13.5 SEPARATING EFFICIENCY FROM REDISTRIBUTION IN GERMAN INCOME TAX REFORM: SOME NUMERICAL RESULTS

In this section we will apply the methodology outlined in section 13.4 in order to evaluate the income tax reform proposals from section 13.3 above. Before presenting and explaining our numerical results, a few qualifications must be mentioned.

In the previous section we illustrated our basic idea by referring to marginal welfare changes. Our numerical welfare calculations, on the other hand, allow for finite changes in tax rates. Finite welfare changes may be obtained from marginal ones by integration. The problem is that, in general, the line integral over the monetary equivalent of marginal utility depends on the path joining before- and after-tax reform prices. Fortunately, the line integral is path-independent if the utility function is homothetic. A second point to note is that, in what follows, we do not express efficiency and redistribution in absolute amounts as we did in Table 13.1. Instead, as is usual in static or dynamic tax incidence, we present all the amounts from Table 13.1 as a percentage of the present value of a generation's disposable full lifetime income (LI). For the old generations living in the reform period t, lifetime income over the remaining life-cycle only is used as the denominator when calculating tax burdens or gains. On the other hand, whenever we refer to aggregate excess burdens or redistributional figures over household groups or generations in the last line of the following tables, we use the present value of full lifetime income over all generations as the reference magnitude.

Our final remark refers to the model assumption under which we compute the efficiency and redistributional effects for the different income tax proposals. We start by considering the small open economy case. Under this assumption, factor prices are given and redistribution between households and generations is only due to changes in tax payments. This helps in understanding the economics behind our numerical calculations. In a second step we consider the closed economy case. Now, changes in gross-of-tax factor prices have to be added to changes in tax payments when evaluating the distributional content of tax policy. For both scenarios, the small open economy as well as the closed economy case, we can describe the time path of the capital stock, GDP, consumption, investment and all other instantaneous equilibrium values. We will, however, give this information for the closed economy case only.

After these preliminary remarks we can now turn to our numerical results.

Table 13.2 Separating efficiency from redistribution for TRP1: small open economy case

Generation	Intragenerational redistribution				Intergenerational redistribution		
	efficiency poor households	redistribution poor households	redistribution rich households	efficiency rich households	redistribution losers	winners	efficiency
−54	−0.02	−2.78	−1.98	0.00	−2.53		−0.02
−50	−0.02	−2.67	−2.06	0.00	−2.49		−0.02
−40	0.13	−2.10	−1.30	0.02	−1.88		0.10
−30	0.21	−1.41	−0.39	0.27	−1.11		0.23
−20	0.25	−0.99	0.04	0.84	−0.66		0.44
−10	0.27	−0.33	0.87	1.45		0.07	0.67
1	0.21	−0.10	1.62	1.18		0.48	0.53
5	0.21	−0.07	1.64	1.18		0.51	0.54
10	0.21	−0.03	1.67	1.18		0.54	0.54
20	0.21	0.03	1.71	1.19		0.59	0.54
50	0.21	0.08	1.75	1.19		0.64	0.54
∞	0.21	0.08	1.75	1.19		0.64	0.54
Σ	0.15	−0.32	0.32	0.35	−0.32	0.32	0.50

Table 13.3 Separating efficiency from redistribution for TRP2: small open economy case

Generation	Intragenerational redistribution				Intergenerational redistribution		
	efficiency poor households	redistribution poor households	redistribution rich households	efficiency rich households	redistribution losers	winners	efficiency
−54	−0.04	−3.91	−2.79	0.00	−3.56		−0.02
−50	−0.04	−3.76	−2.89	0.00	−3.50		−0.03
−40	−0.01	−3.26	−2.52	−0.02	−3.05		−0.01
−30	0.18	−2.49	−1.81	0.23	−2.28		0.20
−20	0.25	−1.38	−0.75	0.63	−1.17		0.37
−10	0.26	−0.03	0.53	0.92		0.16	0.48
1	0.24	0.50	1.59	0.75		0.87	0.41
5	0.24	0.54	1.62	0.76		0.91	0.41
10	0.24	0.60	1.67	0.76		0.96	0.41
20	0.24	0.69	1.74	0.76		1.04	0.41
50	0.24	0.75	1.79	0.76		1.10	0.41
00	0.24	0.76	1.79	0.76		1.10	0.41
Σ	0.15	−0.21	0.21	0.23	−0.57	0.57	0.38

Table 13.4 Separating efficiency from redistribution for TRP3: small open economy case

Generation	Intragenerational redistribution				Intergenerational redistribution		
	efficiency poor households	redistribution poor households	redistribution rich households	efficiency	losers	winners	efficiency
−54	−0.01	−1.09	−0.78	0.00	−0.99		−0.00
−50	−0.01	−1.09	−0.85	0.00	−1.02		−0.01
−40	0.04	−0.49	2.38	0.09		0.31	0.05
−30	0.35	0.09	4.60	0.45		1.44	0.38
−20	0.48	−0.59	3.91	0.77		0.88	0.57
−10	0.31	−0.81	1.56	0.93	−0.02		0.52
1	0.16	−0.89	0.46	0.61	−0.44		0.31
5	0.16	−0.90	0.44	0.60	−0.45		0.31
10	0.16	−0.91	0.44	0.60	−0.45		0.31
20	0.16	−0.90	0.45	0.60	−0.44		0.31
50	0.16	−0.88	0.46	0.60	−0.43		0.31
00	0.16	−0.88	0.46	0.60	−0.43		0.31
Σ	0.16	−0.49	0.49	0.21	−0.26	0.26	0.37

Tables 13.2–13.4 contain the efficiency and redistributional effects of the tax reform proposals TRP1–TRP3 in a small open economy framework. In the left-hand column we list all the generations affected by the tax reform, which is implemented in period 1. The figures above the dashed line refer to previously born generations which are still alive in period one. The negative figures in the first column indicate the number of years which a specific generation has already worked up to this point. The figures below the dashed line refer to generations born in the reform period or later. For example, the figure 20 in the first column means that this generation will be born twenty years from now.

Table 13.2 contains our numerical results when switching to TRP1. Remember that TRP1 is basically a flat tax. Let us consider the efficiency effects first and then speculate a little bit about what is to be expected. There are two countervailing effects on economic efficiency. On the one hand, we will have an increase in efficiency because the marginal tax rates of income tax are reduced over the complete range of the tax schedule. On the other hand, additional distortions are added into the leisure–consumption choice due to the increase in VAT, which is necessary in order to compensate for the revenue losses in income taxes. We should mention that the initial VAT rate of 15 per cent has to be increased to 20 per cent in the first few periods after the tax reform but can be reduced to 19 per cent in the long run. Comparing efficiency losses and gains, there is good reason to expect the efficiency losses from the increased VAT to be dominated by the efficiency gains from the income tax reduction. There are two reasons for this. Both may be attributed to the basic insight that excess burdens vary quadratically with marginal tax rates. First, the reduction in marginal income tax rates is much larger than the increase in VAT rates. Second, and possibly even more important, excess burdens decrease due to intertemporal tax smoothing. Under the present T96, marginal tax rates vary over the life cycle because the income profile is inversely U-shaped. In contrast, under a flat tax the marginal tax rate is time-invariant. Hence, even a revenue-neutral switch from a linear-progressive to a flat income tax schedule would reduce present value excess burdens due to the convexity of excess burdens in marginal tax rates.

Our intuition is confirmed by the numbers in the efficiency columns of Table 13.1. With very few exceptions all generations realise efficiency gains. However, these gains are different for different generations and they are different for poor and rich households. Let us explain why.

The efficiency effects of the tax reform are zero for the very old and rich generations and they are even negative for the old and poor generations. The explanation is that the old and rich people no longer work but have retired earlier. Hence, the increase in VAT induces income effects, but no substitution effects between leisure and consumption. Furthermore, consumption expenditures are mainly financed out of dissaving and only to a lesser extent out of interest income. But due to the high allowances, interest income remains untaxed before and after the reform. For the old and poor, matters are different because they still have to work even during the last periods of their life cycle. In this case, the increase in VAT provokes welfare-decreasing substitution effects between leisure and consumption. Moreover, these house-holds do not gain much from the income tax reduction because factor incomes are small when compared with dissaving. Younger generations, whether poor or rich, realize efficiency gains from the tax reform. These gains increase gradually and reach their peak for generations which started to work about ten or twenty years ago. These households now earn the highest factor income over their life cycle and gain the most by the substantial reduction in top marginal income tax rates. For the newborn and the future generations, efficiency gains are a little bit lower. Their productivity peak and the largest efficiency gains from the tax reform lie in the future, which reduces the present value of total efficiency gains when compared with the current high productivity generations.

Turning to the redistributional effects of TRP1 or, more precisely, to the welfare effects which are due to redistribution, the following results are most noteworthy. First, TRP1 redistributes intergenerationally from the current old and middle-aged generations to the young and future generations. Second, there is a considerable amount of intragenerational redistribution from poor households to rich ones. And third, redistributional effects clearly dominate efficiency effects for almost all generations living in the reform period and for all rich generations born in the future. Both the intergenerational and the intragenerational redistribution profiles are readily explained. As to the intergenerational redistribution, the wage income, interest income and consumption profiles over the life cycle have to be remembered. Consumption expenditures of the old are mainly financed by dissaving and only to a smaller extent by wage or interest incomes. Because revenues from dissaving are not subject to income taxation, any switch from direct to indirect taxation definitely burdens all older generations living in the reform period. Younger generations, on the other hand, gain more the more periods they live after the reform. Replacing income tax by consumption taxes shifts tax payments to future periods, thereby reducing the present value of tax burdens. The intragenerational redistribution from poor to rich occurs because a directly progressive income tax is replaced by a much less pro-gressive flat income tax on the one hand, and an increase in VAT on the other, where the latter is slightly regressive.[12]

As Table 13.3 illustrates, TRP2 basically produces the same pattern of intragenerational and intergenerational tax incidence as does TRP1. The main difference lies in the absolute amounts of redistributional and efficiency effects. Restricting ourselves to a comparison of the aggregate values repro-duced in the last lines of Tables 13.2 and 13.3, the following observations are striking. Aggregate efficiency gains are higher under TRP1 than under TRP2, as is the extent of intragenerational redistribution from the poor to the rich. On the other hand, TRP1 redistributes much less, from an inter-generational perspective, from young to old. For an explanation one has to remember that TRP2 retains the linear-progressive tax schedule. As a con-sequence, TRP2 involves a higher degree of tax progressivity than TRP1, which explains the reduced extent of intragenerational redistribution. A second point to remember is that top marginal income tax rates are reduced less under TRP2 than under TRP1. This is why efficiency gains for all rich generations as well as in the aggregate are lower in Table 13.3 than in Table 13.2. To explain the differences in intergenerational redistribution, the important fact is that TRP2 necessitates an increase in VAT from 15 per cent to 21.5 per cent in the short run and to 20.5 per cent in the long run.[13] Hence we have a more distinctive shift from direct to indirect taxation under TRP2, and a more intense intergenerational redistribution from old to young and future generations.

Our last tax reform in a small open economy context concerns the com-plete abolition of interest income taxation and an equal yield adjustment of VAT. Table 13.4 reproduces the numerical results for TRP3. Whereas gen-eration-specific as well as aggregate efficiency effects are roughly the same for TRP2 and TRP3, redistributional effects differ greatly. Consider the pattern of intragenerational redistribution first. One striking feature is that all poor generations lose whereas almost all rich generations gain. Consequently there is a considerable intragenerational redistribution effect from the poor to rich. This is not too surprising. Due to the high allowances granted on capital income, poorer households do not pay any or only a rather limited amount of taxes on interest income. While being hurt by the increase in VAT, they benefit only to a very small extent from the abolition of the interest income tax. The second interesting point to note is the intergenerational redistribu-tion profile. TRP3 redistributes from the very old, from the very young as well as from future generations to the current middle-aged and rich house-holds – among them, of course by mere coincidence, the passionate suppor-ters of TRP3. For these generations the share of interest income in total income is the highest. Hence, they gain the most by the abolition of capital income taxes. As a final remark we want to add that especially for the poorer generations, but also in the aggregate, intragenerational redistribution effects clearly dominate efficiency effects.

Let us now turn to the closed economy case and check the robustness of our results. The main difference between the small open economy and the closed economy framework is that, within the latter, gross-of-tax factor prices are endogenously determined. Hence, redistributional effects are not only due to differences in tax payments but also to changing factor prices. In Tables 13.5–13.7 we decompose the intragenerational redistribution effects into these two components.

The first point to note is the similarity between all three tax reform proposals of the redistribution profiles which are due to factor price changes.

Table 13.5 Separating efficiency from redistribution for TRP1: closed economy case

| Generation | efficiency | redistribution | | Intragenerational | | | | | Intergenerational redistribution | | efficiency |
		tax payments poor households	factor prices	total	redistribution total	factor prices rich households	tax payments rich households	efficiency	losers	winners	
−54	−0.03	−2.85	0.09	−2.76	−1.97	0.07	−2.04	0.00	−2.51		−0.02
−50	−0.03	−2.70	0.14	−2.56	−1.97	0.12	−2.09	0.00	−2.39		−0.02
−40	0.12	−2.09	−0.12	−2.21	−1.37	−0.10	−1.27	0.01	−1.98		0.09
−30	0.21	−1.28	−0.40	−1.69	−0.66	−0.42	−0.24	0.25	−1.38		0.22
−20	0.23	−0.88	−0.50	−1.38	−0.38	−0.58	0.20	0.80	−1.05		0.42
−10	0.26	−0.30	−0.37	−0.67	0.42	−0.60	1.02	1.42	−0.30		0.65
1	0.31	−0.15	−0.20	−0.35	1.25	−0.45	1.70	1.20		0.19	0.61
5	0.22	−0.18	0.22	0.04	1.29	−0.42	1.70	1.26		0.46	0.57
10	0.15	−0.19	0.60	0.41	1.32	−0.39	1.71	1.31		0.72	0.54
20	0.08	−0.20	1.06	0.86	1.37	−0.35	1.72	1.35		1.03	0.51
50	0.08	−0.20	1.39	1.18	1.41	−0.33	1.73	1.35		1.26	0.50
00	0.08	−0.21	1.42	1.22	1.41	−0.32	1.74	1.35		1.28	0.50
Σ	0.12			−0.21	0.21			0.35	−0.43	0.43	0.47

Table 13.6 Separating efficiency from redistribution for TRP2: closed economy case

Generation	efficiency	Intragenerational redistribution			total	redistribution		efficiency	Intergenerational redistribution		efficiency
		tax payments poor households	factor prices	total		factor prices rich households	tax payments		losers	winners	
−54	−0.04	−3.96	0.09	−3.87	−2.76	0.07	−2.83	0.00	−3.53		−0.03
−50	−0.04	−3.78	0.12	−3.65	−2.80	0.11	−2.92	0.00	−3.40		−0.03
−40	−0.02	−3.25	−0.19	−3.44	−2.65	−0.18	−2.47	−0.02	−3.22		−0.02
−30	0.18	−2.37	−0.51	−2.88	−2.18	−0.55	−1.63	0.21	−2.67		0.19
−20	0.24	−1.22	−0.61	−1.83	−1.28	−0.72	−0.56	0.60	−1.65		0.36
−10	0.26	0.01	−0.44	−0.43	−0.04	−0.60	0.68	0.89	−0.30		0.47
1	0.31	0.43	−0.20	0.23	1.13	−0.53	1.66	0.75		0.54	0.46
5	0.26	0.41	0.27	0.68	1.15	−0.50	1.65	0.78		0.84	0.44
10	0.22	0.40	0.72	1.12	1.18	−0.47	1.65	0.81		1.14	0.42
20	0.18	0.41	1.26	1.67	1.22	−0.43	1.66	0.83		1.52	0.40
50	0.18	0.41	1.68	2.09	1.26	−0.40	1.66	0.82		1.81	0.39
00	0.18	0.41	1.72	2.13	1.26	−0.40	1.66	0.82		1.84	0.39
Σ	0.14			−0.07	0.07			0.22	−0.69	0.69	0.36

Table 13.7 Separating efficiency from redistribution for TRP3: closed economy case

Generation		Intragenerational							Intergenerational		
	efficiency	redistribution		total	total	redistribution		efficiency	redistribution		efficiency
		tax payments poor households	factor prices			factor prices rich households	tax payments		losers	winners	
−54	−0.01	−1.23	0.07	−1.17	−0.84	0.05	−0.89	0.00	−1.07		−0.01
−50	−0.01	−1.12	0.07	−1.05	−0.81	0.06	−0.87	0.00	−0.98		−0.01
−40	0.04	−0.33	−0.27	−0.60	2.26	−0.28	2.54	0.09		0.19	0.05
−30	0.33	0.27	−0.56	−0.28	4.17	−0.62	4.80	0.42		1.05	0.35
−20	0.44	−0.47	−0.59	−1.06	3.31	−0.73	4.04	0.75		0.36	0.54
−10	0.27	−0.78	−0.36	−1.13	0.96	−0.65	1.61	0.95	−0.43		0.50
1	0.28	−0.92	−0.08	−1.00	0.01	−0.43	0.44	0.75	−0.66		0.44
5	0.08	−0.95	0.36	−0.59	0.04	−0.39	0.42	0.87	−0.38		0.35
10	−0.09	−0.97	0.74	−0.22	0.06	−0.35	0.41	0.97	−0.13		0.27
20	−0.25	−0.98	1.15	0.17	0.09	−0.31	0.40	1.05		0.14	0.19
50	−0.26	−0.99	1.39	0.40	0.10	−0.29	0.39	1.03		0.30	0.18
00	−0.25	−0.99	1.42	0.43	0.10	−0.29	0.39	1.03		0.32	0.18
Σ	0.06			−0.34	0.34			0.27	−0.20	0.20	0.33

In all cases these redistribution profiles are U-shaped for the poor as well as for the rich households. While factor price changes favour the very old poor and rich households, they heavily burden the current middle-aged generations. For the rich future generations, this burden is lower than for the middle-aged but continues to be negative, while the poor future generations benefit from factor price changes. Comparing the small open economy with the closed economy context, we realize that the extent of aggregate intragenerational redistribution is reduced in all three cases, whereas the amount of intergenerational redistribution increases further for TRP1 and TRP2.

To explain the above-mentioned redistribution profiles, we have to refer to the time path of factor price changes following the different tax reform programmes. Table 13.8 provides a summary overview of some relevant macro-aggregates and factor prices. Real gross-of-tax factor prices correspond to the marginal products of capital (MPC) and labour (MPL). Due to the negative slope of the factor-price frontier, it suffices to explain the change of either one of the factor prices. Here we concentrate on the time path of the real wage rate. This requires a discussion of labour supply and labour demand reactions to tax changes. Changes in labour demand occur mostly because tax-induced changes in the economy's capital stock shift the marginal productivity of labour. In the following we will neglect this interdependence, however. Labour supply changes are due to tax-induced substitution effects on the one hand, and to income effects on the other. Decreasing the marginal tax load on labour as under TRP1 and TRP2 clearly reduces substitution effects and increases labour supply. As to the income effect, labour supply is inversely related to the change in the present value of disposable income[14] – provided that leisure is non-inferior. Under TRP1 and TRP2 there is a considerable intergenerational redistribution from old to young. Hence, as long as the presently old generations form a relevant part of a period's labour force, total labour supply will increase and the wage rate will fall. As Table 13.8 illustrates, the latter is true for the first two or three periods following the tax reform. During this time span, the interest rate will increase. After the first three or four years, the development of factor prices turns around: the wage rate increases and the interest rate falls.

Now consider the very old generations in the reform period. Because they earn mainly capital income and no or only a modest wage income, they are favoured by the short-run increase in interest rates. On the other hand, for the current high-productivity generations, factor price changes are very unfavourable. They are heavily hurt by the middle- and long-run decrease in interest rates because interest income is more important for them during their remaining lifetime than wage income. For the very young and all future generations, factor price changes are a mixed blessing. But the general direction of redistribution is clear. Poorer households have a higher fraction of wage income than interest income. Hence they benefit more from the long-run increase in wage rates. For the rich and future generations, however, the

Table 13.8 Macro-economic aggregates and factor prices in the closed economy case: percentage rates of change against benchmark equilibrium

Period	Labour supply	Capital stock	GDP	Consumption	MPL	MPC	VAT rate	Savings rate
TRP1								
1	2.5	0.0	1.9	-0.8	-0.6	1.9	19.9	12.7
2	2.3	0.7	1.9	-0.6	-0.4	1.2	19.8	12.6
3	2.1	1.3	1.9	-0.5	-0.2	0.6	19.8	12.5
4	2.0	1.9	1.9	-0.3	0.0	0.1	19.7	12.5
5	1.8	2.4	2.0	-0.2	0.2	-0.5	19.7	12.4
10	1.2	4.8	2.1	0.5	0.9	-2.6	19.4	12.0
20	0.5	7.6	2.2	1.4	1.7	-5.0	19.1	11.5
60	0.0	9.9	2.3	2.3	2.4	-6.8	18.8	11.0
∞	-0.1	10.0	2.3	2.4	2.4	-6.9	18.8	11.0
TRP2								
1	2.5	0.0	1.8	-1.3	-0.6	1.8	21.9	12.9
2	2.3	0.7	1.9	-1.1	-0.4	1.1	21.8	12.8
3	2.1	1.5	1.9	-0.9	-0.2	0.5	21.8	12.7
4	1.9	2.1	2.0	-0.8	0.1	-0.2	21.7	12.6
5	1.7	2.8	2.0	-0.6	0.3	-0.7	21.7	12.5
10	1.1	5.4	2.1	0.1	1.1	-3.1	21.4	12.2
20	0.2	8.9	2.3	1.2	2.1	-6.0	21.0	11.6
60	-0.4	11.7	2.5	2.3	2.9	-8.3	20.7	11.0
∞	-0.5	11.8	2.5	2.3	3.0	-8.4	20.6	11.0
TRP3								
1	1.8	0.0	1.4	-2.0	-0.5	1.4	17.1	13.6
2	1.6	0.7	1.4	-1.7	-0.2	0.7	17.0	13.4
3	1.5	1.4	1.5	-1.5	0.0	0.0	16.9	13.3
4	1.3	2.1	1.5	-1.3	0.2	-0.6	16.9	13.2
5	1.1	2.7	1.5	-1.1	0.4	-1.1	16.8	13.1
10	0.5	5.1	1.7	-0.2	1.1	-3.3	16.5	12.6
20	-0.1	7.8	1.8	1.0	1.9	-5.5	16.2	11.9
60	-0.5	9.5	1.9	1.7	2.4	-6.9	16.0	11.4
∞	-0.5	9.5	1.9	1.7	2.4	-7.0	15.9	11.4

long-run fall in interest rates is decisive because interest income is relatively more important for them over their life cycle.

As a final point we note that, even if redistributional effects due to shifts in tax payment and in factor prices run in opposite directions, quantitatively, total redistribution effects strongly dominate the efficiency effects.

13.6 CONCLUSIONS AND QUALIFICATIONS

The motivation for writing this chapter was our feeling that recent discussions about income tax reforms in Germany almost exclusively focus on efficiency reasoning and largely neglect any redistributional issues. We have developed a methodology which allows us to decompose total welfare effects from a tax, restructuring them into their efficiency and redistributional components. This is one of the many applications where the CGE approach proves to be invaluable. We can scarcely see any other framework in which a quantitative separation of efficiency from redistribution is possible.

It turned out that our scepticism as to the predominance of efficiency arguments in taxation theory and policy is well founded. For the income tax reforms considered here, intergenerational as well as intragenerational redistribution effects, in almost all cases, are quantitatively much more important than efficiency effects. Furthermore, the main differences between the three tax reform proposals do not lie in their efficiency effects, but rather in their intergenerational and intragenerational redistribution profiles. This is important for a summary evaluation of the reform proposals.

Any efficiency-oriented evaluation would concentrate on aggregate present-value efficiency gains and losses. A cursory look at Tables 13.2–13.7 reveals that TRP1, the (almost) flat tax proposed by MP Uldall, is the most favourable one. Aggregate efficiency effects are about 20 per cent higher for TRP1 than for TRP2 or TRP3. Correspondingly, TRP1 is associated with higher employment effects than the other two proposals. There are two reasons for the efficiency superiority of TRP1. The first is the large reduction in (top) marginal income tax rates. The second and probably more important reason is the intertemporal smoothing of tax rates, which is of special importance in a life-cycle context.

Turning to the redistributional effects, all three proposals involve some intragenerational redistribution from the poor to the rich. These effects are highest for TRP3, the abolition of interest income taxes. Our value judgement is that this direction of intragenerational redistribution is undesirable. From an intergenerational point of view, the redistributional effects of the three proposals are different. While TRP1 and TRP2 redistribute from the old to the young and to future generations, TRP3 redistributes in favour of the current middle-aged generations, but burdens younger and future generations. Any evaluation of redistributional effects requires some value judgement. Our view is that the redistribution from old to young following a tax reform countervails the opposite redistributional effects of public debt and pay-as-you-go social security systems. TRP3, on the other hand, reinforces the burdening of future generations. In our opinion, there is hardly any justification for this.

Summarizing, TRP1 seems to be the most attractive reform candidate from an efficiency as well as from a distributional point of view.

As a final remark we would like to stress the importance of our no-bequest assumption. As is well known, an operative altruistic bequest motive would eliminate all intergenerational redistribution. Only intragenerational as well as efficiency effects would remain. We do not want to go into the details of the bequest-motive controversy. In any case, our numerical results can be interpreted as representing the upper limit for tax-induced intergenerational redistribution.

NOTES

1 By way of a special certificate of exemption, it is guaranteed that interest income up to the exemption limit of DM6,100/12,200 annually is not subject to the withholding tax.

2 Actually, Uldall proposed marginal tax rates of 8, 18 and 28 per cent.

3 These are M. Rose (University of Heidelberg), F.W. Wagner (University of Tübingen) and E. Wenger (University of Würzburg).

4 See Schmidt *et al.* (1996) for a more complete description of the Croatian tax system.

5 See, for example, Frankfurter Institut (1996).

6 For a similar welfare decomposition, see Fehr and Kotlikoff (1996).

7 Note that $c_1^{t\,1}$, $l_1^{t\,1}$ and k^t, the capital owned by the old at the beginning of period t, are fixed. The time endowment in both periods have been normalized to 1. λ^{t-1} is the marginal utility of income of the elderly at time t. All other variables are self-explanatory.

8 Without compensation, dc_i^t and dl_i^t give the uncompensated or Marshallian changes in consumption and leisure demand.

9 Note that the following definitions hold: $RD^s := RD_P^s + RD_R^s$ and $EB^s := EB_P^s + EB_R^s$.

10 In the last line of Table 13.1, L and W denote the index sets of those generations which lose and win, respectively.

11 This assumption might appear to be rather restrictive because it seems to ignore the possibility of government borrowing. Kotlikoff (1993) has shown, however, that any government policy involving a positive level of public debt can be relabelled as one in which government debt is always zero.

12 The regressivity of VAT follows from the higher savings rate of the rich households and the lower share of present-value consumption expenditures in present-value lifetime income.

13 Figure 13.2 illustrates that, when compared with TRP1, marginal tax rates under TRP2 are higher in (less-populated) higher income brackets but lower in (densely populated) middle-income brackets. This explains the higher loss in income tax revenue under TRP2, which has to be compensated by a larger increase in the VAT.

14 The effects of a change in present-value income on savings is less clear because it

depends on the time structure of income changes; see, for example, the exchange between Feldstein (1978) and Sandmo (1981).

REFERENCES

Altig, D. and. Carlstrom, C.T. (1995), *Marginal Tax Rates and Income Inequality: A Quantitative-Theoretic Analysis*, Working Paper 9508, Federal Reserve Bank of Cleveland.

Auerbach, A.J. and Kotlikoff, L.J. (1987), *Dynamic Fiscal Policy*, Cambridge: Cambridge University Press.

Fehr, H. and Kotlikoff, L.J. (1996–97), 'Generational accounting in general equilibrium', *Finanzarchiv* NF 53: 1–27.

Feldstein, M. (1978), 'The rate of return, taxation and personal savings', *Economic Journal*, 88: 482–7.

Frankfurter Institut (1996), *Steuerreform für Arbeitsplätze und Umwelt*, Bad Homburg.

Fullerton, D. and Rogers, D.L. (1993), *Who Bears the Lifetime Tax Burden?*, Washington, D.C.: Brookings Institution.

Gravelle, J.G. (1991), 'Income, consumption, and wage taxation in a life-cycle model: separating efficiency from redistribution', *American Economic Review*, 81: 985–95.

Keuschnigg, Ch. (1992), 'Intergenerationally neutral taxation', *Public Finance*, 47: 446–61.

Keuschnigg, Ch. (1994), 'Dynamic tax incidence and intergenerationally neutral reform', *European Economic Review*, 38: 343–66.

Kotlikoff, L.J. (1993), 'From deficit delusion to the fiscal balance rule: looking for a sensible way to measure fiscal policy', *Journal of Economics*, 7th supplement, 17–41.

Kotlikoff, L.J. (1996), 'Replacing the US federal tax system with a retail sales tax: macroeconomic and distributional impacts', unpublished report to Americans for Fair Taxation, December.

Kotlikoff, L.J. and Summers, L.H. (1981), 'The role of intergenerational transfers in aggregate capital accumulation', *Journal of Political Economy*, 89, 706–32.

Sandmo, A. (1981), 'The rate of return and personal savings', *Economic Journal*, 91: 536–40.

Schmidt, P., Wissel, H. and Stoeckler, M. (1996), 'The new Croatian tax system', *Bulletin for International Fiscal Documentation*, 50: 155–63.

14

ARE DESTINATION AND ORIGIN PRINCIPLES EQUIVALENT?

A quantitative evaluation for the European Union

Hans Fehr and Clemente Polo

14.1 INTRODUCTION

The goal of this chapter is to estimate the revenue and welfare effects that European Union (EU) countries would experience if the current value added (VA) transitional system (TS) were to be replaced by a new system based on the origin principle (OP). Here, we analyse the non-reciprocal restricted origin principle (NRROP), a scenario which was recently advocated by Lockwood *et al.* (1994b, 1995). The estimates are obtained by simulating such a policy in a multicountry general equilibrium model of the EU, calibrated to 1992 data. We would like to emphasise that total welfare effects are decomposed into substitution and international income effects, which is, in our view, one of the main contributions of the chapter.

It goes without saying that the issues at stake are important from a practical or policy viewpoint, since VA revenue accounts for more than 10 per cent of fiscal revenues in the majority of EU countries (see Table 14.1), and most of them are currently hard-pressed to reduce the public deficit below the 3 per cent ceiling set in the Maastricht Treaty. On the other hand, some of our results can be looked at as an empirical test of the validity of the equivalence results between VA systems based on the OP and the destination principle (DP), a topic which has received considerable attention in theoretical literature in the last few years.

Before January 1993, VA taxes in the Community were levied according to the DP, that is, at the rates where final consumption took place, providing member countries with tax rebates on their exports and taxing their imports at the national borders. Obviously, the removal of customs barriers on intra-union trade, envisaged in the White Paper for the completion of the internal market, required a major adjustment of the existing DP system. The search for the 'definitive' VA regime reached a high point when the European Single Act was approved in 1987, and the EC Commission revealed its ambitious plans to harmonise VA rates, to apply the OP to all intra-union transactions, and to set up a clearing house (CH) to redistribute VA revenues among countries. Since the transactions of the Community with the rest of world (ROW) would be taxed according to the DP, the 'definitive' system was a restricted OP (ROP) regime, a term coined by Shibata (1967). Clearly, taxing consumption in the EU at the rates which apply where goods are produced or imported from the ROW would make fiscal adjustments on intra-union trade unnecessary.

The Commission plans, however, did not prosper and the current TS system was finally approved in 1990 for the transitional period 1993–6. Under the TS, commodities are taxed at the rate where the purchase takes place, which amounts to applying the DP to most intra-union transactions, while individuals' purchases are taxed according to the OP. The mixed nature of the system has drawn considerable criticism. For some authors, the main problem is the need to maintain fiscal adjustments on intra-union transactions among registered traders; others, however, view cross-border shopping and tax competition among EU countries as the culprit. But currently there is no clear-cut proposal to replace the TS, which has been extended until 1999.

The NRROP is a variant of Shibata's ROP. Under the ROP, countries forming a tax union apply the OP to all intra-union transactions and the DP to transactions with the ROW. In contrast, the NRROP treats transactions of the tax union countries with the ROW as intra-union transactions, effectively eliminating rebates on exports to the ROW and import taxes from the ROW. Notice that although the OP applies to all intra-union transactions, no clearing house is contemplated in this case.

The rationale behind this proposal is the equivalence results derived by Lockwood *et al.* (1994b) between the NRROP and the DP, and their claim that 'although exact equivalence will not hold in practice, it will be sufficiently close to doing so that the differences are unimportant' (Lockwood *et al.*, 1995: 3). If their claim is correct, the application of the same rates to domestic, intra-union and ROW transactions would greatly simplify the administration and reduce private and public costs. But if not, the ROW could retaliate by eliminating rebates on its exports and taxes on its imports, adopting, in other words, the OP as well. This scenario is equivalent to the universal adoption of the OP (UOP).

The NRROP and the UOP reforms are simulated in the static multicountry model developed by Fehr *et al.* (1995), calibrated for this chapter with a new and more comprehensive database of eleven EU countries and the ROW. We want to point out that the model features some standard assumptions in Applied General Equilibrium models – production requires intermediate inputs, similar goods produced in different countries are imperfect substitutes (Armington's assumption), and capital is perfectly mobile – that violate the assumptions made in trade models to derive equivalence results. But if the claim of Lockwood et al., is correct, the departures should have negligible effects. The model disregards other institutional features (tax evasion, transfer pricing, cross-border shopping, etc.), as they do not seem important for our purposes.

A few comments on the simulations performed and the results obtained are necessary. First, the reader should keep in mind that our simulations are differential incidence exercises where tax rates are endogenously determined to keep transfers to consumers constant. Second, we use uniform rates within countries in all scenarios because it is an assumption required to derive the equivalence results between the DP and both the NRROP and the UOP. Third, we first simulate the adoption of uniform rates within countries under the DP and present the effects of a mild harmonisation reform of the current system as our base case. Fourth, our results strongly suggest that equivalence between the NRROP and the DP does not hold in practice. Indeed, the EU will experience large potential gains from the adoption of the NRROP. Finally, if the ROW also adopts the OP, the total gain for the EU is also similar to that in the base case.

The paper is organised as follows. In section 14.2, we provide some historical background on VA taxation in the Community and discuss current proposals for reforming the TS with respect to the equivalence results derived in the trade literature. The features of the Applied General Equilibrium (AGE) model used in this study and the dataset used to calibrate it are briefly described in section 14.3. Section 14.4 includes a discussion of the results obtained in the different policy scenarios. Final remarks and extensions are included in section 14.5.

14.2 VA TAXATION IN THE EU: THE DESTINATION AND ORIGIN PRINCIPLES

In this section, we summarise the proposals and changes VA taxation has experienced in the EU since the introduction of the TS. Then, we discuss the equivalence results between the two international taxation principles: the DP and the OP. Bovenberg and Horne (1992) provide an excellent overview of the issue.

VA taxation in the community

Until 1993, VA taxes in the EU followed the DP, and tax liabilities were calculated with the invoice or tax credit method, which allows the tax paid on input purchases to be deducted from gross tax liabilities. The application of the DP required exports to be zero-rated and imports to be taxed at the same rate as domestic equivalent commodities. Clearly, the existence of border controls where the flows of imports and exports were checked and the corresponding tax adjustments played a key role in the administration of the system. Since the publication of the White Paper (Commission of the European Communities, 1985) and the approval of the Single Act in 1987, it was clear to everybody that the administration of the VA tax would have to undergo a profound change once border controls were eliminated in January 1993.

The current TS (Commission of the European Communities, 1990) approved in 1990 was intended as a temporary arrangement to keep the DP operative after the elimination of border controls in January 1993. However, the difficulties of finding an agreeable substitute based on the OP made necessary the extension of the transitional period for three more years until December 1999. The TS is a hybrid that applies the DP to both intra-union transactions among registered traders and transactions with the ROW, and the OP to most individual purchases. Thus, intra-union transactions among registered traders in the EU receive export rebates in the country of origin and are taxed in the destination country in their first periodic return. In the absence of national customs, fiscal adjustments are made on the basis of accounting records, a possibility already considered by Shibata (1967). In contrast, individuals are free to shop around, although that freedom is limited by the existence of specific tax regimes for exempted persons and legal entities, distance sales and sales of new means of transportation.

The TS has been repeatedly criticised for not treating all intra-union traders equally, having to rely on special regimes and weakening the VA chain. Vanistendael (1995) points out that the tax treatment of international and domestic transactions discriminates against domestic producers who have to pay the tax at the time the transaction takes place. He also indicates that small businesses may be faced with an excessive administrative burden when they are required to have a tax representative in the country of destination. Finally, he argues that the lack of uniformity in the application of the law and the disparity in dual and triple rate structures may produce various types of distortions.

Sinn (1990) emphasises cross-border shopping as one of the major problems that would result from the opening of borders to individuals and tax exempt entities. However, as Keen and Smith (1996) recognise, 'the feared explosion of cross-border activity (not negligible prior to 1993) has not emerged'. It does not matter for our purposes whether it is due to lack of consumer information or the consequences of the special regimes; the fact is that for practical purposes the TS can be viewed as a DP regime.

Finally, the removal of border controls has made the control of export and import activities much more difficult for tax authorities. Keen and Smith (1996) rightly claim that the VA chain which facilitates the collection of the tax may break down more easily when fiscal adjustments on intra-union transactions rely on business records, and its verification requires collaboration among national tax administrations.

Summing up: the current situation is rather confusing. Although it is generally accepted[1] that the 'final' VA system in the EU should be based on the OP (Country of Origin Commission, 1994; European Parliament, 1996), it may not be possible to implement an OP VA system at a reasonable cost if the EU has to set up a transfer system to ensure that tax revenues accrue to the country where final consumption takes place. As we see it, the only way out is to convince EU countries that it is possible to adopt an OP regime without modifying the current distribution of revenues. And for that, we need both theoretical arguments and robust figures.

Equivalence results

The Tinbergen Report (European Coal and Steel Community High Authority, 1953) had already suggested that if rates were uniform within countries, the coordinated substitution of an OP tax for a DP tax would have no real effects after the adjustment of exchange rates. Shibata (1967) showed in a two-commodity model, with homogeneous goods, perfect competition in commodity and factor markets, uniform rates within countries, factor immobility and a flexible exchange rate, that the adoption of the UOP will have no real effects. The result has been recently generalised by Lockwood *et al.* (1994a) to environments with any number of commodities and factors, constant returns, arbitrary factor taxes, transport costs and imperfect competition. Notice, however, that the result does not extend to economies with intermediate goods and factor mobility.

Indeed, Genser, Haufler and Sørensen (1995) pointed out that when there are intermediate commodities, the way in which the OP is administered plays a crucial role. Their results indicate that in order to obtain equivalence, the deduction for the tax on intermediate purchases should be calculated using the notional credit method, deflated by the domestic tax factor. These authors claim that in a simple, small, open economy model, capital mobility does not alter the neutrality of the OP when commodity taxation is of a consumption type. Bovenberg's (1994) analysis of a small economy with capital mobility and overlapping generations indicates that, although neither the OP nor the DP principle distorts the allocation of capital, they are not equivalent since their impacts on the intergenerational and international distribution of resources are different.

The equivalence between the DP and the UOP provides no insights as to what might happen if the EU replaced the TS system by a VA ROP regime. Shibata (1967) showed in a three-country, two-commodity model (under the same assumptions) that the adoption of the ROP by two countries will result in 'real income transfers from the high-tax member country to the low-tax member country'. According to Shibata, harmonisation of tax rates was necessary and sufficient to obtain the same equilibrium. Another way to avoid trade deflection was Shibata's proposal to tax imports at a common rate which would be used also to calculate export rebates. Genser's (1996) unified restricted origin principle is nothing other than Shibata's common external tax. Note also that if the common external tax rate is set equal to zero, imports will be untaxed in the tax union and exports to the third country would be taxed. But this is exactly the NRROP proposed recently by Lockwood *et al.* (1994b).

Berglas (1981) proved that Shibata was wrong. In a three-commodity model, Berglas demonstrated that, even if the two countries forming the tax union have the same tax rate, income will be redistributed unless their trade with the third country was initially balanced. Therefore, full harmonisation of tax rates seems unavoidable in order to obtain equivalence between the DP and ROP. Fortunately, Lockwood *et al.* (1994b) have proved an equivalence result between the DP and the NRROP for rather general economies without requiring full harmonisation. As before, however, intermediate goods and capital mobility are ruled out.

Clearly, the preconditions for equivalence between the DP and the NRROP are not met by the EU: tax rates within countries are not uniform, tax rates are not harmonised across countries, production requires inputs, capital is highly mobile and exchange rates are not flexible. Although the list is quite impressive, Lockwood *et al.* (1994b: 313) claim 'that the only condition sufficient for equivalence of regimes is complete uniformity of tax rates ... across countries in the tax union'. Implicitly, the authors are saying that the other items on the list have a negligible impact in practice. Therefore, uniformity of tax rates in each country is the only assumption we impose in our simulations to test the equivalence result.

14.3 THE MULTICOUNTRY AGE MODEL

The model we use to perform the simulations is the static multicountry model of Fehr *et al.* (1995), calibrated to a 1992 microconsistent database. Here we shall briefly summarise the most salient features of the model, referring the interested reader to the detailed description of the model included in their book.

For this chapter we made some major changes in the database and the type of simulation performed. The base year of the data set is now 1992, all EU member countries of 1992 are included, and only Belgium and Luxembourg are aggregated. In total, we have twelve countries including the ROW.

The model includes eleven produced commodities and two non-produced factors. The last commodity produced in each country is non-marketed services rendered by the government. The two primary factors are labour, immobile across countries, and capital, which is assumed to be perfectly mobile.

Production takes place in the firms which use a nested constant-returns-to-scale technology. At the first level, output is a Leontief aggregate of value added and intermediate commodities. Value added is a CES function of capital and labour, and intermediate commodities are a CES function of equivalent goods produced in different countries. Producers maximise profits and in equilibrium profits must be zero, i.e., revenues must equal costs plus production taxes.

Consumers have homothetic preferences defined by aggregate consumption and leisure. Aggregate consumption is a CES composite of the eleven commodities in the model. Each of the commodities is, in turn, a CES aggregate of domestic production and an aggregate of equivalent imports. Finally, the latter are given by CES functions of equivalent commodities produced in the other countries. Consumers derive income from the sale of their labour and capital endowments. They are subject to income taxes and VA taxes and maximise utility subject to the budget constraint.

The government in each country buys commodities to produce public goods. The government also collects three types of taxes: import taxes, consumption taxes and income taxes. In our model we use statutory VA rates that do not take into account fraud, exemptions, etc. Tax revenues exceed government consumption expenditures in the benchmark, the difference being transferred back to consumers. In all our simulations, tax rates are adjusted endogenously to hold the real level of transfer constant.

The key data used to specify the model numerically are the 1992 inter-regional input-matrix for the eleven EU countries and the ROW. The construction of this table is described in more detail in Fehr (1996). The main sources used for this purpose are Eurostat national input–output tables for the eleven EU countries, and the input–output tables of Japan and the US. First, the tables were updated to 1992 using national account data. Then bilateral intermediate input matrices and final vectors of exports were estimated using information on bilateral trade flows.

Table 14.1 provides a few macroeconomic indicators in the benchmark equilibrium which highlight some important traits of the EU in 1992. Column (1) provides the absolute GDP of each country in millions of ECU and column (2) the relative GDP of each country with respect to the GDP in the EU. In column (3) the ratio of VA revenues to GDP indicates the importance of VA revenues in the EU.[2] The existing trade imbalances for the EU countries in per cent of GDP are given in column (4) while columns (5) and (6) contain the reduced and standard VA rates in the benchmark.

As usual some of the parameters of the model are exogenously specified: elasticity parameters are taken from Fehr et al. (1995) and VA rates from Table 14.1. The remaining parameters are chosen to replicate the observed data as a competitive equilibrium.

Table 14.1 Macroeconomic indicators in 1992

Country	GDP (millions ECU)	GDP (in %)	VA revenue (in %)	Trade (in %)	VA tax rates Reduced	VA tax rates Standard
	(1)	(2)	(3)	(4)	(5)	(6)
B-L	170,605	3.3	12.4	−1.8	6.0	20.5
DK	108,662	2.1	12.8	6.6	−	25.0
D	1,289,278	25.0	8.6	−0.8	7.0	15.0
GR	59,189	1.1	13.1	−11.4	4.0, 8.0	18.0
E	442,438	8.6	9.4	−2.5	4.0, 5.0, 7.0	15.0
F	1,018,945	19.7	10.4	0.8	2.1, 5.5	18.6
IRL	39,483	0.8	9.3	9.5	−	21.0
I	930,227	18.0	11.7	−0.9	4.0	19.0
NL	231,313	4.5	9.8	−2.0	6.0	17.5
P	71,216	1.4	12.0	−11.8	5.0	16.0
UK	799,216	15.5	10.7	−2.8	−	17.5
EU		100.0	10.0	−0.4	−	−
ROW	15,601,425	302.3	7.8	0.4	−	10.0

14.4 SIMULATION AND INTERPRETATION OF RESULTS

In this section we present the results obtained from simulating the fiscal reforms described in the introduction: the adoption of uniform rates within countries under the TS, the substitution of the TS by the NRROP, and finally the shift from the TS to the UOP with uniform rates.

Before presenting the numbers obtained, we want to highlight that for each policy we attempt to explain the change in total welfare (percentage change in Hicks's equivalence variations) in terms of the income and substitution effects at work. An income effect arises whenever the tax revenue of a country differs from the tax burden borne by the domestic consumer: it is positive (negative) when the revenue is greater (smaller) than the burden. In order to isolate substitution effects, we proceed to simulate the corresponding policy, adjusting transfers to eliminate the income effect: we interpret the welfare changes obtained in this simulation as the substitution effects. In turn, substitution effects can be disaggregated into domestic and international substitution effects (Fehr *et al.*, 1995: 104): the former measures the distortions of consumer choices which also appear in a closed economy, while international substitution effects measure distortions in relative prices brought about by the monopoly power that every country can exercise on international markets.[3]

Tax reform under the destination principle

We assume in our benchmark that the TS is a pure DP system, ignoring the fact that under the TS individuals and exempted entities are taxed at the rate where the purchase occurs rather than where consumption takes place; in other words, we disregard cross-border shopping. Then, after the adoption of a uniform tax rate structure within countries, the net tax liability of a firm producing commodity i in country h is calculated using the credit method:

$$T_i^h = \tau^h \left[q_i^h Q_i^h - q_i^h X_i^h - \sum_{k \in W} \sum_{j \in N} q_j^h V_{ji}^{kh} \right] \tag{14.1}$$

where W is the set of all countries; N the set of commodities; τ^h is the uniform tax rate in country h; q_i^h and q_j^k are the producers' prices for commodities i in country h and j in country k, respectively; Q_i^h is domestic production in h, X_i^h exports to both Union and non-Union countries, and V_{ji}^{kh} the intermediate purchases of commodity j from country k. Aggregating firms' tax liabilities and using the market clearing conditions, we obtain after some manipulations the total VAT revenue of each country:

$$T^h = \sum_{i \in N} T_i^h + \sum_{k \in W_h} \sum_{i \in N} \tau^h q_i^k M_i^{kh} = \sum_{k \in W} \sum_{i \in N} \tau^h q_i^k C_i^{kh} \tag{14.2}$$

where W_h is the set of all countries except h. The first term in the above equation is the taxes collected at the firm level; the second is taxes on imports from Union and non-Union countries. Observe that the second equality clearly shows that VAT in the TS is essentially a consumption tax, therefore equivalent to a single-stage retail tax.

The first simulation serves mainly as a pedagogic exercise. Since a fiscal reform of the TS does not produce cross-country income effects, we can easily isolate the distortions implicit in the initial tax rate structure. The total impact on welfare would be the net result of domestic and international substitution effects. One would expect consumers with homothetic preferences to experience positive domestic substitution effects when a uniform rate substitutes the dual or triple VA rate structure in the benchmark. On the other hand, in an open economy it may happen that adopting a uniform tax structure in all countries causes a deterioration in the terms-of-trade of some of them. Therefore, consumers in those countries may end up being worse off. This is exactly what one would expect when the VA system in a country taxes more heavily those commodities with relatively high import shares in domestic consumption; then the adoption of a uniform rate will increase demand for those goods and reduce the demand for domestic goods. The fall in the terms-of-trade simply reflects the lower demand for domestically produced goods. Table 14.2 presents the results of simulating this policy.

The EU as a whole experiences a welfare gain of 7,512 million ECU or

Table 14.2 Uniform taxation within the destination principle

Country	HEV[a]		ToT	VAT rates	
	(millions ECU)	*(in %)*	*(in %)*	*g.e.*[b]	*f.r.*[c]
	(1)	*(2)*	*(3)*	*(4)*	*(5)*
B-L	137	0.64	−0.05	14.69	14.33
DK	13	0.10	0.35	19.47	18.82
D	3,298	2.96	0.55	10.46	10.55
GR	56	0.72	−0.58	14.02	14.27
E	203	0.49	−0.20	11.09	10.99
F	2,270	2.15	0.12	12.88	12.86
IRL	129	3.51	−0.10	12.30	12.43
I	768	0.71	−0.15	14.25	14.03
NL	−514	−2.27	−0.66	11.84	11.25
P	61	0.71	0.05	12.70	12.63
UK	1,092	1.28	−0.09	13.29	13.25
EU	7,512	1.42			
ROW	1,592	0.13	−0.12	9.98	10.00
ΣHEV	9,104				

Notes
[a] Hicksian equivalent variation
[b] General equilibrium

1.42 per cent of the VAT revenues in the benchmark. Notice that the ROW also experiences a modest gain. This is due to the positive domestic substitution effects in EU countries and a slight terms-of-trade deterioration for the ROW. Although it is difficult to estimate welfare changes in fiscal systems subject to various sorts of distortion taxes, it seems that adopting uniform taxes in each EU country would be a move in the right direction for the entire union.

The disaggregated results confirm our expectations as well: total welfare changes (columns (1) and (2)) are positive in all countries except the Netherlands, while changes in the terms-of-trade (column (3)) are either positive or negative. Notice that, in general, countries with small or negative changes in welfare (B-L, DK, GR, E, I, NL and P) are mainly those which experience a deterioration in their terms-of-trade (B-L, DK, GR, E, NL and P). The Netherlands, the sole loser in the game, is the country that suffers the largest deterioration in the terms-of-trade. On the contrary, countries that enjoy the largest welfare improvement (D, F, IRL, UK) show either an improvement in their terms-of-trade (D, F) or negligible reductions (IRL, UK).

The last two columns in Table 14.2 report the uniform VAT rates in each country with (column (4)) and without behavioural reactions (column (5)). Observe that countries which experience a sharp terms-of-trade reduction have to increase the tax rate (B-L, DK, NL) relative to the rate prevailing in the absence of behavioural reactions. The reason for this is that a terms-of-trade deterioration implies a reduction in the real wage rate, which reduces the labour supply and requires an increase in tax rates to balance the budget. Nevertheless, the difference between first round and general equilibrium VAT rates is surprisingly small.

The adoption of the non-reciprocal restricted origin principle (NRROP)

Under the NRROP, ROW countries still keep the DP, providing export rebates and taxing imports at the corresponding rate. In EU countries the tax liability of firm i in country h is now given by:

$$T_i^h = \tau^h \left(rK_i^h + w^h L_i^h \right) = \bar{\tau}^h \left[p_i^h Q_i^h - \sum_{k \in W} \sum_{j \in N} p_j^k V_{ji}^{kh} \right]$$

$$= \bar{\tau}^h p_i^h Q_i^h - \sum_{k \in W} \sum_{j \in N} \bar{\tau}^h p_j^k V_{ji}^{kh} \tag{14.3}$$

where τ^h is the statutory uniform VAT rate, and $\bar{\tau}^h = \tau^h/(1 + \tau^h)$ defines the tax-inclusive statutory tax rate which has to be applied to consumer prices p_i^h. The first calculation corresponds to the so-called addition method, the second to the subtraction method, and the third to the notional credit method. The calculation of tax liability with the notional credit method differs from the credit method used in equation (14.1) in two main respects: first, instead of producer prices we now use consumer prices and the respective tax-inclusive tax rates; second, there is no border tax adjustment with the ROW. Equality between the first and the second or third expressions follows easily from the zero profit condition. Aggregating tax liabilities yields national tax revenue:

$$T^h = \tau^h \sum_{i \in N} \left(rK_i^h + w^h L_i^h \right) \tag{14.4}$$

In contrast to the DP, national tax revenue and consumption taxes paid by domestic consumers will be different. The total tax borne by consumers in country h is given by:

$$\tilde{T}^h = \sum_{k \in W} \sum_{i \in N} \tilde{\tau}_i^k \tilde{q}_i^k C_i^{kh}$$

where $\tilde{\tau}_i^k$ denotes the effective consumption tax rates and $\tilde{q}_i^k$ is the net-of-tax producer price. The vector of effective producer prices, $\tilde{q}$, is calculated using the matrix of intermediate coefficients A and the vector of value added coefficients v:

$$\tilde{q} = (I - A^T)^{-1} v,$$

where I is the identity matrix, A^T is the transpose of the intermediate coefficient matrix, and v is the vector of value-added coefficients $v_i = (rK_i + wL_i)/Q_i$. Since we know the vector of consumer prices p, we can calculate effective consumption tax rates as:

$$\tilde{\tau}_i^k = \frac{p_i^k}{\tilde{q}_i^k} - 1 \quad i \in N, \, k \in W.$$

In contrast to the uniform reform under the DP, the adoption of the NRROP with uniform tax rates within countries involves considerable cross-country income shifting. In order to isolate net tax exports under the NRROP, we compute the effective consumption tax rates and calculate the difference $T^b - \tilde{T}^b$ in the counterfactual equilibrium. In a second simulation run, we keep the tax structure constant[4] and neutralise net tax export by allocating the respective tax burden $\tilde{T}^b$ to every country. As before, the resulting welfare effects are then interpreted as the sum of domestic and international substitution effects. Finally, the terms-of-trade effects reported in the following tables are calculated using the effective producer prices $\tilde{q}_i^k$ in this simulation.

Table 14.3 includes the result of substituting the TS system with the NRROP with a uniform rate structure.

According to Lockwood *et al.* (1994b: 313) 'a switch from a universal

Table 14.3 Uniform taxation within the non-reciprocal restricted origin principle

Country	HEV (millions ECU) (1)	(in %) (2)	Tax export (3)	Subst. effect (4)	Decomp. HEV ToT (in %) (5)	VAT rates g.e. (6)	f.r. (7)
B-L	2,258	10.64	18.70	−9.97	−2.05	14.07	14.15
DK	1,818	13.08	23.49	−12.38	−4.68	17.33	16.58
D	5,450	4.86	8.17	−2.61	−0.95	10.57	10.15
GR	85	1.09	3.31	−1.53	−0.80	16.57	17.84
E	1,118	2.68	3.69	−0.34	−0.25	11.44	11.57
F	6,262	5.93	8.71	−2.09	−1.41	12.85	12.99
IRL	548	14.93	15.79	−0.64	−0.49	10.66	10.71
I	6,081	5.59	8.15	−1.73	−1.04	14.16	13.64
NL	2,080	9.17	14.51	−6.32	−1.43	10.93	11.18
P	−186	−2.18	−0.17	−1.25	−0.68	15.08	15.27
UK	4,439	5.19	10.94	−4.85	−2.88	13.99	13.05
EU	29,952	5.64					
ROW	−4,312	−0.36	−4.07	3.24	3.92	8.81	10.00
ΣHEV	25,640						

275

destination regime to a non-reciprocal restricted origin regime has no real effects. All that is required for equivalence is exchange rate flexibility and uniform taxation of goods within countries.' We have also pointed out that their model excludes intermediate commodities and factor mobility. But they claim 'that although equivalence will not hold in practice, it will be very sufficiently close to doing so that the differences will be unimportant'. If that were true, Tables 14.2 and 14.3 would be 'sufficiently' similar. However, striking differences can be observed between them.

First, the last rows of columns (1) and (2) show that the EU as a whole gains about four times more than in the uniform rate scenario under the DP; on the contrary, the ROW experiences losses under the NRROP. The ROW's losses are the consequence of a negative net tax export (see column (3)), equivalent to a 4.07 per cent reduction of initial VA revenues which is not offset completely by the positive substitution effect (see column (4)), equivalent to 3.24 per cent of initial VA revenues. The ROW loses income to the EU since, under the NRROP, their residents bear some of the burden of EU taxes. But ROW consumers substitute domestic products for imports from the EU, and EU consumers substitute imports from the ROW for domestic products. Demand for ROW products increases everywhere, and the ROW terms-of-trade improve by 3.92 per cent (column (5)). It is ironical that this increase in welfare in the ROW is transferred to EU countries via net tax exports!

Second, all EU countries except Portugal experience substantial positive net tax exports mainly because of the specific treatment of trade with the ROW. However, the negative values of the substitution effects in all EU countries indicate that, when net tax exports are redistributed, the adoption of the NRROP has a negative impact on consumers' welfare in all EU countries. The explanation for the negative substitution effects in the EU is that effective consumption tax rates are much less uniform. Clearly, international income effects in column (3) and substitution effects in column (4) add up to the overall welfare effects in column (2).

The terms-of-trade sign in column (5) also indicates that the international substitution effect is negative in all EU countries. Observe that those countries with the strongest terms-of-trade deterioration are also those with the largest negative substitution effects. The adoption of the NRROP leads consumers in the ROW to substitute domestic goods for EU imports, altering the terms-of-trade in favour of the ROW. The magnitude of the terms-of-trade deterioration in every EU country depends on its VA tax rate and the importance of its trade with the ROW. Denmark, for instance, has the highest VA rate in the EU and strong trade ties with the ROW; it is the country whose terms-of-trade deteriorate the most.

Finally, turning to the VAT rates of the last two columns, we see that countries with a strong trade integration with the ROW, such as Denmark, Germany and the UK, have to increase their VAT rates compared to the first-round level. Other low-tax countries in the EU are able to reduce their taxes slightly.

The adoption of the UOP with within-country uniform tax rates

Our last simulation estimates the effects of the substitution of the OP for the DP in all countries including the ROW, when all countries have uniform rates. As we mentioned earlier, this scenario can be interpreted as the response by the ROW to the adoption of the NRROP by the EU. Such a scenario is not so unrealistic, since the adoption of an OP consumption VA tax has been under serious consideration in the near past, for example in the US (see Grubert and Newlon, 1995).

In contrast to the NRROP, the ROW's tax revenue is now calculated according to equations (14.3) and (14.4) as well. In order to isolate substitution effects, we apply the same compensation mechanism as under the NRROP. Table 14.4 presents the relevant welfare effects due to the substitution of the DP by the UOP with uniform rates within countries.

Our first observation is that, compared to Table 14.3, the EU suffers a welfare loss when the UOP is adopted and the ROW becomes better off. The aggregate gain for the EU is almost the same as in the DP simulation of Table 14.2. At first sight, it may be taken as favourable evidence for the view that the DP and the UOP are equivalent when each country applies a single rate. However, the results for individual countries do not support this view.

High-tax countries such as Denmark and Ireland will experience welfare

Table 14.4 Universal adoption of the origin principle with uniform tax rates

| Country | HEV | | Decomp. HEV | | | VAT |
| | (millions ECU) | (in %) | Tax export | Subst. effect | ToT (in %) | rates g.e. |
	(1)	(2)	(3)	(4)	(5)	(6)
B-L	848	3.99	9.47	−6.73	−1.30	14.67
DK	1,534	11.04	15.84	−6.38	−2.98	17.00
D	823	0.74	−3.10	4.00	1.00	10.54
GR	−461	−5.94	−4.86	−0.79	−0.87	16.76
E	−874	−2.10	−2.82	0.69	0.01	11.55
F	3,634	3.44	2.24	1.33	−0.28	12.80
IRL	410	11.18	6.18	4.94	0.31	10.63
I	2,171	2.00	3.26	−1.09	−0.73	14.32
NL	−611	−2.69	1.60	−4.34	−0.83	12.04
P	−696	−8.15	−6.95	−1.14	−0.42	15.16
UK	456	0.53	2.07	−1.37	−1.13	13.90
EU	7,233	1.36				
ROW	10,543	0.87	−0.57	1.38	0.78	9.47

gains in excess of 10 per cent of total initial VAT revenues; Greece and Portugal are at the other extreme of the spectrum. Columns (3) and (4) provide a disaggregation of welfare effects in terms of net tax exports (income effects) and substitution effects. As expected, net tax exports are definitely very important in countries with the highest tax rates (Belgium-Luxemburg, Denmark and Ireland), positive in other high tax countries (France, Italy, and UK), and negative in countries with low tax rates (Greece and Portugal).

When we neutralise all net tax exports by redistributing them, we obtain the substitution effects reported in column (4). We expect that the domestic substitution effects will be negative in general, since the spread of the effective consumption tax rates which are relevant for consumer decisions increases under the OP. As for the international substitution effect, it may be positive or negative depending on whether the change in the terms-of-trade (column (5)) is positive or negative. Notice that Belgium and Denmark experience the most extreme terms-of-trade reduction and are also the countries with the highest negative substitution effects. Adding up the aggregate substitution effects in column (4) and the net tax export effects in column (3) yields approximately the total welfare changes reported in column (2).

14.5 CONCLUSIONS

What can be learned from our chapter? First, we hope that our simulations serve as a methodological tool for a better understanding of the welfare effects of alternative VAT reform schemes. Second, we think that the chapter provides useful insights into the current policy debate on the 'definitive' VA system.

Our decomposition results show that effective consumption tax rates are a very valuable tool for estimating income and substitution effects under both the NRROP and the UOP. They provide an intelligible disaggregation of total welfare effects, which increases our confidence in the numbers obtained from a single simulation.

The results obtained have theoretical and policy implications. In our opinion, the results obtained do not support the view defended by some authors that the shift from a DP VA system to an OP VA system has no real effects. We have pointed out that our model includes features (intermediate commodities and capital mobility) ruled out in the trade models used to prove equivalence results. But the proponents of the NRROP, for instance, believe that equivalence will hold in practice. Our results show that these assumptions are quite relevant in practice and that one should expect substantial real effects after the move.

Turning to the policy implications, it might seem at first that the results suggest that the EU should apply the NRROP since the welfare gains under this system are enormous. It must be remembered that, first, the welfare improvement in the EU is generated in the ROW and transferred via tax exports; and, second, that the efficiency (substitution) effects are very negative for the EU. Moreover, it is very unlikely that non-EU countries would not react after the introduction of the NRROP in the EU. Probably most ROW countries would introduce some measures to prevent these huge revenue flows towards the EU: we have considered the adoption of the OP by the ROW. In this case, most EU countries end up being worse off than with a DP regime with uniform tax rates within countries.

NOTES

1 Laux-Meiselbach (1990) is an exception. He argues that the adoption of the OP will be barred by technical difficulties, may induce tax setting and distort investment decisions if there is uncertainty on the future rates of the tax.
2 Note that since investment expenditures are also included in the tax base of the model, our VA revenues are higher than those reported in national input–output tables.
3 For example, under the DP, a country could improve its terms-of-trade by taxing its imports at a higher rate than its exports.
4 In other words, we run a budget incidence simulation. A differential incidence with endogenous tax rates was technically not possible since in this case net tax exports fluctuate too strongly.

REFERENCES

Berglas, E. (1981), 'Harmonization of commodity taxes: destination, origin and restricted origin principles', *Journal of Public Economics*, 16: 377–87.
Bovenberg, A.L. (1994), 'Destination and origin based taxation under international capital mobility', *International Tax and Public Finance*, 1: 247–73.
Bovenberg, A.L. and Horne, J.P. (1992), 'Taxes on commodities: a survey', in G. Kopits (ed.), *Tax Harmonization in the European Community*, Occasional Paper 94, Washington, D.C.: International Monetary Fund.
Commission of the European Communities (1985), *Completing the Internal Market* (COM (85) 310), Brussels: Commission of the European Communities.
Commission of the European Communities (1990), *Amendment to the Proposal for a Council Directive Supplementing the Common System of Value Added Tax and Amending Directive 77/388/EEC. Transitional Arrangements for Taxation with a View to Establishment of the Internal Market* (Com(90)182), Brussels: Commission of the European Communities.
Country of Origin Commission (1994), *Formulation of the Definite Scheme for Improving Turn-over Tax on the Intra-Community Trade of Goods and Services and for a Functional Clearing Procedure*, Bonn: Federal Ministry of Finance.
European Coal and Steel Community High Authority (1953), *Report on Problems Raised by the Different Turnover Systems Applied in the Common Market*, Brussels: ECSC.

European Parliament (1996), *Options for a Definitive VAT System*, Economic Affairs Series E-5, Luxembourg: European Parliament.

Fehr, H. (1996), 'Construction of a microconsistent data set for the EU 1992', University of Tübingen, unpublished.

Fehr, H., Rosenberg, C. and Wiegard, W. (1995), *Welfare Effects of Value-added Tax Harmonization in Europe: A Computable General Equilibrium Analysis*, Berlin: Springer-Verlag.

Genser, B. (1996), 'A generalized equivalence property of mixed international VAT regimes', *Scandinavian Journal of Economics*, 98: 253–62.

Genser, B., Haufler, A. and Sørensen, B. (1995), 'Indirect taxation in an integrated Europe: is there a way of avoiding tax distortions without sacrificing national tax autonomy?', *Journal of Economic Integration*, 10: 178–205.

Grubert, H. and Newlon, T.S. (1995), 'The international implications of consumption tax proposals', *National Tax Journal*, 48: 619–47.

Keen, M. and Smith, S. (1996), 'The future of value added tax in the European Union', *Economic Policy*, 23: 375–420.

Laux-Meiselbach, W. (1990), 'Value-added tax and international trade', in V. Tanzi (ed.), *Public Finance, Trade and Development: Proceeedings of the 44th Congress of the International Institute of Public Finance*, Istanbul, 1988, Detroit: Wayne State University Press, 125–35.

Lockwood, B., de Meza, D. and Myles, G.D. (1994a), 'When are origin and destination regimes equivalent?', *International Tax and Public Finance*, 1: 5–24.

—— (1994b), 'The equivalence between the destination and nonreciprocal restricted origin regimes', *Scandinavian Journal of Economics*, 96: 311–28.

—— (1995), 'On the European VAT proposals: the superiority of origin over destination taxation', *Fiscal Studies*, 16: 1–17.

Shibata, H. (1967), 'The theory of economic unions: a comparative analysis of custom unions, free trade areas and tax unions', in C. Soup (ed.), *Fiscal Harmonization in Common Markets*, New York: Columbia University Press.

Sinn, H.W. (1990), 'Tax harmonisation and tax competition in Europe', *European Economic Review*, 34: 489–504.

Vanistendael, F. (1995), 'A proposal for a definitive VAT system: taxation in the country of origin at the rate of the country of destination without clearing', *EC Tax Review*, no. 1: 45–53.

15

WELFARE EFFECTS OF VAT RATE HARMONISATION IN THE EUROPEAN UNION

Barbara Cavalletti and Anna Ruocco

15.1 INTRODUCTION

The free circulation of goods and services in the European Union started on 1 January 1993, and consisted of the physical elimination of the border controls between member states. This event represented the first step towards the construction of a single market. The abolition of internal boundaries implied, as a consequence, the modification of indirect taxation. Up to now a hybrid system, the so-called *transitional system*, has been in effect. The main feature of the transitional system is that, while for the final consumer the origin principle applies (except for distance sales, cars, boats and planes), for commercial transactions the destination principle remains in use. The dissatisfaction caused by the current system is based on many grounds. Here we must note that the ultimate goal for the *definitive system* would be to base VAT on the origin principle. Then, two crucial political questions arise: the harmonisation of rates and the allocation of revenues to the member states.

In this chapter, we focus in particular on the question of the harmonisation of tax rates. There are at least two reasons to harmonise tax rates across countries. First, any compensation mechanism between member states would be much simpler and would require less administrative costs. Second, it can be seen that allowing each country to have different tax rates, especially when the origin principle applies, could lead to similar results as having internal tariffs. In other words, internal taxation would have the nature of indirect protection. The alignment of indirect taxes, then, might be a way of eliminating this type of trade distortion.[1]

Another point of view suggests that rate harmonisation is a limitation of national fiscal sovereignty and, therefore, market competition itself should be allowed to lead gradually to uniform taxation.

Up to now, the member states have only agreed on an adequate approximation of rates within a harmonised structure of two rates. In one of its latest documents,[2] the Commission, while not saying anything precise about the reduced tax rate – for which its previous suggestion was the recommendation of a minimum tax rate equal to 5 per cent[3] – reconfirms a range for the normal rate between 15 per cent and 25 per cent. A spread of 10 percentage points seems to be too wide to prevent distortions in competition and it can hardly be seen as a band at all.

The reason why little has been done in this respect is because it is not just a political and technical problem. Rather it stems from theoretical ambiguities which are at the very heart of VAT. The literature dealing with the harmonisation of tax rates focused mainly on the possibility of proving that this policy is Pareto-improving. Studies have been conducted considering VAT under the destination principle (Keen, 1987, 1989) and under the origin principle (Lopez-Garcia, 1996). The conclusion they arrived at is that, 'under normal circumstances, there exist harmonising reforms that generate a potential Pareto improvement provided that they are supplemented with the appropriate international transfers'.[4] The model used in both papers is a standard model of international trade (Dixit and Norman, 1980) with two countries, where only a consumption tax is levied, whose revenue is returned to the consumer as a lump-sum payment. Crucial assumptions are that no income effects as well as no binding revenue constraints for the government are considered, and that no other tax distortions are present in the benchmark equilibrium. Our aim is, then, to test the differing relevance of tax rate uniformity in efficiency terms under the destination principle (DP) and origin principle (OP), when more complexities are added into the model. The analysis here is carried out within an international trade general equilibrium model, in which each government provides a certain level of public goods and where national fiscal systems are rather complex.

Finally, given that no compensation mechanism for revenue displaced by the system of taxation takes place, welfare effects depend on the way in which we finance the policy at issue. There are many ways to neutralise the revenue effects of the harmonisation process: several taxes are already in place and new ones can be introduced. In this study three alternative options have been considered: lump-sum taxes; taxes on the use of labour input; and income taxes.

Results show that the OP option is a crucial feature of a harmonised VAT regime; in particular, rate harmonisation is supported as potentially welfare improving compared to the actual VAT regime. Conversely, when the DP option applies, the harmonised VAT structure is unlikely to generate a Pareto improvement for the European countries as a whole. Furthermore, income taxation proves to be a viable tool for the financing of a harmonisation policy.

Given the complexity of the analysis, the issue is investigated by means of applied simulation analysis. This choice is also based on the empirical features of the questions addressed, which are greatly affected by the detail of representation of the fiscal complexities of the domestic system.

The chapter is organised as follows: section 15.2 contains a short description of the structure of the model; section 15.3 sketches the efficiency implications of the different policy reforms we are dealing with; section 15.4 presents the results of the numerical simulations as well as detailed economic explanations; while comments and conclusions are drawn in section 15.5. Sensitivity analysis concerning the tax rates is contained in the appendix.

15.2 MODEL STRUCTURE

The analysis concerning the switch to a uniform indirect tax system between the member states of the European Union (EU) has been carried out in an applied, static, multicountry general equilibrium model. The model represents seven of the EU member countries and an aggregate of all the other countries, commonly named 'rest of the world' (ROW). For the model description we refer to Fehr et al. (1995) (the FRW model) and Ruocco (1996). In particular, we refer to the latter for the notation. The Armington (1969) assumption applies; labour is assumed to be variable in supply but internationally immobile, while capital is fixed in supply and moves freely across countries. On the consumer side, each country is represented by a single representative agent. Subject to his or her budget constraint, the domestic representative consumer maximises a well-behaved utility function, which is assumed to be weakly separable between leisure and aggregate consumption and homothetic in consumption goods. Revenue accrues to the consumer from labour and capital endowments and from transfer payments received by the national government. Each national production side is characterised by production functions which depend on a value added aggregate (labour and capital), combined at a higher level with an aggregate of intermediate inputs. Producers are assumed to minimise their costs (or, alternatively, to maximise their profits).

The national fiscal system of each country is represented by: (a) VAT with differentiated tax rates, depending on goods and on countries; (b) a progressive income tax, whose base is given by labour and capital income (transfers are exempted);[5] (c) tariffs on intermediate consumption and final consumption, differentiated between member states and ROW; (d) a proportional tax on the use of labour, differentiated by countries but uniform across sectors;[6] and (e) differentiated production taxes, depending on goods and on countries.

We construct two different benchmark equilibria which differ only with respect to the VAT: in one scenario the VAT is based on the DP, and in the second scenario on the OP. We want, in fact, to concentrate only on the rate harmonisation process and not on the switch itself from DP to OP.

15.3 THEORETICAL BACKGROUND

As we mentioned in the introduction, the goal of this chapter is to evaluate the welfare effects implied by imposing a unique reduced tax rate and a unique standard tax rate within and across countries,[7] at first under DP and then under OP. In addition, we investigate to what extent results depend upon the way in which we finance this policy. To understand more fully the economic implications of these policy questions, in this section we highlight their different allocative properties and we give an evaluation of their potential welfare effects.

Let us consider indirect taxation under DP. In the benchmark equilibrium, VAT rates differ within a country (depending on goods) and across countries, implying that consumer decisions are distorted for two different reasons: tax rates drive a wedge (a) between the marginal rates of substitution (MRS), and the marginal rate of transformation (MRT) between any two consumption goods, and (b) they distort the choice between aggregate consumption and leisure. International allocation is distorted as well, because domestic tax rates drive a wedge between the MRS of any two different goods produced in one country and consumed in other countries. Therefore, a simple switch to a uniform tax rate within countries would eliminate both domestic and international distortions. Clearly, there seems to be no necessity for uniform tax rates across countries as well.

Although different options concerning the structure of VAT under OP exist, here we adopt the so-called *subtraction method*, which has been translated into the model as a tax on value added. The marginal conditions for domestic resources are the same as under DP. But under OP consumers and producers face tax-inclusive prices. Hence, consumers pay: (a) the tax of the country of origin on imported goods; and (b) the national tax rate on domestic goods. The international allocation of goods is not distorted, but we introduce two additional international distortions, namely the first is a wedge between international MRS and MRT, and the second is a wedge between the marginal rates of technical substitution (MRTS) between tradable factors. Under OP the switch to uniform tax rates across countries eliminates the international distortions due to VAT and, therefore, it can possibly be said to be welfare-improving.

Since the uniformity across countries implies the reduction of the number of tax rates within each country, the harmonisation policy would reduce the number of domestic distortions under the DP as well as under the OP system.

Given that our analysis considers different ways of financing tax rate harmonisation, we should say a few words about the allocative effects of the tax instruments we use. As already mentioned, we first perform the analysis in budget incidence, then in equal yield, allowing the tax rates on labour or, alternatively, the tax rates on income to vary endogenously. While transfers do not introduce any allocative distortions, labour taxes create a wedge between the marginal productivity of labour and the MRS between consumption goods and leisure. Given that labour is internationally immobile, no other distortions take place. Since capital is fixed in supply, income tax is equivalent to a labour income tax plus a lump-sum tax. Therefore, it introduces the same allocative distortion as a labour tax.

Although the description of the allocative distortions implied by each fiscal tool allows for a better understanding of the direction in which we are moving, it is, nevertheless, difficult to derive welfare results from it. The benchmark equilibrium represents, in fact, a very highly distortive tax system, due to both the tax structure and the high level of public expenditure and transfers that each government has to finance. Distortions then compensate for each other, and eliminating one of them might even be welfare-worsening.

Broadly speaking, welfare effects in a multicountry model are driven by domestic, as well as by international, income and substitution effects. International income effects are due to tax export, which arises whenever the tax burden is partly shifted to foreign residents while the tax revenues still accrue to the national government. In the model the international effects are captured by changes in the terms of trade (ToT).[8]

Imposing a uniform tax system across countries would implicitly mean, an increase in tax rates for some countries and a decrease for others. If we do not consider repercussions on other markets, an increase in the VAT rate under DP reduces the domestic demands and leads to a decrease in the producer's prices. Then the expected effects are a reduction of the domestic consumer surplus and a worsening in the ToT. However, in a general equilibrium framework the final result depends upon market interdependencies. In particular, repercussions are expected both on the uses side and on the sources side of income: leisure demand will increase and labour supply decline. If the decline of the labour supply is higher than the corresponding decrease of the labour demand, eventually, due to the final demand and production reduction, the wage rate increases. In turn, this will augment both production costs and disposable income. The final impact on demand (and production) and on producer prices depends upon the prevailing effects. When the effects on the side of uses of income prevail, an increase of the VAT rate under DP implies a decrease in producer prices and, consequently, a ToT deterioration. When the effects on the side of sources of income prevail, then producer prices are augmented as a consequence of the tax increase; the ToT improve and the tax revenue increases. Key parameters are the elasticity of demands for goods, the elasticity of labour supply and the possibility of technical substitution.

Under the OP, an increase in tax rates on domestic goods (which are all tradable) implies, in the first round, an increase in producer prices and, therefore, an improvement in the ToT. Given the interactions between markets, we cannot be sure about the final impact. In addition, when the OP applies, remarkable tax export phenomena can occur, which greatly affect welfare results.

Let us turn now to the labour taxes and consider the first-round effects. An increase in the labour tax rate leads to a decrease in labour demand and to a decrease in the net wage rate. The cost of labour, on the other hand, increases and, therefore, we expect an increase of producer prices and positive effects on the ToT. Also, in this case, the final effects depend on the interactions between the markets. It is worth noticing that a labour tax generates international income effects. It is well known, in fact, that if labour supply is variable and has a positive slope,[9] a tax on labour input cannot be fully shifted on to the wage, but rather is partly shifted on to producer prices. *Ceteris paribus*, the forward shift is lower the more inelastic the labour supply is and the more factors are substitutes. Clearly, the part of the tax which is shifted forward will be borne by the final consumers: if the purchaser is not a domestic resident then a part of the tax on labour is exported.

Finally, the usual assumption is that income taxation is less distortive than labour taxation: while it creates the same allocative distortions, the same tax revenue is charged both on labour and capital income. Hence, we could expect that when a tax has to be reduced because VAT revenue increases as a consequence of the harmonisation process, then it would be more convenient to reduce the tax on labour. Vice versa, when a tax rate has to be increased it would be better to increase the income tax rate.

There are, however, at least two reasons why a labour tax could be less distortive than an income tax. On the one hand, the tax base for income tax is given by labour and capital income minus allowances; hence, depending on the level of the allowances, the difference between the two tax bases may be quite small. In an extreme case, we could assume that the allowances are exactly equal to capital income, and the trade-off between labour and income taxes will simply depend upon the level of the initial tax rates. In fact, in the benchmark equilibrium, wage and income tax rates differ substantially for some countries.[10] Therefore, even when financing the same change in the fiscal revenue, the excess burden implied by the two taxes differs greatly: as is well known, the excess burden approximately varies quadratically with an increase in tax rates. On the other hand, since capital is fixed in supply, only the tax on labour can be partly shifted on to producer prices, so that labour taxation is expected to have a stronger positive effect on the ToT in comparison to income taxation. In conclusion, while income taxation may have a stronger positive effect on domestic distortion (but not necessarily), labour taxation will definitely cause stronger positive effects on international distortions.

As a final remark, it must be noted that, when comparing VAT and income taxation under OP, the difference in the tax base is given by the net capital import or export. For those countries which are net exporters, the harmonisation is expected to be welfare-improving if it implies an increase in VAT, compensated by a decrease in income tax.

To conclude this section, let us make some general remarks from a normative point of view. Within our model, the non-uniformity of the optimal consumption tax structure is due to the presence of international effects, reinforced by considerations regarding the domestic fiscal system, in which several distortions are present. Therefore, the optimal indirect tax structure is characterised by differentiated tax rates across and within countries. An argument which can be used in favour of the uniformity issue across countries is that the level of benchmark tax rates is based on redistributive considerations rather than on efficiency grounds. One could then advocate uniformity across countries as possibly welfare-improving with respect to the benchmark equilibrium, which is, at any rate, far from optimal.

In conclusion, even if the optimal tax theory did not suggest moving towards a fully harmonised case, the impossibility of achieving the optimality allows us to say that there is no *a priori* ground for believing that the harmonisation of the tax rate across countries should be Pareto-inferior in respect to our benchmark case. If the benchmark equilibrium is characterised by a high level of indirect protection, removing the protection could lead to substantial welfare gains.

It would be most confusing to try to consider all of the distorting taxes at the same time. Even in a more simplified context, analytical solutions are hard to come by or do not yield remarkable insights. In this case numerical simulation analysis offers a convenient alternative to analytical model solutions.

15.4 SIMULATION RESULTS

In this section we present our simulation results and their economic explanations. The first simulation group is related to the case in which VAT is based under the DP; the tax rates are harmonised across countries, distinguishing between reduced and normal rates. The uniformity across countries is achieved by an additional simplification of each domestic indirect tax system. In fact, we start from a benchmark equilibrium where commodity taxation is differentiated also within countries and we impose a unique reduced and a unique standard tax rate. Each government, while imposing the new VAT tax rates, alternatively: (a) adjusts the level of transfer payments (budget incidence, SIM1a); (b) fulfils its budget constraint by using labour taxes (SIM2a), or (c) by using income taxation (SIM3a). The results of the simulations are summarised in Tables 15.1 and 15.2. The same analysis has been carried out by assuming that VAT is charged according to the OP (SIM1b, SIM2b, SIM3b). Simulation results are shown in Tables 15.3 and 15.4.

Our base case is obtained imposing a 5 per cent reduced tax rate and an 18 per cent standard tax rate across the EU member states. In the appendix we report the sensitivity analysis concerning the level of the standard tax rate,

Table 15.1 VAT under the destination principle ($t_R = 5\%$, and $t_N = 18\%$): simulation results

	SIM1a Budget incidence		SIM2a Equal yield – labour tax			SIM3a Equal yield – income tax		
	ToT	ΔVAR%	ToT	ΔVAR%	ΔT$_L$%	ToT	ΔVAR%	ΔT$_I$
F	−0.40	−24.90	1.37	−24.15	47.63	0.35	−24.58	78.75
BL	−0.26	−10.85	0.08	−10.42	20.33	0.02	−10.54	8.23
NL	−0.07	−13.88	0.32	−13.47	28.48	0.17	−13.67	16.69
D	0.19	0.98	−0.12	0.87	−1.15	0.03	0.90	−0.69
I	0.33	26.07	−0.91	25.30	−28.73	−0.27	25.68	−21.65
UK	0.72	15.58	−0.27	14.98	−32.80	−0.04	15.07	−8.17
DK	−1.52	−36.21	3.84	−54.44	2,958.74	1.45	−55.23	40.83
ROW	−0.10	−0.07	−0.47	−0.10	—	−0.20	−0.08	—

Notes

t_R	Reduced VAT rate
t_N	Normal VAT rate
ToT	Terms of trade variation (%)
EV%	Monetary welfare changes as a percentage rate of national VAT revenues in benchmark equilibrium
EV^{EU}	Sum of the equivalent variations of the European Union members. Here and in general, the absolute values refer to ECU millions
EV^{EU+ROW}	Sum of the equivalent variations of the European Union members and the ROW
ΔVAR%	VAT revenue changes (%)
Δt$_L$%	Labour tax rate changes (%)
Δt$_I$%	Income tax rate changes (%)

Table 15.2 VAT under the destination principle ($t_R = 5\%$, $t_N = 18\%$): equivalent variations

	SIM1a Budget incidence		SIM2a Equal yield – labour tax		SIM3a Equal yield – income tax	
	EV%	EV	EV%	EV	EV%	EV
F	0.25	206.17	−0.8	−665.74	−0.07	−63.87
BL	−2.40	−206.57	−1.41	−121.09	−1.14	−98.19
NL	−0.18	−30.42	0.56	95.55	0.40	67.67
D	−0.76	−371.18	−1.86	−911.88	−1.30	−622.6
I	−0.33	−96.92	−1.49	−435.02	−0.77	−223.99
UK	0.90	271.34	−1.08	−326.92	−0.53	−105.11
DK	−1.43	−130.97	0.15	11.88	0.05	4.75
ROW	−0.16	−935.53	−0.45	−2,518.74	−0.25	−1,354.61
EV^{EU}		−356		−2,352		−1,040
EV^{EU+ROW}		−1,291		−4,870		−2,394

Note
For notation, see Table 15.1.

Table 15.3 VAT under the origin principle ($t_R = 5\%$, $t_N = 18\%$): simulation results

| | SIM1a | | SIM2a | | | SIM3a | | |
| | Budget incidence | | Equal yield – labour tax | | | Equal yield – income tax | | |
	ToT	ΔVAR%	ToT	ΔVAR%	ΔT$_L$%	ToT	ΔVAR%	ΔT$_I$
F	−2.56	−22.8	0.54	−20.98	87.34	−1.29	−22.07	134.73
BL	−0.36	−9.07	0.87	−7.01	56.77	0.56	−7.65	22.31
NL	−0.89	−12.65	−0.58	−12.21	33.1	−0.66	−12.42	19.14
D	2.32	8.07	1.46	7.66	−6.97	1.78	7.74	−3.77
I	1.91	26.27	0.8	25.59	−18.22	1.42	25.94	−13.66
UK	1.94	12.99	0.56	12.19	−40.87	0.93	12.3	−10.26
DK	−7.41	−53.99	−1.05	−51.23	3,726.53	−3.95	−52.5	48.32
ROW	−0.59	−0.07	−1.31	−0.12	—	−0.78	−0.09	—

Note
For notation, see Table 15.1.

Table 15.4 VAT under the origin principle ($t_R = 5\%$, $t_N = 18\%$): equivalent variations

| | SIM1a | | SIM2a | | SIM3a | |
| | Budget incidence | | Equal yield – labour tax | | Equal yield – income tax | |
	EV%	EV	EV%	EV	EV%	EV
F	−4.05	−3,036.11	−6.67	−5,001.34	−4.79	−3,590.68
BL	−3.29	−255.17	2.21	171.84	1.64	127.35
NL	−3.21	−610.61	−3.18	−604.61	−2.89	−548.55
D	7.15	3,991.98	4.83	2,695.57	5.89	3,291.55
I	3.79	1,145.9	2.35	710.89	3.44	1,039.74
UK	4.93	1,765.04	2.46	881.89	3.51	1,255.92
DK	−13.87	−1,245.57	−12.74	−1,144.09	−12.33	−1,107.22
ROW		−2,895.24		−6,275.15		−3,833.51
EV^{EU}		1,755.42		−2,289.85		468.11
EV^{EU+ROW}		−1,139.82		−8,565.00		−3,365.4

Note
For notation, see Table 15.1.

for which we chose the two extremes of the band proposed by the Commission: 15 and 25 per cent.[11] As for the ROW, we use the non-reciprocal approach: the ROW does not adjust to the fiscal changes in the EU. This hypothesis, especially under the OP, affects the welfare results substantially, since the ROW represents a significant numerical component.

Let us start the analysis by considering the simulation results of SIM1a. As we have already noted, the rate harmonisation itself is not neutral: while adapting to the common policy concerning VAT harmonisation, high-taxing countries expect some revenue losses. On the contrary, low-taxing countries should gain some revenue from the increase of the tax rates. In the simulation performed, the hypothesis concerning rate harmonisation implies a reduced rate for F, BL, NL and DK, lower than that which would be necessary to maintain the existing VAT yield unchanged, while the normal rate remains substantially unaltered. D diminishes the reduced rate but raises the normal rate,[12] while I and UK increase both the reduced and the normal rate. Those countries in which VAT harmonisation implies some revenue loss (F, BL, NL and DK) experience a worsening in the ToT. The results are exactly reversed when the countries face a VAT revenue gain (D, I and UK): positive ToT effects take place, a result which is basically reconfirmed[13] by the sensitivity analysis. The explanation relies on the fact that the sources side-effects prevail over the uses side-effects. When VAT increases, the impact on the labour market is always stronger than the impact on the demand side. The labour supply decline is such that the final result is an increase in the net wage rate, and producer prices increase. In this sense, an increase in the VAT generates an increase in producer prices and, hence, has a positive impact on the ToT.

Now, we can look at the welfare effects. For the European countries, the *a priori* advantages from undertaking the harmonisation process are limited to domestic harmonisation; and looking at Table A15.2 we notice that they cannot be particularly relevant. Apart from F and UK, the switch turned out to be welfare-worsening. The UK case is quite interesting because the increase in VAT rates leads to such a strong positive change in the ToT that the final result proves to be welfare-improving. It shows that a switch from a lump-sum tax to VAT can even be welfare-improving, a result which is not new in the literature (Dixit, 1975). F is the only case in which the harmonisation process reduces the domestic distortions: despite a negative ToT effect, welfare improves. Nevertheless, the reason can be the significant decrease of VAT revenue (and of the fiscal burden). For opposite reasons, the domestic distortions in D and I are exacerbated.

Let us turn to SIM2a: the same policy is now financed by labour taxes. According to the results of the previous simulation, F, BL, NL and DK increase their labour tax rates. As expected, the effects on the source side outweigh those on the uses side: so that an increase in the labour tax rate corresponds to an increase in producer prices and, consequently, to an improvement in the ToT. This effect is also reinforced by the fact that taxes on labour have a direct impact on producer prices – due to the forward tax-shift effect. As before, the total welfare outcome depends on domestic, as well as on international, effects. Although the changes in the ToT are positive for F, BL, NL and DK, the policy is welfare-worsening for F and BL. The latter results can be explained by the fact that, for both F and BL, the harmonisation process has a negative effect on domestic distortions. In fact, looking at the sensitivity analysis we find that a further increase in the tax rates on labour (Table A15.3) in respect of that in Table 15.1 implies smaller welfare losses. For D, I and the UK, the policy implies a reduction of the tax on labour, a consequent reduction of producer prices and a worsening in the ToT, to such an extent that the final result for all these countries is a welfare reduction. This could be seen as a suggestion that the proportional tax on labour input is less distortive than VAT with two harmonised tax rates, so that, in substituting labour taxation with VAT, we increase domestic distortions. Therefore, taxes on labour reduce international distortions and can have a positive effect on domestic distortions, at least in respect to VAT taxation. This idea is also supported by the comparison of the results of SIM1a and SIM2a: switching from VAT to a labour tax, welfare losses are smaller in SIM2a when compared to the corresponding results of SIM1a or they turn out in welfare gains. The only exception is F, for which the gain in SIM1a must be basically linked with the dramatic reduction of VAT revenue.

Results do not change too much when VAT harmonisation is financed by a change in income taxation (SIM3a). Only the magnitude of the effects varies compared to those of SIM2a: both the positive and the negative variations of the ToT are smaller. Furthermore, welfare gains and losses are smaller. When we reduce the tax on labour, the welfare effects are worse than those obtained by reducing the tax on income, a result which, as mentioned in section 15.3, could be justified by the progressivity of income tax (exemptions in this respect are F and BL).

In conclusion, there seems to be no plausible reason for supporting the harmonisation of tax rates under the DP option, which causes positive welfare effects only when accompanied by a relevant reduction of the tax burden. In fact, the only case in which harmonisation results in a welfare gain for the European countries as a whole[14] is when we apply the lowest normal tax rate. But this result is evidently linked to welfare improvement due to the reduction in the tax burden obtained in budget incidence. As for the financing of this policy, surprisingly enough, in many cases labour taxation seems to be a less distortive tool compared with income taxation, but as a whole the income taxation is superior. Of course, the convenience of using one tax instrument instead of another one strictly depends on whether we have to recover or decrease some yield. A better choice would be to leave the countries free to choose their fiscal tools depending on their needs: new asymmetries in the fiscal system within the Union will take place, but will also improve total welfare results.

Let us now consider the second group of simulations: VAT is based on the OP and the subtraction method applies. The first thing we notice is that the direction of the ToT effects under the OP is basically the same as under DP, but welfare results are quite different. As under DP, for F, BL, NL and DK the harmonisation implies a decrease in tax rates, while for I, UK and DK the tax rates increase. On the basis of the results obtained under DP, where the sources effects prevail over the uses side-effects, it is clear that an increase in VAT rates under OP will also increase the producer prices and, therefore, lead to an improvement of the ToT.

As for the comparative analysis of the equal yield simulations compensated by labour or income taxation, we can refer to the corresponding cases under the DP option. As already noted, however, in this case the interpretation of the welfare results is closely linked to the tax export phenomena. Applying the non-reciprocal approach, the EU countries increase their imports from the ROW, whose goods remain untaxed, exports of EU products to the ROW dramatically decrease because goods are charged twice: by VAT under OP within the country of production and by VAT under DP in the ROW. In spite of this, the revenue which accrues to the EU countries from the ROW is still substantial, as can be seen in Tables A15.5 and A15.6: increasing the level of the harmonised VAT rate causes greater improvements, both in the ToT and in welfare effects within the European countries. Through the impacts on the ToT and due to the non-reciprocal approach, it is clear that the costs of the harmonisation are shifted on to the rest of the world, which pays for the welfare gains of the EU.

In conclusion, when the OP applies, VAT harmonisation proves to be Pareto-improving whenever it is linked with an increase in tax rates and provided that transfer payments can be made between the member states. But this result seems to rely heavily on the crucial assumption that the ROW does not adjust to that policy.

As far as the financing of this policy goes, similar to the results of the simulations under DP, a reduction of income tax rates is more strongly welfare-improving than a decrease in the tax rate on labour, and we can claim that the result depends on the progressivity of income taxation. On the whole, welfare losses are smaller (or turn out to be welfare gains) when the harmonisation process is financed by income tax.

15.5 CONCLUSIONS

In considering VAT rate harmonisation in the ongoing completion of the EU, this chapter has focused on the efficiency effects of switching to uniform tax rates across countries when the DP and OP apply, respectively. Furthermore, in light of the problems raised by the financing of the policy at issue, the implications of switching from indirect to direct taxation have been analysed. While no support for uniformity across countries was found under the DP, when the OP system applies, it is possible that the EU may find a way to render this policy potentially Pareto-improving with respect to the case in which each country applies its own tax rates. The presence of a binding budget constraint for national governments greatly affects the magnitude of gains and losses and, as a whole, might negate the advantages and the welfare gains of the harmonisation process. The equal yield analysis contributes to the discussion of several important aspects of VAT harmonisation, which affect the possibility of making this policy a viable option for the

EU countries. First of all, the OP option is necessary for achieving substantial welfare gains from the harmonisation process. Even though the application of the reciprocal approach, although relatively unrealistic, might partly cancel out the gains of the European countries as a whole. Lastly, the choice of the fiscal tools for financing the harmonisation process depends on the needs of each single country and on the features of the new harmonised VAT structure. In conclusion, despite the asymmetries in the fiscal systems, income tax proves, in general, to be a superior tool.

APPENDIX

Table A15.1 Tax rates (%)

	Income tax rate	Labour tax rate
F	6.1	29.9
BL	16.8	14.9
NL	9.83	14.9
D	19.9	13.7
I	10.73	20.9
UK	18.21	6.5
DK	27.12	1.1

Table A15.2 Benchmark VAT rates

	1	2	3	4	5	6	7	8	9	10	11	12	13
F	7	17.6	17.6	17.6	17.6	17.6	17.6	33.3	17.6	7	17.6	17.6	8.6
BL	6	16	16	16	16	16	16	25	16	6	16	16	7.1
NL	4	18	18	18	18	18	18	18	18	4	18	18	7.3
D	6.5	13	13	13	13	13	13	13	13	6.5	13	13	7.3
I	3.5	15	15	15	15	15	15	20	15	3.5	15	15	3.4
UK	0	15	15	15	15	15	15	15	15	0	15	15	5.8
DK	22	22	22	22	22	22	22	22	22	22	22	22	15.4
ROW	10	10	10	10	10	10	10	10	10	10	10	10	10

Table A15.3 VAT under the destination principle ($t_R = 5\%$, $t_N = 15\%$): simulation results

| | SIM1 | | | | | SIM2 | | | | | SIM3 | | | |
| | Budget incidence | | | | | Equal yield – labour tax | | | | | Equal yield – income tax | | | |
	ToT	ΔVAR%	ΔEV%	EV	ToT	ΔVAR%	T_L%	ΔEV%	EV	ToT	ΔVAR%	ΔT_I	EV%	EV
F	−0.39	−31.77	1.16	964.19	1.69	−30.90	62.60	−0.72	−602.93	0.40	−31.42	1.00	0.38	317.43
BL	−0.35	−19.57	−1.78	−152.94	0.22	−18.88	36.86	−0.51	−44.18	0.07	−12.10	14.71	−0.39	−33.77
NL	−0.18	−21.68	0.02	3.5	0.23	−21.13	45.67	0.15	26.41	−0.01	−21.41	26.18	−0.02	−4.00
D	0.02	9.08	0.09	46.2	0.12	−8.80	13.24	−0.74	−360.62	0.29	−3.80	6.39	0.09	42.45
I	0.29	13.99	1.28	372.89	−0.70	13.59	−15.80	−0.44	−128.91	−0.21	13.79	−11.73	0.42	123.26
UK	0.43	4.23	1.20	361.41	−0.17	4.06	−6.90	−0.88	−266.76	0.06	4.10	−1.77	0.04	13.34
DK	−1.64	−59.73	−1.22	−111.84	3.95	−57.99	3219.19	−0.21	−19.02	1.40	−58.78	43.49	−0.09	8.7
ROW	0.12	0.01	0.07	396.91	−0.20	−0.06	—	−0.64	−3,594.9	−0.36	−0.04	—	−0.30	−1,704.92
EV^{EU}				1,461					−1,694					544
V^{EU+ROW}				1,857.91					−5,288.9					−1,160.9

Note
For notation, see Table 15.1.

Table A15.4 VAT under the destination principle ($t_R = 5\%$, $t_N = 25\%$): simulation results

	SIM1 Budget incidence				SIM2 Equal yield – labour tax						SIM3 Equal yield – income tax			
	ToT	ΔVAR%	ΔEV%	EV	ToT	ΔVAR%	T_L%	ΔEV%	EV	ToT	ΔVAR%	ΔT_I	EV%	EV
F	−0.42	−9.88	−2.28	−1,904.43	0.70	−9.53	14.44	−1.63	−1,362.86	0.22	−9.73	30.6	−1.63	−1,355.18
BL	−0.07	8.31	−4.45	−382.01	−0.21	8.00	−13.89	−4.08	−349.96	−0.08	8.13	−6.00	−3.45	−295.84
NL	0.18	3.31	−1.18	−200.54	0.55	3.30	−6.50	0.76	129.06	0.56	3.34	−4.00	0.70	119.59
D	0.56	23.07	−3.40	−1,662.3	−0.62	21.90	−31.21	−5.10	−2,497.2	−0.53	22.00	−16.88	−5.00	−2,434.4
I	0.42	52.47	−4.77	−1,388.7	−1.40	50.73	−55.36	−4.77	−13,890	−0.40	51.59	−43.40	−4.26	−1,242.7
UK	1.34	40.63	−0.59	−177.50	−0.48	38.82	−86.84	−2.39	−721.13	−0.24	39.03	−22.20	−2.02	−613.11
DK	−1.27	−48.52	−2.19	−200.71	3.63	−46.72	2,425.17	0.47	42.80	1.57	−47.50	35.03	0.04	3.48
ROW	0.59	−0.21	−0.68	−3,815.5	−0.24	−0.17	—	−0.05	−282.16	0.16	−0.17	—	−0.11	−615.18
EV^EU				−5,916.2					−6,149.3					−5,818.2
EV^EU+ROW				−9,731.7					−6,431.4					−6.433.4

Note
For notation, see Table 15.1.

Table A15.5 VAT under the origin principle ($t_R = 5\%$, $t_N = 15\%$): simulation results

	SIM1 Budget incidence				SIM2 Equal yield – labour tax					SIM3 Equal yield – income tax				
	ToT	ΔVAR%	ΔEV%	EV	ToT	ΔVAR%	T_L%	ΔEV%	EV	ToT	ΔVAR%	$ΔT_I$	EV%	EV
F	-2.96	-30.64	-30.64	-2,992.9	0.35	-7.71	101.76	-7.71	-5,779.6	-1.72	-29.9	153.26	-1.72	-4,005.3
BL	-0.6	-18.35	-18.35	-268.69	0.76	1.64	71.66	1.64	127.04	0.38	-16.88	27.69	0.38	81.99
NL	-1.26	21.51	21.51	-904.44	-0.97	-5.42	52.21	-5.42	-1,028.7	-1.14	-21.22	29.56	-1.14	-977.14
D	1.02	-4.89	-4.89	1,954.93	0.75	1.62	10.95	1.62	905.89	1.08	-4.66	5.15	1.08	1,607.91
I	0.99	12.89	12.87	866.52	0.16	0.54	-4.39	0.54	162.48	0.59	12.77	-3.34	0.59	538.44
UK	0.66	-0.59	-0.59	689.19	-0.18	-0.59	-8.66	-0.59	-212.71	0.16	-0.74	-2.25	0.16	217.99
DK	-7.72	-58.16	-58.16	-1,246.7	-1.24	-13.42	3,972.34	-13.42	-1,205.4	-4.26	-56.73	50.6	-4.26	-1,149.4
ROW	1.00	0.09	0.09	3,916.50	-0.37	-0.41	—	-0.41	2,299.81	0.33	0.05	—	0.33	915.2
EV^{EU}				-1,902.1					-7,031					-3,685.5
EV^{EU+ROW}				2,014.36					-4,731.2					2,770.3

Note
For notation, see Table 15.1.

Table A15.6 VAT under the origin principle ($t_R = 5\%$, $t_N = 25\%$): simulation results

| | SIM1 | | | | | SIM2 | | | | | | SIM3 | | | |
| | Budget incidence | | | | | Equal yield – labour tax | | | | | | Equal yield – income tax | | | |
	ToT	ΔVAR%	ΔEV%	EV	ToT	ΔVAR%	T_L%	ΔEV%	EV	ToT	ΔVAR%	ΔT_I	EV%	EV
F	-1.67	-4.98	-4.26	-3,195.1	1.02	-3.4	57.08	-4.67	-3,503.1	-0.32	-4.32	92.87	-3.8	-2,826.8
BL	0.17	12.23	-3.05	-236.42	1.11	13.68	24.59	3.26	252.76	0.96	13.32	10.03	2.79	216.62
NL	-0.05	7.64	0.01	2.75	0.3	7.59	-7.05	1.55	294.76	0.42	7.68	-4.43	1.96	371.82
D	5.32	37.95	15.02	8,388.99	3.12	35.64	-45.16	11.72	6,543.67	3.42	35.87	-24.11	12.39	6,919.35
I	4.03	56.84	6.34	1,915.14	2.28	54.74	-47.5	5.97	1,803.05	3.31	55.75	-37.05	6.8	2,054.63
UK	4.88	44.34	11.32	4,050.0	2.28	41.74	-110.02	8.98	3,213.44	2.7	42.05	-28.55	9.71	3,476.3
DK	-6.74	-44.5	-13.96	-1,253.7	-0.6	-41.55	3,200.61	-11.38	-1,021.8	-3.22	-42.86	43.16	-11.4	-1,023.9
ROW	-4.13	-0.08	-3.3	-18,582.0	-3.44	-0.06	—	-2.75	-15,529.0	-3.29	-0.05	—	-2.62	-14,781.0
EV^{EU}				9,671.61					7,582.74					9,187.93
EV^{EU+ROW}				-8,910.6					-7,946.6					-5,593.5

Note
For notation, see Table 15.1.

NOTES

1 See Keen (1987, 1989).
2 CEC (1996).
3 CEC (1989).
4 Angel and Lopez (1996: 91).
5 See simulations in section 15.4; the domestic income tax rates are shown in Table A15.1 in the appendix.
6 See Table A15.1.
7 As one can see from Table A15.2, the benchmark equilibrium is characterised by different reduced tax rates and different standand ones.
8 The evaluation of the ToT is done by using a Laspeyres price index, where we take the ratio between the benchmark quantity of export and import at the new equilibrium prices and divide by the ratio between the benchmark value of export and import.
9 Leisure is a normal good and the total price effect for leisure is negative (the substitution effects outweigh the income effect).
10 See Table A15.1.
11 The relevance of the reduced tax rate is far less important because it only applies to three goods. Results are contained in Tables A15.3–A15.6.
12 The tax rates still refer to 1982.
13 For comparison, see the results of the sensitivity analysis on the value of the normal rate: Tables A15.3–A15.6 in the appendix.
14 As a measure of the aggregate welfare we consider the sum of the EV across all the EU member states.

REFERENCES

Armington, P.S. (1969), 'A theory of demand for products distinguished by place of production', *IMF Staff Papers*, 16: 159–76.

Commission of the European Community (1989), *Completion of the Internal Market and Approximation of Indirect Taxes* (COM(89)260), Brussels: CEC.

Commission of of the European Community (1996), *A Common System of VAT: A Programme for the Single Market* (COM(96)328 final), Brussels: CEC.

Dixit, A.K. (1975), 'Welfare effects of tax and price changes', *Journal of Public Economics*, 4: 103–23.

Dixit, A.K. and Norman, V. (1980), *Theory of International Trade*, Cambridge: Cambridge University Press.

Fehr, H., Rosenberg, C. and Wiegard, W. (1995), *Welfare Effects of Value-added Tax Harmonization in Europe: A Computable General Equilibrium Analysis*, Berlin: Springer.

Keen, M. (1987), 'Welfare effects of commodities tax harmonisation', *Journal of Public Economics*, 33: 107–14.

Keen, M. (1989), 'Pareto improving indirect tax harmonisation', *European Economic Review*, 33: 1–12.

Lopez Garcia, M.A. (1996), 'The origin principle and the welfare gains from indirect tax harmoinization', *International Tax and Public Finance*, 3: 83–93.

Ruocco, A. (1996), *A Multicountry General Equilibrium Model for the European Union: The Basic Features and the Coding Structure*, Discussion Paper No. 83, University of Tübingen.

INDEX

For Product Safety Concerns and Information please contact our EU
representative GPSR@taylorandfrancis.com
Taylor & Francis Verlag GmbH, Kaufingerstraße 24, 80331 München, Germany